WE'RE HERE TO HELP

WE'RE HERE TO HELP

When Guardianship Goes Wrong

DIANE DIMOND

Brandeis University Press
Waltham, Massachusetts

Brandeis University Press
© 2023 by Diane Dimond
All rights reserved
Manufactured in the United States of America
Designed and composed in Charis and Playfair type
by Chris Crochetière, BW&A Books, Inc.

For permission to reproduce any of the material in this
book, contact Brandeis University Press, 415 South Street,
Waltham, MA 02453, or visit brandeisuniversitypress.com

Library of Congress Cataloging-in-Publication Data
available at https://catalog.loc.gov/
hardcover ISBN 978-1-68458-167-2
e-book   ISBN 978-1-68458-168-9

5 4 3 2 1

This book is dedicated to the countless people—from all races and ethnic backgrounds, women and men, old and young, rich and poor, the abled and disabled, and their suffering family members—who have been irreparably damaged by a government system that was created to help the most vulnerable citizens. The nation's guardianship and conservatorship system ran off the rails decades ago, and those who could set it straight have failed to act.

This work is also dedicated to my loving family, especially my incredibly supportive soulmate-husband Michael Schoen, and my extraordinary, proofreading daughter Jenna Lamond. Thank goodness one of us knows where the commas, semicolons, and hyphens are supposed to go.

Thanks to all my family for understanding why I must do what I do.

CONTENTS

PREFACE

This book is *not* about the guardianships and conservatorships that run smoothly. They are plentiful and certainly necessary for those who have no family or close friends to care for them in their time of need. Every citizen should applaud the work that public guardians perform on behalf of the indigent, as their selfless compassion is evident. Those guardians earn a small state-supplied stipend for taking care of the poor who have no one else to assist them. In addition, every state has a system whereby a judge can bypass willing family members and appoint a professional for-profit guardian or conservator to supervise the life of an at-risk person. Many of these court appointees are well meaning and selfless, extremely helpful and noble. But many are not, and the cases revealed in this book will prove that point. The stories you will read here may shock or outrage you. Some are unforgettable.

Nothing in this book should be construed as legal advice. The information presented here is merely reflective of the court documents, source material, personal testimonials, and other evidence gathered during years of investigation into the legal system dedicated to protecting our most vulnerable citizens.

Investigative journalists don't write about the houses left intact after a tornado. We don't chronicle the trains that stay on the tracks and arrive on time. We often write about the things that have gone wrong in society. We focus on the people whose lives are torn apart by unexpected storms, the souls whose very existence swerve off the expected track of life and end in tragedy.

ACKNOWLEDGMENTS

Credit for this work ever seeing the light of day goes to my longtime agent and dear friend Wayne Kabak. We were stymied about how to convince a publisher that the topic herein was worthy of a book, and Wayne suggested I write a longform piece in a magazine or newspaper. Editor Kent Walz of the *Albuquerque Journal* came to understand the dire situation surrounding abusive guardianships in New Mexico, and in 2016 he commissioned me to write a six-part series. Huge appreciation goes to Walz for truly opening the door for beleaguered families to find me and tell me their stories.

I never stopped writing about the court-instigated system that has so negatively affected so many Americans. And when the time was right, the retiring Kabak introduced me to one of the best literary agents in the business, Jane Dystel, and her partner Miriam Goderich. Many thanks to them and the team at Dystel, Goderich and Bourret for helping me find a home for this book.

Also, enormous gratitude to Sue Berger Ramin, director of Brandeis University Press, who instantly saw the need for the public to learn about the ugly side of a little-understood legal system that could unexpectedly overtake any one of us. In addition, sincere thanks to the extraordinary team at Brandeis who helped make this manuscript better going out than it was coming in to them: Rosalind Kabrhel, Daniel Breen, Anthony Lipscomb, Natalie Jones, and Chris Crochetière.

This book would not have been possible without the tireless coopera-tion from reform activists Rick and Terri Black, founders of the Center for Estate Administration Reform; Tom Coleman, executive and legal director of the Spectrum Institute; Dr. Sam Sugar, founder of Americans Against Abusive Probate Guardianship; Kerri Kasem, founder of Kasem Cares; Elaine Renoire and Marcia Southwick of the National Association to Stop Guardianship Abuse; and dogged Washington state attorney Cheryl Mitch-ell. Many thanks also go to private investigators Shannon Tuloss and Dan-iel "Danno" Hanks for their probing prowess, which helped uncover many important details for this book. Most importantly, recognition must go to the earliest pioneering whistleblowers who defied court gag orders to tell me their stories and share important documents: Nancy Herrmann Hart; Mary, Emily, and Cliff Darnell; and David Winstanley. There were many others who confided their stories but wish to remain anonymous, and I re-spect their privacy.

Finally, a very special thanks goes to my good friend and neighbor, Catherine Whitney, a prolific *New York Times* best-selling author. I am in total awe of her many talents. Her encouragement and assistance with this project have been a treasured gift.

WE'RE HERE TO HELP

Introduction

The idea of taking care of family and fellow citizens who cannot physically or mentally support themselves has long been a part of the fabric of American life. But somewhere along the line, that noble notion began to fade. Following World War II, young people in extended families began to move away from rural homes in search of postwar opportunities in big cities. At the same time, many left childhood inner-city areas in search of stylish suburbs. The traditional multigeneration style of living—a daughter and her husband and children living with grandparents, for example—was diminished as the younger folk chose alternatives to staying close to home. Cultural and economic developments during this time, coupled with major advances in medical care, resulted in longer life expectancy, and the number of elders who had been left alone soared. Society then turned to the courts to help these at-risk citizens. That is when the long-established legal process known as guardianship began to morph into something it was never meant to be.

The adult guardianship system we know today was originally established during the early twentieth century. Called conservatorship in some states, it is a court-initiated and court-supervised system that was designed to help the nation's most vulnerable citizens who cannot care for themselves. Many of these arrangements are made necessary after a family quarrels, sometimes bitterly, over what is best for their at-risk loved one, be they an elderly parent, a sibling with a mental illness, or a relative living with a physical or intellectual disability. When a concerned family member turns to a lawyer for help to settle the dispute, the outcome can be shocking. The client may be led to believe that a judge will name them to the position of guardian, but once in court, reality hits. After hearing about the family's dispute, the judge might appoint a rival family member to be guardian. But when there is family strife, judges frequently rule that the situation is "dysfunctional" and they appoint a for-profit outsider to be the guardian. The relative who initiated the guardianship might argue against appointing a professional by explaining to the court that only they know the dependent person's deepest desires and what they had planned for the future. They may inform the judge that their name is specifically mentioned in an existing will, a trust, a power of attorney document or an end-of-life directive. But often none of that matters, because in this astonishing world, the court and its appointees can simply ignore previously prepared legal documents if it is determined that they are no longer in the vulnerable person's "best interest." Suddenly, the family member who sought a solution from the court realizes the system has turned on them, and henceforth an outsider will be in charge, a total stranger who makes their living controlling the lives and finances of so-called wards of the court. Welcome to the part of the justice system where the usual criminal and civil rules of procedure simply do not apply.

The criminal justice system is predicated on the idea that a person is "innocent until proven guilty," but in a guardianship or conservatorship court, that is not the standard. Rulings are based on whether a person is seen as "incapacitated." Too often there is no presumption that a potential ward has the capacity or is competent to handle their own affairs, for if an attorney brings forth a petition declaring someone to be mentally deficient, judges who hear guardianship cases tend to take their word for it. Frequently and frighteningly, these declarations of mental impairment are not accompanied by any definitive or trustworthy medical findings.

Before an adult is conscripted into this system, a judge must be presented with a "petition for guardianship" and agree that the person in question is incapacitated by either a mental or physical condition and unable to adequately take care of themselves. After that finding, all life decisions automatically transfer to the appointed guardian (defined as someone who manages all health and welfare decisions for another), and/or a conservator (a person who oversees a ward's finances). Family and friends come to realize that every aspect of the "protected person's" life will be decided by someone else. Wards are, for all intents and purposes, held captive to the will of another. For some dependent citizens this is a positive step. For too many it is exactly the opposite.

Initiating the guardian or conservatorship process is unbelievably simple. All that need be done is for a lawyer to draw up a petition for guardianship and present it to the proper judge.[1] In recent years, attorneys have begun to more frequently insert the word "emergency" in the title of the document. An "emergency petition for guardianship" asserts that the prospective ward is in imminent danger and in immediate need of protection from either self-harm or outside exploitation. In the rush for a ruling (because it's an emergency!), no time is taken to vet the petition for accuracy. The judge simply takes the word of the officer of the court who filed it. The petition's allegations about the would-be ward's situation or their family members' behavior can be exaggerated, contain mere suspicions, or be outright false. My investigation into the system revealed there is no shortage of attorneys willing to fabricate facts on these petitions. They know busy or uncaring judges will likely just rubber-stamp their request. And due process is routinely nonexistent, especially during hearings on emergency petitions. There is no jury involved. No witnesses are called to refute the petition's accusations. The targeted person is not even in the courtroom to be seen by or speak to the judge, and family members of the proposed ward often have no idea that a legal proceeding is being held. While these emergency guardianships are temporary, they nearly always become permanent.

Cases involving a nonemergency petition are more cumbersome and take more time to conclude. In those instances, the judge usually orders psychological testing, in-person interviews with both the at-risk person and individuals closest to them. The judge may entertain listening to arguments from lawyers hired by family members opposing the guardianship. There are no reliable statistics on how many of these emergency or nonemergency petitions are rejected by judges, but the number is believed to be small.

Once a person is placed under either type of guardianship—temporary or permanent—their money and material goods are confiscated and they are stripped of their civil rights. Among the many restrictions: they are not allowed to access their money, freely travel, vote, sign a contract, marry or divorce, have a baby, choose where to live, or decide when to go to church, go shopping, or go to a doctor. Many wards find themselves isolated in their own homes or involuntarily moved into assisted-living situations. Currently, there are only a few states that allow guardianized adults to choose their own lawyer; instead, the judge appoints one for them, and the role of that attorney is murky. Are they there to truly represent the ward's wishes, or are they appointed to decide what is in the "best interest" of the conscripted person? Once in the system, the ward has fewer rights than a prisoner on death row. It has become a shameful, yet tolerated, fact of life in America, and it has gone on for decades.

Perhaps most frightening is the knowledge that a guardianship can target anyone and be initiated by any outside party. The petitioner who starts the process could be a family member, but they could also be a social worker, an angry neighbor, a business rival, a former lover, a real estate agent or antiques dealer who has their eye on your property. In one outrageous case in Rockwall, Texas, a local mechanic claimed an elderly local doctor owed him $40,000 for unpaid work, and he filed an application for guardianship with the court.[2] The judge never laid eyes on the doctor nor alerted his family to the proceeding. There was no hearing or medical evidence presented. Despite this obvious lack of due process, the judge granted the mechanic's request to become the guardian.[3] The doctor's family was forced to spend some $100,000 in legal fees for a lengthy fight to undo the mess.

This is no small problem. Best estimates from the National Center for State Courts put the number of adult Americans under active guardianship at 1.5 million, but that does not include those consigned under the banner of conservatorship. And that number is from a 2011 analysis.[4] Informed reform advocates—particularly those who have been ensnared in abusive guardianships and have spent years trying to get corrective state and federal laws passed—believe the correct figure is now closer to two million people. Just what percentage of these wards are subjected to an exploitative guardianship is not known. Reliable and up-to-date statistics are impossible to come by because no organization or state or federal government entity keeps an official tally of those citizens who have been ordered into this system and thereby stripped of the right to make decisions about their own lives. An exhaustive investigation by BuzzFeed News in September 2021 concluded that at the pace the population is aging, there could soon be as many as two hundred thousand new guardianship cases opened in the United States each year.[5] And, of course, for nearly every guardianized person, there are multiple family members and close friends who are also affected by this sometimes-heartless system.

Life under guardianship or conservatorship has changed considerably over the decades. It has, in many instances, become a criminal enterprise that targets vulnerable people—most often those with significant wealth—and manipulates the courts into conscripting them into guardianship or conservatorship. In the process, massive amounts of wards' assets are put into play. Consider that every year, new guardianships or conservatorships place more than $50 billion under the control of others, and with the average case lasting about six years, that makes for an accumulated $300 billion pot at any given time. This is money that is being controlled by largely unsupervised court appointees.[6] With that much money available, is it any wonder that such a legally sanctioned system would attract the criminal element? Informed critics estimate that predatory players illegally divert multiple billions of dollars from this monstrous cache of money each year.[7]

Many of those billions have traditionally come from the hard-earned portfolios of older Americans, many of whom scrimped all their lives so they could leave selected heirs a healthy inheritance. Once guardianized, a large part, if not all, of their anticipated bequeathment is diverted to the strangers who operate within this mysterious guardianship system. But today the scandal is much more pervasive as the dishonest have gone far beyond targeting just the elderly. Like other scams, the victim base has grown over time to include young people who have earned or inherited substantial money; injured employees who have won sizable workers' compensation settlements; victims of birth accidents targeted for control of their hefty medical malpractice awards; those with intellectual or developmental disabilities who receive generous monthly government disability payments; military and government workers with attractive pensions; and citizens with money who suffer from mental illness, even if it is only a temporary handicap (e.g., pop star Britney Spears). Citizens from a wide range of groups have now been unwittingly conscripted into this court-activated alternative existence.

As a journalist trained to present "both sides of a story," I quickly learned about the veil of secrecy that envelops the guardianship and conservatorship system. Beginning in 2015, and after listening to heartbreaking stories from family members who watched helplessly as strangers took over the lives of their loved ones, my efforts to get the "other side" were almost uniformly stonewalled. In many cases, judges had established wide-ranging gag orders that sealed all court records from public scrutiny and sternly warned participants to stay mum about what had occurred during hearings. Those who refused to remain quiet faced contempt of court charges and substantial fines. For example, a woman in Santa Fe, New Mexico, who tearfully told a girlfriend about her longtime boyfriend's guardianship case was sanctioned $25,000 after the friend posted about the situation on Facebook. When I requested interviews with lawyers who wrote and presented guardianship petitions, they demurred, citing a standing gag order. After contacting guardians or conservators to ask for comment on specific cases, I quickly learned that transparency is not a hallmark of this system. Even when there was no gag order in place, nearly all insiders shrugged off requests for comment and invoked the idea that since the mental or physical health of the ward was at issue, federal HIPAA privacy laws precluded them from providing any information.

In one of the earliest cases I investigated, family members who had been provided copies of the court docket (schedule of events) and other pertinent legal documents defiantly ignored the judge's command to stay silent. They courageously passed on their files to me, and I began to write about the indignities and civil rights violations suffered by their guardianized mother.[8] Soon, other desperate-to-be-heard individuals contacted me asking that I help expose their guardianship horror stories. These people may have lived thousands of miles apart, but their stories of guardianship exploitation were achingly similar. A nationwide pattern became evident. There were times when I marched myself into court hearings as if I belonged so as to get a firsthand look at how the system operated, only to be promptly removed. I also heard from concerned caretakers, court employees, and those who worked inside corporate guardian offices, who generously provided me with confidential information and paperwork to prove the validity of their stories. Still more anxious relatives of wards sent me shocking photographs of their loved one's deteriorating condition under guardianship. The photos depicted massive bruises on naked bodies, untreated bed sores, withering limbs, and the blank, sad stares of the overmedicated. I received surreptitiously recorded cell phone videos in which wards tearfully begged to be rescued from their guardian's control.

Yes, there are always two sides to every story, but in questionable case after questionable case the only response I got from the court-appointed guardianship community was either "no comment," vague complaints about family dysfunction causing the unfortunate situation, or the rote pronouncement that that the ward was being "protected" in the eyes of the law. My eyes were telling me something different. My brain came to the conclusion that when there is institutionalized secrecy and silence, as has been the central feature of guardianship, meaningful change is unlikely to occur. To my muckraking mind this was an issue crying out for the white-hot glare of public scrutiny.

To be sure, many guardianship arrangements are truly beneficial, especially if a judge names a trusted person to be in control of the at-risk person. In fact, the majority of court-appointed guardians are family members who make sure their loved one is able to live a safe and comfortable life, surrounded by friendly faces who are devoted to their well-being. This is a best-case scenario. Yet, while it might sound ideal—a dependent person enveloped in the bosom of his or her loving clan—this arrangement doesn't always ensure a positive outcome. The truth is that some family guardians have also been known to take cruel advantage of their guardianized relatives, stealing money or property from them, physically, mentally, and even sexually abusing them. It is rare for a judge to learn of this maltreatment because the conscripted and isolated person has no communication pipeline to reach the court. It is left to other family members to complain to the judge. That said, after following disputed guardianship cases for years now, I can report that many judges refuse to allow family members to speak in court, ordering them to hire a lawyer to address the bench for them. It is not unusual for a judge to dismiss family complaints as coming from the disgruntled, ill informed, or even duplicitous. The personalities in charge of administering this court system tend to be an insular bunch who are routinely dismissive of those who have questions or objections about the way things work.

Over the years, numerous cases have been identified in which a money-driven professional guardian deliberately aligned him or herself with the most disruptive and untrustworthy member of a family. This ensures the family fights will continue. Angry opposing relatives will file multiple complaints with the court about how their conscripted kin's life is being negatively affected by the guardianship. They may express concern about the way the ward's money is being spent, the foods or medicines being administered, or the guardian's sudden declaration that certain relatives can no longer visit because they "upset" the protected person. Each time a complaint is filed, a hearing is called and the guardian must respond to the grievance in court. Time spent preparing for court, or appearing in court, or writing a post-hearing report allows the guardian to charge for more and more billable hours. With an average hourly rate ranging between two hundred to six hundred dollars an hour, it is in the guardian's financial interest to keep the conflicts brewing. And once a guardian comes under personal attack from the family, they are allowed to hire their own attorney to represent them. They may also ask the court for a psychiatric evaluator to step in to examine the ward or even the person making the complaint. The family may insist that home health aides be dismissed and replaced, or that a certified public accountant (CPA) be hired to examine the way the ward's finances are being handled. And guess who is responsible for paying the ever-mounting fees for all these outside players? It is the ward, as their confiscated money is used to pay all the bills.[9] When a frustrated family member fights what they see as an unjust system, they may very well be depleting their own inheritance.

It is profoundly important to understand the complete authority that guardians and conservators have. These court appointees can wield enormous power, and they may exercise it almost unchecked.[10] The system was originally designed to help citizens who can no longer live independently, and the overriding standard has always been to assist the ward using "the least restrictive measures," and with an eye toward "conserving the person's estate."[11] But often the first step a professional guardian takes is to put all financial assets under their own name, and then to cocoon their charge away from the outside world. This means the protected person becomes completely dependent on the guardian and the support staff hired on to care for them. Lonely wards have been inaccurately told that their family and friends no longer want to see them; guardians have erroneously told home health aides that a particular relative must be kept away because they have threatened to kill the ward so they can inherit the estate sooner.[12] If family visits are allowed, aides are often directed to hover over the conversation and take copious notes for the guardian's edification. Guardians have been known to twist the contents of those notes when seeking permission from a judge to ban certain people from visiting. Those stripped of visiting rights are usually the same people who have complained about the guardian's management techniques. And if the magnitude of this isolation results in anxiety for the ward, a guardian has the power to make sure prescription medications are administered. Overmedicating a ward to ensure compliance is not unusual, and with the elderly it can hasten their death.[13] In many states there is no legal obligation for a guardian to stay in touch with the family about the health or ultimate fate of a ward. Guardians have been known to keep a ward's death secret, order up cremation and keep the cremains in storage rather than pass them to a family member.[14] Why would a guardian take such draconian steps? The short answer is because they can, and no authority steps in to stop them. Punishment of court appointees who engage in such inhumane acts has been maddingly rare.

Other examples of egregious guardian behavior have occurred because judges simply assign too many cases to one appointee. For example, a guardian in Florida, with more than four hundred people to keep track of, used her power to initiate Do Not Resuscitate (DNR) orders on time-consuming hospitalized wards. In one instance, her unwanted DNR on a military veteran who had difficulty swallowing was coupled with another order to cap the man's feeding tube. He died slowly over the course of a week while helpless nurses and doctors stood by.[15] Conversely, there are cases on record in which a guardian ignored a ward's DNR request, kept the person alive, and thereby insured no interruption of their fees.[16] In Ohio, a guardian assigned to care for hundreds of wards simultaneously parked his charges in nursing homes, ignored them, and then publicly asked for more clients since the nursing home staff was doing his job for him. He ultimately pleaded guilty to multiple counts of stealing from his wards and falsifying court records.[17] A guardian in Nevada was convicted and sent to prison for stealing at least $200,000 and expensive belongings from her wards to help bankroll both her unemployed boyfriend and her gambling habit.[18] The sadistic nature of some guardians is difficult to comprehend.

It is not humanly possible for a judge to adequately monitor the multitude of machinations within each individual case, and the number of wards grows each year. Judges who handle the guardianship and conservatorship caseload routinely complain of being overworked, underfunded, and understaffed. It is easier for them to listen to one voice—that of their own appointee—rather than entertain family members who are almost always painted as being at the crux of the problem. This needs to change. Judges stand as the creators of guardianships. They must be held accountable for what their chosen appointees do. If they need more funding to do the job properly, state legislatures are responsible for making sure that money is available. Adequate funding is ever more urgent as the so-called Silver Tsunami of aging Americans is upon us.

There is an inherent conflict of interest built into this long-neglected system. Guardians are supposed to protect the incapacitated person for as long as they need help, yet there is absolutely no incentive for them to ever report to the court that the ward no longer needs their assistance. To do that would be to deprive themselves of lucrative fees. But a guardianized person who once suffered a brain injury, for instance, can recover and overcome the need for outside intervention. A victim of a debilitating car accident can learn to live an independent life. A person with a physical disability, like cerebral palsy, may need help with transportation or navigating stairs, but that doesn't mean they lack the mental ability to live their life guardian-free. Sadly, while it is fairly easy to establish a guardianship for citizens like these, it can be next to impossible for them to escape court control.

There are no federal laws specific to guardianships, and state laws are a mishmash. Most states do not require guardians to have a college degree in fields that would enhance their ability to perform their court-ordered duties, subjects like banking or estate planning, psychology or psychiatry, physical or intellectual handicaps, geriatric medicine, social work or family dynamics. Only in recent years have some states begun to require credit and criminal background checks before a guardian can be appointed.[19] Surprisingly, many states do not explicitly prohibit chronic debtors or convicted felons from holding such a sensitive position. At this writing, only three states require professional guardians or conservators to be licensed to operate: Alaska, California, and Nevada.[20] In the remaining states, a hairdresser or masseuse must pass a far more stringent set of licensing requirements than a court appointee who, quite literally, takes control of another person's life.

Some state-level reforms are being adopted to improve the system, but critics uniformly agree they are Band-Aid solutions that ignore the big-picture problems. Many believe the federal government must step in; the US Congress has held hearings on guardian atrocities dating back to 1987, yet no definitive legislation has ever emerged. That lawmakers haven't seriously tackled the obviously systemic problems inherent to guardianship and conservatorship leaves the public wondering just who is fighting against improvements—and why.

This book will take you through the process, from beginning to end, dissecting the secretive, complicated, and complicit industry of for-profit individuals who make a living off the confinement of others. You will read real-life, almost unbelievable stories about wards and families who lived through the often-incomprehensible tactics employed by predatory players as they schemed their way through the guardianship system and lined their pockets in the process. At the time of this writing, some of the cases mentioned within these pages were still unfolding or working their way through the legal system, but they are included here to help the reader understand the complexity—and sometimes the depravity—of the guardianship system. All the true life stories presented here are offered in hopes they will help you and those you love avoid becoming entrapped in an unwanted, court-sanctioned situation that can strip a person of their most basic civil rights. We think this sort of thing couldn't happen in the United States, but it happens all the time, to all sorts of people. The sheer numbers of these abusive cases—reported by loving family members and worried friends across the United States—screams for attention to be paid.

1

The Floodgates Open

"Nancy, slow down. I don't understand. What do you mean your father was stripped of his civil rights by—who did you say? A guardianship judge there in Albuquerque?"

The story pouring out of my childhood friend regarding her late father, Dr. Jack Herrmann, a prominent doctor and philanthropist, just didn't make sense. How could a judge take away someone's constitutionally guaranteed civil rights? I thought to myself, *That can't happen in the United States of America.* And what was this legal procedure she called "guardianship"? I thought guardians were only appointed for children under eighteen.

As a longtime investigative reporter specializing in true crime stories, I was used to getting calls from people telling me all sorts of wild and complicated tales, asking me to follow up on what they were sure was a "Pulitzer Prize–winning story." But as I listened to Nancy Herrmann Hart that fall day in 2013, I quickly realized I had never heard anything like what she was telling me. Her story revolved around a family war among the six survivors of Dr. Herrmann's eight children. Nancy, a nurse by trade, alleged that some of her siblings had been looting their father's investment accounts and using the cash to pay off houses and take overseas vacations. She also suspected some of Dr. Herrmann's financial advisers were mishandling his $7 million estate. As the doctor became more mentally challenged by advancing dementia, the siblings became locked in an ever more vicious fight for control of their widowed father's fortune before he died.

Nancy was stuck in a terrible situation as she attempted to fully understand the financial aspect of what was happening to her father while trying to protect him at the same time. And the legal quagmire got worse after she hired an elder law/estate attorney to help her. Sometime around June 2012, Nancy said, she poured out all the emotional and financial details of her father's situation to this lawyer. He assured her he could help. Nancy insisted to me that the attorney never told her that he planned to take the information she had given him and petition the court to appoint a guardian, a conservator/trustee, and someone called a "court visitor" to evaluate the situation and make medical and financial decisions for Dr. Herrmann. Nancy told me this lawyer did not fully explain the process to her. She said she was never informed that within weeks her father would become a "ward of the court" and be declared "incapacitated," then stripped of his civil rights. But that is exactly what happened.

When presented with the attorney's petition for emergency guardianship, district court judge Beatrice Brickhouse rubber-stamped the document, declared Dr. Herrmann was incapacitated, and agreed to appoint all the people recommended by the lawyer—effective immediately.[1] There was no due process hearing, the judge never laid eyes on Dr. Herrmann, and no witnesses were heard. On that day, August 16, 2012, Nancy had no way of knowing she had walked, chin first, into a well-established industry of friendly and professionally connected court appointees who earned a living by "protecting" the vulnerable. Judge Brickhouse named a court visitor to investigate the Dr. Herrmann situation. She appointed a temporary guardian (with a permanent guardian appointed soon after). And the judge designated attorney Darryl Millet to act as a separate conservator/trustee to handle the considerable Herrmann estate.[2] This controversial conservator would figure prominently in multiple high-stakes cases in New Mexico, repeatedly accused by family members of employing needlessly harsh, heartless, and financially sloppy tactics. He developed a reputation for dragging out a case for months, even years after the ward had died, which allowed him to continue to charge the estate his fees. This is precisely what would happen in Dr. Herrmann's case.[3]

Nancy said it was terrifying to watch as her eighty-seven-year-old father suddenly became an object to be handled by strangers. He was not allowed to see his regular physician anymore; the guardian chose one for him. Round-the-clock nurses were hired. Then a landscaper was employed to water the doctor's few outdoor plants, many of which had withered long before in the hot southwestern sun. Someone else was paid to regularly clean the unused swimming pool and, inexplicably, to install a costly electric pool cover. A dog walker was engaged to take care of the doctor's tiny Yorkshire terrier. A separate "pooper-scooper" was put on the payroll to tend to the backyard. Fees were paid to a messenger service to pick up groceries and prescription medicines even though the doctor's pharmacy had a free delivery service. Nancy said that after she and one of her concerned brothers began to question the financial arrangements and the medical care their father was receiving, the guardian hired an attorney to protect her interests in court as she sought the judge's approval to ban family visits. Dr. Herrmann's money was used to pay for the guardian's new lawyer to fight against his own children. Shortly thereafter, Nancy and her brother were prohibited from seeing their father because, as the guardian told the judge, they upset the ward by discussing his situation with him. The judge authorized the visitation ban and, again, entertained no testimony from any of the Herrmann clan. Nancy didn't realize at the time that some guardians invite conflict because that results in more court appearances and more hourly fees they can charge. And Dr. Herrmann had plenty of money left to be spent.

Much of my career has been dedicated to reporting on the plight of victims. While I surely didn't want to get involved in a Herrmann family squabble, this was obviously much bigger than that. Had I uncovered a flaw in the justice system? How could I best investigate this? The Dr. Herrmann I knew from my days growing up in Albuquerque—the handsome and charismatic World War II veteran who went to Catholic mass daily and spent sixty years ministering to the sick and volunteering his time to take care of prisoners and the poor—must have had a last will and testament, a designated power of attorney and an ironclad estate plan. Surely he would have spelled out exactly what each of his surviving adult children would inherit. Could a guardian circumvent all those legal safeguards? If what Nancy was telling me was true, the guardian and the conservator must have either been inexcusably unaware of the doctor's legal documents or deliberately ignored them with permission from the judge. Either way it was troubling. I figured that if I checked court records, that would surely shed some light on what had happened.

Much to my surprise, I discovered that New Mexico judges who heard guardianship cases routinely sequestered the proceedings. At that time, all aspects of these cases were kept sealed and secret. Gag orders were in place and everyone involved in guardianship cases was instructed to keep quiet about developments or face contempt charges and hefty fines. It was an unexpected layer to the process that, effectively, blocked me—or any-one else—from learning how it all worked. I came to discover that secrecy was the name of this guardianship game in many states nationwide. And none of the court-appointed players would ever come forward to explain the inner workings, or to report malfeasance, because to do so would jeop-ardize their own ability to participate in this lucrative enterprise. In other words, they would lose their place at the trough if they spoke the truth about how it all worked.

I also discovered that one of the playbook maneuvers conveniently available to conservators is a requirement to transfer a client's unen-cumbered money into what's called an Interest on Lawyer Trust Account (IOLTA). The IOLTA program now exists in every state. A lawyer is not allowed to benefit financially from their client's money, so interest-bear-ing accounts were long prohibited. Once IOLTA regulations were put in place, beginning in 1980, law firms were encouraged to pool client funds—usually nominal amounts like retainers, client refunds, or government checks—in interest-bearing accounts. The interest is then supposed to be passed on to the state's bar association to provide free legal assistance to the poor, to fund legal education, and to make improvements in the state's justice system.[4] There are suspicions that some conservator attorneys mis-use IOLTA and park ineligible funds there, but the secrecy of the system makes it almost impossible for an outsider to confirm that. Nancy told me she had reason to believe the conservator/trustee of her father's estate was illegally parking large sums of money in an IOLTA and possibly misusing the funds. Since a conservator works for the ward and not the family, they are not required to reveal details about the financial health of an estate, including what amounts are held in IOLTA. As a journalist, if I can't get my hands on corroborating documents, look at financial spreadsheets, or con-duct on-the-record interviews with primary players, I simply cannot write about a topic as fact. I had to tell Nancy that I was at a dead end. While I could find no reason to disbelieve what she was telling me, there was just no way to adequately confirm the details. Sadly, it was one more big dis-appointment for this determined daughter who refused to give up fighting for her father's legacy.

On August 16, 2013, Dr. Jack Herrmann suffered a stroke and died in Presbyterian Hospital in Albuquerque, the hospital in which he had prac-ticed for so many decades. When Nancy first contacted me, she was sure her family battle wouldn't take much longer. That was not the case. More than ten long years would pass before Dr. Herrmann's estate would be closed. Why would it take so long to finish work on this account? One reason was that Nancy continued to fight what she believed was sloppy administration of the estate and unjust treatment of her at the hands of conservator Millet. According to a confidential court transcript supplied to me by Nancy, conservator Millet described various roadblocks to closing the Herrmann estate. He told the judge about a lengthy legal dispute over how one of the brothers would repay the estate for moneys he had taken before Dr. Herrmann's death. He also mentioned that "one of the most time-consuming issues was mineral rights held by the trust for property located in West Virginia. It took nearly a year to resolve this matter so that the Trust could be terminated."[5] Nancy continues to suspect that there was chicanery on the part of the conservator, specifically with his handling of her father's funds held in the IOLTA. She shared two court-registered documents outlining the IOLTA transactions for Dr. Herrmann's estate from August 2012 to September 2013. Another IOLTA spreadsheet covered the time period between April 2019 and February 2022. Together these documents show that instead of the nominal amounts of money that are supposed to be held in an IOLTA, this account looked more like a wealthy person's check registry, with hundreds of thousands of dollars being deposited and withdrawn over the course of a year. For example, the opening balance in April 2019 showed that the conservator had deposited a whopping $1,043,899.71 into the Herrmann IOLTA. According to multiple legal experts schooled in the process, that is not a proper use of IOLTA. Regrettably, there is little to no judicial supervision of these accounts.

At one point in this long odyssey, Nancy won court permission to have a full-blown forensic audit of her father's estate conducted—at her own expense. But by his own admission to the judge, conservator Millet refused to turn over financial records to the auditor. The court then appointed an independent forensic account to conduct another audit. For some unknown reason, that examination languished for more than three and a half years. After the court-appointed examiner finally submitted some seven hundred pages of documents and spreadsheets, it was determined that the audit was "unverifiable" as it was done without access to the IOLTA bank statements controlled by the conservator/trustee. Any time there is such a delayed and inconclusive audit, heirs are left to wonder whether their loved one's estate was fairly and honestly administered. When they get that final disbursement from an uncooperative conservator, how can they be sure they've received the correct amount? The answer is they can't. Not in a system that is so steeped in secrecy and rife with judicial decisions that so often go in favor of the court's handpicked appointee.

To Nancy there was a long-standing and obvious lack of enthusiasm to wrap up her father's accounts. "What a joke," she told me. "The last hearing was April of 2019, [and] the judge told [the conservator] then to close the estate." But that didn't happen. And, of course, as long as the estate remained open, the conservator was free to continue to charge fees. In May 2022, Nancy filed a motion for "contempt of court with sanctions" against conservator Millet for this failure to obey the judge's order and wrap up the estate. Two weeks later, on July 15, 2022, district court judge Erin O'Connell finally issued the final order terminating the trust. O'Connell denied the contempt motion. Nearly nine years had passed since Dr. Herrmann's death.

AROUND CHRISTMASTIME 2015, a private investigator I know came to me with a sad story about a brother and sister from Maryland who were fighting a third sibling in Pennsylvania over where their newly widowed mother should live. As with so many of these cases, one of the siblings decided to take the matter to court. The brother from Pennsylvania didn't want the responsibility of caring for his mother, but he didn't want his brother and sister to win that right either. So he hired a lawyer and asked the court to appoint an outside guardian. The court agreed.

As I researched the story, the similarities between the case of ninety-four-year-old Elizabeth "Betty" Winstanley and that of Dr. Herrmann were evident. They both had considerable estates. They both had been declared incapacitated, unable to care for themselves, and stripped of their civil rights. They were forced to live at the mercy of total strangers appointed by the court. Although they lived thousands of miles away from each other, what the court system did to them was frighteningly similar. However, unlike the closed and secretive New Mexico justice system, I was able to learn many details about the procedures that Pennsylvania courts used to keep Mrs. Winstanley (and her money) in the state against her will. With plenty of court documents at my disposal, help from a dedicated lawyer representing Mrs. Winstanley, and interviews with the major players, I was finally able to start publishing stories about this mysterious and exploitative court system called guardianship. My first nationally syndicated column on the topic ran in February 2016. Under the title "Elder Guardianships: A Shameful 'Racket,'" I recounted for readers what I had learned about the elegant and eloquent ninety-four-year-old widow Betty Winstanley.[6] Via telephone calls, she and I had developed an open and robust relationship. Using the cell phone her youngest son gave her, and speaking from the privacy of her apartment at the Masonic Village retirement facility in Elizabethtown, Pennsylvania, Betty expressed profound frustration at her situation.

"I feel like I am in prison," she told me during an early call. "My life is a living hell."

Mrs. Winstanley's conversational feistiness and spirited candor about her children's bickering, and the untenable predicament it put her in, made me immediately suspicious of the Pennsylvania court's ruling that she was an "incapacitated person." She very lucidly lamented about losing her right to freely travel where and when she wanted. She was righteously offended that she had lost the sacred right to vote. "And here I am a member of the Daughters of the American Revolution," she said with a huff in her voice. She told me her husband had left her with an estate worth about $1.9 million and she wondered why she was being forced to live in a place she did not want.

Betty wistfully told me about her seventy-two-year marriage to the late Dr. Robert Winstanley, an ophthalmologist who I thought bore a striking resemblance to popcorn peddler Orville Redenbacher. Robert had piloted his own plane during their frequent trips to Cuba and other far-flung locales so he could deliver free eye care to the needy, Betty said. She told me all about the circumstances surrounding their first meeting, their long-distance romance, and their long life together. While Robert had gone off to serve his country during World War II, she diligently continued with her university education. At a time when her contemporaries were getting married, having babies, and were content to be housewives, Betty Winstanley was a rare breed. She earned an advanced degree in chemistry and got a job with a chemical laboratory in New Jersey. "My parents always taught me to live an independent life," she said. "And that's what I always did." Late in their lives, the couple decided to take a "lovely" apartment at the independent-living retirement facility in Pennsylvania. The cost was $3,300 a month, which included some meals. They enjoyed getting out on their own for frequent motor trips and sometimes took advantage of planned excursions offered by Masonic Village. For seven years the Winstanleys lived their well-planned retirement dream. And they felt confident that when the time came, they could rely on the skilled nursing staff at the compound. That time came, rather unexpectedly, in early 2014.

As Betty explained it, she was using a rolling walker to get around, and one day she felt faint as she moved down a long hallway. Seeing no staff nearby, she decided to lower herself to the ground until she felt stable. "They said I fell," she told me. "But that is a bad, bad word around here. Once you fall, they decide you aren't capable of taking care of yourself anymore." Tests revealed a small fracture, which may or may not have been a preexisting condition, and Betty was sent to the medical section of the facility for rehabilitation. Robert was left alone in their apartment in another area of the sprawling campus. Soon he fell ill, and about the time Betty was ready to return to the apartment, Robert was transferred to the medical ward. Betty chose to stay there with him, and soon administrators at Masonic Village labeled her as a resident who could no longer live independently. Betty maintained that despite her walker and her need for hearing aids, she would be just fine back in her own apartment. This is the point at which her free will evaporated. Over her protestations, Betty was transferred to a small room where nurses could monitor her 24/7. At a cost of $8,500 a month, it was nearly triple the price of her private apartment.[7] Sadly, Robert died of heart failure in the medical ward in June 2014. Betty and the youngest son, David, were at his bedside.

Several sources confirmed that within three weeks, the eldest Winstanley son, Richard, was in court claiming his mother needed a guardian to make decisions for her. Betty described Richard, her oldest son, as "long troubled" and one who held tight to childhood sibling rivalries.[8] In addition, Betty believed Richard was angry because she had recently moved to transfer her power of attorney away from him to her other two children. Betty had made it clear she did not want to remain at Masonic Village without her beloved husband. She wanted to move near her son David and her daughter Betsy, who both lived in Maryland. Even before Robert's death, Betty had come to despise Masonic Village and its bullying administrators. "They make me feel like a piece of protoplasm on a deserted island here," Betty told me on the phone one day. "I just want to move to an assisted-living home in Annapolis, Maryland, so I can be near David and Betsy. I have no family around here except Richard, who rarely comes to visit. I just want to be near my family, is that too much to ask?"

On July 17, 2014, at the all-important first court hearing on the guardianship request, Betty was without her hearing aids, as a Masonic Village attendant had collected them "for cleaning" the day before and had not returned them. Betty told me she believed the session had something to do with the court accepting the terms of her late husband's will, so she was content to sit quietly. Betty described herself as being consumed by continuing grief over the loss of Robert during this court proceeding, and she insisted that her court-appointed lawyer never told her what the court proceeding was for, or that she had the right to speak before the judge made a decision on her mental capacity. The judge never directly addressed her or asked her to offer comment. Common Pleas Judge Jay Hoberg of Lancaster County, Pennsylvania, heard testimony from one doctor and one nurse from Masonic Village that day, and promptly declared Betty was "a totally incapacitated person." The decision was reached despite other conclusions presented to the judge from two independent neuropsychologists David had hired to examine his mother. Those two doctors conducted individual tests of Betty and declared she was of sound mind. Depressed? Understandably, yes, as her husband of more than seven decades had just died, they said. Affected by dementia or Alzheimer's? No.

Those positive findings on Betty's capacity didn't seem to matter to Judge Hoberg. Mrs. Winstanley was appointed a guardian and a conservator and immediately felt cut off from the rest of the world. Her family visits were curbed, her checkbook was confiscated, and she was restricted from leaving the Masonic Village campus. Her court-appointed guardian, Robert Stump, did not allow Betty to go to town for lunch when David or Betsy were approved to visit. She was also denied her annual drive around the community to see her cherished displays of Christmas lights.

Judge Hoberg's order was set in stone. Betty's guardian was steadfast that she remain in Pennsylvania, despite a state law mandating that guardians must consider the wishes of their ward. David, a flight attendant, told me he had spent his entire life savings on attorneys to fight for his mother's wishes. The battle went on month after month and would ultimately stretch into years.

"I get the impression they just plan to wait her out until she dies," Betty's outside attorney, Candace Beckett, told me. "I've watched my client decline during this prolonged fight . . . she is like a flower who is dying on the vine."

I was able to attend one of Mrs. Winstanley's court sessions in Judge Hoberg's courtroom and watched as her new guardian, Patricia Maisano, and the guardian's court-approved attorney tried to get judicial permission to take away Betty's cell phone—her lifeline to friends and family—

since it was learned she had been communicating with a reporter (me). This pair insisted to the judge that they had Mrs. Winstanley's best interests at heart. What if the ward put herself in danger by accidentally revealing her net worth to a stranger, or some of her own HIPAA-protected medical information, they asked?[9] Douglas Earl, an attorney hired by David, stood and asked the judge in an exasperated tone whether he was the only one who saw "the irony" of the situation. Here, he said, with a gesture toward Maisano, was a guardian who professed to protect and care for a ward while, at the same time, trying to strip Mrs. Winstanley of her only connection to the outside world. Why, he asked, was that a priority? The guardian's attorney rose to complain that my syndicated columns had been published "without permission" from Ms. Maisano, which, considering the First Amendment and freedom of the press, was an absurd thing for him to say. When my presence in the courtroom was pointed out to Judge Hoberg, he instructed the bailiff to immediately remove me, even though it was a public hearing. I once again marveled at the secrecy surrounding the guardianship process. Ultimately, Mrs. Winstanley was allowed to keep her phone.

"I'm ninety-five years old," Betty said, in an exasperated tone, a few weeks shy of her actual ninety-fifth birthday. "I just want to spend my remaining months and years near people who love me." After a pause and heavy sigh, she added, "I don't know what's happened to me . . . and why my son Richard would put me in a position like this." Family friend R. B. Adams believes he knows the reason. "It's all about the money," he told me. "They won't let her leave because they haven't spent all her money yet!"

I did not stop writing. Follow-up columns on Mrs. Winstanley's plight included a detailed summary of the exorbitant fee of $600 per hour her self-described "Master Guardian," Patricia Maisano, charged for services rendered. Using court documents and guardian-generated daily logs and spreadsheets provided to me by Betty's team, I reported on the almost unbelievable drain on the Winstanley estate.[10] During the first three months guardian Maisano was in charge of managing Mrs. Winstanley's life, she billed $50,599.18 for services rendered. I highlighted some of the more outrageous charges, including two phone calls the guardian listed as having been made to one of Betty's children to discuss "dates for [a] Christmas visit." For those two calls, the estate was charged a total of $1,560. After Betty was rushed to the hospital with an unknown health problem, the guardian's logs show that she made no calls to any Winstanley offspring to inform them of their mother's setback. Three days later, the guardian noted making a couple of phone calls to Betty to see how she was doing. Maisano calculated that the time she devoted to those communications was worth $990. Then there was a $1,000 bill incurred because, as Maisano noted, her "computer emails appear[ed] to be breached . . . [and] extensive work [was] done on my phone and computer as a result." The charge included time spent calling her IT department and a consulting attorney. There was no written explanation as to why Mrs. Winstanley should have been billed for technical or legal assistance on Maisano's devices, which were surely used for more than just keeping track of her estate.

The court battle to free Betty from her confinement in Pennsylvania went on for years. In 2016, during an appeal to the Pennsylvania Superior Court, Justice Jack Panella expressed disbelief at Judge Hoberg's decisions in the Winstanley case, saying, "This woman should have been moved to Maryland two years ago. Is this the United States of America?"[11] Nevertheless, nothing changed for Betty. She remained at Masonic Village. Her estate dwindled and then was reported to have been entirely consumed. She died, still trapped at the Lancaster, Pennsylvania, location she loathed, in July 2019, just shy of her ninety-eighth birthday. She lived the last five years of her life angry, depressed, and under the control of strangers.

My columns on Mrs. Winstanley's situation opened a floodgate of complaints. I was inundated with emails, letters, and phone calls about cases just like Mrs. Winstanley's and Dr. Herrmann's. Worried family members from across the country begged for public exposure of their situation in the belief that publicity would help return their family to normal. Most who reached out explained that they had nowhere else to go in their quest to put a stop to the mistreatment of their guardianized loved one. They explained that police would not take a report because it was a "civil matter" as a judge had already issued a final ruling. Neither their district attorney nor their state's attorney general would respond to their pleas, they said. Hiring an attorney to help them fight was impossible since no lawyer relished fighting other lawyers in court, especially in such a chummy and specialized area like guardianship. These anxious relatives told me that not even their local chapter of the American Civil Liberties Union (ACLU) would help; the group routinely chose not to become involved in guardianship cases. One anxious woman told me it was "as if the whole process is bulletproof." An anguished son whose mother had suddenly been guardianized said the judge overseeing the case refused to allow him to speak in court, instructing him to hire a lawyer he couldn't afford if he wanted to address the court. Most people who wrote to me described a system designed to thwart any effort to make it accountable to the citizens it supposedly served.

Now, after years of writing about the predatory pitfalls resulting from judges appointing strangers to manage the lives and money of others, I have come to realize two important things. First, it is no longer just the elderly who are being targeted for guardianship. Cunning players within the system have figured out ways to pursue a wide field of vulnerable people. Second, I came to understand that nothing opened the public's eyes to the inherent downside of the guardian/conservator system like the case of a celebrity caught in the system's clutches.

Pop star Britney Spears was that celebrity.

2

The Case Heard 'Round the World

If it could happen to someone as visible and idolized as Britney Spears, what chance do mere mortals have to avoid the surprise grip of guardianship?

Britney Spears wasn't elderly, and she hadn't inherited a pile of money from a rich relative. She was a beautiful and multitalented girl-next-door type from the Deep South who, as a child, had traveled first to New York and then to Los Angeles to see if she could make it big. And, boy, did she succeed! After early stints off-Broadway, appearances in several television commercials and TV series (including the *Mickey Mouse Club* from 1992 to 1994), she finally broke through as a megastar singer and dancer. Britney's first best-selling album, *Baby One More Time*, was released in 1999 when she was just sixteen years old, and it debuted at number one on the US Billboard 200. Five more of her award-winning albums landed on that chart over the next few years, catapulting her to global pop icon status. To date, Britney Spears has sold over one hundred million records worldwide, seventy million of them in the United States.

While her professional life was soaring, her personal life was a mess. She married and divorced twice (her first marriage was annulled after just fifty-five hours), and by the age of twenty-five she had two sons with her second husband, Kevin Federline. Somewhere along the line, the stress became too much. There were reports of suspected drug and alcohol abuse, and she surrounded herself with shady entertainment-industry types. A pack of paparazzi followed Britney everywhere, and during this time she filed for divorce from Federline. In November 2006, she began to act in bizarre ways. And when Britney began to publicly melt down, cameras were there to immortalize her downfall. She was photographed driving dangerously with her infant son in her lap, she was videotaped manically attacking a cameraman's car with an umbrella, and in the most notorious caught-on-tape episode, she entered a Tarzana, California, hair salon one evening, stood in full view of the front window, and dramatically shaved off her long hair down to the scalp. Britney appeared to be suffering a very public mental breakdown, acting out as if to prove she was in control when obviously she wasn't. Ardent fans, however, saw the defiant act differently. They interpreted the public shearing as a signal that Britney was retaking command of both her personal life and her physical appearance.

Whatever the motivation behind the haircut-seen-'round-the-world, few were surprised when Jamie Spears, Britney's father, stepped up in early 2008 and asked the court to appoint him as conservator of his daughter's person, and an attorney named Andrew Wallet to be co-conservator of her very lucrative estate.[1] Los Angeles Superior Court judge Reva Goetz agreed there were adequate grounds to establish a conservatorship. That judge's fateful decision to conserve Britney Spears, and the controversial process she used to put the process into motion, would surface more than a decade later in a most explosive way. Britney's father was legally installed as the person through which all decisions about her life would flow. But there is a mysterious backstory to how Jamie Spears—a man who had long battled substance abuse, held only menial jobs, and had been estranged (and ultimately divorced) from his wife for many years—came to learn about the legal avenue called conservatorship. Once he chose to pursue that path for his famous daughter, it resulted in her estate automatically paying him more than $16,000 a month for his services.[2] In June 2021, *Forbes* estimated that over the course of the conservatorship Jamie Spears was paid at least $5 million.[3] The *New York Times* reported that in addition to his monthly fee, Britney's father also got a percentage of his daughter's entertainment and marketing earnings. The extra income he derived from Britney's worldwide *Femme Fatale* tour in 2011 and her four-year residency in Las Vegas beginning in 2013 was reported to be at least another $2.6 million.[4]

Who was first to educate the unsophisticated Jamie Spears about the conservatorship route? Several insiders and media reports indicate that the idea originated with entertainment business manager Louise "Lou" Taylor, owner of Tri-Star Sports and Entertainment Group.[5] In her memoir *Through the Storm*, Britney's mother, Lynne Spears, wrote about Taylor's active involvement in the planning of her daughter's conservatorship.[6] And perhaps not coincidentally, once the court appointed Jamie Spears as co-conservator, he hired Lou Taylor to be the manager for Britney's 2009 *Circus* tour, and later for Britney's entire estate, according to the *New Yorker*.[7] Taylor would hold that lucrative position until her abrupt resignation in November 2020. At that time, Taylor had a guaranteed minimum salary of $500,000 a year, paid for out of Britney's estate. According to several accounts, Britney always resented Taylor's involvement in her life. In an email, Britney reportedly referred to the business manager as a "crazy lady" and a "stalker." Britney would later say the email was faked, but her disdain for Taylor was reported by many insiders.[8]

Although a lawyer for Taylor categorically denies she had anything to do with influencing Mr. Spears's choice of conservatorship, journalist Liz Day with the *New York Times* took to Twitter to reveal a lengthy series of court documents and emails from Taylor that disputed that assertion.[9] One email to Jamie Spears dated January 17, 2008, has Taylor assuring Britney's dad that attorney "Andrew Wallet . . . and tri star will serve as co's [co-conservators] w you." There was also an email on January 30, 2008, from Jamie Spear's lawyer to Taylor discussing the preference to go before a judge who would "give Jamie the power to administer psychotropic drugs to B." Britney was officially placed into conservatorship on February 1, 2008. In addition, other celebrities or their family members came forward to say that Taylor pushed the conservatorship route with them too. The father of actress Lindsay Lohan said his ex-wife and Taylor conspired to conserve his daughter in 2010.[10] And singer Courtney Love said Taylor once tried to put her under a "mutated strain" of conservatorship, but she was able to successfully block the move.[11] Like Britney, both those young women had had troubled personal lives and considerable estates at the time these alleged efforts were made. Taylor's lawyer sent out a barrage of legal letters demanding retractions from fan websites and news organizations that reported the talent manager's alleged attempts to conserve either Lohan or Love.[12] (Many of those articles have subsequently disappeared from the internet.) The *New Yorker* quoted Charles Harder, an attorney representing Taylor, as saying, "At no time did Ms. Taylor ever make any effort to put anyone into a conservatorship. Not Britney Spears. Not Lindsay Lohan. Not Courtney Love."[13]

There may have been a more sinister motivation driving Jamie Spears as he chose to first conserve, and then periodically institutionalize, his daughter. It might have had something to do with a dark family history, and a tactic he learned from watching his own father. *New York Post* reporter Dana Kennedy spent time in the Spearses' tiny neighboring hometowns of Kentwood, Louisiana, and Osyka, Mississippi, and discovered that Jamie was not the first of the Spears clan to take such an action against a female member of the family.[14] After doggedly trying to get reluctant locals to talk, Kennedy located Jamie's half brother, John Mark Spears, who declared that the father he and Jamie shared "was a monster, but nobody would say a bad word about him outside the family." Their father's name was June Austin Spears, and he had ten children with three wives. Jamie's mother was Emma Jean Spears, and at age thirty-two after being institutionalized by her husband, Emma Jean took a shotgun to the gravesite of her infant son and died by apparent suicide. Who actually pulled the trigger on the long gun used that day is still hotly debated among the locals.

"These Spears men are something awful," Britney's uncle told the *Post*. "They've gotten away with so much, especially to their women, for years." Reporter Kennedy found another half sibling, Leigh Ann Wrather, to back up the sordid stories about June Austin Spears. Leigh Ann also spoke of her father's sadistic streak and added that he had sexually abused her from the age of eleven. June Spears died in 2012, and these half siblings said that he not only viciously beat his children but also physically and mentally abused his wives, which reportedly resulted in both women suffering a mental breakdown. "He shipped them both off to Mandeville [the state's former notorious mental hospital] from time to time," according to John Mark. "So, I'm not too surprised about what Jamie's done to Britney. It's all about control with the Spears men." The *Post* reported that at least once during her stay at Mandeville, Emma Jean was put on the powerful drug lithium. A half century later Britney would say she was also involuntarily dosed with lithium just as her grandmother had been.

In November 2018, ten years into Britney's court-ordered confinement, Jamie Spears suffered a major health scare. His colon spontaneously ruptured and he was hospitalized for nearly a month. After a decade as the domineering, go-to person in charge of all aspects of his famous daughter's life, Jamie was suddenly out of the picture, for the most part. This would be a pivotal event in Britney's life as a conservatee, the point at which she began to gather courage to take her fight public. The void caused by her father's absence resulted in the singer announcing on Twitter in early January 2019 that she was taking an indefinite work break and would delay her much-anticipated second Las Vegas residency. "I had to make the difficult decision to put my full focus and energy on my family at this time," she wrote. "I hope you all can understand."[15]

Alert fans, especially those in the active #FreeBritney movement (which had gained momentum over the years of their idol's conservatorship), noticed the singer specifically mentioned devoting time to her "family," but not necessarily to her father. Now that Jamie's overwhelming presence was gone from her daily life, and her Las Vegas shows were canceled, some wondered whether Britney was finally exercising her greatest leverage— to simply say no to the grind of constant work. There were conflicting reports about why Britney stepped away from the stage, including one unconfirmed story that it was Jamie Spears who canceled the Las Vegas performances as punishment after his daughter refused to take certain medications and took an unauthorized solo drive to a local Starbucks.

In March 2019 a second surgery to further repair Jamie's colon lengthened his recovery, and the media reported that he had been "near death" at times. By April, *People* magazine reported that Britney had checked into a program for "all-encompassing wellness treatment," which would last several weeks.[16] Some reports indicated that the facility was actually a mental health treatment facility, and that from his sick bed Jamie had ordered his daughter to be institutionalized. Some Britney supporters worried that in exercising her newly felt freedom, Britney may have slipped in her sobriety, but no evidence of that surfaced. Details of all these developments were known to the court, but the veil of secrecy surrounding California conservatorships kept the facts from the public.

Britney has consistently been described by insiders as a loving and truly attentive mother to the two sons she co-parents with ex-husband Kevin Federline. On August 24, 2019, the unsettling drama that seemed to perpetually swirl around her life erupted again. Britney took her young sons, Sean Preston, thirteen, and Jayden James, twelve, to visit their recuperating grandfather at his condo. A police report obtained by *Us Weekly* briefly detailed a confrontation between the older boy and Jamie Spears, which led to a fearful Sean Preston locking himself in a room.[17] Jamie Spears reportedly managed to break down the door and he "shook" the boy, according to the magazine. After Federline learned of the incident, he filed a complaint with police, alleging that the older man had "abused . . . [and] physically assaulted" Sean and that his sons "felt unsafe" around their grandfather. Reports noted that Britney had done the right thing after the traumatic event, promptly removing the children and returning them home to their father to explain what had happened.[18] Within days, a domestic violence restraining order against Jamie Spears was granted. This was another crucial event that would directly affect Britney's conservatorship arrangement.

On September 6, 2019, in what looked like a preemptive move, Jamie Spears asked the court for permission to "temporarily relinquish the powers of conservatorship" until January 31, 2020, due to "personal health reasons."[19] He recommended that professional fiduciary Jodi Montgomery take his place as she was already attached to the case as Britney's care manager. At a hearing three days later, the judge agreed to Montgomery's temporary appointment.[20]

Britney Spears had been privately telling therapists and court investigators for years that she felt the conservatorship should end because her father was forcing her to take too much medication and she had to endure unnecessary psychiatric evaluations that were "oppressive and controlling." The *New York Times* revealed that an investigator dispatched by the judge in 2016 reported back that Britney "is 'sick of being taken advantage of.'" Further, the investigator wrote, "[Britney] is the one working and earning her money but everyone around her is on payroll."[21] The investigator's report to the court made no difference, and the stringent terms of Britney's confinement did not change. She was still considered incapacitated, yet she had clearly proven herself competent enough to earn multiple millions by performing a worldwide concert tour, appearing as a judge on the television program *The X Factor*, and starring in a grueling four-year run of shows in Las Vegas. Britney Spears supported not only her family but also scores of staff and court-appointed minders, including no fewer than thirteen lawyers. Yet she was not able to convince the court that she was capable of taking care of herself. In the meantime, Britney was reportedly kept to a rigid weekly allowance of two thousand dollars a week, and that amount didn't change no matter how much she earned.[22] It is interesting to note that Britney's court-appointed guardian, attorney Samuel Ingham—a prominent figure and favorite court appointee in Los Angeles conservatorship cases—never called the court's attention to California probate code 2601, which states: "If the ward or conservatee is employed at any time . . . the wages or salaries for such employment shall be paid to the ward or conservatee and are subject to his or her control to the same extent as if the guardianship or conservatorship did not exist."[23]

Spears's private battle became quite public in the summer of 2021. It is extremely rare for a ward to speak in an open court setting, but Spears got the chance to give the public a glimpse into her personal anguish. On June

23, 2021, she delivered a passionate and explosive statement to California Superior Court judge Brenda Penny via telephone, during which she forcefully outlined the many civil rights she had been denied. The world was listening. Among the Britney bombshells were revelations that she has long wanted to marry her boyfriend Sam Asghari, have more children, take a break from working, and stop being forced to take mood-altering medications like lithium.[24] "I was told, right now in the conservatorship, I'm not able to get married or have a baby. I have an IUD inside of myself right now so I don't get pregnant," Britney said, addressing Judge Penny. "I wanted to take the IUD out so I could start trying to have another baby. But this so-called team won't let me go to the doctor to take it out because they don't want me to have any children, any more children."[25] It is a fact that the power bestowed upon these court appointees allows them to legally force a ward to be put on birth control. They can order a protected person to be sterilized. If a ward has a child, the guardian can put it up for adoption.[26] Perhaps buoyed by the massive public attention, and the always present and super loyal #FreeBritney fanbase, which had gathered outside the courthouse the day of the hearing, Britney, then thirty-nine years old, poured out her grievances. "I worked seven days a week, no days off, which, in California, the only similar thing to this is called sex trafficking," she told Judge Penny. "Making anyone work against their will, taking all their possessions away—credit cards, cash, phone, passport—and placing them in a home where they work with the people who live with them. They watched me change every day—naked—morning, noon, and night. My body, I had no privacy door for my room." A documentary series titled *The New York Times Presents* would soon reveal that the situation was even worse than the pop star described. "Controlling Britney Spears," an episode of the series that aired in October 2021, detailed how security teams hired by Jamie Spears allegedly engaged in wide-ranging and ever more intrusive surveillance of Britney. According to the documentary, these individuals monitored and recorded Britney's private communications, even those from her bedroom, via a secretly planted audio device. The primary source for this information was Alex Vlasov, a former trusted employee from the firm Black Box Security, and he was prominently featured in the documentary.[27] "Her own phone and her own private conversations were used so often to control her," Vlasov said. He provided emails, texts, and some 180 hours of audio recordings stored on a USB drive as proof that Britney's personal conversations with boyfriends and her children; text messages to her mother, her lawyer, and others; her FaceTime calls; her digital notes; photographs; and her browser history had all been captured during clandestine surveillance missions. According to Vlasov, all of the information was instantaneously provided to Jamie Spears via "a clever tech setup" that fed a mirror device in Jamie's control. Everything that Britney said or did on her phone showed up on an iPad or iPod that her father was able to monitor in real time. The documentary alleged that the intrusive surveillance had continued for years.

In 2019, during Britney's aforementioned stay at a mental health treatment center, she was adamant that she didn't want to be there. The *New York Times* obtained text messages sent from Britney's phone clearly stating she was there against her will, yet her father denied he had forced her to go. "Mr. Vlasov shared digital communications that showed how Ms. Spears, while in the facility, had tried to hire a new lawyer to replace her court-appointed lawyer—and that Mr. Spears and others had monitored that effort," the *Times* reported. In a companion article, the newspaper released portions of Britney's communication with the unidentified lawyer. He had asked to come talk to her in the treatment facility and Britney said she didn't think security would allow it. "They will say no for sure to me seeing a new lawyer on my side," she wrote. She suggested the lawyer pose as a plumber to try to gain entry, but that idea was quickly rejected. The attorney called her inability to meet him before potentially hiring him, a "Catch-22 situation." A week later, Britney reached out to the lawyer again to say her father had confiscated her phone after he learned she was seeking outside counsel. The lawyer confirmed to the *Times* that the digital correspondence Vlasov provided was accurate. There seems to have been no limit to how Britney's father sought to control and manipulate his famous daughter.

Many curious members of the public wondered why Britney hadn't simply petitioned the court to end the conservatorship, which was her right. To that, Britney told the judge during the June 2021 hearing, "Ma'am, I didn't know I could petition [for] the conservatorship to end," she said in a halting tone. "I'm . . . I'm sorry for my ignorance, but I honestly didn't know that." Apparently, none of the well-paid court-appointed lawyers on Britney's payroll had bothered to inform the singer that there was a legal route available to her that could possibly end her lengthy confinement.

During that thirty-minute court appearance, Britney often spoke in a breathless torrent of words. More than once, Judge Perry had to ask her to slow down so the court reporter could make an accurate transcript. In the end, Britney's message was firm and clear. This conservatee was no longer the Britney of 2008, in danger of suddenly attacking the paparazzi or shaving her head. The Britney of 2021 was able to unambiguously speak from the heart, state her complaints, and outline her future goals, simple as they sounded. "I'd like for my boyfriend to be able to drive me in his car, and I want to meet with a therapist once a week, not twice a week," she said. "Basically, this conservatorship is doing me way more harm than good. I deserve to have a life. I've worked my whole life," she said. In closing, Britney Spears spoke to the judge as if she desperately needed a friend. "I wish I could stay with you on the phone forever because when I get off the phone, all of a sudden, I hear all these no's. No, no, no, and then all of a sudden, I feel ganged up on, and I feel bullied, and I feel left out and alone, and I'm tired of feeling alone. I deserve to have the same rights as anybody does by having a child, a family, any of those things, and more so." An unidentified member of the #FreeBritney movement was interviewed outside court after the dramatic hearing and succinctly summed up the opinion of many fans when she said, "If Britney is so ill that she needs this conservatorship, then they sure as hell shouldn't have been propping her up on a stage to perform and make money for them for [all these] years."

The powerful aftershocks of Spears's statement to the court began to be felt about a week later. On July 2 Bessemer Trust, the wealth management firm involved in the conservatorship, asked the court for permission to withdraw from the case, citing "changed circumstances," specifically "the fact that the Conservatee claimed irreparable harm to her interests." The judge approved the request.[28] On July 6 Samuel Ingham, the controversial probate lawyer who was originally assigned as guardian after Britney's chosen attorney was kicked out of court in 2008, announced he wanted to resign from the conservatorship.[29] At the outset of the case, Ingham had told Judge Reva Goetz that Spears was so incapacitated she "did not understand" why she needed representation, and that proffer to the court helped cement the permanent conservatorship. At the time of Ingham's resignation, his annual salary was reported to be more than $520,000, and he had been on the case for thirteen years. Ingham's legal colleague David C. Nelson also sought to be excused. Both were given the court's permission to step aside.

Also jumping ship was Spears's manager, Larry Rudolph. He quit, saying he firmly believed Britney when she announced on July 17, 2021, that she would not perform as long as her father remained her conservator.[30] The white-hot global spotlight on the Spears case, absent in all other conservatorship and guardianship cases I have studied, cut through the legalese to reveal the harsh human toll the system caused. Once eager participants in the Spears conservatorship suddenly wanted no part of it. Asked to comment on the slew of resignations from the Spears conservatorship case, celebrity lawyer Christopher Melcher likened the situation to a "sinking ship," and he said the court appointees had "no where to go hide at this point in the case."[31]

In most of the abusive guardianships cases I have investigated—going back to 2015—worried loved ones said they had contacted their local ACLU office asking for legal assistance in their fight to restore at least some of the civil rights of their conscripted person. In every instance, I was told that local chapters of the ACLU routinely declined to become involved in guardianship and conservatorship cases. It was interesting to see, then, that on July 13, 2021, the national office of the ACLU was out front filing an amicus brief with the court supporting Britney Spears and her right to select her own legal representation.[32] Twenty-five other civil rights and disability rights organizations also signed the brief. The ACLU's sudden involvement (and the press release the group issued to announce it) left the impression that the ACLU only cared about such cases if they involved a worldwide celebrity and guaranteed their organization's name in the headlines. But Zoe Brennan-Krohn, ACLU staff attorney representing the ALCU's Disability Rights Program, which sponsored the brief, defended the group when asked to comment for this book. "Because we are such a small team working on such a large range of issues," she said in a written statement, "we aim to take cases and engage in work in ways that can have a broad impact. The Britney Spears case was an instance in which filing an amicus brief . . . had the potential to change the conversation about conservatorship and guardianship nationwide. This single brief had the potential to raise awareness of the reality that Britney's case was not an anomaly, that guardianship and conservatorship are deeply problematic institutions nationwide."[33] Of course, the long-running and highly publicized Spears case had already raised awareness about the issue worldwide.

The next day, July 14, 2021, there was another extraordinary development for a conservatorship/guardianship case. After pondering what the conservatee had told her, Judge Penny announced she would allow Spears to hire a lawyer of her own choosing.[34] Did that, in effect, mean that Britney was no longer incapacitated? The judge did not say. Attorney Mathew Rosengart, a former federal prosecutor with a reputation as a fierce litigator, promptly appeared on Britney's behalf. Among Rosengart's long list of other celebrity clients were Steven Spielberg, Sean Penn, and Julia

Louis-Dreyfus. Rosengart hit the ground running by immediately requesting to replace all court appointees and to conduct a full audit of Britney's estate. *Forbes* had estimated Spears's worth at the time to be $60 million and called that amount suspicious and "shockingly low compared to her pop peers."[35] Rosengart obviously agreed, and he wanted an accounting of exactly where his client's money had gone.

Two weeks later, court documents revealed Rosengart had tapped a new, licensed fiduciary for Spears. Jason Rubin, a well-respected CPA with no apparent ties to the cliquish California conservatorship industry, came on board to try to untangle exactly who got what from the millions Britney had earned during the previous thirteen years.[36] Rubin had his work cut out for him, and he may have started inspecting invoices from 2008, which showed the hourly rates for some of Jamie Spears's lawyers. Jeffrey Wexler charged $535 per hour; Geraldine Wyle, $495; Gerald Cohen, $460; Vivian Lee Thoreen, $315; and Jonathan Park, $250. During the first six months of the conservatorship, this legal brain trust charged Britney's estate $550,000.[37] That, of course, was in addition to the $10,000 per week being invoiced by Britney's court-appointed attorney, Samuel Ingham.

On July 29, 2021, Rosengart, along with Britney's medical team, asked the court to remove Jamie Spears from any participation in his daughter's life. One month later, Judge Penny agreed to completely remove Britney's father from the roster of court appointees. Rosengart's end goal, of course, was to get the court to terminate the conservatorship—permanently. That milestone was reached on November 12, 2021, ending the nearly fourteen years of unwanted (and perhaps mostly unwarranted) confinement of Britney Spears.[38] "The conservatorship of the person and estate of Britney Jean Spears is no longer required," Judge Penny announced to a hushed courtroom. "The conservatorship is hereby terminated." To say Britney was thrilled, tearful, and grateful would be an understatement. She quickly announced her engagement to longtime boyfriend Sam Asghari, and shortly after Britney's fortieth birthday, the couple said they planned to try to have a baby.[39] Britney would soon announce that she had suffered a miscarriage.

Any record of this case would be incomplete without mention of another "friend of the court" brief that went largely unreported during the flurry of media coverage. It's a shame that this legal maneuver didn't make headlines, because it spells out, in detail, how the conservatorship of Britney Spears might very well have been fraudulent from the beginning. The so-called amici curiae brief was filed on September 29, 2021, by California conservatorship lawyer Lisa MacCarley, the executive director of a non-profit group called Betty's Hope. MacCarley has long advocated for serious reforms in the state's conservatorship system, and she came to have a particular interest in Spears's case. MacCarley's brief, a copy of which she supplied for this book, sought to terminate Spears's conservatorship and establish public hearings to determine how the entirety of the California system "ran roughshod over Ms. Spears's constitutional rights, thus depriving her of life, liberty, and property for over thirteen years." MacCarley maintained that the very creation of the February 2008 conservatorship was not legal because Britney was never physically served with a notice, called a citation of conservatorship, as mandated by the California Probate Code. Such a document, MacCarley wrote, is to be handed to every person facing conservatorship without exception, because "the California Legislature specifically wanted the Proposed Conservatee to have [it] in order to ensure fairness and a chance to be heard." These mandatory citations were designed to ensure courtroom due process is followed. Attached to MacCarley's brief was paperwork showing the citation was served on the court-appointed attorney Samuel Ingham via fax but was not personally delivered to Britney, as required by law.

In one particularly succinct passage, MacCarley writes, "Despite her fame, fortune, beauty and talent, Ms. Spears was forced to be represented by an attorney she did not choose who testified AGAINST her with respect to issues of capacity, and then who signed off on orders that violated Ms. Spears' right to due process. Soon afterward, Mr. Ingham began receiving *$10,000 a week* for his efforts."[40] Further, MacCarley revealed that Britney had not been given five days' notice of the hearing to "conserve" her, as is also required by law. During that time, Britney happened to be held at UCLA Medical Center for a mental health evaluation, but she was accessible enough and well enough to order in and eat In-N-Out Burgers and make several telephone calls. One of those conversations put her in touch with her chosen lawyer, Adam Streisand.

The most intriguing section of the MacCarley document has to do with the behavior of Judge Reva Goetz and Samuel Ingham during one of the initial 2008 conservatorship hearings. As MacCarley lays out the developments of that day: Judge Goetz and attorneys Samuel Ingham and Adam Streisand were in the courtroom. The record from that hearing, called the Minute Order, shows that Mr. Streisand, who announced he was there representing Britney Jean Spears, was "ejected" from the proceedings. The brief then refers to Streisand's February 5, 2021, appearance in "Framing

Britney Spears," another episode of the documentary presented by the *New York Times*. In that episode, Streisand said the judge had fired him as Britney's lawyer during that 2008 hearing. To quote Streisand: "The judge said, 'I've got a medical report, and you haven't seen it, Mr. Streisand, and I'm not going to show it to you. And it shows that she is not capable of retaining counsel and directing counsel on her own.'" Streisand said he explained to the judge that he had spent time with Britney, found her of sound mind, and disagreed with the judge's conclusion. No matter. Judge Goetz immediately dismissed Britney's choice of attorney, installed Samuel Ingham as Britney's legal representative instead, and Streisand reluctantly left both the courtroom and the case.

"That is the day justice died for Britney Spears," attorney MacCarley declared. This experienced conservatorship attorney also said she had never heard of another California case where a judge had fired a defendant's lawyer. MacCarley's brief continues, "A thorough investigation should be made by Ms. Spears's present counsel as to 'how' Judge Goetz obtained 'a report' in the first place." MacCarley notes the publicly available court record shows that all parties to the case had written numerous and detailed declarations regarding their actions during the run-up to the conservatorship hearing, but "not a single declaration by any attorney or party mentions Dr. James Edward Spar." That doctor's name is important because it first surfaced publicly during an interview Streisand gave to CNN in June 2021. During that appearance, Streisand recalled the mysterious "report" Judge Goetz said she had obtained about Britney Spears's mental capacity, and that Goetz had said it was "a report from Dr. Spar."

Dr. James Edward Spar is well known within the conservatorship court, having been involved as an expert witness on competency in numerous cases. For twenty-five years, Dr. Spar has practiced geriatric medicine in Los Angeles. His specialties include assessing elderly patients with depression or dementia.[41] He was, for example, tapped to determine whether former Viacom/CBS CEO Sumner Redstone, then ninety-three, was of sound mind when he fired two top executives who then filed wrongful termination suits.[42] Dr. Spar would seem to be ill suited to have evaluated a twenty-six-year-old superstar.

Dr. Spar is, of course, bound by patient confidentiality rules, but in the Netflix documentary *Britney vs Spears* (2021), he said with a broad smile, "I'm not going to acknowledge that I was ever brought in to evaluate Britney Spears."[43] But on the popular British podcast *Defiance*, Dr. Spar gave a long, generic explanation of how the conservatorship evaluation process unfolds in California, including how wards who have been conserved for temporary mental problems could go back and ask the judge to review their case. Then Dr. Spar spontaneously told host Tom Pattinson, "I don't know what the hell is going on with Britney Spears. I don't know why she still has a conservatorship. I don't know any more than you do."[44] That doesn't sound like the doctor who wrote a most memorable, blockbuster report concluding Britney Spears was "not capable of retaining counsel and directing counsel on her own," as Judge Goetz insisted.

"I don't believe a report from Dr. Spar was ever sitting on Judge Goetz's desk," attorney MacCarley said during a phone interview from her Los Angeles County office. Question: So, is it possible that Judge Goetz simply invented the existence of such a report as a reason to dismiss outside counsel and install Samuel Ingham? Answer: "There is no other explanation that makes any sense," MacCarley said. Attorney MacCarley has been practicing conservatorship law in California for thirty years, and when asked about Judge Goetz's relationship with attorney Ingham, she replied simply, "He was one of her favorites." It was well known that the most lucrative conservatorship cases were frequently assigned to Ingham. Calls for comment to Judge Goetz (now retired), attorney Ingham, and Dr. Spar were not returned.

Could it be that the lengthy conservatorship of pop star Britney Spears began illegally, was unethically manipulated by officers of the court to deprive her of her right to private counsel, and was predicated on a mental evaluation that never happened? As of this writing, none of the players in question have ever denied the contents of MacCarley's amicus brief. If MacCarley's suspicions prove true, then the case of Britney Spears should be publicly dissected for all to see. Violators of professional ethical standards should be exposed and punished. Depriving an American citizen of their rights for as long as Spears was held under court control should not happen in the United States of America. And any serious public scrutiny of this system must include the group at the center of this system—the judges. Only a judge can declare incapacitation. Only a judge can begin a guardianship or conservatorship and keep it in motion. Only a judge can undo a misguided guardianship or remove a dishonest appointee, but that rarely happens. Judges routinely enjoy immunity from prosecution for the actions they take on the bench. Perhaps in some egregious instances—like when someone's constitutional rights are wrongfully suspended—that blanket protection should be lifted.

Some critics of the guardianship and conservatorship system refer to it as legalized human trafficking; others call it a rigged system or akin to an organized crime racket. Distraught relatives who participate in support groups have compared notes and come away speaking of a "playbook" of court-appointee maneuvers designed to isolate the ward from familiar people and places (like church, for example), with the goal of creating maximum compliance and Stockholm-syndrome-like dependence. These frustrated families have taken up a descriptive mantra for what routinely happens to victims at the hands of predatory players: Court appointees, they say, "Isolate. Medicate. Take the estate." Those determined relatives who seek to pursue legal action against a guardian or conservator after their loved one has died will find it is not only the judge who enjoys immunity. Before closing out a case, it is standard operating procedure for the family to be asked to sign a "waiver of liability" before receiving any moneys or possessions left in the estate. That waiver acts to protect the court appointees from all future civil actions. It does not protect a court appointee from future criminal charges.[45]

Sadly, most of the general public has no idea about this part of the judicial system. They have no inkling that someone they love, or they themselves, could easily be conscripted. It is time for the veil of secrecy to be lifted—not just for Britney Spears, but for everyone.

3

The Players

The nation's court system can be confusing. There are many different divisions within federal courts, but they do not hear guardianship and conservatorship cases because there are no federal laws specifically governing these arrangements. There are also many types of state courts: criminal, civil, divorce, family or drug courts, the appeals court—and more. Most states refer the cases discussed here to their probate court. That said, other states funnel guardian and conservator cases through the family court, surrogate court, common pleas court, or even the orphan's court, as it's called in Pennsylvania. No matter which specific name is used, judges who deal with these cases most frequently operate under what is known as "equity court" rules.

State probate courts are a unique feature of the justice system. The traditional mission of that court has been succinctly described this way: "The probate court process is simply the legal process by which the court oversees the settlement of an estate after someone dies."[1] But in more recent times, probate judges have been assigned to oversee a range of different cases, including guardianship or conservatorship cases that involve *living* people and their estates. In those circumstances the issue is no longer a *settlement* of a person's estate but the *control* of the ward's estate. This transformation of probate court responsibility has caused many an upset family member to describe their guardianized loved one as being "dead in the eyes of the law."

There are fundamental differences in the way equity-oriented courts and courts of law are conducted. Perhaps most surprising, a citizen's right to due process is not necessarily guaranteed, and in many state probate courts, jury trials are not allowed.[2] In all courts operating under equity court rules, the judge is the final authority. While he or she is expected to operate within the legal system, a judge in a court of equity can, as one legal description put it, "weigh many different sides to a case and explore different perspectives to arrive at a judgment, rather than having to rely on the narrow confines of the law."[3] As many guardianship reformers have put it, "A judge in this kind of court can do pretty much as he damn well pleases." By the way, to qualify for the bench a typical judgeship candidate has only to be of age, a US citizen, and a legal resident of the state. Surprisingly, while many judges who hear guardianship cases are trained lawyers, some are not.[4] Qualifications vary from state to state.

It is difficult for a layperson to understand all the legal machinations that go on inside any courtroom. And different areas of law—be it corporate, civil rights, bankruptcy, consumer protection, or estate/guardianship—spawn their own peculiar language and intrigues. Even newbie attorneys are at a distinct disadvantage until they gain experience and learn the courtroom tricks of the trade in their chosen field.

Law schools spend major amounts of time teaching student lawyers all about legal theory, principles, and process. They probably don't teach about the dastardly tactics some attorneys have been known to use in guardianship and conservatorship cases. Those questionable methods have developed organically over the years and are known to be shared and honed among like-minded colleagues when they meet privately or gather at legal conventions. (These techniques will be revealed and explored throughout this book.) It also seems obvious that law schools have been unwilling or unable to educate students about how best to help a client avoid an unwanted or exploitive guardianship, how to help fight off unnecessary guardian controls, or how to adequately explain to a helpless family watching their conscripted loved one's decline that there is little hope. These officers of the court are left with only one explanation: the judge initiated the guardianship and only the judge can dissolve it, which is highly unlikely. End of story.

The terminology used in this area of the justice system can be confusing, perhaps deliberately so. To simplify, imagine a sheet of paper with the heading "Guardianship" or "Conservatorship." Below the title is a flowchart listing the players in the process in order of importance. The judge sits alone at the very top of the chart, and that person appoints all the other participants and, in theory, authorizes their actions. The appointees listed below the judge on the chart share a puzzlingly similar sounding set of titles. They might be called a guardian, a guardian ad litem (GAL), or a conservator. Or one person might be assigned to multiple roles. The system certainly would have been easier to understand if different titles had been adopted from the get-go, but that was not the case.

As previously mentioned, the court proceedings begin when a petition for guardianship (or conservatorship) is presented to a judge usually by an elder law or estate law attorney. That action puts in motion the need for a host of others who will enter the picture as soon as the judge approves the petition and declares the ward to be "incapacitated." Generally, these are the positions a judge most frequently appoints, and a summary of their duties.

* *The Guardian*: This is the person tapped to assume control of all personal and health decisions for the ward (also called the "inca-pacitated person" (IP) or the "respondent"). This includes compli-cated tasks such as preparing an inventory of all the ward's material goods for the court, deciding whether and when to remove the pro-tected person from their home and place them in a care facility, and selling the ward's home or other property to help pay for their care. Other more mundane chores involve opening mail, paying bills, tak-ing calls from family and caretakers, and making medical appoint-ments for the IP. This position might be filled by a trusted relative or friend, or it might be assigned to a person well known to the court, such as a solo for-profit guardian or a professional care com-pany specializing in what is called "life management services." In some cases, the judge will grant a guardian "plenary control," which means they have complete authority to decide both the ward's personal and medical matters and their finances. In other words, they would act as both the guardian and the conservator. Anyone anointed to a plenary post is in a very powerful position as they will control every aspect of the ward's life.

* *Conservator*: In many cases that involve a ward with meaningful assets, the judge will appoint a separate conservator to manage the person's finances. Conservators are responsible for determin-ing the value of all holdings in an estate—from bank accounts, trusts, stocks and bonds, homes, automobiles, property hold-ings, heirlooms, and valuables such as artworks and coin or stamp

collections—and reporting the collective value to the court. To adequately manage the assets over the protected person's lifespan, conservators may use a mathematical calculation to project a ward's life expectancy and determine which holdings need to be liquidated to meet current and future needs. One calculation assumes that 4 to 5 percent of a ward's estate can prudently be spent on their care each year. For, say, a relatively healthy elderly person with a $5 million estate, that would work out to a likely unnecessary $200,000 to $250,000 a year. Yet there are cases in which that amount, and more, has been spent on a ward in one year. There is no officially accepted calculation equation for conservators to follow.

* *Guardian Ad Litem:* This person is an attorney who is assigned to represent the ward. But there can be confusion regarding the precise role of a GAL. Traditionally, a lawyer takes direction from their client. But in the case of a guardianship or conservatorship where the client has been—or is about to be—declared incapacitated, what then? Can such a client really make good choices and adequately direct their GAL to provide them with "zealous advocacy"? In some courts, GAL lawyers are instructed by the judge to be the eyes and ears for the court and make decisions based on what they perceive is in the ward's "best interest." It's a gray area, not fully or uniformly defined from state to state.

* *Court Visitor or Court Investigator:* This appointee often has training in medicine or social work. They are there to help determine whether the guardianship is truly necessary and whether it should be made permanent. They are assigned by the court to interview the petitioner, the potential ward, the prospective guardian or conservator, family members and other relevant individuals (like the respondent's doctors or therapists), and report to the court their unbiased findings. Some court visitors and investigators are more diligent than others.

* *Qualified Healthcare Professional:* The qualifications of this appointee differ depending on the state. They may be a licensed physician, like a family doctor, or they may be required to have an advanced degree in clinical psychology or neuropsychology. They normally spend a few hours with the respondent interviewing and testing their cognitive ability, speech, judgment, memory, and "executive

function" (e.g., their ability to carry out daily tasks in proper order). The psychological examiner is required to write a report for
the judge to study before a final ruling on capacity is issued. Such
evaluations may be ordered more than once during the course of a
guardianship.

* *Court Clerk*: This is one of only two positions within guardianships
  and conservatorships not paid for out of the ward's estate or from
  generous monthly government payments. Both the court clerk and
  the judge work for the county or state and are compensated by the
  taxpayers. Simply put, the clerk is the keeper of the records. Any
  family member or other interested party worried about a guardianship and contemplating possible legal action should become acquainted with the court clerk. Upon written request, the clerk can
  often provide valuable copies of documents, including the docket
  for the case (a dated, chronological listing of events), lawyer's motions, rulings from the judge, financial reports and audits entered
  into the record, and more. Clerks are instructed not to release records regarding a ward's medical or mental health as that would vi-
  olate federal HIPAA privacy laws.[5] It benefits concerned outsiders
  to gather as many court documents as possible and keep them in
  chronological order in a secure binder.

* *Caretakers*: Once the guardianship is ratified by the judge, the
  guardian can hire any number of outside staff to care for the ward.
  These can include home health aides, licensed practical or registered nurses, drivers, housekeepers, cooks, personal shoppers, gar-
  deners, maintenance workers, painters, carpenters, car mechanics,
  and more. As for the hands-on caretakers, there are many dedicated
  and loyal people working in the field. There are also the inexperienced or uncaring types who, at best, do the minimum to help the
  guardianized person and, at worst, mistreat, physically abuse, and
  even steal from them. There is no state that keeps a central registry
  of disreputable caretakers, and there are no checks and balances
  on guardians who decide to hire their own unqualified relatives or
  friends for caretaker positions.

* *Financial Consultants*: Just as a guardian cannot personally perform all the necessary tasks for a ward and may hire outside help,
  a conservator can do the same. They may engage financial audi-

tors, experts in the stock or bond market, trust companies, income tax preparers, real estate analysts, accountants, or appraisers who determine the value of antiques, artworks, or other possessions of the ward. In short, any specialist the conservator believes is needed may be hired. And like a guardian who may feel threatened by family complaints about their performance, a conservator may also hire a personal attorney to represent him or her during court proceedings. The ward pays for all these services whether they truly need them or not.

When the lawyer first presents a guardianship petition to the judge, it is not unusual for him or her to have a list of recommended appointees to offer up at the same time. In fact, the attorney may have already contacted their favorite guardian, conservator, court visitor, or healthcare professional to check on their availability. Those chosen cohorts may actually be in court with the lawyer the day the petition is filed. While it is the judge who makes the final decision on filling positions, such suggestions from counsel are usually welcomed and readily accepted by overworked, understaffed jurists with bulging dockets.

As for how much each of these players usually charge—generally speaking—the fee a ward must pay for their own physiological evaluation can be as high as $2,000. A court visitor charges, on average, about $150 an hour. Fees for guardians ad litem, guardians, conservators, and financial advisers range from $250 up to as much as $600 dollars an hour. The fees for lawyers who initiate the petitions vary from state to state, of course, but in large metropolitan areas, rates as high as $800 an hour have been reported.

Because these arrangements have flown under the public radar for so many years, and because the process is so cloaked in secrecy, families have no way of knowing how interconnected these appointees are. They are supposed to be there to serve the best interests of the ward, but they also instinctively look out for each other, as they frequently wind up working together again and again. It is human nature to want to work with familiar and cooperative people, but as anguished family members will attest, the tight-knit group of for-profit guardianship teams frequently seem to have more than just camaraderie in mind. Relatives of the conscripted say it often appears more like a "you scratch my back, I'll scratch yours" cronyism where the participants readily go along to get along, and the primary motive is money. This group of largely unchecked professionals are often part of a chummy clique of familiar courtroom faces, their financial and professional futures intricately intertwined.

Although it has been shown that some attorneys have inserted false statements in guardianship petitions to ensure the judge approves them, I could find no case in which a lawyer was disciplined or sanctioned for such a fib. Court documents and criminal indictments reveal that guardians have engaged in double-billing or have illegally claimed government benefits for ineligible wards. A guardian may sell an unsuspecting ward's car, home, or other property and underreport to the court the actual amount received. Where the unreported funds wind up is left to the imagination because no in-depth auditing of guardian transactions takes place. Court visitors and psychological evaluators are known to have been biased by pre-interview pronouncements from a lawyer or guardian that the ward has obvious dementia, is mentally unstable, or that the family is dysfunctional. With a preconceived notion in mind, these appointees may then scrimp on time devoted to a case and simply rubber-stamp the idea that a guardianship is crucial. Perhaps most alarming, judges have been known to receive campaign contributions from those who they name to guardianship or conservatorship positions. Critics of the system say that this smacks of a pay-to-play arrangement.

As the cases reported in this book illustrate, these transgressions are just the tip of the iceberg when it comes to the dastardly deeds done in the name of protecting a ward of the court. Yet the players within the system rarely report a fellow appointee for bad or even criminal behavior. Insider whistleblowing is virtually unheard of since such an action would result in the immediate loss of position within this profitable enterprise. To lodge a complaint about wrongdoing against a colleague would mean certain expulsion from this most lucrative and exclusive inner circle.

4

Britney Is Not Alone

Britney Spears isn't the only celebrity to discover that fame is no protection against being conscripted into a conservatorship or guardianship. Over the past few decades, many Hollywood types have had their final days guided by restrictive court orders. Attentive celebrity watchers have seen a stream of fan magazine stories about their favorite star's battle with this court-ordered system. One early example: in July 2012 Zsa Zsa Gabor's daughter, Francesca Hilton, asked the court for conservatorship of her mother's estate when she suspected the star's ninth husband was over-medicating, deliberately isolating, and financially exploiting the ninety-five-year-old star. The court obliged.

In addition to celebrity cases, there has been no lack of media exposure about the problematic guardianship and conservatorship system. Documentaries like *The Guardians* (2019), *Pursuit of Justice* (2018), and the Academy Award–nominated *Edith+Eddie* (2017) have presented graphic and disturbing guardianship stories. And the award-winning 2021 Netflix movie *I Care a Lot*, starring Rosamund Pike, presented a true-to-life portrayal of a quintessentially diabolical guardian—though the film eventually veered off into a fanciful storyline only Hollywood could have created.[1]

Dedicated print and television reporters, many in sunny, retirement-friendly states like California, Florida, Nevada, Arizona, and New Mexico, have routinely delivered compelling and instructive horror stories about guardianized civilians and their frustrated families who have been trapped by the system. Several long-form exposés have been published in recent years, including in the *Los Angeles Times*, *Seattle Times*, *Columbus Dispatch*,

Sarasota Herald-Tribune, Albuquerque Journal, Buzzfeed News, and the *New Yorker.* Yet after all that very public negative exposure, some of it involving top celebrities, few steps have been taken to substantially change the shamed system. The meaningful but scattershot way the topic has been reported has simply not resulted in a collective hue and cry demanding change to this civil rights–crushing process.

One of the earliest modern-day mentions of a newsmaker being placed under conservatorship didn't involve a famous person but, rather, involved an infamous one: serial killer David Berkowitz, New York's "Son of Sam," or the ".44 Caliber Killer." Beginning in 1976, Berkowitz engaged in a series of random fatal shootings of young couples sitting in cars at night—he seemed to target women with long dark hair—and as the media breathlessly reported on the unknown shooter's deadly spree, widespread panic resulted. After Berkowitz's headline-grabbing arrest in August 1977, on charges that he murdered six young people and wounded nine others, the public was riveted about his motive for the brutal killings. However, it is likely that few people noticed that three months after his capture, a judge placed Berkowitz under a conservatorship. The move came after savvy lawyers anticipated that Berkowitz's crimes would spark lucrative offers from moviemakers and publishers. They were right. While money did come into the defendant's bank account, most of the Berkowitz-based projects eventually evaporated or failed to generate much profit.

The fact that Berkowitz was under a conservatorship had been sealed by the court, but the news was made public after the Associated Press successfully argued for release of the conservator's records. It was then learned that when the twenty-four-year-old Berkowitz was taken into custody he had about $1,000 in the bank. By October 1980 that balance topped $102,000. The court-appointed conservator kept good care of the account, and as interest, tax refunds, and Social Security payments added up over the years, Berkowitz's bottom line swelled to more than $190,000. Shortly after his arrest, New York's legislature had hastily passed the "Son of Sam" law, which prohibited criminals from profiting from their crimes, and Berkowitz's ill-gotten gains were confiscated by the court. Naturally, there was a lengthy legal battle over where that money should go. In the end, Judge Dominic Lodato denied claims from the various lawyers in the case who, collectively, submitted invoices for more than $120,000. Judge Lodato ordered that all funds be distributed to the grievously wounded survivors.

ON FEBRUARY 13, 1983, the highly acclaimed Broadway producer David Merrick suffered a stroke at age seventy-three. This occurred at about the same time he planned to end his nine-month-long marriage to his fifth wife, chorus-line dancer Karen Prunczik, who at twenty-six was nearly a half century younger than her husband. Lawyers for Merrick, who was known for producing some of Broadway's biggest hit musicals, such as *Gypsy, Hello, Dolly!, The Fantasticks, I Do! I Do!, Promises, Promises,* and *42nd Street,* asked the court to name a conservator to handle their client's finances while he recuperated and tried to regain his power of speech. After hearing from several witnesses about Merrick's condition, the judge tapped Merrick's business partner, Morton Mitosky, to be the conservator. The outgoing Mrs. Prunczik-Merrick promptly filed a motion claiming that her husband had been unduly influenced by Mitosky and had become unreasonably paranoid since his stroke. She wanted her estranged husband to come home and live with her. Instead, the headstrong producer had already moved back in with his third wife, Etan Merrick, whom he would soon remarry. At stake was Merrick's estate, worth over $50 million. The judge dismissed Prunczik-Merrick's complaint that the producer was being "held against his will," and found that Mr. Merrick was "happy there with his former wife, living at her home." In fact, after about a year, Etan Merrick would assume the role of conservator after Mitosky stepped aside. Ultimately, Prunczik-Merrick dropped all legal actions and said she would not contest the divorce after an undisclosed, and presumably very healthy, monetary settlement was reached.

One anecdote from this case emphasizes just how powerfully the court can assert itself into a private citizen's affairs. David Merrick's condition so improved that Etan Merrick asked the court to end the conservatorship. She quickly learned that undoing such an arrangement was not so easy, even after explaining to the judge that David had recovered to the point that he was already preparing for a London premiere of *42nd Street.* When she asked permission to release $1.5 million of her husband's money to cover costs for his UK project, the judge refused. He determined it would not be a wise investment. Imagine a jurist with no experience in the theater being able to dictate to such a successful and prolific producer!

"He said it was an inappropriate investment," Mrs. Merrick recalled. "Here we had a show that was a proven property—in four years it had grossed $21 million on Broadway—and the judge told me it was [an] illegal [expenditure]." The Merricks appealed the decision, certain that a London residency—and another planned for Australia—would be highly profitable. The appellate court upheld the lower court decision to withhold funds. However, one of the three judges on that appellate panel wrote a blunt dissenting opinion. He said that given Merrick's astounding record of success with theatrical ventures, the court's intervention was akin to telling Henry Ford he could no longer make automobiles or instructing John D. Rockefeller to step away from the oil business.

In January 1985, nearly two years after the court action began, David Merrick appeared in court to prove he was capable of handling his own affairs. He engaged in what was reported to be "a show-stopping performance," including a rousing discussion with the judge about who would win the upcoming Super Bowl. Though Merrick's prediction was wrong (the San Francisco 49ers beat the Miami Dolphins that year), the judge was so enchanted with the courtroom conversation that he terminated the conservatorship. Etan Merrick would appear on Capitol Hill in 1987 to give testimony about the hoops they were made to jump through, and the vast cost of dissolving Merrick's conservatorship. "How very fortunate that David had worked a lifetime and amassed enough money to pay all these people to 'protect him,'" she told the House Select Committee on Aging. "The cost of the termination procedure alone could probably have supported a small South American Country for a year."

A final note: David Merrick died in London on April 25, 2000, at the age of eighty-eight. His London production of *42nd Street* at the Royal Drury Lane Theatre opened August 8, 1984, and packed houses were reported during the next five years. The production was considered a major success, garnering top theatrical awards, and was credited with launching the career of actress Catherine Zeta-Jones.

ACTOR PETER FALK is best remembered for portraying Columbo, the brilliant but rumpled—and sometimes forgetful—homicide detective who would invariably start to leave a suspect's room and turn back with hand to forehead to say, "Oh, uh . . . one more thing . . ." But by 2008 Falk had been diagnosed with dementia, probably caused by Alzheimer's disease. He may have been incapable of remembering his most famous character. On a sunny day in April of that year, Falk was found wandering the streets of Beverly Hills wearing wrinkled khaki pants and a long-sleeved plaid shirt unbuttoned at the belt, exposing his belly and the top of his blue boxer shorts. Falk's hair and expression were wild as he tugged at his pants pockets and threw his hands in the air while shouting that he'd "lost his car keys." Oblivious to his surroundings, Falk wandered into the street as cars swerved to avoid him. According to the book *Beyond Columbo: The Life and Times of Peter Falk* (2017), a police officer, and then two actor friends, Charles Durning and Joe Mantegna, rescued him and took him home. Photographs from this disturbing episode splashed across the airwaves and in newspapers worldwide and caused Falk's fans to wince in embarrassment and sympathy.

Falk was married twice and had two daughters, Catherine and Jackie, who were adopted during his first marriage. A year after his divorce, when Catherine was five years old, Peter married Shera Danese, who was twenty-two years his junior. Whether Falk stayed in regular touch with his girls after the second marriage is a matter of dispute. Catherine writes, "For thirty years, Mr. Falk maintained a loving relationship with Catherine despite constant interference by his second spouse." Shera Danese insists nothing could be further from the truth. Catherine admits that she once sued her father to force him to continue to pay for her college, but she maintained they had reconciled. How that reconciliation was achieved is unclear, since Catherine also claims that every time she and her sister went to visit their father, their stepmother refused them entry and slammed the door in their faces.[2]

In December 2008, after Falk's very public episode in Beverly Hills, Catherine began what would be a seven-month-long court battle. She wanted the right to visit with her dad, but under California law, as she explained during an interview for this book, "I had to go into court, and basically, petition for conservatorship, which I didn't even really want. But it was the 'umbrella' to being able to go into court and say, 'and can you (also) give me visitation?' It's the only place to go to ask to see your parent." Catherine's petition asked Los Angeles County Superior Court judge Aviva K. Bobb to appoint two conservators: one to look out for her father's person, and another to take control of his $100 million estate to protect against "fraud and undue influence." Catherine also prominently asked the court to officially affirm her right to spend quality time with her ailing father.[3] During a court hearing, Shera Danese, the actor's wife of thirty-two years, testified that her husband thought his daughter was trouble. She told the court the two had never been close.[4] "He didn't want a relationship with her. He has no relationship with her," Danese said. "His visits with her are confrontational. I'm questioning her motives for coming here."[5]

Catherine presented telegrams and postcards her father had written her years earlier as proof that they once had a closer relationship than her stepmother realized. By all accounts, it was a brutal, argumentative two days of testimony, concluding with Judge Bobb ordering attorneys for both sides to retreat and hammer out an agreement.[6] In the end, Shera was declared the guardian-conservator of her husband, but she had to agree to allow visitations.[7] Those encounters with Catherine and her father occurred in a friend's nearby home, and Shera Danese was not allowed to be there. Since sister Jackie had not been a party to the court action, she was unable to see her father during the last three years of his life.

During a telephone interview, Catherine Falk said she learned of her father's death on June 23, 2011, from the media. Neither she nor her sister had any idea that their dad had been hospitalized with pneumonia earlier that month. She alleged that Shera Danese denied the sisters information about the funeral and buried their father without notifying them. No matter the dysfunctional family dynamics, the most compassionate course in a situation like this would have been to allow children the opportunity for a final goodbye with their parent. "There were definitely bumps in the road," Catherine told the television program *Inside Edition* a few weeks after Falk's death. "But we had reconciled and I had a very loving relationship with him. I adored him, he adored me."[8]

That painful experience propelled Catherine to become an outspoken activist in the field of guardianship reform. She established the Catherine Falk Organization and partnered with the National Association to Stop Guardian Abuse.[9] Together they have campaigned in various states to pass Peter Falk's Law. It reads in part: "A guardian may not restrict an incapacitated person's right of communication, visitation, or interaction with other persons, including the right to receive visitors, telephone calls, personal mail or electronic communications."[10] The law also requires court appointees to alert family members when their loved one's residence changes, when the ward develops a life-threatening condition, or when the ward dies.

ANOTHER DYNAMIC ACTIVIST in the guardianship reform movement is Kerri Kasem, the daughter of famed radio personality Casey Kasem. She, and to a lesser extent her two siblings, also battled a stepmother for the right to be with her father in his last years. Kerri's very public campaign to end the elder abuse that can occur during conservatorships and guardianship has been going on for years.

Casey Kasem is best remembered for his distinctive voice and weekly *American Top 40 Countdown* radio music program. He was also an accomplished voiceover artist, appearing as various characters on *Sesame Street*, the *Transformers*, and the *Scooby Doo* cartoon series, and was the "voice of NBC" for many years. Kasem was a major force in the radio world from 1970 to 2009, and his many charitable and political endeavors endeared him to Hollywood and beyond. In 1972 Casey married and had three children: Mike, Julie, and Kerri. He and his wife Linda Myers Kasem divorced in 1979. The following year, he married actress Jean Thompson and they produced one daughter, Liberty Jean.

The public didn't realize it, but Casey's health began to deteriorate in 2007, and he was incorrectly diagnosed with Parkinson's disease. In 2009 his voice began to falter, and Kerri said it took him "hours and sometimes a couple of days to get through a simple script." Speaking from her home outside Tampa, Florida, Kerry remembered that was the year her father was forced to quit his show. "His voice was really going by 2009," she said, "I think he wanted to keep working, but I think his wife convinced him to stop." Sometime later—Kerri isn't sure exactly when, because Jean Kasem did not inform her husband's adult children—doctors diagnosed Casey with a much more invasive disease: Lewy body dementia. It is a progressive Alzheimer's-like condition marked by memory loss, visual hallucinations, problems with movement, and severe sleep disruptions.

The three oldest Kasem children had never been close with their stepmother. Brother Mike moved away to Singapore, and the two sisters were reduced to sneaking visits with their father at locations outside of his home. Casey longed to have a unified and happy family, but with Jean in the driver's seat, that apparently wasn't possible. "She could have had a family who loved her, but she didn't want that," Kerri said about her stepmother during a televised interview. "She called us 'the old family,' whereas she was 'the new family.' It was a divide that she created."[11] On the other hand, Jean was quoted as saying, "Casey's adult children, Kerri, Julie, and Mike, from a prior marriage . . . grew up with their mother and have a deep-seated hatred towards me."[12] It could be that both sides were correct.

Once Casey became too ill for clandestine meetings, the Kasem sisters pushed to visit him at home. Kerri was particularly upset and publicly outspoken after Jean isolated Casey and refused his older children any visitation. On October 1, 2013, Kerri, Casey's brother, Mouner, childhood friend Jason Thomas Gordon (grandson to Danny Thomas), and other Casey supporters staged a protest outside the elder Kasem's home. Large homemade signs reading, "Jean, why won't you let me see my dad?," "I miss my brother!," and "Casey's best friend of 63 years" greeted Jean.[13] Her response was to call the police. On October 7, daughter Julie Kasem and her husband, Dr. Jamil Aboulhosn, filed a conservatorship petition asking the court to put Casey in their care. Los Angeles Superior Court judge Lesley Green denied the request, saying there was no convincing evidence that the eighty-one-year-old Kasem was at immediate risk.[14] Months of bitter accusations followed, some in court, some over the airwaves. Jean said her husband's children and their lawyers had "blood on their hands" and were part of a "conspiracy" to kill Casey.[15] Kerri alleged that immediately after Jean made that statement outside the courthouse, "she drove to Malibu and was spotted by the neighbors making out in a car with her boyfriend."[16]

Casey's condition worsened, and he was moved from his home to a convalescent hospital in Santa Monica. Logan Clarke, a private detective hired by the estranged Kasem children, reported a disturbing and dangerous episode that occurred at the hospital on May 7, 2014. Jean arrived with a caretaker and ordered that her husband's feeding tube be removed. "The doctor warned her that this could be fatal," Clarke said, "She told them all to go to hell." A doctor and nursing staff caring for Casey Kasem confirmed that story.[17] Casey was loaded into one of two waiting SUVs, without his wife, and was driven away. Thus began the radio icon's final journey. During interviews for this book, Kerri said her investigation determined that the grievously ill Casey was driven to Nevada, then to Arizona, back to Nevada, and then to Montreal, which Kerri said was the hometown of Jean's unidentified boyfriend. Casey was finally located in Washington State, and just how he survived the arduous road trip is unclear. Back in California, Kerri argued to the court that Jean Kasem was guilty of elder abuse and had put her father's life in danger. This time the court agreed, and in mid-May 2014 superior court judge Daniel Murphy appointed Kerri as her father's conservator. Her first step was to file an official missing person's report, which automatically enlisted law enforcement cooperation. Kerri's next step was to secure a court order demanding Jean relinquish Casey's passport and allow doctors in Washington State to examine her ailing father. The judge agreed to those requests. Because it took time to get all the players in order, Kerri was not able to see her dad until the evening of May 30, 2014. She said he was alert, but barely so.

The next day, Kerri, accompanied by medical personnel and an ambulance, arrived at the private Washington State home where her father was being held. The plan was to transport him to St. Anthony's Hospital in Gig Harbor. At first, Jean reportedly refused to let the paramedics enter, and she was videotaped talking about "the honor of King David" and throwing a block of frozen hamburger meat at Kerri, who was waiting in the street to follow the ambulance to the hospital.[18] Eventually, the transfer to the hospital was successful and doctors were finally able to evaluate Casey's condition. Kasem was found to have serious open bedsores on his back as a result of his three-week-long odyssey. Kerri described them to me during one of our many conversations as being "as big as a salad plate." He also had infections in his lungs and urinary tract. Casey Kasem died at the hospital on June 15, 2014, at the age of eighty-two. During his last fifteen days, he was surrounded by loved ones, including his three oldest children, Mike, Julie, and Kerri; his brother Mouner and his wife, Mary; and his dear friend Gonzalo Venecia. Although a court order stipulated that all members of the family could visit, Kerri said Jean and daughter Liberty came only once, "for about ten minutes."

Kerri Kasem, a successful television and radio performer in her own right, has dedicated her life to Kasem Cares, a nonprofit foundation that she established after her father's death. On the group's website, Kasem-Cares.org, its stated mission is to fight elder abuse and isolation. Although Kerri fell short of her quest to confront her stepmother in court, she did produce an eight-episode Apple podcast called *Bitter Blood: Kasem v. Kasem*, which she describes as "what you would have heard at trial, if there had been a trial . . . all the depositions, all the sworn statements."[19] Kerri is joined in her activism by other reformers who put their faith in the legal system and emerged heartbroken. Among the Kasem Cares team are the adult children of Glen Campbell and Mickey Rooney who say they also were denied the right to a full and loving relationship with their fathers before they died. Today, Kasem Cares presses state legislators to pass laws designed to ensure elders can live in dignity and with their chosen family members at their side. Kerri reports that twenty-one states to date have either passed the Kasem Cares Visitation Bill or have adopted their own version of the legislation.[20] While there is much to fix within the guardianship/conservatorship system, laws that ensure continued involvement of family and friends in a ward's life are an important step toward ensuring outside monitoring of this often-abusive process.

MOST CASES IN THIS BOOK feature the same basic elements: questionable court decisions, bad actors motivated by money or power, yearslong legal fights, and painful family betrayals too complex to fully document. But the end-of-life stories of Glen Campbell and Mickey Rooney were a bit different and deserve specific mention here. In both instances the children born to the first wives of these celebrities felt powerless to help their fathers escape what they saw as tragic and allegedly exploitative circumstances.

Glen Campbell, the legendary singer, songwriter, and host of his own television show in the 1960s and '70s, was a prolific performer. Many in the industry considered him to be a master musician, a superb guitarist without peer. Over a career that spanned parts of seven decades, he produced sixty-four albums and sold nearly fifty million records worldwide. In 1968, one of Campbell's most lucrative years, his records outsold those of the Beatles. Among the long list of his most popular, award-winning songs are "Gentle on My Mind," "By the Time I Get to Phoenix," "Wichita Lineman," "Galveston," and "Rhinestone Cowboy." Campbell married four times and fathered nine children. In 1982 he entered into his last marriage, to Kimberly Woolen, a former Radio City Music Hall Rockette, and they had three children. Glen told interviewers that Kim was instrumental in helping him kick his dependency on alcohol and cocaine, and they shared a deep religious faith. As the years went by, Campbell's career slowed down but he never left the public eye.

In late 2010 the singer was diagnosed with Alzheimer's disease, and he disclosed the sad news to the world shortly after his diagnosis. An interview Campbell granted in early February 2012 was most revealing. Speaking with a reporter from the CBS television affiliate in Dallas, touted as his last sit-down interview, Campbell turned to his wife and asked, "How old am I now? Forty-five? Sixty-five? Ninety-five?" When Kim replied that he is seventy-five years old, he shrugged and said, "Oh, it's just a number. I'm getting very forgetful." With his trademark smile, he added, "That's why I go out and play golf."[21] Campbell told *Rolling Stone* magazine later that year, "I don't feel any different at all. I haven't been to the doctors where they said, 'You got Alzheimer's.'"[22] Of course, that wasn't true. He had forgotten. Despite the devastating diagnosis, an ambitious concert tour was launched to promote Campbell's final album, *Ghost on the Canvas*. It was billed as his farewell tour. In 2012 Campbell was joined on stage by his oldest daughter, Debby, singing harmony and prompting her father during performances if he forgot lyrics or lost focus, and his daughter Ashley playing banjo. The tour was rocky at times, according to multiple reports. After one concert, during which Glen called for his closing song "Rhinestone Cowboy" just ten minutes into the program, Debby suddenly lost her job as a backup singer, along with several other musicians.[23] Stepmother Kim reportedly took control, and the youngest two Campbell children joined the show. There are reports that this final tour was only supposed to span five weeks; instead it last nearly two years, prompting some to wonder if such a nonstop lifestyle was good for a man in Campbell's declining condition. Kim insisted that performing the music that had defined his life was the best and most therapeutic way for her husband to stay mentally alert for as long as possible.

Soon after his diagnosis, cameras seemed to follow Glen Campbell everywhere. He was filmed going to doctor's appointments, during his MRI tests and intravenous treatments at the Mayo Clinic, while he played his guitar and interacted with other patients in the hospital, and backstage during the tour.[24] Then it became clear that the footage was to be used in a documentary entitled *Glen Campbell: I'll Be Me*. The trailer for the film, released in 2014, was a slick promotion promising to chronicle the singer's "425 days" on the road, his 151 concerts, "from Carnegie Hall to the Hollywood Bowl."[25] The documentary was advertised as the first time a major celebrity had shared such a devastating diagnosis with the world, and it received high praise. One reviewer opined, "The family should be applauded for allowing the public to see Glen Campbell's fight to continue to perform." But not everyone in the far-flung Campbell clan agreed it was really all about Glen's fight against Alzheimer's. Some of his children thought their father was the victim of a well-planned marketing strategy designed by Kim to exploit Glen, to force him to work under the pretext that it was his choice. The goal, these Campbell family members believed, was to monetize fan devotion with a final tour and documentary, and to fatten the elder Campbell's bank account before he was no longer able to perform.

On January 13, 2015, after Kim made the solo decision to institutionalize her husband so he could have round-the-clock care at a facility in Nashville, Glen's two oldest children filed a petition for guardianship with the Tennessee Court. Debby Campbell-Cloyd and her brother Travis Campbell were listed as petitioners.[26] Although the case was sealed, the Associated Press obtained a copy of the petition. The siblings claimed that Kim was not providing their father with needed toiletries and clothing, not visiting him regularly, and possibly mishandling his $50 million estate. They also alleged that several of Glen's eight surviving children were not on the list of those who had permission to visit him. And finally, the petition complained that their stepmother was allowing her husband to be interviewed on camera at the facility even though his progressive disease made such appearances inappropriate.

The court rejected the sibling's plea to name an outside conservator and assigned the role to Kim Campbell, Glen's wife of more than thirty years. But the order also stipulated that visitation would be granted to the Campbell children. They were allowed two four-hour sessions per month. More court battles relating to the conservatorship would follow, adding to the legal fees for both sides. In the back-and-forth family bickering that so often takes place in these cases, Kim said stepson Travis hadn't visited his father in twenty years and only resurfaced during the last year and a half of Glen's life. Travis said Kim wouldn't allow her husband's "old family" children to visit and made staying in touch impossible. Travis explained that after he had suffered a near fatal heart attack, he realized the urgency of mending family ties before it was too late. It is, of course, a shame that fractured families feel their best course of action is to turn to the courts to settle disputes. Conservatorships and guardianships tend to complicate matters and further inflame resentments.

Glen Campbell died in Nashville, Tennessee, on August 8, 2017, at the age of eighty-one. It is very likely that at the end of his life, after struggling with Alzheimer's symptoms for seven years, Campbell was not aware of the family enmity festering around him.

ACTOR MICKEY ROONEY had eight wives and nine children. Yet with all those loved ones surrounding him, his life did not end in family bliss. Primarily because, as those who got to know him well explained, Rooney did next to nothing to stay in touch with his biological children. History will record that in the end he was broken and humiliated by those closest to him—his last wife and one of her sons. Only a late-in-life conservatorship salvaged Rooney's final years. This case underscores how court intervention can work to the benefit of an at-risk person and help them escape a truly harmful situation.

Rooney's career in show business began during the days of vaudeville and silent films and continued through nine decades. He was born in Brooklyn, New York, in 1920 and christened Joseph Yule Jr. His mother was an American chorus girl and his Scottish father was a vaudevillian. When the boy was four years old, his parents divorced and his mother took him to live in Hollywood. There, after adopting the stage name Mickey Rooney, he got his first film role at the age of six. In his teens, he was cast as the precocious son of a judge in the Andy Hardy sixteen-film franchise and won the hearts of movie fans across American for his boy-next-door quality. Rooney would go on to appear in more than three hundred films, alongside the biggest stars of the day.

In June 1944, after his first failed marriage to then teenaged starlet Ava Gardner, he was drafted into the military and served almost two years. When Rooney returned to Hollywood in his mid-twenties, he could no longer play teen roles, but at just five feet and two inches tall, he wasn't suitable for casting as a leading man either. His career faltered, but over the following decades, he would remain a popular personality on radio, television, movies, and Broadway. Along the way he would marry a series of beautiful (and always taller) women, mostly singers or actresses, and each union would end after a short time. One marriage was over after just a hundred days.

One of the most devastating moments in Rooney's life came in 1966 as he worked on a movie set in the Philippines. His then wife, Barbara Ann Thomason, said by some to have been the love of Mickey's life, was found dead in her master bedroom suite. Milos Milosevics, an actor friend of Mickey's, was also found dead next to her, and the murder weapon was Mickey's own gun. It was reported that Barbara and Milos were lovers, but that has been disputed by some of the children born of this marriage. "Dad tried to protect us kids from a lot of stuff back then," daughter Kelly said during a televised interview. "We really loved him and we cherished him. Growing up we came to realize that the world loved him too. So, we did have to share him with the world."[27]

Rooney married his last wife in 1978. Jan Chamberlin, a former nightclub singer, had two adult sons. The most troubled and troublesome son was Chris Aber, who was alleged to have financially exploited and physically abused his famous stepfather. It has been reported that to get to Mickey Rooney, one had to pay Chris for the opportunity, and he often committed Mickey to demeaning engagements, far beneath Rooney's celebrity standing. "Chris forced him to work during his later years," Kelly Rooney said during a telephone interview from her home in California. "Dad couldn't even read the teleprompter. It was horrible to see him belittled and embarrassed like that." At one point, stepson Chris became Mickey's de facto "manager" by insinuating himself into Rooney's production company and naming himself the treasurer. That's when he allegedly began to siphon off Mickey's investment and pension funds.

Why Chris's mother didn't stop her son from taking advantage of her husband is a mystery. Insiders have also accused Jan, a woman significantly taller and heavier than her husband, of physically abusing the diminutive actor. "When I would call my dad, I would hear her screaming in the background," daughter Kelly told me. "And when my sister Kerry and I visited their house, there was Jan screaming at my father. I said, 'What is going on here? Dad doesn't deserve this,' and she said, 'Oh, you don't know what goes on in this house!'" Yet, Kelly said, every time the "old family" children would ask about his situation, an upbeat Mickey would simply tell them everything was fine and not to worry. Just when the abuse began, and how many years it lasted before becoming common knowledge, isn't known.

Perhaps Mickey Rooney really did think everything would work out fine, just like in the Hardy Boy movies. But in early 2011, when he was ninety years old and decades into his last marriage, Rooney finally found the courage to reach out for help. While filming *The Muppets* (2011), he confided in an unnamed Disney executive about the physical, emotional, and financial abuse he was suffering. That began a process in which probate estate and trust attorney Michael Augustine was hired.

Augustine is a man who is fond of snappy sayings such as, "Being rich and famous doesn't make you smart," but he would soon discover that his famous new client was far from rich. During a telephone interview for this book in the spring of 2022, Augustine said he once asked Rooney's New York agent where all the star's money went. "And he said, 'Let's just say he didn't lose it at the two-dollar window.' Mickey could not get away from the ponies," Augustine offered. "And when he was younger, he had a lot of drug and alcohol problems. He and Judy [Garland] were some of the original stoners."

In late February 2011 Augustine filed a complaint with the Superior Court in Los Angeles asking to be awarded conservatorship over Rooney and his estate. In addition, Augustine laid out several reasons why stepson Chris and his wife, Christine Aber, should be ordered to stay away from the aging actor. The *Hollywood Reporter* revealed the contents of the legal filing, which alleged that Chris "threatens, intimidates, bullies and harasses Mickey," and refuses him information about his own finances, "other than to tell him that [he] is broke." Court papers maintained that the Aber couple had withheld medicines, food, and proper clothing from Rooney, leaving him "extremely fearful that Chris will become physically threatening against Mickey and may even attempt to kidnap Mickey from his home." Judge Reva Goetz granted both the conservatorship request, naming Augustine as the man in charge, and the demand for a stay-away order for the Abers.[28]

None of these legal machinations were known to the public at the time, but shortly after Augustine's appointment, on March 3, 2011, there was Mickey Rooney on Capitol Hill testifying before the US Senate Special Committee on Aging. The world-famous actor had found the strength to take his very private situation public. Visibly shaking, and looking somewhat embarrassed, he read from a prepared statement about the need to stop elder abuse.

> I know because it happened to me. My money was taken and misused. Over the course of time, my daily life became unbearable. Worse, it seemed to happen out of nowhere. At first, it was something small, something I could control. But then it became something sinister that was completely out of control. I felt trapped, scared, used, and frustrated. But above all, I felt helpless. For years, I suffered silently. I couldn't muster the courage to seek the help I knew I needed. Even when I tried to speak up, I was told to be quiet. It seemed like no one believed me.[29]

Rooney delivered the final paragraphs of his statement with a raised fist and an earnest tone. "Ladies and gentlemen of the committee, I didn't tell you my story so you would feel sympathy for me. I came here for you to think of the millions of us seniors" in abusive situations. He closed with a direct message to all elderly citizens and veterans in particular, "Tell your story to anyone who will listen, and above all, HAVE HOPE. Someone will hear you."

"I had no idea he was going to speak there," daughter Kelly said. "But I was cheering him on!"

Mickey returned to California likely comforted by the fact that he had gone public, and finally had an attorney looking out for his best interests. He went back to the home he shared with his wife, Jan, in Calabasas. Rooney's financial circumstances were being sorted out, but unfortunately his personal situation did not improve. In July 2012 Augustine said he noticed several incidents that led him to conclude that his client was still being physically abused. "Mickey had a tooth knocked out, he had a black eye, he ostensibly fell down the stairs," Augustine said. "So, Mickey, I felt, was physically in peril." The lawyer would later tell the *Hollywood Reporter* that he had written up an agreement to keep Jan away from Mickey, and she had signed it. Speaking from his Los Angeles office in early 2022, Augustine revealed that to get his famous client away from the danger in Calabasas, and to help Mickey find some peace, he quietly rented a house for Rooney in the Universal Studios area of North Hollywood. Mickey had convinced his other stepson, Mark Aber, and his wife to come back to California from New York to help him. They soon moved in too. Attorney Augustine said that after Mickey got away from his eighth wife and her abusive son, Chris, "all of a sudden, Mickey's appearance and everything about Mickey improved. He started working again and he was doing much better."

There were many layers to this court battle, and before the case was closed, stepson Chris would be accused of stealing millions of dollars from his stepfather's estate over the years. Mickey's lawyer considered the loss uncollectible since Aber and his wife had declared bankruptcy in 2012. "We had evidence that [Chris] had stolen between $8 and 10 million, but we knew that we were not going to collect it," Augustine said. In October 2013 the Abers agreed to a settlement Augustine devised. The abuse charges that had been leveled against them would be dropped in return for a "judgment" of $2.9 million. If Mickey was never going to get his money back, at least there would be a court record of his stepson's misdeeds.

Mickey Rooney died of natural causes on April 6, 2014, at the age of ninety-three. He left his entire estate to stepson Mark. It was valued at just $18,000. To settle outstanding debts, an auction of Rooney's memorabilia was held. A kind benefactor bought the Emmy Award that Mickey won for his portrayal of an intellectually disabled man in the television movie *Bill* (1981) and gave it to Kelly and her siblings. To date, there seems to be no trace of the Lifetime Achievement Oscar award that Rooney won in 1982.

Kelly said she wishes her stepmother would have been less resentful of her father's children. "Why didn't she just reach out? We could have helped care for him. But she never did. Instead, she kept us from him until the end."

Seven of Mickey Rooney's surviving children filed suit to challenge their father's will, which had been drawn up just two or three weeks before he died. "We were suspicious since his signature didn't look the same," Kelly said. "We wanted to know some kind of truth since we were unable to see him or talk to him" during his final months. The cash left in Rooney's bank accounts was a paltry amount, but the money that could be made from auctioning off his memorabilia, or from future royalties, or the sale of Mickey's likeness rights could produce significant revenue in the future. Attorney Augustine said that as soon as he stepped into the case, he began getting phone calls from Mickey's adult children, "asking about the money, their dad's money." Kelly disputes that. "We knew for a long time that we kids weren't getting anything. We all have our own lives. Our calls were just about seeing him." Ultimately, the lawsuit the adult children filed was not pursued. Jan and her son Chris also filed a challenge to the will, alleging Mark and his wife had tricked Mickey into signing a new document just three weeks before his death. The mother-son duo asked the court to order an exhumation of the body to prove that Mickey had been "poisoned." Online records of the outcome of that suit cannot be located, but Augustine said, "It went nowhere." There was no exhumation. "The suit just died."

MANY OF THESE CELEBRITY CASES played out in private. It was only after death that the most alert fans learned of the internal family struggles these stars endured, including the imposition of a conservatorship or guardianship. But the court-controlled process was only vaguely described by the media, and it's likely the public did not fully grasp how court involvement could either restore family connections or be used to keep adult children at bay even during a ward's final weeks or days of life.

Many more celebrities have been placed under court-ordered protection over the years. Some arrangements have worked well; others have not. A partial list includes musicians Joni Mitchell, Randy Meisner of the Eagles, Brian Wilson of the Beach Boys, and British-born singer Amy Winehouse, who was conscripted into the UK system called deputyship. Among those conserved in California were actresses Nichelle Nichols of *Star Trek* fame, Edie McClurg (*Ferris Bueller's Day Off* [1986] and *Planes, Trains and Automobiles* [1987]) and actress Amanda Bynes (*Easy A* [2010], *Hairspray* [2007], and *She's the Man* [2006]), whose nine-year conservatorship was dissolved in March 2022. In New York, famed pop artist Peter Max was guardianized in 2015, as was talk show host Wendy Williams in the spring of 2022. In addition, guardianships or conservatorships were reportedly considered, or unsuccessfully attempted, on behalf other celebrities, including recording artists B. B. King, Mariah Carey, the late Aaron Carter, Demi Lovato, and Ray Price, and actors Lindsay Lohan and Charlie Sheen.

For the celebrity cases explored in this chapter, late-in-life court intervention was a positive development, a pathway for "old family" adult children to be able to spend time with their parent during their final days. Court rulings in the Peter Falk, Casey Kasem, and Glen Campbell cases are illustrative of that. For Mickey Rooney, conservatorship may have increased his lifespan by removing him from an allegedly dangerous situation. The conservatorship established to oversee the money of serial killer

David Berkowitz was successful in diverting his cash to actual victims and their families. However, in a majority of other cases you will read about in this book, guardianships and conservatorships involving regular citizens have had the opposite effect. Family members have frequently been permanently barred from being with their loved ones by uncaring court appointees who concoct all manner of excuses for isolating the ward. Once loving and trustworthy relatives are kept away, a layer of watchfulness disappears and unscrupulous court appointees are free to act in questionable—sometimes criminal—ways.

5

Mercenary Methods and Practices within the System

Much like other successful businessmen and women, players in the guardianship or conservatorship system network with each other. They give out and take in business cards, and they remember who is friendly and eager to work with them. They are attracted to those who think outside the box, and they like to make money. While an honest entrepreneur will have a set of ethical and moral standards, an unethical participant in the guardianship racket doesn't care if their actions cause human suffering. The worst of this bunch are propelled by either the powerful feeling of controlling others, or by the idea that they can steal from their wards and then explain away their actions to a friendly judge who will very likely take no action to punish them.

Based upon years of collecting evidence about how these predators operate, here is a composite synopsis of a how the players come together and interact with each other. Let's focus on a hypothetical guardian. We'll call her Susan, since it's believed a majority of guardians are women.

Susan runs a medium-sized guardian company in a popular retirement state. She's been successful over the years but recently noticed that her caseload is down, and she worries that she might have to start laying off some employees. So, she devises a multipronged business plan to drum up new clients. First, Susan sets up a dinner with the two emergency room nurses she met at last month's guardianship conference. Over a nice meal and lots of wine, she fills them in on what she does. She suggests that when the nurses come across physically or intellectually disabled patients or senior citizens who seem a bit disoriented, they should call her right away. Susan says she is especially interested in cases where there is no family in attendance because, as she tells her dinner guests in her most sincere-sounding voice, "Those poor people left all alone in the world, they really need an advocate." Susan tells them she can run right over to the ER no matter the time of day or night, and with a quick signature from the patient, "They will have a guardian to speak for them." To sweeten the pot, Susan leans across the table and tells the nurses in a hushed voice that she will give them a hundred dollars for each referral. To button up the hospital connection, Susan will follow up by reconnecting with two young orderlies working at another facility and make them the same offer. She calls this pair her "hospital trolls" because they have handed over names and addresses of at-risk solo patients in the past. None of these sources know that Susan already has similar deals with staffers at several geriatric doctor's offices in town. She makes a mental note to check in with those connections, too, so they don't forget her.

Next day, Susan is off to see administrators at a few of the local nursing homes. Her company already oversees a hundred fifty "protected people" and, hoping to get a referral fee of her own, she wants to let them know that some of her wards will soon be ripe for institutionalization. Susan knows that nursing home and assisted-living operators can bill insurance companies and Medicare for lots of different tests and services (pssst, even for tests and services that are never actually rendered). The homes can also count on generous monthly checks for eligible Medicaid clients, government money that often exceeds what it actually costs to care for a resident. With that profit margin in mind, Susan knows her wards are valuable to these facilities, so she makes it a point to stay in regular touch with their top bosses. And as Susan has learned, if her caseload gets too heavy and she can't make her regular visits with her wards, she can always rely on the staff at these nursing homes to pick up the slack. Susan wants to keep everyone from the top administrators to the head nurses happy, so she never forgets to send them birthday and Christmas gifts.

Susan also makes plans to renew her visits to senior centers in the most well-to-do neighborhoods. She will again convince them to sponsor her as a guest speaker, and she'll give her spiel about the need to preplan for guardianship, even add it to their estate plan if possible. During these presentations, Susan, with folded hands clasped to her chest, adopts a very earnest tone when she says, "You don't want to be a burden to your children. Let them have their own lives, am I right? So, make guardianship part of your advanced directives package." At the end of her pitch, Susan is pleased when so many in the group ask for her business card. In turn, she collects contact information from those who appear most interested or stay on to ask questions. She will quietly pass on these names and phone numbers to a few elder law and estate attorneys she knows. If the contact results in business for the lawyer—say, from someone who wants to draft a new will or an end-of-life document—then Susan is in line for yet another referral fee. She is careful to maintain the best of relations with these lawyers because they have the power to suggest to the court which guardians are appointed. Susan's continued contact with these lawyers is an "I'll grease your palm, you grease mine" association in which all the professionals win.

The real money comes from the ward's estates, of course, and Susan is lucky enough to be friendly with several Probate Court judges in her area, and she faithfully contributes to their reelection campaigns. They frequently appoint her as the "plenary guardian," meaning she is anointed to handle all the personal and financial matters for the incapacitated person, at an hourly fee of $300. Of course, Susan can't do everything a ward might require. She is, in effect, the supervisor of a crew of people, and the size of the team is whatever Susan decides is necessary to maintain the homebound protected person's lifestyle. The in-home aides and housekeepers make twenty-five dollars an hour, but Susan charges it out to the ward's account as forty dollars an hour. After all, she rationalizes, she needs to be compensated for the time she spent vetting, hiring, and supervising these people.

There is one ward Susan sees face-to-face on a regular basis. This extraordinary attention is due to the fact that this elderly widow has an estate worth multiple millions. Much of it, however, is tied up in untouchable trust accounts, and Susan has formulated a plan. Since the woman has mild dementia that will likely get worse with every passing month, Susan will soon ask the judge for permission to sell the ward's home. She knows exactly how she will justify the sale. Susan will tell the court the woman is only in her mid-seventies, and in otherwise good health, so she might live for many more years. Susan will remind the judge that the ward's trusts cannot be tapped, and so to make sure the woman will have the necessary funds to live out her life under long-term assisted care, selling the house is the prudent thing to do. The judge will most likely approve the idea. Judges almost always accept her recommendations, no questions asked.

Susan doesn't put the home on the open market. Instead, while the ward is away at a doctor's appointment, she calls her girlfriend, a real estate agent, to alert her to their next deal. "Hey there, I've got another one. Meet me at 456 School Street and I'll show you around!" The ward's four-bedroom home is in good shape and on a sizable lot with decent land-scaping, an attached two-car garage, and top-ranking schools nearby. It's appraised at $450,000. Inside the house, Susan's trained eye quickly spots several valuables—signed artworks that adorn the living room wall; sets of expensive china, silverware, and glassware; antique Tiffany lamps in the bedrooms; the assortment of porcelain figurines from Spain; and sev-eral neat stacks of coin collection books—so many different coins! Susan knows just the interested buyers to contact for these items. She can sell them individually, take a cut, and when her annual report to the court is due, she can explain that she simply liquidated the entire contents of the home during a financially unsuccessful estate sale. Susan has it on good authority from the court clerk that guardian's financial reports are rarely audited because the state simply doesn't have enough auditors to analyze the reports. Besides, the clerk has told Susan, if a discrepancy is found, guardians are notified so they can "fix it."

Susan's annual statement on the wealthy widow's estate will also list the sale price of the house at just $300,000. Susan will explain that the reason it sold for a below market price was because in the thirty years the widow lived there, she neglected to update the interior, thus making it worth less. She's sure no one will question the discrepancy between the appraised value and the sale price. Then, when Susan's friend quickly flips the house and sells it for $450,000 where does all that profit go? Take a guess. These real estate transactions are so lucrative, Susan is considering going for her own realtor's license, just like other guardians she met at a national guardianship conference last year. When they told her how much money they made cutting out the middleman on these real estate deals, Su-san's jaw just about hit the floor. She ponders the possibility of helping her son and daughter-in-law buy one of these underpriced homes. But back in the moment, Susan has spotted the widow's low-mileage late model car in the garage, and she reminds herself to call her other pal who buys gently used cars at a low price and sells them for top dollar. He doesn't mind a surreptitious split of the profits either.

Back at her office, Susan takes one more step to try to boost her bottom line. She calls a meeting of her case managers and bookkeepers to chew them out for shortchanging the company. "Never," she says in her stern voice, "never, ever charge a ward's account for a fifteen-minute phone call! I work by the hour, you got that?" Waving a sheaf of the latest company invoices, Susan adds, "Remember, everything I do is invoiced at a minimum of $300!" She reiterates that every chore listed on her daily activity list—from opening a piece of mail, calling a personal shopper to pick up a pair of slippers for old man Johnson, or reading an email from widow Simpson's agitated daughter—every action is to be recorded as taking at least one hour. At $300 a shot. No exceptions. And don't worry, she tells her workers, if the number of billed hours exceeds the number of hours in a day, no one will notice. They never do.

6

Guardians from Hell—and Lawyers and Judges Too

No one can definitively say how many professional for-profit guardians are operating in the United States at any given time. No agency or organization tracks how many guardians are licensed lawyers or fiduciaries, or how many have gone through some sort of guardianship training or education program. The National Guardianship Association, which touts itself as being the "leading national resource" for professionals, reports a membership of just a thousand, and that number includes volunteer guardians, conservators, and fiduciaries.[1] Florida reports there are some five hundred fifty registered guardians in just that one state.[2] As mentioned, the latest available statistics from the National Center for State Courts put the current number of adult wards of the court at about 1.5 million, and many consider that to be an undercount.[3] Since neither the states nor the federal government keeps track of the guardianship/conservatorship system, it is up to informed journalists to make educated guesses. In a deeply researched series on the topic in 2021, *Buzzfeed News* reported there could be up to two hundred thousand new guardianship cases established in the US every year. Who will be assigned to look out for the well-being of these at-risk citizens?

Many working inside the system have said there are just not enough people willing to serve as a guardian to vulnerable adults and, therefore, judges are forced to appoint, and reappoint, the relative few who make themselves available. Because the courts try to fast-track cases whenever possible, there seems to be no opportunity for a judge to thoroughly vet a potential guardian's background, and no central complaint bureau for the court to consult to learn about problematic guardians. Few jurists bother to simply ask a guardian candidate how many wards they are already responsible for. In multiple cases identified during research for this book, it was not unusual to find one guardian assigned to multiple dozens and sometimes hundreds of cases simultaneously. In some instances, the wards assigned to a particular guardian were scattered statewide, making it next to impossible for any meaningful monitoring or face-to-face visits. This status quo is a recipe for disaster.

The astounding depth of deception and exploitation that some guardians have engaged in is mind-boggling, and it has gone on for decades. And while the judges who appoint disreputable guardians frequently shrug and explain that they simply took the recommendation of the petitioning attorney, the public should realize the system begins and ends at the bench. Those who wear the black robe must be held accountable if they routinely appoint rogue actors, ignore legitimate family complaints, and refuse to recommend punishment for those duplicitous appointees caught red-handed.

In the following examples of criminal guardianship, it is important to note that it was most often the news media that unmasked the worst of the worst, and not the police, prosecutors, or the sitting judge. Nationwide, in case after case, it was a local reporter who took the time to listen to a worried family's complaint, investigate it thoroughly, and write about it in the newspaper or broadcast it on television or radio. Only after an obviously abusive guardian was exposed to the public in this way did the responsible regulatory or law enforcement agency decide to act. Well, sometimes anyway.

Arguably one of the most boldly brazen guardians of modern times is April Parks of Las Vegas, Nevada,[4] a state that has been justifiably criticized about widespread corruption within its guardianship system for decades.[5] Parks, a stout woman with a wide face and an aggressive manner, is said to have been the model for Rosamund Pike's devastatingly deft portrayal of a scheming guardian in the Netflix movie *I Care a Lot* (2021). The April Parks scandal, as first reported by the *Vegas Voice* and then by the *Las Vegas Review-Journal*, was the spark that energized the Rick Black–led guardianship reform movement in Nevada.[6] The local ABC affiliate KTNV-TV and other media organizations joined in the coverage. Black helped victimized family members focus on the most newsworthy aspects of their case so reporters could grasp the enormity of the problems in Nevada. Suddenly, citizens in that state realized how easily they too could be caught up in guardianship's grip.

April Parks was assigned to protect some four hundred elderly and disabled wards over the course of a dozen years. She was one of the busiest professional guardians in Clark County, juggling numerous complex cases simultaneously. Parks devised a business plan that assured she would continue to get a fresh set of wards, and to handle her heavy caseload she concocted an expedient routine. First, Parks had people in the legal and medical community feeding her names of potential wards and providing her with the required paperwork to file along with a petition for an emergency guardianship. She took advantage of a lackadaisical court practice that allowed a total stranger—like herself—to simply present a judge with a medical report declaring that a person was no longer able to care for themselves. Her petition would also assert that the targeted person, most often a retiree with money, was not well enough to appear at the hearing and no family could be located. With that, the court would immediately establish a temporary guardianship and name Parks as the interim person in control. Parks most often appeared before Clark County guardianship commissioner Jon Norheim, a lawyer who had presided over nearly all guardianship cases in that area since 2005. Norheim reportedly appointed Parks to a new case, on average, almost once a week. He had the power to rein in any guardian who stepped out of line, and it seems inconceivable now that he had failed to hear any of the mounting number of complaints about Parks's bullying nature. Perhaps he acted more out of friendship with Parks than in his professional supervisory capacity. It was reported that at one hearing Norheim praised Parks, and two other familiar guardians, as "wonderful, good-hearted, social worker types," and he added, on the record, "I love April Parks."[7]

After being appointed as guardian, the court record shows Parks would waste no time. She would immediately swoop in, inform the unaware ward that she had a court order and they must do as she commanded. The person, or in at least one case a husband and wife, would be moved to a prearranged assisted-living facility that very day. Some of these "protected people" would be heavily medicated and have no idea that Parks was back in their residence deciding what to sell off, what to keep, and what price to ask when she put their home up for sale. Within a short time, Parks would be back in court applying for permanent guardianship, telling the court the ward's family was either out of town or incapable of taking care of their relative themselves. Commissioner Norheim would quickly approve her application, and Parks was anointed with the permanent power to control each ward's finances, estate documents, and medical decisions. Bank accounts, investment portfolios, and other valuable assets were quickly transferred into Parks's name, ward's homes and belongings were sold off, invoices for incredible amounts of hours and services were created, and double-billing was not uncommon. On one calendar day, for example, Parks billed various wards for a total of twenty-five hours of her time. She got away with her scheme for years because oversight of the Nevada system was nearly nonexistent.[8]

Sometime around April 2016, likely worried that increasing media coverage had sparked a serious investigation into her activities, Parks and her husband left Nevada for parts unknown. She abandoned dozens of her wards and left the Clark County guardianship system to pick up the pieces. Parks twice failed to appear in a Las Vegas court to answer charges that she had deliberately overcharged her wards, and a frustrated judge issued a bench warrant for her arrest. An attorney representing one of her wards begged for an official, full-scale investigation.

Once the prosecutor's office got involved, a grand jury was impaneled. The *New Yorker* reported that an assistant to the notorious Parks "testified that she and Parks went to hospitals and attorney's offices for the purpose of 'building relationships to generate more client leads.' Parks secured a contract with six medical facilities whose staff agreed to refer patients to her—an arrangement that benefited the facilities, since Parks could control the fates of a large pool of their potential consumers. Parks often gave doctors blank certificates and told them exactly what to write in order for their patients to become her wards."[9] For facilities that were saddled with low-paying Medicare patients, or long-term patients whose insurance had run out, having someone like Parks help them guardianize a person, move them to assisted living, and free up a hospital bed was a godsend.

In March 2017 April Parks was indicted on 270 felony charges that included racketeering, theft, exploitation, and perjury.[10] Three others were also accused: Parks's business partner, Mark Simmons; her attorney, Noel Palmer Simpson; and Parks's husband, Gary Neal Taylor. By this time the conspirators had mostly scattered. Parks and Taylor were located in Pennsylvania, extradited back to Nevada, and jailed in mid-May. Simmons was found and brought back from Indiana. Clark County district attorney Steve Wolfson held a news conference to announce the indictments and made it clear that his office believed Parks was the mastermind in a fraudulent billing scheme that stole at least $560,000 from a hundred fifty victims over a five-year period. The DA proclaimed that professional guardian April Parks was always "the number one target in this investigation."[11]

The news shocked the community. People entrusted with caring for society's most vulnerable had, instead, victimized them. And then, less than a week later, the depths of Parks's cruelty made headlines again. Billy Smith, a man who often bid on abandoned storage rooms, took possession of a unit last rented by April Parks. What he discovered inside made his jaw drop—twenty-seven urns filled with human cremains. "This is the most bizarre thing I've ever found in a unit," Smith told KVVU-TV. "Somebody had the gall to store a family member in a storage unit like that." Accompanying paperwork showed that several of the urns were just a few years old, but some had been in storage years longer.[12] It was determined that after Parks ordered deceased wards to be cremated, she chose to toss their remains into her secret depository rather than make the effort to locate a loved one and transfer the ashes in a dignified manner.

There was no trial. And no swift justice. More than a year and a half would elapse before Parks, then fifty-three, accepted a plea agreement and pleaded guilty to reduced charges.[13] On November 5, 2018, she appeared in court wearing an inmate's faded black jumpsuit adorned with a waist chain to which her handcuffs were loosely attached, and her once brassy red hair was now gray. With her hand on her hip at times, Parks told the judge she took full responsibility "but never intended harm." She spoke of her "great passion" for guardianship work and maintained that she had taken "great care and concern" with her wards. "Things could have been done better," she said, "We were a group practice, and honestly I think some things got ahead of us."[14]

The most genuine-sounding comments in court came on January 4, 2019, when Parks was sentenced by district court judge Tierra Jones. Many of Parks's victimized wards had died, but nine people were allowed to give victim impact statements before her sentence was handed down. Karen Kelly, with the Clark County public guardian office, read out a long list of victims' names who she said had lived in "intense anxiety and anguish" for the final years of their life under Parks's dictates. "The choices she made were out of greed," Kelly said. "She didn't see them as people. They were paychecks." Herman "Bill" Mesloh, an elderly and blind former ward, told the court that Parks deliberately isolated him from his wife, Kathy. "For six months I didn't know if my wife was dead or alive," he told the judge. "There are some evil people in this world," he said. "And April Parks is a predator of the worst kind." Rudy North, eighty, who had been suddenly and involuntarily enrolled in guardianship along with his wife, Rennie, in 2015, compared April Parks to Hitler.[15] He likened her tactics during the couple's two-year ordeal to those he said he experienced living in the Nazi concentration camp, at Auschwitz, during World War II. "We were taken without announcement, without the ability to make a phone call," North said. "The only thing we beat them on, really, is we are alive today."[16]

"She was not a guardian to me," former ward Barbara Ann Neely said. Parks had isolated her from her family so no loved one knew about her dire situation. "She did not protect me. As each day passed, I felt like I was in a grave, buried alive." Others spoke of guardian Parks depriving wards of adequate food and clothing. Some said their loved one had lost their entire life savings, their home, or their precious family heirlooms to Parks's greed. Judge Jones intently listened to the heartbreaking victim statements. She then turned her attention to April Parks, the woman who had spawned such misery. "You told us you never meant any harm," Jones told Parks. "But after hearing these stories of people Scotch-taping their shoes, people being charged for Christmas gifts, and nothing to eat, how is that not harm?"

Parks was sentenced to sixteen to forty years in the Nevada state prison. She was also ordered to pay almost $560,000 in restitution.[17] Her accomplices pleaded guilty. Business partner, Mark Simmons, was sentenced to seven to eighteen years in prison; Parks's husband, Gary Neal Taylor, got two to five years; and Parks's attorney, Noel Palmer Simpson, got no jail time, was not required to pay restitution to the victims, and was required to pay only a nominal fine. In November 2019 Simpson was stripped of her license to practice law.[18]

THE STATE OF NEVADA is not alone in ignoring outrageous conduct within the ranks of those who populate the guardianship system. Florida also has a long and dismal track record of reining in rogue actors like judges, guardians, guardians ad litem, and attorneys. For the purposes of dissecting one of Florida's most shocking guardianship cases, let's focus on a court appointee named Rebecca Fierle, aka Rebecca Fierle-Santonian. In February 2020 she was arrested arrest on charges of abuse and neglect related to the death of one of her wards, a Vietnam veteran named Steven Stryker. But it quickly became clear that the questionable activities of Rebecca Fierle went much deeper and wider than the extraordinarily sad case of Mr. Stryker. After his untimely death on May 13, 2019, multiple county and state agencies launched investigations. Taken together, the official conclusion was that Rebecca Fierle—a guardian with responsibility for multiple hundreds of wards spread out across thirteen far-flung Florida counties—had been gaming the system and enriching herself for more than a decade.[19] A close examination of her activities brings into sharp focus the interconnected players within the guardianship industry, and their collective habit of ignoring a ward's problems by claiming that oversight and responsibility lies elsewhere. It also raises questions about why Fierle would be charged in connection with just *one* of her guardianship cases.

In the summer of 2018, Stryker, a seventy-five-year-old US Army veteran who suffered with several health issues, including a history of mild dementia, was admitted to the AdventHealth Orlando hospital. That facility then petitioned the court for an emergency guardian for Stryker because "the alleged incapacitated person is unable to make decisions that would be safe and reasonable for his plan of care and is not able to effectively manage his finances."[20] In that same motion, the hospital recommended the judge appoint Rebecca Fierle as guardian, and the judge complied.[21] Why a hospital would presume to suggest to a judge the name of any one particular guardian is unknown. The judge was apparently unaware that the hospital was also paying Rebecca Fierle to act as a guardian in a sweetheart deal that went against state regulations.

Among the various maladies Steven Stryker suffered was a chronic condition called esophageal stricture. His throat muscles would constrict, often so aggressively that he would choke. Swallowing food or even his own saliva was sometimes so difficult that medical personnel employed a procedure known as an upper endoscopy to help him get the nourishment he needed. Despite his frail condition, guardian Fierle moved him multiple times to various assisted-living locations. The Stryker family believed those care homes were ill equipped to handle Steven's specific health issues. They worried that he was put at "a greater risk of aspirating" in these facilities.[22]

On May 9, 2019, Kim Stryker, the ward's daughter, filed an urgent complaint with the Ninth Judicial Circuit Court, the same court that had guardianized her father the year before. She wrote of her objections to guardian Rebecca Fierle's intransigent behavior as her father laid in a Tampa hospital. "His guardian has insisted on including a DNR [Do Not Resuscitate] order on his medical records, despite his vocal opposition," Kim wrote. "He is doing much better and is quite lucid and extremely upset that this woman has full control over his medical and financial records." Kim made it clear that she was also strongly against any DNR order and had made her opinion known to the guardian. The court forwarded the grievance to a state agency known as the Office of Public and Professional Guardians (OPPG). Why such a life-and-death complaint went to an already overburdened agency like the OPPG, which focuses on long-term investigations of guardian's activities, has not been explained publicly.

Five days later, Steven Stryker died. As he aspirated and went into cardiac arrest, the medial team at Tampa's St. Joseph's Hospital could only watch, their hands tied by two directives from Fierle. Not only had this guardian issued the unwanted Do Not Resuscitate mandate, but she had also ordered Stryker's feeding tube be capped. Absent any means of nutrition or medical resuscitation efforts, Stryker slowly and painfully passed away on May 13, 2019. Only after the death was there an investigation into daughter Kim Stryker's complaint.

The media pounced on the story and the scandal sparked a whirl of official response. Within a short period of time, the Florida Department of Law Enforcement (FDLE) announced it was conducting a criminal investigation into Fierle's actions; the director of the Office of Public and Private Guardians was forced to resign; and circuit court judge Janet Thorpe declared Fierle had "abused her powers" in the Stryker case. The judge also found that this guardian was not personally bonded as the law required, and she began the process of removing Fierle from the ninety-five cases she supervised just in Orange County. Judge Thorpe further revealed that Fierle had filed "numerous" Do Not Resuscitate orders on her wards without family or court permission.[23] The judge immediately revoked all the outstanding advanced directives Fierle had filed. There had long been news reports about abusive and exploitative guardianship cases in Florida, but the case of Steven Stryker elevated the topic to nuclear status.

On one particular day, July 26, 2019, there was a firestorm of news about the controversial case. First, Rebecca Fierle officially resigned all her guardianship cases statewide, and she promised to leave the profession forever. Governor Ron DeSantis called for the Elder Affairs Department to conduct a "vigorous" investigation of the state's guardianship program, and he pledged legislative changes to toughen enforcement laws. The head of the Elder Affairs Department announced "immediate" changes to the speed with which complaints were handled and passed along to appropriate authorities. Also, on this day the Orange County Comptroller's Office investigation into a representative sample of thirty of Rebecca Fierle's cases was released. It revealed that as of that month, judges in thirteen counties had appointed Fierle as guardian to some four hundred fifty wards, and that was in addition to the more than four hundred cases she had also controlled in Orange and Osceola counties since 2007. As the Comptroller investigators dug into those eight hundred fifty cases Fierle had handled, they discovered that in multiple instances Fierle had misappropriated ward's funds and spent the money in ways that benefited her own family members and friends—all the while concealing the activity from the court. She failed to follow state regulations that required her employees to undergo criminal background checks and be duly registered with the state. Further, it was found that Fierle routinely failed to notify family members when there was a court proceeding affecting their loved one or before she sold off the ward's assets. On August 7, 2019, it was reported that a law enforcement search of Fierle's Orlando office discovered the cremains of nine unidentified individuals, presumably her deceased wards, and one family pet.[24] Reports would surface about at least one family member who had fought in vain with Fierle to receive their loved one's remains.

By September 2019 a full audit by the Orange County Comptroller's office would expose another Fierle scheme. Investigators said that over a ten-year period she had billed $3.9 million to the AdventHealth medical system for acting as guardian to another 682 incapacitated patients. About a third of those clients were known to, and protected by, the Florida court's guardianship system, and Fierle was already charging them $65 an hour for her services. AdventHealth was paying her $130 an hour for the same wards. That Fierle might have allegedly entered into a double-dipping side deal with a hospital was astonishing, as those types of arrangements are clearly forbidden under state law.[25] For handling this lucrative batch of wards, known as "Group 1" clients, Fierle was paid $2.8 million. The audit concluded she never reported those payments to the court as required. The rest of the group of 682 wards—referred to as "Group 2" patients—were unknown to the court, and therefore unsupervised by anyone other than Fierle. She received compensation of $1.1 million for the Group 2 wards.[26] The comptroller's audit stated, "It is clear how guardianship is (supposed to be) established under Florida law. However, it is not entirely clear how Ms. Fierle obtained the authority to act and exercise discretion over the Group 2 patients."[27]

It is also not clear why AdventHealth would find it acceptable to pay out millions to someone who would so flagrantly skirt state regulations on guardianships. Administrators there must have liked her work since they would then go on to recommend that she be appointed as guardian to Steven Stryker.

Florida, like other states, had no one dedicated agency to accept family complaints about suspected guardian abuses. So, a group called the Clerk's Statewide Investigation of Professional Guardians Alliance was formed, a wordy-sounding organization comprised of those county clerks interested enough to join and willing to investigate guardianship complaints.[28] There are sixty-seven counties in Florida, and clerks of only six counties currently participate in the group. It was the Okaloosa County Clerk who looked into the Stryker case, and the *Orlando Sentinel* broke the story about the findings.[29] The clerk's report made it clear that Fierle had been repeatedly asked to remove the Stryker DNR and refused, despite Steven Stryker's expressed desire for lifesaving actions, the pleas from his daughter, and from Linda Lanier, a business associate and family friend who held Stryker's power of attorney. It was also the educated opinion of one of the last medical professionals attending to Stryker that the DNR should be dropped.

Kim told investigators that just a week before her father died, Fierle told her the DNR would remain in place because "quality of life, rather than quantity of life" mattered most. Kim adamantly believed her father would have survived if not for the end-of-life orders from his court-appointed guardian. Okaloosa investigators also interviewed Dr. Kirtikumar Pandya, a psychiatrist who tended Stryker at St. Joseph's Hospital. Dr. Pandya said he became concerned about the situation and thought Fierle's insistence on the DNR was "not rational" because Stryker's condition was generally not considered to be terminal.[30] The doctor requested that the hospital take steps to remove the DNR and order up an ethics consult. Fierle attended that ethics meeting, but she wielded the power of the court, and she ultimately decided the DNR would remain in place, along with her order to cap Steven's feeding tube.[31]

Okaloosa investigators confirmed Kim's complaint that the guardian had moved Stryker to various assisted-living facilities that were not capable of meeting his medical needs, and he always wound up back in a hospital emergency room. When the officials questioned Rebecca Fierle about why her ward had been sent to such inadequate places, locations that necessitated his hospitalization so many times, the *Orlando Sentinel* reported that she answered, "It was difficult to find facilities for Stryker because he was a registered sex offender for lewd exhibition."[32] The clerk's final report concluded, "Even though it was difficult to find a facility willing to accept him due to his sex offender status, as court-appointed guardian, it remained Fierle's responsibility to ensure the ward's medical care needs were met." When investigators asked her why she filed the DNR order in the first place, Fierle gave the same rote answer she had given Kim: it was "an issue of quality of life rather than quantity." She also dubiously insisted that Steven Stryker had agreed to the Do Not Resuscitate order after she conducted a solo bedside conversation with him. An interesting postscript to this investigative report: the hospital's case manager and the attending physician who called the time of death refused to speak to county investigators conducting this probe.

When Steven died, guardian Fierle did not bother to inform his family or friends. An official state report includes an email from Kim Stryker to Fierle, dated two days after the death. The subject line reads, "My father is dead." The message goes on to ask, "Were you even going to tell me?" It was family friend Linda Lanier who first learned of Steven's passing. She told the *Orlando Sentinel* she had sent flowers to Steven at the hospital, along with a cheery note informing him that Fierle had agreed to step down as his guardian. A nurse told Lanier her friend was dead, and it was Lanier who passed on the bad news to Steven's daughter.

The breadth and depth of Rebecca Fierle's questionable actions cannot be adequately communicated by simply relating the Stryker saga. She had been active in the guardianship community in Florida since 2007, and family complaints about her practices and harsh decisions began to surface almost immediately. Fierle was undaunted. She orchestrated a widespread network of spotters—social workers, employees at hospitals and nursing homes, even first responders at police and fire departments—who informed her of individuals who seemed ripe for guardianship. Fierle became known to judges across a wide swath of the state. Apparently none of the judges realized, or were concerned, that her vast territory and heavy caseload made it impossible to adequately tend to each of her wards. And there's no way to know whether judges were aware that multiple serious complaints had already been lodged against Rebecca Fierle.

The media's coverage of the Steven Stryker case emboldened others who had had negative experiences with Fierle to come forward. On the same day Fierle officially resigned as a professional guardian, the *Orlando Sentinel*'s reporter Monivette Cordeiro wrote of her exclusive interview with psychotherapist Marci Elliott.[33] Elliott had been part of the Orange County Guardianship Examining Committee, a group of medical professionals and other experts in the field who visit with potential wards to determine whether guardianship is warranted. They then report their findings to the judge.

In May 2016 Elliott met with a woman named Connie Rae Tibbetts, seventy-one, and determined she needed a dedicated guardian. The court assigned Rebecca Fierle to the Tibbetts case. Over the next nine months, this ward of the court would complain that she was routinely ignored by her guardian. As a cancer patient, Connie Rae needed to see a doctor. She also badly needed the attention of a dentist. But Tibbetts said her multiple calls asking Fierle to schedule medical appointments were disregarded. In frustration, psychotherapist Elliot and Tibbetts's out-of-town daughter, Christine, repeatedly complained about the guardian's neglect. First, they contacted the newly formed Office of Public and Professional Guardians. The OPPG wasn't fully operational yet so it was suggested they hire a lawyer, call the Florida Abuse Hotline, or write to the court. Their next round of complaints went to the Ninth Circuit Court judge in charge of the case. They explained how Connie Mae was stricken with cancer, and that Fierle had lied to them when she insisted that Mrs. Tibbetts had refused medical treatment. Their repeated protests went nowhere. (In a typical deflection, a spokesperson for the circuit court would later say the Tibbetts complaint had been forwarded to the OPPG.)

Marci Elliott was beside herself. The system she had dedicated her time and effort to was so obviously flawed that she wanted no more part of it. In December 2016 Elliot resigned. In a letter to Frederick Lauten, the chief judge of the Orange-Osceola Circuit Court, and circuit judge Jose Rodriguez, she said, "I cannot continue to participate in any kind of action that could possibly put another human being under Rebecca Fierle's control. I can no longer stand by and be silent."[34] Nothing was done to discipline or stop Fierle back in 2016, and she continued to be appointed as guardian for some of Florida's most vulnerable people.

On March 25, 2017, Connie Rae Tibbetts died at age seventy-two. And some two and a half years later, Steven Stryker would die under the same guardian's dubious supervision. Therapist Elliott called Stryker a "sacrificial lamb," and revealed that she had recently been contacted by a state inspector general investigator who said her 2016 complaint about Fierle was finally being addressed.

It turns out the state of Florida had received at least eight documented complaints about Rebecca Fierle as far back as 2008. That's when Angela Woodhull, the determined daughter of Louise Falvo, a Fierle ward, filed a lawsuit against the guardian and two nursing homes claiming they had been involved in embezzlement and Medicaid fraud in connection with her mother's care. Woodhull, of Gainesville, Florida, is a unique person with a colorful background. She plays the accordion, writes original music, and is known in the entertainment field as Angelina the Polka Queen. She even appeared in the HBO movie *Recount* in 2008 as her accordion-playing alter ego. But Woodhull also has a master's degree and a PhD in educational psychology, she teaches English as a second language, and is a licensed private detective. In short, while Angela is eclectic, she is smart as a whip and nobody's fool.

Woodhull's guardianship saga is full of eyebrow-raising details, including an estranged cousin who Angela says "kidnapped" her wealthy mother and took her to Ohio, a duplicitous lawyer who instructed Angela on how to surreptitiously whisk her mother back to Florida, and the mysterious establishment of an unwanted guardianship. The first thing Angela wants people to know is that she did not agree to a guardianship, and she never signed the required papers to establish one. She readily displays the guardianship petition's signature filed with the court and has declared it "a forgery," offering samples of her handwriting as proof. To back up her assertion, Woodhull provides the sworn statements of two court-qualified forensic document examiners she hired. Both experts concluded the signature on the guardianship petition was not consistent with her handwriting.

So, who perpetrated this fraud upon the court? During a series of interviews for this book, Woodhall says the false document was prepared by the attorney she consulted in an effort to get her mother back from Ohio and away from the clutches of her "money-hungry cousin."[35] According to Angela, upon hearing that her mother had a substantial estate, this lawyer proceeded—without permission—to file for guardianship. The petition was readily approved by Seminole County Circuit Court judge Nancy Alley. Angela says she quickly informed the court, in writing, that the guardianship was filed under false pretenses and neither wanted nor needed. But, she says, the petitioning lawyer got to Alley first, falsely explaining that this was really a case of a daughter trying to steal her mother's $1 million estate. The judge believed the lawyer, and the guardianship of widow Louise Falvo stuck. The person Judge Alley appointed to be in control of the elderly woman's life was guardian Rebecca Fierle.

"My mother wasn't incapacitated. She should never have been put into guardianship," Woodhull told me. "My mother was a handful . . . but she was very independent. She knew what she had in the bank, she was very active and took public transportation whenever she wanted to go some-where, she got out and raked the leaves every day." Once put under guard-ianship, Louise was relegated to a nursing home on Rebecca Fierle's orders. That was the point at which the embezzlement from her mother's estate began, according to Angela. She said guardian Fierle immediately put her mother on Medicaid even though she did not qualify. "That's Medicaid fraud, pure and simple," Woodhall said.

Angela also believes her mother was routinely overmedicated. Louise Falvo, ninety-two, died on July 21, 2008, just three months after being put under guardianship. Angela flat-out declared, "My mother was mur-dered." Asked for proof of that allegation, Angela related a deathbed story. "At the nursing home, they had cleaned up my mother and left the room," she said. And then Angela's investigative instincts kicked in. "I noticed the urine bag still hanging there, so I emptied the contents into a glass coffee cup and smuggled it out." Angela said she immediately took the specimen to Gainesville Police Department sergeant Ray Barber, and the sample was frozen and kept by police as evidence. Four months later, Angela wrote to Sergeant Barber to ask about test results. He mistakenly told her the speci-men wasn't there and suggested she had picked it up. She had not. A more complete search quickly located the frozen evidence, which had inexpli-cably remained untested. Angela picked up the urine sample and rushed it home to her freezer. Angela said she was "overwhelmed and exhausted" by her continuing efforts to find justice for her mother and to prove the guardianship had been a fraud from the very beginning, and so the frozen evidence stayed put. "Every time I opened my freezer there would be my mother's urine," she said.

Months went by, and finally Angela acted, obtaining an "unknown sub-stance drug scan" test conducted by ExperTox Analytical Laboratory in Winter Park, Florida. The results were shocking. Louise Falvo, an elderly woman who wasn't even five feet tall, had three opioids in her system when she died: morphine, propoxyphene, and norpropoxyphene. The Na-tional Institute of Health recommends propoxyphene use by the elderly "should be avoided."[36] And norpropoxyphene comes with a warning that it can accumulate in tissues, especially in the elderly, and can prove lethal even in low doses.[37] "I phoned the lab for an explanation and spoke with the man who certified the report," Angela said. "He told me there were enough drugs in my mother's body to kill an entire football team." Angela shared an email she then wrote to Sergeant Barber in November 2009, in-forming him of the test results. "This is called 'negligent homicide,'" she declared. "What do you plan to do about this?" There was no response from the Gainesville Police Department, apparently no investigation, and no charges were ever filed in the death of Louise Falvo.

It's important to mention that the official autopsy report of Louise Falvo, shared with me for inclusion in this book, also lists the same three opioids as being present in her bloodstream, along with other medications, including one for controlling depression and anxiety. And it notes that Falvo was already suffering from hypertensive disease and congestive heart failure when she was put into guardianship, thus making her a candidate for what should have been a very carefully prescribed medication regime.

Angela had always had a fraught relationship with her headstrong mother, but she could not stand to let Louise's death be in vain. For four years she methodically gathered evidence against the petitioning lawyer, guardian Fierle, and the nursing home. She investigated some thirty cases in which Fierle was guardian, and said she personally visited with about fifteen of those wards in nursing homes or with their relatives. Woodhull chronicled their "horrific experiences" dealing with the controlling guardian. There was an allegation that a deceased ward's diamond wedding rings were given by Fierle as a "payoff" to the head of nursing at one facility. Another claim alleged Fierle had changed the will of a ward and named the nursing home as the beneficiary. According to Woodhull, that ward's three children challenged the change to their parent's last will and testament, and they won in the court of appeals. Other wards complained of Fierle charging them for services never rendered, like a $500 automobile paint job (allegedly done at the auto body shop of Fierle's brother) on a car that had already recently been painted.

In 2012 Angela took all her investigative findings and presented a sixty-six-page document to the Florida attorney general's office. She also provided nearly two hundred pages of backup evidence. She got no definitive response. She spoke to agents of the FBI, but as she said during one of our many telephone conversations, they left Angela with the impression that "they were investigating me" to see if she was a threat to the judge or others in the guardianship system. She showed her discoveries to the Orange County white-collar crime unit, which in turn handed her report over to Rebecca Fierle for her comments. Angela said she approached federal and state agents about her claim of Medicaid fraud. They got her an audience with investigators schooled in welfare and food stamp fraud. "These guys were used to investigating people who spent food stamps on wine," Angela recalled when we spoke one day. "What I had was beyond them. They said they wouldn't know how to even start. So, like usual, it all winds up in the ozone." Angela said she reached out to a top Medicaid official in Atlanta to report her suspicions, but "it ended up going nowhere too." Every state or federal lawsuit Woodhull filed was lost, including one that went before the US Supreme Court. The lawyer for guardian Fierle successfully argued to the high court that Angela's complaint was "a state issue, not a federal issue." The problem was, no state entity would act on her information, apparently choosing to believe the guardian's claim that Angela was "a crazy woman." Then came February 10, 2020, the day Rebecca Fierle was arrested in connection with the death of Steven Stryker.[38]

Within weeks Angela was invited to the attorney general's office to meet with agents of the Florida Department of Law Enforcement. "They told me, 'We would like to talk to you. We would like to learn from you as we continue to investigate Fierle,'" Angela recalled. "So, I went into the meeting ready to be the educator, to tell them exactly what I'd found." Instead, she says she got a decidedly icy reception from a state lawyer who was the initial point of contact. On hand for the March meeting with the FDLE were representatives from the Seminole County sheriff's department, the Orange County white-collar crime unit and the Gainesville Police Department. "They said they had looked over my report, and then they proceeded to shoot holes in it." Angela said she has no idea if the information in her carefully constructed report was ever investigated by Florida law enforcement. An important note: the Louise Falvo estate stayed open for five years after her death, with two probate judges in a neighboring county presiding over the estate. Judge Victor Hulslander and Judge Toby Monaco failed to close out the estate and, in the end, all the assets were depleted by court appointees. Angela Woodhull received no inheritance.

As for the ultimate fate of her mother's guardian, Angela continues to believe that since Rebecca Fierle was so intricately involved with prominent judges, lawyers, first responders and hospitals, and nursing home operators, she will never receive the punishment she deserves. "Since she can threaten to spill the beans" in open court, Angela theorizes, "the system will probably protect her." Woodhull may have a point. After all the evidence county and state investigators gathered that seriously called into question the tactics of guardian Rebecca Fierle, and after the intense public outrage about her activities, prosecutors ultimately decided to try her only on reduced charges of aggravated abuse and neglect of an elderly or disabled adult in the death of Steven Stryker. On September 19, 2022, after just three and a half days of testimony, a jury in Tampa, Florida, deliberated for about twelve hours before announcing they were deadlocked. Judge Samantha Ward did not insist they keep deliberating; instead she declared a mistrial. Perhaps one reason for the jury's inability to reach a decision was that no autopsy of Stryker was performed before his body was cremated. The defense insisted there could therefore be no definitive cause of death linking Rebecca Fierle to Stryker's passing. As the date of her retrial on two felony charges neared, prosecutors gave Fierle a deal. She pleaded "no contest" to one lesser charge of simply neglecting an elderly ward. At this writing she has not been sentenced.

THE TWO IN-DEPTH CASES described in this chapter—Parks from Nevada and Fierle from Florida—are by no means isolated incidents. They may not even be the worst of the worst guardians to have preyed on their wards. They are presented here to give readers an idea of how intricately manipulative and duplicitous some guardians can be, and how easy it is for all those involved in the guardianship system to dodge responsibility. From judges and lawyers, guardians and conservators, to state and federal investigative agencies, very few participants ever raise a hand to say, "Mistakes were made. Let's fix this."

In the relatively few cases where an official investigation is launched, the public is often disappointed in the outcome. Take the case of judge Martin Colin and his wife, Elizabeth Savitt, of Palm Beach County, Florida, for example.[39] This scandal featured a circuit court judge with an apparent gambling problem who oversaw guardianships, and his tennis-pro wife who suddenly switched jobs and became a guardian. As the *Palm Beach Post* admirably reported in a long series of in-depth articles, Savitt's career change came at a time when the couple was having significant financial troubles. When the question of possible conflict of interest arose, Judge Colin explained that the arrangement was perfectly fine because his spouse never appeared in his courtroom.[40] That was true, but Elizabeth Savitt was a regular in the courtroom of her husband's closest probate court colleagues—specifically judge David French, who oversaw most of her cases. Also, various lawyers appointed to guardianship cases allegedly sought out guardian Savitt to join their team, while at the same time they were asking her husband to approve their costly fee sheets attached to other probate cases. One local attorney, Sheri Hazeltine, publicly admitted that Judge Colin had taken her aside at the Delray Beach courthouse one day and point-blank asked her to recommend his wife for probate cases that required a guardian. Hazeltine accepted the unorthodox suggestion, and the judge then appointed her as the lawyer-of-record on multiple profitable guardianship cases. In return, attorney Hazeltine recommended Savitt be brought on board as guardian in nearly a dozen instances.

Then there were Judge Colin's mysterious financial dealings. The *Palm Beach Post* got its hands on state investigative documents and concluded that "when it came to smoke, the judge's checking account was a forest fire."[41] There was a steady stream of thousands of dollars in cash and checks streaming in and out of Colin's account, about $120,000 in cash during the five-year period Savitt served as a guardian. According to the *Post*, Savitt would write checks from her Savitt Guardians business account to her husband, totaling more than $47,000, and these payments came at a time when Savitt had helped herself to tens of thousands of dollars from her ward's estates without first getting court permission to do so.[42] The checks from Savitt Guardians to Martin Colin, especially one with a bottom note that read "loan," raised suspicions that the judge was personally profiting from his wife's judicial appointments.

During the same period, thousands of dollars flowed between the judge and four local probate and family law lawyers, two of whom had been appointed by Judge Colin to cases. The Florida State Code of Judicial Conduct clearly states it is a violation for a jurist to accept a loan or a gift from any party "who has come, or likely will come, before the judge."[43]

In one jaw-dropping instance, Colin appointed his former law partner to the $20 million probate case of Wet n Wild cosmetic founder Stanley Acker. Over the course of the next eight years, that attorney would make at least $700,000 as he worked to settle inheritance disputes between Acker's heirs. There was a paper trail indicating that the judge had received a loan from that attorney's elderly mother.

And last, Judge Colin was discovered to have been a regular patron at area casinos. Bank statements and court documents painstakingly analyzed by *Palm Beach Post* reporters John Pacenti and Holly Baltz revealed that the judge "withdrew a total of $115,000 at Broward County casinos" during the five years he heard probate cases. The reporters also discovered payments Colin had made to a bookie who was busted in an illegal online gambling ring.[44] After all these *Palm Beach Post* revelations, Judge Colin was removed from hearing guardianship cases. He resigned from the bench in November 2016.

Taken together, this information about the judge and his guardian wife certainly seemed to warrant an official investigation.

Reporter Pacenti was able to retrace the investigative history of the Colin-Savitt saga and discovered the first complaints about guardian Savitt were lodged in 2012 after a call to a hotline operated by Palm Beach County Clerk & Comptroller's office, which was tasked with overseeing grievances against guardians. No action was taken against Savitt. In 2014 several more hotline tips about Judge Colin's wife were received, but no disciplinary action was initiated against Savitt. In 2016, after the newspaper's bombshell revelations about the couple were made public, aggrieved family members were hopeful that some state agency would launch a serious investigation with an eye toward possible criminal prosecution.

It wasn't until late 2018 that the state attorney assigned his public corruption unit to investigate. They were assisted by Anthony Palmieri, deputy inspector general in the Palm Beach County Clerk & Comptroller's office. It turned out Palmieri had quietly investigated those past complaints about guardian Savitt and had written up a confidential and very detailed twenty-five-page report in March 2017.[45] Once the state attorney's corruption unit became interested, Palmieri shared his findings with the state investigators. He included a detailed memo explaining how Florida's complex guardianship system worked, and the Hazeltine/Savitt connection. Palmieri, a man who had audited some two thousand guardianship cases during the course of his career, painstakingly outlined several "substantiated charges" against Savitt in connection with thirteen of her cases. Included was the finding that she had taken retainer fees without permission and had perpetuated a serious conflict of interest by not always disclosing that she was the wife of a sitting judge. Palmieri also named more than a dozen circuit court judges who had engaged with Savitt in questionable ways. The report concluded there had been "corruption and collusion of judges and lawyers in Delray Beach for financial gain."[46] If state investigators read all the available investigative information, they would also have learned specific details about the multiple serious complaints from families of Savitt's wards. They had claimed numerous judges would simply wave off family worries about Savitt's excessive retainers; many worried relatives filed grievances over Savitt's alleged overbilling; there was a report that Savitt had attempted to annul a marriage to exclude a rightful heir; and there were complaints about Savitt's contrived disagreements designed to generate more fees for herself and those who worked with her. There was also a claim that $400,000 had gone missing from the estate of one of Savitt's incapacitated senior wards about the time the

Savitt-Colin's home faced foreclosure. The allegation that estate money had been illegally diverted to save the guardian's home was ultimately labeled as "unfounded."[47] But many other grievances were substantiated and the Palmieri report concluded there had been "major violations of guardianship law."[48] Yet guardian Savitt remained untouched by law enforcement for several more years.

On June 30, 2019, nine months after the state attorney's Public Corruption Unit had opened its inquiry, the office issued a memorandum that read in part, "This investigation focused on whether the relationship between Judge Colin and Elizabeth Savitt resulted in Savitt receiving an unfair financial advantage or if she or her associated attorneys received unfair favorable rulings from Judge Colin." The state attorney's conclusion found "no evidence to support any of the allegations."[49] To those citizens who had followed the scandal, the finding was a major letdown when it was made public. To them the story was about more than whether Elizabeth Savitt got preferential treatment within the court system. It was about whether Savitt, or other people—like guardianship judges and attorneys—had conspired to guardianize and then cheat vulnerable people out of their hard-earned estates. It appeared as though no state or federal prosecutor in Florida was willing to risk their careers by taking on a case involving an entire section of the justice system.

Palm Beach Post reporter John Pacenti was not deterred. With the state's so-called Sunshine Laws on his side, he petitioned for—and finally got—the entire investigative file from the state attorney's office. It took a threat by the newspaper before the files were released.[50] The *Post* uncovered a web of questionable financial machinations the Savitt-Colin couple had engaged in. And it was journalist Pacenti, along with his colleague Holly Baltz, who revealed the Public Corruption Unit's slapdash investigative techniques.[51] The decision not to prosecute was reached, according to the newspaper, even though state investigators failed to interview crucial witnesses. Investigators never subpoenaed Savitt's business bank account to try to determine exactly where she got the money she funneled to her husband; they never questioned the four attorneys who had given money to the judge; they failed to interview Ms. Hazeltine about whether she felt pressured by the judge to work with Savitt; the bookie to whom Judge Colin had made payments was never interviewed; and state investigators did not speak to any family members of wards who had complained of possibly illegal activities on the part of probate judges and Elizabeth Savitt.

And, most glaringly, the public corruption unit detectives never bothered to question either the judge or his wife to specifically ask them to explain where all the cash that had flowed into their household had come from.

Family members who hoped Savitt would have to pay for what she had done got one bit of positive news. In March 2019, more than three years after the *Post* first revealed allegations of financial wrongdoing by the judge and his wife,[52] the Department of Elder Affairs finally exercised the legislative power it had been given years earlier and filed an administrative complaint against Elizabeth Savitt.[53] This would mark the first time the department targeted a professional guardian for discipline. Relying on the findings from Anthony Palmieri's twenty-five-page report, which concluded Savitt had violated three sections of the state's guardianship statute, it was decided Elizabeth Savitt's registration to act as a guardian should be revoked. In announcing the action Elder Affairs secretary Richard Prudom said, "Revoking Ms. Savitt's registration is simply the right thing to do based on her repeated bad behavior and shows our seriousness and commitment to removing those self-service bad actors who act unlawfully." Savitt was immediately removed from all her current, as well as any future, guardianship cases. The public would never have known about these court-approved misdeeds had it not been for the dogged determination of the *Palm Beach Post*'s reporters. As for Savitt's husband, the controversial judge was allowed to quietly retire with no disciplinary action taken against him. He then opened Colin Mediation in Lake Worth, Florida. His website's front page boasts of Colin's forty years of legal experience and informs potential clients that "courts are very busy and in certain situations, it may be quicker and more efficient for issues to be referred to retired Judge Colin for a prompt and knowledgeable result."[54]

IT WOULD BE IMPOSSIBLE for one book to relate every instance of an outrageous action taken by a judge, a lawyer, a guardian, or other court appointee. Stories of destructive, humiliating, and sadistically cruel behavior have been documented in states across the nation. The following is a brief summary of some more cases.

* In January 2006 Gary Harvey, of Horseheads, New York, fell down the basement stairs and was left profoundly disabled. He was in his fifties at the time and happily married to his wife, Sara. He had

not executed any advanced directives, so Sara was advised to file
for guardianship. The Department of Social Services of Chemung
County, New York, was appointed guardian and Gary remained under their control for eleven long years, miraculously surviving in
a near-comatose state. Sara was Gary's closest advocate, and she
often alleged that her husband was left to lie in his own waste and
that his feeding tube was clogged or dislodged, and made other criticisms of his 24/7 care. At one point, Sara noticed Gary's discomfort
with his trachea tube and reported it to the nursing staff. For two
weeks the complaint went unaddressed until Sara—by this time at
the end of her patience—said something to the effect that if she had
a pair of scissors she would cut the tube, thus forcing them to fix
it. The nurse gave her scissors, and Sara followed through. Victory!
The faulty trachea tube was replaced, and Gary was never in any
medical danger. But Sara was then accused by the guardian of trying to kill her husband. Sara's visitation hours were drastically cut
and she was ordered to be strictly supervised. Sometimes the guardian would deny any spousal visits. In July 2009, without Sara's
knowledge the guardian petitioned to take Gary off all life support.
Sara went public, and the resulting media coverage got the guardian
to withdraw the petition. The guardian retaliated in various ways,
according to Sara. The most heartless act occurred on February 27,
2013 (a rare visiting day for Sara), and was captured in a memo
from guardian Elizabeth Beckwith written to the visitation monitor:

> Sara Harvey is permitted the following actions:
> Kiss Gary two times on the cheek.
> Hold hand under the following conditions:
>
>   1. Hands are visible at all times by the monitor (CIS staff person
>   and camera).
>   2. Sara's hand should NOT be moving at all when holding Gary's
>   hand.
>
> Please note that the above two actions shall only be permitted under
> the above conditions. IF Sara deviates at any time during today's
> visit from these stated expectations, then all touching should stop
> immediately. These permitted actions cease at the end of the visit
> today.

For the last four years of his tightly restricted life, Sara says she was only allowed to see Gary for twenty minutes. Gary Harvey died in the hospital on April 23, 2017, at the age of sixty-six.

* In Columbus, Ohio, attorney Paul Kormanik, a guardian for some four hundred wards, bragged that he had more business than any other guardian in the nation. "And I could take another thousand if they were in nursing homes," he once said, adding that the home's staff could serve as his eyes and ears and pick up the slack when he wasn't there.[55] In May 2014 a five-part series in the *Columbus Dispatch* unmasked Kormanik and other guardians accused of heartless behaviors and billing irregularities. The Dispatch reported Kormanik had been removed from cases for taking questionable-sized fees without prior court approval, and that he had double-dipped when he paid himself with money from ward's estates and then also charged the state's indigent fund for servicing the same client. He regularly failed to get his wards on the Medicaid rolls, which in at least one case led to a married couple being needlessly separated when the wife was sent to a nursing home. A short time after the husband was finally allowed to join his wife, she died, unaware that he was at her side. Some Kormanik wards told the court their guardian was needlessly isolating them from their families. Others said they never once laid eyes on the man who was supposed to be protecting them. A retired probate judge told the newspaper he had tried to "rein in Kormanik's caseload" years earlier by contacting the Ohio Supreme Court about the guardianship system's problems, but no official review of the controversial Kormanik (or the state's system) was ever undertaken.[56] In January 2015 Kormanik was indicted on eleven criminal charges of engaging in a pattern of corrupt activity (racketeering), stealing from his vulnerable clients, and tampering with records to conceal his crimes from the court.[57] Guardian Kormanik was offered a plea deal and eventually pleaded guilty to just four counts of falsifying records, taking public money under false pretenses, and absconding with almost $50,000 worth of items taken from ward's homes—from cash and a riding lawn mower to jewelry and family heirlooms. Kormanik faced the possibility of spending up to four years in prison. On the morning of his scheduled sentencing in October 2015, he died by suicide.[58]

* An elderly Ohio woman's attempt to simply update her power of attorney resulted in an unwanted guardianship that would cost ninety-year-old Rita Cole nearly all the money she had. Rita regularly traveled to Richmond, Rhode Island, for visits with her niece, Karen Nelligan. In November 2015, during a trip to see Karen, Rita told her niece she wanted to update her estate documents since her elderly brother could no longer fulfill the duties as her POA. Rita's plan was to name her very good friend, Dr. Mary Bender of Cincinnati, Ohio, as her primary power of attorney. But that is not what happened. Karen took her aunt to see a Rhode Island estate attorney, and he convinced the elderly, unmarried, and childless Rita to name him as her POA for financial matters and niece Karen as POA of her person (for medical care). At this point in time, Ms. Cole's estate was valued at $127,050. Rita received a small monthly pension of $190 and her monthly Social Security check was $1,626. Her condo in Cincinnati was valued at $95,000.

A few months later, in January 2016, Rita and her niece were vacationing in Florida when they went to a bank branch and, according to advocates of Rita's, they discovered that $117,000 was missing. Karen began to ask pointed questions about charges, balances, and transactions on her aunt's account and a bank teller got suspicious of this younger woman probing around regarding an older person's money. The bank manager was alerted and called Winter Park Police to report a "possible fraud in progress." Rita and Karen were separated, and according to a police report, "Ms. Cole said that her niece was trying to take her money." Karen would tell the responding officers, "She was just trying to take money out of her aunt's account to buy a plane ticket to send her home to Ohio." But such a withdrawal was apparently impossible because the Rhode Island lawyer now had control of Rita's money. He was listed with the bank as having the "power of attorney" for the account, and Winter Park Police immediately called to inform him about the incident. Armed with that sketchy and contradictory information, the attorney filed a temporary guardianship petition with the Rhode Island probate court saying Rita's family was "exploiting her" and she needed court protection. The only evidence of exploitation provided was that brief and seemingly contradictory police report, and there was no medical evaluation offered to the court indicating that

Rita was incapacitated. No matter; Judge Christine Engustian read-ily approved the temporary petition without a due process hearing or prior notice to either Rita or her niece. Three days later, on May 13, 2016, police escorted a shaken Rita away from Karen's home and placed her in the Highland Memory Care and Assisted Living facil-ity in Providence, Rhode Island. Dr. Bender traveled from Cincinnati to help her friend, and she, along with Karen Nelligan and others, waged a battle to free Rita. They were not successful. Rita would remain confined, mostly isolated, and allegedly overmedicated at times for the next thirteen months.

Administering too many drugs to elderly patients to render them compliant is not uncommon. (It's often referred to as "chem-ical restraint.") One 2014 estimate concluded that "as many as 1 in 5 patients in the nation's nursing homes are given antipsychotic drugs that are not only unnecessary, but also extremely danger-ous for older patients."[59] Rita Cole spent Fourth of July, Thanks-giving, Christmas, and her ninety-first birthday locked away from the outside world. Every month, her finances were depleted by ongoing legal fees and the $6,700 that was taken to pay her bill at the Highland facility. Suddenly, on Memorial Day weekend 2017, Dr. Bender was finally allowed to take Rita home to live with her in Ohio. Why was Rita finally freed? The question was put to the Rhode Island attorney who initiated the guardianship. Via email he responded, "Due to the amount of time I had put into this matter and the ongoing acrimony with the family, I personally decided to withdraw from the case rather than continuing to add charges to the invoice."[60] This attorney also said his firm's normal hourly fee is $325 for such matters. Financial spreadsheets provided by the lawyer's office show a final balance in Rita's account of just $500, certainly not enough to cover even two more hours of legal service. The paperwork notes that the $500 was forwarded to the "successor guardian," presumably Dr. Mary Bender. Yes, Rita was freed, but her money was gone and she had lost more than a year of freedom.

Many questions spring from the case of Rita Cole. If a family member in Rhode Island is actually exploiting a visiting relative from Ohio, how is it good public policy to lock away the alleged vic-tim in an institution far away from her home? Exactly how was Rita Cole "protected" by keeping her from going home to Cincinnati? Who, besides the for-profit players in the guardianship system and the senior care facility, truly benefited from the arrangement? If the allegation of elder exploitation was real, why was there no police investigation or charges filed? Several calls to Dr. Bender to get an update on Rita's well-being went unanswered. Then it was learned that Rita Cole passed away on April 8, 2022.[61] She was two weeks away from her ninety-sixth birthday.

* In Colorado Springs, Colorado, conservator Andria Beauvais faced a possible twelve years in prison after being charged with sixteen felonies related to her illegal handling of several of her ward's finances. Her victims ranged in age from thirty-one to ninety-seven, and her criminal acts took place over the course of about five years. Beauvais's unlawful activities might have gone undetected had it not been for the diligence of one elderly ward's daughter, Barb Dowski, who got a call from a family doctor asking about her mother's unpaid bill. She began to investigate and discovered Beauvais had not only allowed her mother's Medicare coverage to lapse; Beauvais had also illegally siphoned off some $118,000 from her mother's accounts. Dowski took her evidence to the Colorado Springs Police Department, and after a lengthy investigation it was discovered that Dowski's mother, Barbara Moore, was far from the only victim.

A dogged detective named Robert Campbell determined that Beauvais had stolen more than $402,000 from various wards, including money from the estate of a young man who had received a substantial settlement after having been badly burned in a childhood accident. Among Beauvais's other wards were those who had been diagnosed with developmental disabilities or Alzheimer's. Beauvais told the court her husband was addicted to drugs and regularly drained her bank accounts. In addition, she said her adult son had been injured in an assault, and she had to pay his medical bills since he had no health insurance. "If I could go back and undo what has been done, I would," she said, "I can't explain why I did it . . . I'm embarrassed beyond words." Court records show that in the midst of her illicit check-writing spree, Beauvais bought a new home and a car, and her family enjoyed Disney vacations. In the end, a controversial plea deal reduced Beauvais's sixteen felony counts to just one count of theft. In early April 2022, despite hearing several emotional victim impact statements, and a plea from the prosecutor to sentence Beauvais to the maximum six years in prison, judge William Moller sentenced Andria Beauvais to just ninety days in jail. After her release, she was ordered into a ten-year supervised economic probation program, meaning all her financial accounts and activities will be subject to constant monitoring. Her disappointed victims and their families hope that an outstanding civil suit and two other pending investigations—one conducted by the Castle Rock Police Department and another by the federal Department of Veterans Affairs—will deliver to them a more palatable sense of justice.

Every once in a while, victims of a predatory guardian will be surprisingly satisfied with the prosecution of their court-appointed adversary. Thus was the case of Susan K. Harris, who, at seventy-four years old, received the harshest punishment ever meted out to a guardian—so far, anyway. Her day of reckoning came on July 15, 2021, and it occurred after the US Department of Justice moved in to stop her decade-long crime spree. Harris had been the president of Ayudando Guardians, a "nonprofit corporation" based in Albuquerque, New Mexico. Yet Harris lived a lifestyle as if she was rolling in profits. The Spanish word *Ayudando* means "helping" in English, and according to the DOJ, Susan helped herself to at least $11 million that wasn't hers.[62]

Federal investigators concluded that Susan had schemed with her sixty-year-old husband, William Harris, her adult son, Craig Young, and chief financial officer Sharon Moore. Their big mistake was to illegally divert federal dollars that came to their clients with special needs via Social Security or Veterans Affairs checks. In the summer of 2017, federal officials shuttered the business and charged that in the decade between November 2006 and July 2017, the gang at Ayudando, led by "ringleader" Susan Harris, used the stolen money to "fund an extravagant lifestyle, including the purchases of homes, vehicles, luxury RV's and cruises, as well as a private box at 'The Pit' [to watch college basketball] at the University of New Mexico. The stolen funds were also used to pay for more than $4.4 million in American Express charges incurred by the defendants and their families."[63] It was revealed in court that each time Ayudando's $300,000 luxury box at UNM was occupied, the visitors racked up a catering tab of between $3,000 and $5,000.

Ultimately, all the defendants pleaded guilty to various combinations of charges, including conspiracy, conspiracy to defraud the United States, money laundering, mail fraud, and aggravated identity theft. Their sentencing hearing was set for March 2, 2020.[64] Numerous victims attended to give impassioned impact statements, and the judge said she had received letters from many of the almost one thousand Ayudando clients who had been victimized. However, instead of showing up in court to receive their agreed-upon sentences of seven years for William and between thirty years and life for Susan, the couple went on the lam. Six weeks later, the US Marshals Service found them holed up in a nondescript apartment complex in Shawnee, Oklahoma. When the Harrises fled their luxury home in Albuquerque, they took their pet Chihuahua with them. Marshals reported it was the dog's incessant barking that helped them locate precisely which apartment the couple was using as their hideout.[65]

On July 15, 2021, US District Court judge Martha Vazquez threw the book at the Harrises. Calling it a case of "unbelievable greed" and citing the couple's lack of remorse for leaving many of their clients destitute, homeless, and unlikely to ever recover financially, Vazquez sentenced William to fifteen years in federal prison. Susan, described as "the engine" of the operation, got what amounted to a life sentence—forty-seven years. Given her age, it is unlikely she will ever serve the three years' probation the judge tacked on. The couple was also ordered to pay the entire amount of stolen money as restitution, also unlikely to happen since both will be behind bars and unable to earn for a considerable period. Ayudando's former chief financial officer, Sharon Moore, received a twenty-year sentence, and Susan's son, Craig Young, was sent to prison for just under six years. Ayudando might have been listed as a nonprofit on paper, but a former accountant for the firm told investigators the firm served as a "family ATM" for Susan Harris.[66]

Some court watchers opined that if the bad actors at Ayudando had just stuck to stealing from clients who did not receive federal funds, they might have gotten away with their crimes. County and state law enforcement agencies rarely pursue the intense forensic investigations needed to crack financial crimes committed by guardians, conservators, and the attached lawyers. Such probes are costly and require specialized auditors. And it's a sure bet that suspected court appointees will always defend themselves by claiming a judge sanctioned their actions. Many law enforcement administrators—from police to prosecutors—simply don't want the political headache that comes with investigating a case that could uncover crimes committed by officers of the court or evidence of dereliction of duty on the part of a sitting judge.

7

How Do the Bad Actors
Get Away with It?

The most common question that arises from abusive guardianship cases is, "How do these court appointees get away with it?" The answers are simple. Sometimes it is a matter of an exasperated, overworked, or inattentive judge who relies on the honor system and blindly believes all court appointees act with integrity. Those who sit on the bench almost always accept the recommendations of the lawyers, guardians, and conservators and approve their actions with no questions asked. Also, in many states, the system is simply not designed to keep track of the ever-increasing volume of guardianship cases, and judicial follow-up falls through the cracks. And to put it bluntly, sometimes abusive players get away with it because of who they know.

The most enterprising players in the guardian game make it part of their business plan to build a web of high-level connections, people they can call upon for protection should they ever get stuck in a sticky situation. Those who help shield the bad acts of guardianship appointees have been known to come from within law enforcement and the legal community, and from the ranks of elected officials. Since the founding of the republic, questionable characters pulling political strings has been a fact of life. Getting a state lawmaker, a member of the US Congress, or an influential businessperson to place a call to just the right person can work wonders in making a legal problem go away.

Perhaps no one in the professional guardianship industry has used their top-shelf political, judicial, and business connections to better personal advantage than one Mr. Jared E. Shafer of Las Vegas, Nevada. Suspicions of questionable and perhaps illegal activity swirled around him for about as long as he worked in the guardianship arena. Shafer, a man with a large frame, balding head, patchy gray beard, and a somewhat slovenly appearance, has been variously described as arrogant, antagonistic, and demanding. He's known as the never-benevolent Granddaddy of Guardianship in Nevada, and his reign lasted nearly four decades. The insider power Jared Shafer was able to so brazenly assert over the Silver State's guardianship system should act as a red flag warning to other jurisdictions where highly connected and suspect guardians operate.

To fully understand Shafer's reach, it is necessary to summarize his personal history and how he came to be centermost in the state's lucrative and scandal-scarred guardianship system. According to the *Las Vegas Review-Journal*, Shafer had been a "travel consultant" for several years in the early 1970s and then was named vice president of Rom-Amer Pharmaceuticals.[1] The *Los Angeles Times* reported that some of Shafer's Rom-Amer associates were accused of bribing a Nevada politician to sponsor a law that would make one of their products—a so-called antiaging drug called Gerovital H3—available for purchase without a prescription.[2] Shafer had left the company by the time the allegations of impropriety surfaced publicly, and he was never charged with a crime.

In the late 1970s shortly after his departure from the world of pharmaceuticals, the unemployed Shafer was in touch with his longtime pal, Clark County Commission chairman Manny Cortez. The two men were so close that in the early '60s Cortez reportedly chose Shafer to be godfather to his newborn daughter, Catherine.[3] (Remember her name.) In 1979 Chairman Cortez was instrumental in getting his out-of-work friend named to the post of public administrator and public guardian in Las Vegas. Shafer would hold that position for almost a quarter century. He would remain an active player in the Nevada guardianship system long after his retirement from public office.

During a brief telephone interview with Shafer, conducted in August 2022, I asked him if he was indeed the godfather of Catherine Cortez. "Oh, fuck no. Jesus Christ! That's the stupidest goddamned thing I've ever heard," he replied in a raised voice. Our conversation would best be described as contentious.

In June 1982 an audit of Shafer's public guardianship office found a widespread failure to properly inventory wards' estates, leaving doubt as to where money and property had gone. After that, as the *Review-Journal* put it, "Nothing much changed, and auditors and critics periodically questioned Shafer's operating methods throughout his tenure in public office."[4] In 1983 two of Shafer's estate management executives were arrested by the FBI on charges that they had stolen at least $60,000 from the accounts of dead people. The pair pleaded guilty to similar charges in Arizona and were sentenced in the Grand Canyon state to five years in prison. Shafer maintained the thefts in Nevada took place without his knowledge, and investigators concluded they lacked "enough evidence" to pursue the public guardian, Jared Shafer.

To call Shafer a combative and hostile figure would be an understatement. As far back as 2005, he was the focus of a multitude of family complaints to the Las Vegas Police Department about his alleged mistreatment of wards—complaints that were not investigated. When asked whether he was aware of the numerous grievances about his behavior as a guardian, Shafer said, "Yeah. I know." Asked what he might like to say to those who criticized his actions, he simply said, "Nothing." Later in the conversation he said, "People who hate me hate me because I took the money away from them. Everything was done with the judge's approval."

In 2009 Shafer and two CPAs who worked with him were accused by the US Securities and Exchange Commission (SEC) of engaging in a Ponzi scheme that "fraudulently offered and sold some $180 million in unregistered notes to more than 800 investors, many of whom were senior citizens."[5] The trio reportedly wriggled out of being prosecuted by agreeing to return some of their ill-gotten gains. Shafer's extensive network of high-level statewide contacts over the years, including several career politicians, lawyers, and judges, coupled with his Teflon-like persona, reportedly helped him dodge numerous attempts to curb his questionable conduct.[6] In sheer frustration, dozens of aggrieved relatives of Shafer's wards flocked to the online complaint organization RipOffReport.com to post allegations about guardian Shafer's unsavory and exploitative tactics.[7] Many complaints also mentioned Shafer's long time protégé, Patience Bristol, and Commissioner Jon Norheim, the man who took the bench and heard nearly all guardianship cases in Clark County, Nevada. Hearing Master Norheim was accused of routinely ignoring family grievances and siding with court appointees, specifically Jared Shafer. Those who post at RipOffReport.com are identified only by the town in which they live, so trying to contact them to attempt to confirm their stories is impossible. That said, within the posts a pattern of alleged bad behavior emerged.

Guardians Shafer and Bristol were blamed of excessive billing, outright theft, corrupt practices, and brutal treatment of their many wards, including isolating them from loved ones and ordering them to be overmedicated. Some of the complaints blamed Shafer and Bristol for "killing" or "murdering" their loved one. The autopsy of one elderly ward reportedly concluded he died of starvation; another wrote to say her deceased aunt suffered from malnutrition.[8] One distraught adult wrote from Utah, "Dad killed himself. He slashed his wrists. The note left behind stated he couldn't stand what Patience Bristol and Jared Shafer had done to him and his family."[9]

The law caught up with Patience Bristol. She was widely seen as the obedient underling who did Shafer's dirty work for him. She was ultimately charged with fifteen counts of exploiting the elderly, selling the homes and cars of unsuspecting elderly wards, stealing a reported $150,000 in cash from one of her charges, and pilfering expensive jewelry from wards and selling it for nearly $50,000. Bristol confessed to authorities that she used the money to pay her mortgage and credit cards, and to finance her gambling addiction.[10] Her unemployed boyfriend was also a beneficiary.[11] Inexplicably, the Clark County district attorney, Steve Wolfson, agreed to negotiate a plea agreement and dropped all but one of the fifteen charges. On May 28, 2014, Bristol was sentenced to serve three to eight years in prison for exploitation of an elderly person.

Another pattern had emerged—one in which those working under Jared Shafer got tangled up with the law and had to pay the price for their offenses while their boss remained unscathed. Asked about whether he bore any responsibility for his underlings' crimes, Shafer replied, "You're reading the bullshit of the world."

Question: It seems as though people around you, those you supervised, kept going down.
    Answer: That's their problem, not mine. Those two guys stealing things, [in 1983,] they were tied to the mob, the real mob. And they got caught.

Question: But you always seem to escape the trouble.
    Answer: Well, that's the way it was. [Patience Bristol] worked for me as a [freelance] guardian on good cases. She got caught on her own outside cases.

Various published reports, including a lengthy *New Yorker* article on the Nevada guardianship system, recounted numerous allegations of misdeeds by guardian Shafer.[12] The magazine described Shafer this way: "In the course of his thirty-five-year career, Shafer has assumed control of more than three thousand wards and estates and trained a generation of guardians. In 1979, he became the county's public administrator, handling the estates of people who had no relatives in Nevada, as well as the public guardian, serving wards when no family members or private guardians were available. In 2003, he left government and founded his own private guardianship and fiduciary business and he transferred the number of his government-issued phone to himself."[13] Among the cases mentioned by the *New Yorker* was one in which a concerned family member tried mightily to persuade a judge that guardian Shafer had made an unfair business decision on behalf of her mother. As reporter Rachel Aviv wrote:

> When Concetta Mormon, a wealthy woman who owned a Montessori school, became Shafer's ward because she had aphasia, Shafer sold the school midyear, even though students were enrolled. At a hearing after the sale, Mormon's daughter, Victoria Cloutier, constantly spoke out of turn. The judge, Robert Lueck, ordered that she be handcuffed and placed in a holding cell while the hearing continued. Two hours later, when Cloutier was allowed to return for the conclusion, the judge told her that she had thirty days in which to vacate her mother's house. If she didn't leave, she would be evicted and her belongings would be taken to Goodwill.[14]

The *New Yorker* also mentioned Terry Williams, another angry and determined daughter of one of Shafer's wards. Williams was shocked when the court allowed guardian Shafer to ignore her status as executor of her elderly father's estate. She was also outraged at Shafer's overall poor treatment of her dad. Williams took it upon herself to research dozens of Shafer's past cases and, in 2006, went to police with a list of nearly two dozen statutes she believed Shafer had violated. Police told her it was a civil matter and they would not investigate. Eventually, Williams filed a federal racketeering (RICO) lawsuit against Shafer. Her pro se effort was not successful.

Journalist and former Las Vegas City councilman Steve Miller wrote about another RICO conspiracy lawsuit, which also named Shafer, Patience Bristol, Wells Fargo Bank, employees of Shafer's billing company, and several others. It was filed in the US District Court (Southern District of Nevada) in May 2015.[15] The estate of World War II veteran Guadalupe Olvera demanded a jury trial and alleged Shafer had embezzled "in excess of $420,000 . . . for services and reimbursements from the Estate of Guadalupe Olvera without court approval, accounting or oversight," and that he did so with the help of the other defendants. The suit also claimed Shafer's compensation "was dramatically higher than that authorized by statute." The Olvera saga began in late 2009 when Olvera's daughter, Rebecca "Becky" Schultz, became alarmed after her well-to-do father came under the spell of a female stranger who took him out of his home in Henderson, Nevada, isolated him from family, and allegedly "proceeded to convert much of his assets to her own use and benefit."[16] Becky, a resident of California, reached out for help and ultimately came in contact with Shafer. He counseled her that the best way to rescue her dad was to name him as temporary guardian. Becky agreed. But Becky said that once installed, Shafer took almost immediate steps to legally and permanently tether her father and his money to Nevada. After almost a year, and after guardianship Hearing Master Norheim denied the ninety-three-year-old Olvera's plea to leave the state,[17] the old soldier quietly ordered his only child to come get him and take him back to California. After Becky complied, Shafer sought a kidnapping charge against her.[18] Nevada Family Court judge Charles Hoskin, a colleague of Norheim's who heard all guardianship appeals and disputes, issued a bench warrant for Becky Schultz's arrest after she failed to return to the state for a court appearance.[19]

An expensive three-year battle ensued, with guardian Shafer continuing to control Guadalupe Olvera's estate. According to court documents he used thousands of dollars of his ward's money to fight Becky. As journalist Miller wrote, "Totally fed up, on December 3, 2011, Mr. Olvera's daughter Rebecca authored a six-page formal complaint to Nevada's Attorney General Catherine Cortez-Masto to document that her elderly father was being exploited by guardian Jared Shafer and to ask that Olvera be released into his family's care in California. Cortez-Masto refused to take action."[20]

Yes, Commissioner Cortez's now-adult daughter, Catherine Cortez, followed in her father's political footsteps and had become Nevada's attorney general. By then she was married and sporting a new hyphenated last name.[21] As the state's top cop, Cortez-Masto simply took no action to look into complaints about close family friend Shafer or any other guardian. In one letter to a family member, she reportedly explained that such an investigation would be outside her purview. When Cortez-Masto ran for the US Senate seat in 2016, her habitual lack of response to families of the guardianized became a campaign issue. A Super Pac called the Freedom Partners Action Fund bought more than a million dollars' worth of television commercials for her Republican opponent with the message that Cortez-Masto had "let Nevada seniors down." At the same time, Charles Pascal, the distraught relative of a Shafer ward came forward with details of a conversation he'd had with his mother-in-law's court-appointed minder, Jared Shafer. Pascal told the *Free Beacon* that he confronted Shafer about $350,000 in questionable fees that had been paid out and promised to take up the issue with A. G. Cortez-Masto. "He says, 'Go ahead.' He says, 'Let me tell you something, Catherine's father put me in as a guardian, we were friends for years. Try filing a report and see what happens.'"[22] Indeed, Pascal said when he phoned the attorney general's office for help, a staffer told him, "We don't take reports on Jared Shafer or any guardian." Despite the ad campaign, Cortez-Masto went on to win election to the US Senate in 2016.

So, what happened to Becky Schultz's RICO suit against Shafer and his colleagues? In a series of emails with me, Becky said details were confidential, but that "it was settled out of court. We received a bit of money . . . from [defendant] Wells [Fargo] and Shafer."[23] And, she said, defendant Patience Bristol also had to pay up, but restitution was deferred while she served her prison sentence. Now that Bristol is free, and when she is employed, Becky said Bristol's paychecks are being garnished to satisfy terms of the settlement agreement. During our telephone interview, Jared Shafer steadfastly denied there was any settlement.

In July 2017 a third RICO-based lawsuit was filed against Shafer, his private for-profit company Professional Fiduciary Services of Nevada, PFSN's longtime attorney Elyse Tyrell, and several others who worked on the guardianship case of victim Jason Hanson, a man with cerebral palsy and who is wheelchair bound.[24] The suit claimed that when Hanson turned eighteen in 2007, his juvenile guardianship status was declared terminated, and he should have been given control of an irrevocable trust fund set up for him by his paternal grandmother. In addition, after his father died unexpectedly in 2008, he should have received an estate worth an estimated $200,000.[25] Court appointees never transferred the money to Jason, a young man who is educated, well spoken, and intelligent, and so as a practical matter his guardianship continued. Jason lost the childhood house he stood to inherit and was forced to live in a group home funded by taxpayers.

On a videotape recorded by a family friend, Jason explains that when he was just eighteen, and after his father died, he foolishly believed his guardian had his best interests at heart. Instead, guardian Shafer sold his father's house and everything in it. "Jared Shafer is a thief, a crook, and if I believed in the devil, he would certainly look a lot like Jared Shafer," Jason said to the camera. "It's like Shafer put a gun to my head and I didn't realize it until it was too late. I don't understand how people like him can go to sleep at night with a clear conscience."[26] At the age of twenty-seven, Hanson finally found an attorney willing to help. His lawsuit against Shafer and the others alleged that together the defendants acted to charge "excessive fees" and committed "multiple fraudulent acts of embezzlement." Unfortunately, the attorney who agreed to take Jason's case died a short time after filing the suit. As a close friend of Jason's put it to me, "In his absence, his associate botched the next hearing by coming to court completely unprepared, and the uninterested judge dismissed Jason's case." Jason's future remains in doubt, and he will apparently continue to survive thanks to public assistance.

Shafer's close association with US Senator Cortez-Masto was not the only political alliance he enjoyed. Another reason his political protection ran so deep in Nevada was his association with a company called Signs of Nevada. This company reportedly offered up in-kind contributions to certain political candidates in the form of eye-catching, get-out-the-vote highway billboards and large A-frame posters.[27] Free advertising of that sort is a boon to cash-strapped candidates who might otherwise not be able to afford such a visible campaign. Such gifts can also forge lasting and loyal political contacts. A search of the Nevada Secretary of State's online archive shows Signs of Nevada and Shafer's Professional Fiduciary Services of Nevada shared the same post office box in Henderson, Nevada, for many years. It also lists the company's Annual Contributions and Expense Filings, which show hundreds of thousands of dollars going to various Republican and Democratic state candidates over the years. Included were a district court judge, members of the state assembly and senate, the Clark County Commission, and political action committees.[28]

Not surprising, then, that Shafer is considered to have been the force behind the passage of at least two guardianship-related pieces of legislation adopted by the Nevada legislature that did not benefit wards of the court. Journalist Steve Miller said around the statehouse they are quietly referred to as "Shafer bills." One law declared that no person living out of state could be named as a guardian for a resident of Nevada. That was a major impediment to outsiders with parents who had retired to that sunny state and suddenly needed assistance. In 2003 another Shafer-backed bill was approved; this legislation erased the requirements that private guardians had to provide actual receipts for expenditures on behalf of their wards, and that they had to file mandatory annual reports with the court. Passage of that bill occurred about the same time that Shafer retired as the public guardian and became one of those private guardians. As a for-profit professional, he continued to win numerous court appointments to be a guardian. Many recommendations came from attorney Elyse Tyrell of the now-defunct Trent, Tyrell and Associates law firm, a practice that specialized in estate planning, probate, elder law, and guardianship cases.

One past victim of the Las Vegas guardianship system I spoke with referred to Jared Shafer as a "protected species" in Las Vegas legal circles. Shafer is a man who made it a habit of forcefully inserting himself into lucrative guardianship cases and coming away decidedly wealthier for his efforts. He wielded such heft that he seemed to be able to command the system at will. A case in point: Hearing Master Norheim was once presiding over a proceeding that questioned how Shafer handled the estate of his ward Kristina Berger. As the courtroom's fixed camera rolled, a Berger family attorney wanted to know why there was "no money left and no records to explain where it went."[29] The barrel-chested Shafer suddenly blurted out, "Your honor, close the courtroom!" As if to underscore the power Shafer enjoyed within the system, a cowed-looking Commissioner Norheim simply said, "Okay." The room was suddenly emptied of spectators and the camera was shut off. "The bottom line in Nevada is that guardianships are private ... so we can discuss sensitive things," Shafer said on the phone when I asked about that particular courtroom command to Commissioner Norheim. "Health and finances are discussed in private," he said. When it was pointed out that a ward's finances are not covered under any privacy laws, Shafer shot back, "You can complain about me all day, but in the end we do the right thing for the ward. The family is not my priority. Who's the person I work for? The ward!"

Toward the end of Shafer's long career managing the lives of the incapacitated, his colleague Elyse Tyrell worked with him on what is believed to be his last professional guardian case. It had to do with an itinerant construction worker who became a millionaire many times over, but by the time he got the money, the man was in no condition to fully enjoy it. Given

Jared Shafer's past practice of aligning himself with financially rewarding guardianships, it's likely he was enthusiastic and grateful to be attached to the case by his collaborator, Tyrell.

Not much is publicly known about the life Ramiro Hernandez led before his life-altering accident. On December 5, 2009, at a casino construction site in Las Vegas, he accidentally plunged into the abyss of an unprotected eighty-foot-deep elevator shaft. His injuries were catastrophic. He sustained multiple fractures in his back, in various areas of his pelvic circle, and in his toes. Once hospitalized, he suffered a severe stroke, causing a cerebral hemorrhage that necessitated a craniotomy. Ramiro was left with a devastating and permanent traumatic brain injury. At the time of the accident, he was fifty-four years old and the father of three adult daughters, Karla, Maribel, and Christina. None of the women responded to multiple phone calls seeking comment about their father's case.

Ramiro Hernandez (aka Ramiro Hernandez Solis) was so profoundly injured that he required hospitalization in Las Vegas for nearly a year. On November 13, 2010, he was finally discharged and moved back to California to live with his daughter Christina. The rigorous care he still required, amid an already bustling family with small children, proved to be too much for his family. When Ramiro's health began to decline, it was decided to move the ailing patriarch to the Casa Colina Transitional Living Center in Pomona, California. He took up residence there in June 2011, and his expenses were paid through California's version of workers' compensation. Over time, the diminutive Ramiro became completely paralyzed on his left side, and he is now confined to a child-sized wheelchair. He suffers from chronic kidney and urinary tract infections. Without his mood-stabilizing medications, depression and anxiety sometimes take hold, and during one frightening episode he tried to attack a fellow resident with a tomahawk. Yet, as of this writing, Ramiro is described as a mostly happy resident who enjoys visits from relatives and going on off-campus lunch dates with his family. He frequently and enthusiastically partakes of the boating, shopping, and movie field trips offered by his caretakers.

After their father's 2009 accident, Ramiro's family hired the Las Vegas–based Richard Harris law firm to initiate a personal injury/negligence lawsuit on behalf of their father. The goal was to win an award large enough to finance the gravely injured man's care for the rest of his life. The lawsuit was filed on January 31, 2011. Traditionally, these types of actions take time to adjudicate, and many end with out-of-court settlements. The Hernandez case was no exception. Negotiations between the injured man's lawyers and the several entities involved dragged on month after month, year after year.

Then, more than two years after Ramiro's crippling accident, on January 23, 2012, a person he had never met petitioned Nevada's guardianship court for appointment to the case as the "general guardian." The request came from Jared E. Shafer via a petition written by attorney Elyse Tyrell. A familiar face immediately signed off on the appointment—district court judge Charles Hoskin. His order appointed Shafer to be Ramiro Hernandez's guardian as well as his power of attorney designee.[30] In one judicial swoop, Shafer got himself attached to a lawsuit that was destined to result in a payout of multiple millions of dollars to the injured man.

Why would a prestigious law firm like Richard Harris (founded by the late US senator Harry Reid) want to associate with such a controversial figure as Jared Shafer? Well, according to the lead plaintiff attorney on the case, Benjamin Cloward of Las Vegas, the firm did not choose Shafer. During a phone interview in late August 2022, Cloward explained that his firm specializes in personal injury and wrongful death lawsuits, not in matters involving incapacitated clients. Cloward said that since Mr. Hernandez was unable to state his desires to him, "I didn't have the legal ability to make decisions for him. I was required to get my client a guardian." Based on a colleague's recommendation, Cloward said, "We hired the Trent Tyrell law firm because they had the expertise in guardianship and incapacitation that we didn't have." (Bringing in an outside firm to provide expert guidance is an accepted procedure in the legal community.) Elyse Tyrell joined the Hernandez case, and having had a long association with Jared Shaffer dating back to at least the early 2000s, it was no surprise when he was tapped to act as guardian.[31] Since Tyrell worked with Shafer for so many years, she had to have been aware of the numerous controversies and complaints surrounding her choice, but that apparently did not deter her from recommending him for and representing him in new appointments.

During the time the Hernandez lawsuit remained unresolved, the Nevada Supreme Court became convinced that there were major problems within the guardianship system, especially on Shafer's home turf of Clark County, which handled about eighty-five hundred guardianship cases every year. After so many headline-making complaints, including the very public prosecution of Patience Bristol, the high court announced the creation of a new commission to investigate how guardianships were established, the court's records keeping system, how judges monitored their appointees, and judicial training methods. Almost simultaneously, in May 2015, the Eighth Judicial District Court took surprise action and officially removed commissioner Jon Norheim and family court judge Charles Hoskin after apparently deciding the pair had been mishandling guardianship cases.[32] The district court's most senior judge, Dianne Steel, was appointed to try to restore order to that department of the judiciary.

A final settlement for Ramiro Hernandez was reached on January 8, 2015, according to attorney Cloward. He also said there were a multitude of lawyers representing both the plaintiff and the various defendants and insurance companies involved in hammering out the final agreement, and that "Jared Shafer was just a placeholder" who had nothing to do with the settlement negotiations. Nonetheless, copies of court documents obtained from a source during research for this book reveal that at a hearing on February 4, 2015, Shafer was back before the not-yet-removed Judge Hoskin to report that "he has received a settlement offer from the liable parties." In one document submitted by lawyer Tyrell, Shafer asked the court for "the authority to accept" the offer. "Petitioner has been informed that this offer is fair and reasonable," the document read in part. "The terms . . . are confidential and will be provided to the court in camera." Judge Hoskin immediately okayed Shafer's request. Just why this guardian would claim to have gotten a settlement offer nearly a month after the actual settlement had been reached is unknown. According to attorney Cloward, it may simply have been a necessary courtroom procedure that Shafer was tardy in carrying out. And the way the deal was structured, none of the settlement money would ever pass through Shafer's hands. The funds were to go directly to a licensed fiduciary in California. For a guardian used to calling all the monetary shots and setting his own fees, this arrangement likely proved frustrating for the seasoned Shafer.

During our phone interview, Shafer first said he didn't recall the name Ramiro Hernandez or the particular case. Later in the conversation he said, "Oh, yeah. He was a vegetable if I remember correctly." Shafer termed his participation in the lawsuit as merely a "facilitator."

Meantime, Judge Steel was trying to whip the guardianship court into some semblance of order. It took Steel eight months, until August 31, 2015, to notice something was amiss in the still-open guardian case of Ramiro Hernandez. On that date, Judge Steel issued a show cause order demanding Jared Shafer appear before her and "show cause, if any, why you should not be held in contempt for being out of compliance with Nevada Statutes."[33] Apparently, no inventory of the ward's estate had been filed with the court, as is required. Of course, Hernandez was a laborer with few assets before his accident. But a settlement had been reached in his personal injury lawsuit months earlier and the court had no record of it. Judge Steel's order warned Shafer that she had the power to have him arrested if he did not comply. "Guardian's failure to appear may result in the dismissal of the Guardianship and/or issuance of a Bench Warrant."

According to the Clark County Court docket, on September 10, the team of Shafer and Tyrell filed "The First and Final Account and Report of Guardian." It declared that Ramiro Hernandez's assets on hand—his so-called inventory value—was $8,453,652.89. A settlement of almost $8.5 million was more than enough to cover the living expenses for this now sixty-one-year-old disabled man, even after paying attorney's fees of $1,197,757.48 and setting aside a portion of the award to reimburse the insurance company for its workers' compensation outlay. However, the docket shows that five days later attorney Tyrell filed an errata with the court. Translated from the Latin, an errata is a "correction of errors" in the first filing. It turns out the actual settlement amount awarded to Hernandez was $10 million. The errata document does not explain why there was such a discrepancy, but it did include a forgotten $1,546,347.11 annuities account. Was this just a clerical error or was there potentially something more sinister at play? How could such an experienced lawyer and guardian overlook a discrepancy of $1.5 million?

Benjamin Cloward thinks it was an honest, albeit embarrassing mistake. He ran down the list of the many watchful attorneys involved in the case. There were his lawyers from the Richard Harris law firm; two expert attorneys from Reno who specialized in the complications surrounding workers' compensation; at least two California-based law offices involved, including one hired by Hernandez's daughter Christina; and, of course, there were several attorneys representing the two allegedly negligent casino companies, as well as lawyers working on behalf of the business's insurance companies. "I think, for Shafer, he decided, 'Oh, geez, there are way too many eyes on this case. I can't get away with anything here,'" Cloward said. During one phone interview, the attorney looked back in his files and confirmed that Jared Shafer netted just $2,500 for his participation in the Hernandez case. Elyse Tyrell got $8,000.

There had been buzz throughout the legal community about the potential size of the upcoming Hernandez settlement, and his meager payday was probably not what Shafer had in mind when he first agreed to join the case. That his career would end with such a financial dud had to be disappointing for Shafer. It is likely, however, that there is a sizable group of people who have had firsthand experience with guardian Shafer and who, upon reading this, will believe it is a fitting comeuppance for a man who finally met a case he couldn't dominate. Attorney Elyse Tyrell did not respond to multiple written requests for comment.

8

Washington Could Help—But It Hasn't

Back in 1987, as the trend toward living longer became apparent, the Associated Press (AP) released a chilling six-part series called "Guardians of the Elderly: An Ailing System."[1] The findings of the AP's yearlong investigation of probate and guardianship courts in all fifty states and the District of Columbia was a shock to those who cared about such things. After studying more than twenty-two hundred randomly selected cases in which an elderly person had been placed under legal guardianship, the primary authors, Fred Bayles and Scott McCartney, concluded that 43 percent of the time, senior citizens were taken through court proceedings with no lawyer to represent them. They also concluded:

> [It is] a dangerously burdened and troubled system that regularly puts elderly lives in the hands of others with little or no evidence of necessity, then fails to guard against abuse, theft and neglect.
>
> In thousands of courts around the nation every week, a few minutes of routine and the stroke of a judge's pen are all that it takes to strip an old man or woman of basic rights.
>
> The court entrusts to someone else the power to choose where they will live, what medical treatment they will get, and, in rare cases, when they will die.
>
> While guardianship procedures vary, even from county to county, the laws follow a pattern: A petition is filed, usually by a family member, alleging a person is incompetent and no longer able to care for himself or herself. The person is evaluated, and the court rules

on the petition. If granted, guardianship reduces these "wards of the court" to the status of legal infants who may no longer drive a car, vote or, in many states, hire an attorney. A prisoner has more legal rights, said Winsor Schmidt, a Memphis State University professor who has studied guardianship in thirteen states.

Over the course of its six-day series, the AP reported case after horrific case of elderly Americans unwittingly caught up in a system that not only virtually imprisoned them but was funded by their own hard-earned money. And in so many instances, guardianship insiders arrogantly maintained that their actions were to "protect" the elder person, either from themselves or from dodgy family members. The AP revealed a deeply flawed system that was often slow to punish—or failed completely in punishing—those guardians found guilty of what the courts called "unjust enrichment." Civilians would simply call it "stealing from old people."

The widely reported findings so concerned Florida Congressman Claude Pepper, a member of the House Select Committee on Aging, that he called a special hearing of his Health and Long-Term Care subcommittee. Pepper, then age eighty-seven, had always been an outspoken elder advocate, and he hailed from one of the country's premiere retirement states. It was clear the findings of the AP investigation about abusive guardianships angered him.[2] "It is, in one short sentence, the most punitive civil penalty that can be levied against an American citizen, with the exception, of course, of the death penalty," Chairman Pepper said during his opening statement. "You would think, given the severity of restrictions guardianship imposes upon one's civil rights, that great care would be taken by the States and the federal government to safeguard against abuse and exploitation. Sadly, the findings of over ten years of research by this subcommittee reveal that guardianship . . . fails miserably in accomplishing that objective."[3]

In that moment, on September 25, 1987, Pepper revealed that the United States Congress had known since at least 1977 that the nation's guardianship system was fraught with problems and only some sort of government intervention could fix it. Pepper's opening comments also mentioned the lack of due process afforded potential wards, including no prior notice of a guardianship attempt, no guarantee that they could appear in court before being conscripted, no right to their chosen counsel, and loss of material goods and property.[4] "Thirty-three states allow 'advanced age' as a ground for appointing a guardian," the elderly Pepper told the room in his erudite Southern drawl. "I wonder if they would get me. I am eighty-seven. I will have to be on the alert that somebody doesn't go in, in my absence and without my knowledge, and without my having an attorney, and ask to have a guardian appointed for me."[5]

Chairman Pepper, who had previously served his state as a US senator for fifteen years, also railed against the many cases in which there had been no medical evidence presented to prove that a ward was mentally unfit to care for themselves. And he told a story about a Michigan janitor who answered a newspaper ad to become a guardian, left his $14,000 annual salary, and was suddenly managing more than $1 million of wards' assets. That man kept the job for eight years, Pepper explained, until it was discovered he had been using funds from his four hundred wards for personal purposes.

Pepper had invited the Department of Justice to participate in the hearing, believing that anything pertaining to the civil rights of the American people would be of interest to the DOJ. "They told us they didn't have any contribution to make on this subject," Pepper announced, "I am sorry that they didn't feel that it was a subject within their jurisdiction—I wish they had . . . it is a matter of grave concern."[6]

Among the witnesses who testified before the subcommittee on that September day were four elderly Americans, each of whom had a sorrowful story to tell about their own experience with an unwanted and abusive guardianship. Also on hand was one Mr. John Hartman, the aforementioned former janitor, now a convicted felon, who was transported to Capitol Hill for the occasion from his prison cell in Detroit, Michigan. Hartman told the panel that in 1977, at the young age of twenty-three, and with no expertise or training, he had been hired as a public guardian in Bay County, Michigan. Within a year he began to commingle wards' funds with his own. Hartman took full responsibility for illegally misappropriating some $130,000 over the years. He pleaded guilty and was ultimately sentenced to serve five years in prison. "How was I able to so abuse the guardianship authority I was given?" Hartman asked the question on so many lawmakers' minds. "It was very simple. No one bothered to really check what I was doing. Occasionally I would get a call from the court administrator saying, 'Some of [your] figures don't add up. Can you fix it?' And I would fix it." Hartman said the system was so unchecked that it encouraged otherwise honest people "to act in an illegal, reprehensible manner." He recommended better training for guardians, tighter controls over their activities, and setting a limit on how many wards could be assigned to one guardian.[7]

It is important to revisit this hearing to understand just how the guardianship system's most serious problems—clearly identified in the 1970s and '80s—are virtually the same issues that plague the nationwide system today. Suggested solutions are still the same as well. Except now the number of citizens affected by guardianship or conservatorship has tripled, and those of a criminal nature have discovered target groups that extend well past just the elderly.

Over the years, chairs of other congressional committees have appeared to be interested in learning more about the complicated issues surrounding guardianship and conservatorship. But each hearing seemed to simply cover ground already explored. At the US Senate Select Committee on Aging's hearing in 2016, chaired by Senator Susan Collins, witnesses called to testify were asked to explain the already obvious problems they encountered with the system.[8] Not consulted was the nonprofit group Americans Against Abusive Probate Guardianships (AAAPG), which at the time was the premiere reform group gathering data on abusive guardianships. Following that 2016 hearing, AAAPG's founder Dr. Sam J. Sugar, MD, wrote on the group's website: "For some strange reason the only witnesses that were called to testify before this advisory Senate committee were stakeholders in the system, each of whom makes a living in the guardianship sphere. Not a single advocate or victim was called to testify, despite the fact that the committee had been deluged with complaints and requests for appearances from members of our group, and others, for years."

Dr. Sugar, who had become involved as a reform activist after his mother-in-law was involuntarily conscripted into what would become an exploitative guardianship, also took exception to testimony indicating that since a majority of appointed guardians were relatives of the ward, the predatory nature of guardianship must be assigned to family members and not to stranger appointees. "Nearly all members of the committee are content to believe that abusive guardianship is all the fault of greedy family members, family guardians and fiduciaries." Sugar wrote. "Only in passing was it even mentioned that professional guardians are guilty of abuse and theft of family funds in this professional guardianship racket." Sugar went on to correctly point out that family-controlled guardianships do not automatically strip a ward of all their civil rights. Further, if a relative is found to be abusing or financially exploiting the ward, criminal charges can be filed against them. Not so with a professional guardian, because "law enforcement refers to these very same acts as civil matters," and any complaints are adjudicated by the judge who appointed the suspect person.

It is extremely unusual for a judge to admit that they appointed a greedy guardian or conservator. It is just as rare for a judge to pursue criminal charges against one of their own appointees.

In November 2018 Senator Collins called another public hearing on ways to strengthen the nation's guardianship system.[9] Once again, the committee heard recommendations from various state officials and system insiders. Again, Dr. Sugar was not asked to appear before Congress, but he was invited to answer a list of written questions. First, he was asked what recommendations he had for collecting data to better inform federal, state, and local officials. Sugar shared his communications with the committee for inclusion in this book. He began his answer by pointing out that one of the main reasons there was a lack of solid information was because most guardianship cases are sealed on the grounds that the files contain protected medical or mental health material. "How absurd is it to protect an individual's name when you are taking their life in the form of a guardianship," the doctor wrote. Sugar recommended the creation of a common-sense-based four-point national database with mandatory reporting from the states.

* The total number of all existing guardianships, specifically citing how many wards were controlled by a family member versus a for-profit professional.
* The number of new guardianships created annually, sorted by zip code.
* The number of cases closed annually and the reason for termination—restoration of rights or death?
* The value of the ward's estate prior to guardianship or conservatorship and the remaining value at termination.

The committee's second question asked Sugar how best to protect wards from exploitation and abuse by their guardians. After having reviewed hundreds of complaints coming into AAAPG, Sugar told the committee that the most common complaint was the court's haphazard revocation of advanced directives like wills, powers of attorney, and estate plans. Judges, he said, should be forced to scrupulously adhere to these preplanned documents. Sugar also focused on the fact that victims' family members and friends have no central complaint department where they can register their concerns about the treatment of a guardianized loved one. The police don't respond to citizens' concerns in civil matters, and offices of district attorneys and attorneys general have traditionally been unresponsive as well.

So, the founder of AAAPG suggested setting up a federal watchdog organization with the power to refer criminal charges to local prosecutors. Sugar also stressed that "guardians are not licensed and therefore not concerned with losing such a license," and he suggested establishing a national licensing program that would have the power to yank licenses and mete out specific penalties. And finally, Dr. Sugar proposed that the Department of Justice turn to the federal racketeering statutes (RICO) to prosecute guilty guardians and conservators because "federal RICO [conspiracy] actions are the only possible way to address what is, in some cases, a Mafia-like ring of predatory court insiders that prey on the unsuspecting elderly." He pointed out that exploitations were especially notable in popular retirement states, like his home state of Florida, as well as California, Nevada, Arizona, Texas, and New Mexico.

In response to other questions, Dr. Sugar suggested that federal funds be withheld from any court system that failed to comply with its own state's elder abuse laws, and that there be a cap on legal fees to thwart lawyers who overbilled. Perhaps most importantly, this medical doctor declared that a citizen's mental incapacity should never be determined or declared by a nonprofessional. "The concept of incapacity is so fluid and so poorly defined," Sugar wrote, "that it is much too easy for an examiner who is paid handsomely by the court, and makes his living doing these examinations, to blithely declare what the judge expects him to, thus depriving an innocent individual unnecessarily of his rights and starting down the path of being owned by a total stranger."

Senator Collins's opening statement at the 2018 hearing mentioned the aging Baby Boomer population, and the urgent need to reform the guardian system since the number of Americans over the age of sixty-five is expected to skyrocket to nearly a hundred million by 2060.[10] To help eliminate flaws in state programs, Collins announced that following a year-long committee investigation, she and senator Bob Casey were introducing the bipartisan Guardianship Accountability Act. "Preventing guardianship abuse requires law enforcement and social service agencies at all levels of government to work together," Collins said. She maintained that the proposed legislation would promote that kind of collaboration.[11] As of this writing, that Senate bill has gone nowhere.[12]

Before he retired from the US House of Representatives in late 2022, Florida congressman Charlie Crist introduced no fewer than four guardianship-related bills, the latest entitled the Guardians Aren't Above Prosecution (GAAP) Act. None of Crist's proposed legislation ever advanced very far.[13] In March 2021, as the Britney Spears conservatorship case remained undecided and was generating worldwide news, two Republican congressmen—Matt Gaetz and Jim Jordan—asked the House Judiciary Committee to hold hearings on the controversial court-ordered process.[14] Their letter to democratic chairman Jerry Nadler read in part, "If the conservatorship process can rip the agency from a woman who was in the prime of her life and one of the most powerful pop stars in the world, imagine what it can do to people who are less powerful and have less of a voice."[15] Whether the requested House inquiry was ignored because of the divisive partisan atmosphere that had settled over Congress, or due to simple indifference on the issue isn't known. But no Britney-inspired guardianship hearings were held on that side of Capitol Hill.

In September 2021 the Senate Judiciary Committee announced its hearing entitled "Toxic Conservatorships: The Need for Reform."[16] It was a play on the title of Britney Spears's hit single "Toxic," and it was likely so named to attract maximum media attention. Five witnesses were heard: two representing disability rights groups; a clinical professor; an official from the National Center for State Courts; and Nicholas Clouse, a man from Huntington, Indiana.

Clouse told senators that at age eighteen he had been in a debilitating car accident and sustained a traumatic brain injury that caused the loss of much of his memory and left him with constant headaches and frightful nightmares.[17] In the fall of 2012, his parents sued Nicholas's teenage friend who had been driving, and in the expectation that there would be a sizable settlement to protect, his parents had their son sign a legal document. The agreement named Nicholas's parents as legal guardians of both his person and his estate. The lawsuit suit resulted in an undisclosed amount of money, and it was reportedly enough to set up an annuity that would yield monthly payments for the rest of young Clouse's life. He testified that in 2014 he met Chelsi, the love of his life. On Valentine's Day 2016, he proposed marriage. "I was excited to start a family," Clouse told the committee, "But my parents were extremely hesitant to allow me to work, let alone get married." Two months later Chelsi became pregnant. "This was unquestionably the best thing that ever happened to me," Clouse said. "I am not sure my parents would have ever allowed me to get a job and move out of [their] house were it not for a baby on the way."[18] Even after he relocated, Nicholas said his mother and stepfather refused to terminate the guardianship. He had no control over the paychecks he earned and had to get permission to buy diapers and formula for his daughter. His trust money was kept from him and remained under the tight-fisted management of his parent-guardians. Nicholas said his stepfather demanded explanation for even the smallest grocery store purchase. After Nicholas repeatedly asked to end the guardianship, his parents' lawyer falsely told him that "it was impossible" to undo. When bills that should have been paid by his trust were listed as past due, Nicholas began to suspect his stepfather was misappropriating funds. Indiana law does not provide for a path to review guardianships to determine whether they are still needed, and with his trust fund moneys held hostage, Clouse had no way to hire his own attorney. Ultimately, the Indiana Disability Rights group offered him free legal representation, and after an intense months-long back-and-forth, the court finally approved the termination of guardianship petition on August 24, 2021. At twenty-eight years old, Nicholas Crouse was finally free to make his own decisions and manage his own money.

Once again Congress had heard firsthand stories about the loss of civil rights, the lack of due process, the sorrow of exploitation, and the growing state struggle against the ever-expanding grip of guardianship. It was a day of poignant testimony, but after the "Toxic" hearings, no serious steps toward guardianship reform were taken.

It is not as if Congress was operating in a vacuum. The Government Accountability Office is often called "the congressional watchdog," as it conducts bipartisan investigations on behalf of House and Senate members. Beginning as far back as July 2004, the GAO had warned lawmakers about the lack of governmental oversight of the easily exploitable guardianship system.[19] In its report to Congress that year, the office stressed the need for the federal government to help states "develop cost-effective approaches for compiling, on a continuing basis, consistent national data concerning guardianships." To translate the GAO's oh-so-obvious conclusion: society cannot control a system if it doesn't know what it is dealing with. Since no state or federal agency kept track of how many guardianships were in effect, the age and gender of the conscripted, or the most common complaints about the behavior of those in charge, the clear remedy was to start collecting that kind of data immediately. As of 2023, no national database has been established.

In 2010 the GAO investigated the system again, and reported to Congress that it had "identified hundreds of allegations of physical abuse, neglect, and financial exploitation by guardians in 45 states and the District of Columbia between 1990 and 2010."[20] An audit of just twenty closed cases revealed that multiple millions of dollars had been stolen from wards, judges had failed to adequately screen their guardians—"appointing individuals with criminal convictions or significant financial problems to manage high-dollar estates"—and courts and federal agencies did not communicate, thus allowing questionable guardians "to continue the abuse of the victim." More than a decade later, these same complaints about the system are common. Arguably the most shocking example of predatory guardianship summarized in the 2010 GAO report was the case of a Kansas City, Missouri, taxi driver who had been appointed a guardian for an elderly man suffering from Alzheimer's disease. The eighty-seven-year-old man was "found living in the guardian's filthy basement and wearing an old knit shirt and a diaper." It was determined the guardian had embezzled more than $640,000 from the old man, which he used to buy a Hummer and to cover checks he had written to exotic dancers. That driver-turned-court-appointee was sentenced to eight years in prison and ordered to pay $640,000 in restitution.[21]

Another GAO report, issued in July 2011, warned that only thirteen states bothered to conduct criminal background checks on potential guardians.[22] In November 2012 the office reported on the need for a national strategy to effectively combat financial exploitation by court-appointed guardians.[23] And in case lawmakers had forgotten past GAO findings, there was this reminder: "We have also reported that few states conduct criminal background checks on potential guardians. Moreover, we have noted concerns with weak court oversight of appointed guardians, as well as poor communication between the courts and federal agencies that have enabled guardians to chronically abuse their wards."

A November 2016 GAO report on guardianship abuse repeated an observation the office had first offered years earlier.[24] "The extent of elder abuse by guardians, nationally, is unknown due to limited data." Again, these federal investigators were stressing the fact that lawmakers can never get their arms around a problem as widespread and pervasive as guardian and conservator exploitation if they don't have adequate information. The 2016 report offered stark examples of criminally minded guardians abusing their dependent wards.[25]

* In Ohio, a professional guardian-attorney who was addicted to drugs stole more than $200,000 from wards over a six-year period. He was sentenced to four and a half years in prison, ordered to pay restitution, and was indefinitely suspended from practicing law.

* A for-profit guardian in Oregon mistreated or stole money from twenty-six wards, including twenty-one disabled veterans.[26] After what prosecutors called her "post-death money grab," she was convicted of criminal mistreatment, aggravated theft, money laundering, and tax evasion. She was sentenced to four years in prison and ordered to pay more than $117,000 in restitution to the victims or their survivors.

* A Texas guardian was appointed to care for more than fifty wards, some of whom lived four hundred miles away from her home. The guardian went months without contacting many of these protected people, failed to provide them with shoes, clothing, and their monthly allowances, and was late in paying their medication and nursing home bills. As punishment she was fined $25,000 and was ultimately stripped of her guardian certification.

It is a wearying exercise to wade through the voluminous pages of GAO findings and recommendations and realize that after all these years, many of the same systemic troubles still exist. The situation begs two major questions. What are taxpayers getting in return for these expensive and repetitive GAO investigations—a massive collection of reports from 2004, 2010, 2011, 2012, and 2016—and why hasn't anyone in Congress taken the lead to change the status quo?

Reform activist Rick Black, founder of the Center for Estate Administration Reform (CEAR), believes he knows why—intensive lobbying efforts on Capitol Hill and the conspiracy of silence from insiders. "We are up against an army of attorneys who actively spread their gospel of propaganda, and who are the largest political campaign contributors," Black opined. "Estate, trust, family, elder guardianship and probate attorneys, and the professional guardians they sponsor, all know that these cases routinely happen. But they will not openly admit it to the public or to Congress."

Black and his wife, Terri, cofounded CEAR from their home base in Charlotte, North Carolina. They became prominent guardianship reform advocates after living through the painful guardianship of Terri's father, Del Mencarelli, who was financially and emotionally manipulated by a female companion in Nevada. Mencarelli and Helen Natko, a woman with a gambling habit, had a long relationship, and there came a time when Natko successfully petitioned the court to become Del's guardian. During a trip to see her father, Terri Black realized something was wrong, specifically with her father's finances. She was right. According to the Blacks, once they questioned Natko's activities, she "literally kidnapped" Del, isolated him from his family, berated him in public, made bad medical decisions on Del's behalf, and stole from him. As the guardian, Natko had access to Mencarelli's money and court records show she transferred about $220,000 out of a joint account. In July 2017, after a four-year battle during which the outraged Blacks spent some $1.3 million in travel and legal fees to fight on behalf of Del, a jury finally pronounced Helen Natko guilty of criminal exploitation and theft.[27] Justice Court judge William Kephart ignored the prosecutor's recommendation for prison time, instead sentencing Natko to pay a $10,000 fine and serve five years' probation. The judge also admonished Natko with the final command, "No gambling allowed."[28] That wasn't the end to the Black's entanglement with the controversial Nevada court system. On Christmas Eve 2019, adult guardianship judge Linda Marquis overlooked the criminal conviction and awarded the last $58,000 of Del's estate to go to Natko and her attorney, Dan Foley, for "the work they had done." Del's only child and intended heir, Terri Black, received nothing. Terri said her greatest regret is not about money, but rather losing the right to be with her father during the final part of his life. Del Mencarelli never escaped Natko's control and died in her care on July 3, 2015.

The Blacks' sorrowful experience in Nevada prompted Rick to leave his executive-level engineering job—a career that had taken him around the world—and dedicate himself to advocating against the current guardianship and conservatorship system. This soft-spoken and determined reform activist has called judge-instigated guardianships "the perfect crime," because once the civil court is involved, law enforcement almost always shies away from pursuing any criminal investigation. The tireless Blacks have become leaders in the nationwide grassroots effort to combat the system. They keep track of thousands of cases, stay in regular contact with both state and federal lawmakers and their staffs, and are always ready to provide evidence of specific instances of exploitation in guardianship cases. They travel to states across the nation from their home in North Carolina to show the flag and to testify against the current system whenever asked. "We victims have done a terrible job organizing, defining our messaging, and maintaining a sustained voice," Rick Black said during one of our many conversations. "Most victims' families [just] bitch about other family members and professional guardians, which only aids the true villains. Until equity court litigators fear they will go to prison . . . things will only get worse."

It was hoped that a bipartisan bill sponsored by then eighty-four-year-old Republican senator Chuck Grassley and cosponsored by Democratic senator Amy Klobuchar might be the catalyst for real reform of the guardianship system.[29] The Elder Abuse Prevention and Prosecution Act (EAPPA) became law on October 18, 2017, and it was seen as finally forcing what congressman Claude Pepper had sought thirty years earlier. It compelled the Department of Justice to become seriously involved in investigating and prosecuting abusive elderly guardianships.[30] The legislation instructed the DOJ to designate elder justice coordinators within their ninety-six regional offices, and at department headquarters in Washington, DC, deputy attorney general Antoinette "Toni" Bacon was appointed to supervise this new team of prosecutors.[31] The DOJ was also tasked with training FBI agents on how best to investigate predatory guardianship and conservatorship cases. Perhaps most importantly, the legislation stated, "The DOJ must collect and publish data on elder abuse cases and investigations. . . . [and] DOJ must publish best practices for improving guardianship proceedings and model legislation related to guardianship proceedings for the purpose of preventing elder abuse." In addition, the Department of Health and Human Services was required to keep track of abuse cases that involved state's Adult Protective Services agencies.

Activists in the guardianship reform movement were hopeful that any positive changes that were adopted to safeguard elderly wards would automatically trickle down to protect other guardianized people as well, no matter their age or health condition. They were optimistic that with a so-called guardianship czar at the helm, in the person of Antionette Bacon, criminal prosecutions under the EAPPA would become the new standard, a much-needed federal deterrent that would serve to scare off abusive and dishonest court appointees.

But as Dr. Sam Sugar wrote again to the Senate Special Committee on Aging, the response of the DOJ's nationwide elder justice team was dismal at best, nonexistent at worst. "Personal attempts by yours truly to present hundreds of cases to Director Antoinette Bacon at the Department of Justice have been ignored," Sugar said. "This level of impertinence cannot stand." He called the government's failure to respond to multiple thousands of legitimate complaints "a stain on our country." Ms. Bacon did not respond to Sugar's complaints nor return multiple calls from this inquiring journalist.

In addition, Rick Black said he tried to interact with Ms. Bacon, hoping to share his vast experience with guardianship exploitation. During one of our many telephone conversations, Black told me, "I made contact with Ms. Bacon in early January 2018, via phone and email. Her overtures on the DOJ's commitment to prosecute guardianship fraudsters were originally quite encouraging." Both Rick and Terri Black had diligently worked both sides of Capitol Hill to make passage of the EAPPA a reality. "We felt we finally had an ally in the DOJ's executive suite. . . . We thought action was finally being taken," Rick said. In June 2018 the Blacks met Ms. Bacon during a private get together on Capitol Hill, and while they found Bacon "engaging," they report that their relationship cooled after that. Attorney general William Barr began to publicly focus on prosecuting internet-based scammers, and Antionette Bacon, according to Rick Black, followed her boss's lead. "She leveraged her alliance with Barr and was awarded the US Attorney position for the Northern District of New York, moving to Albany in September 2020." The role of National Elder Justice Coordinator was passed to career federal prosecutor Andy Mao. At a DOJ-hosted Elder Abuse Prevention Conference in Tampa on March 3, 2020, Mao was in attendance, and as Rick Black described it to me shortly after that session, "He [Mao] worked too hard at convincing me I didn't have compelling evidence of any crimes being committed." After having many discussions with Mao in several different forums, Black concluded that he "lacks the courage to fight this battle or demand justice for this class of marginalized adults. Very few in the DOJ want to prosecute attorneys, especially those who are fully blessed by equity court jurists."

So, since the passage of the EAPPA in the fall of 2018, how much progress has the Department of Justice actually made in fulfilling its mandated role? A deep dive into the 163 pages of the DOJ's 2021 report finds this section: "The Department . . . brought over 220 criminal and civil enforcement actions, in 46 federal judicial districts, against conduct that targeted or disproportionately affected older adults."[32] While this seems encouraging, the rest of the section makes it clear that abusive guardianships—which can wipe out life savings, cruelly isolate wards from loved ones, and even hasten death—are lumped in with much less devastating crimes. In summarizing the two hundred twenty cases, the report states: "These included matters involving tech support fraud, romance scams, and telemarketing fraud; and matters involving guardians or persons with powers of attorney who abused their authority and defrauded their wards—including cases against nursing homes that provided their residents with grossly substandard care and deprived them of the skilled nursing care to which they were entitled." To be sure, there are heartbreaking DOJ cases mentioned in the report, including those in which elderly citizens were ruthlessly victimized by nursing homes or in-home healthcare aides, taken advantage of by dishonest financial advisers or persons who finagled power of attorney from a senior, and criminally minded scammers selling everything from nonexistent home repairs to phony gift cards. But a dedicated reader discovers the DOJ prosecuted only three cases that involved a court-appointed guardian who had ripped off their wards. In other words, the DOJ spends much more time looking at the bad guys coming at elders from the outside, rather than investigating the bad guys on the inside of their own judicial system. Of course, investigating the actions of judges, lawyers, and other court personnel can be politically tricky and take institutional courage, but it doesn't mean those cases should be ignored. Of the three guardianship-related prosecutions outlined in the latest DOJ report, one of them almost seemed like an afterthought.

Case #1: On June 30, 2021, the DOJ office in Philadelphia indicted three people—one in Pennsylvania and two in Virginia—on multiple charges, including bank fraud.[33] Guardian Gloria Byars was reported to have stolen hundreds of thousands of dollars from dozens of her elderly wards and then laundered the money through shell companies controlled by Virginia residents Carlton Rembert and Alesha Mitchell. Byars was also alleged to have stolen gold Krugerrand coins from one elderly victim's safety-deposit box and $131,000 from his bank accounts. Apparently that wasn't enough for the sixty-year-old Byars. Prosecutors also charged her with stealing $756,000 from a retired federal employee's estate, among other crimes. For the frequently appointed Byars, this was not her first run-in with the law. The state of Pennsylvania had been investigating her for years, and she had been the focus of a *Philadelphia Inquirer* investigative series in March 2018, which revealed she had become a guardian in 2015 even though she had been convicted of fraud and passing bad checks years earlier.[34] In October 2019 Byars, her sister, Carolyn Collins, and her husband, Keith Collins— who were court-appointed guardians themselves—were indicted on state charges of stealing more than $1 million from 108 wards in six Pennsylvania counties.[35] The case lingered, unadjudicated, until federal officials stepped in and took over. As of this writing, Byars's trial, along with those of her four codefendants, is still pending.

Case #2: Wayne Jerome Houston, sixty-one, of Kitsap County, Washington, pleaded guilty to stealing as much as $280,000 from twenty-one different clients of his Cross Point Services guardianship organization.[36] His business served the elderly and other vulnerable adults, and according to the DOJ, Houston "stole from those he was supposed to protect at least 240 separate times" over an eight-year period. One of the victims was a tribal leader who was bilked out of $50,000. Federal investigators became involved because some of the money Houston pilfered was from Social Security and arrived as monthly payments destined for wards of the court. Ultimately, Houston was sentenced to just one year and a day in prison and was ordered to pay restitution of $256,336.[37]

Case #3: This federal indictment was different because it did not center on guardianship yet it contained a guardianship component. Jeffrey Siegmeister, a former Florida state attorney, was charged with conspiracy, extortion, bribery, wire fraud, and filing false tax returns. Also indicted was a defense attorney named Marion Michael O'Steen. To summarize, this pair was alleged to have fixed prosecution cases so O'Steen could charge clients higher fees. Siegmeister was charged with seeking bribes in return for favorable handling of criminal defendants, including those arrested for attempted murder, driving under the influence, and keeping a gambling house. In addition, during his tenure as a state attorney, Siegmeister allegedly suggested the owner of a tractor dealership give him a $20,000 discount on a new tractor in exchange for dropping two DUI charges against a family member. He got the discount and the charges were dropped. At the end of the DOJ's press release about the indictment, one additional charge was mentioned.[38] Siegmeister, *acting as a court-appointed guardian*, was alleged to have "engaged in a scheme to defraud his ward by, among other things, transferring the victim's assets for his own benefit . . . and creating a Last Will and Testament for the victim which designated a Siegmeister relative as the sole beneficiary of the victim's estate." In February 2022 Siegmeister pleaded guilty to diverting more than $500,000 from his ward's estate, defrauding the probate court, and failing to report the diverted funds on his tax returns.[39]

The DOJ's 2021 report also touted the four hundred elder justice training and outreach events the department held during the year designed to educate the public about the myriad of scams targeting senior citizens. Also mentioned was the Elder Justice Initiative's "renowned webinar series" for professionals, which features experts on various topics related to elder abuse.[40] Finally, the report mentions the Elder Justice Initiative website,[41] which offers "plain language content . . . specifically addressing guardianship and mistreatment by guardians," which the public can access to understand the various strategies used by predatory players.[42] While raising public awareness and alerting bad actors that their tactics have been exposed is a good thing, victims of guardian exploitation will tell you that prosecuting abusers and putting them in prison would be a much more satisfying outcome. Many family members of conscripted wards believe that if state or federal prosecutors would simply uphold laws already on the books, the word would spread among the corrupt, and there would be far fewer guardianship victims.

In February 2022 Senator Grassley, one of the primary authors of the EAPPA, was asked whether he was satisfied with the DOJ's lack of prosecutorial progress on criminally abusive guardianships. "It's always a concern," he wrote in response to an inquiry for this book. "Considering it appears that conservatorship (and guardianship) doesn't catch the attention of the media unless it's a very high profile subject. While I'm disappointed it took so long for the media and the Justice Department to become interested in the subject, it is important that they are committed to exposing it and ending it."

A final note. Nowhere in the last DOJ report is there mention of a need for a national database to keep specific track of guardianship cases, abuse complaints, and a list of corrupt guardians or prosecutions. Establishing such a database—one that Congressman Pepper said so long ago was crucial to controlling the problem—remains undone.

Professor Pamela Teaster of Virginia Tech studies guardianship trends. She lays the blame for the lack of one centralized registry firmly at the feet of politicians. She believes such a system is critically needed to keep track of the important trends and statistics inherent to guardianship. "I can tell when people are coming down the street to deliver shoes to me," she said, referring to the tracking system that retailers use to monitor deliveries. "And [yet] we can't get some kind of government database set up to tell us at least who these people in guardianship are? Just their genders, just their ages, how long they've been under guardianship, when [financial] reports are filed and when they aren't . . . and whether the guardianship is still appropriate? We can't have that? It's the political will, quite frankly, and it's because it cost[s] money."[43]

Attorney Bradley Geller has worked within the guardianship system for thirty-five years. He resides in Michigan, a state he believes has a disproportionate percentage of adult guardianships. But, of course, absent an official database there is no way to confirm that dubious distinction. Speaking from his home in Ann Arbor, Michigan, Geller said compiling nationwide guardianship and conservatorship statistics would be relatively easy. "It's just a matter of each county in a state counting up their guardianship files—one, two, three, four—and adding them all up. It would be as easy as that." Asked why he believes the decades-old call for a national database hasn't happened yet, Geller was blunt. "Because no one gives a shit about older adults. They are not valued in this society, and the same goes for kids. We care about people who are employed . . . and if they don't work and don't vote, we don't care. The reason we don't know the number is that we don't want to know."[44]

9

Weaponizing Guardianship
to End a Marriage

Guardianships and conservatorships are powerful legal tools. They can be applied to help truly vulnerable people navigate life, but they can also be used to "overprotect" those who only need minimal help. It makes no logical sense to fully guardianize someone who simply needs assistance with, say, getting to the grocery store, keeping their medications straight, or maintaining a checking account.[1] Yet highly restrictive guardianships and conservatorships have been established for those in minimal need. And some judges have allowed the system to be used to unfairly marginalize and silence people who are not, in fact, incapacitated.

One of the most surprising and shocking uses of guardianships can be found in situations where the future of a marriage is at stake. Case in point: a Florida couple in their fifties and sixties had dated for nearly a decade. Finally, Robert and Rene decided to marry. Robert was a wealthy man, and the couple enjoyed not one but two houses in different locations in the Sunshine State. Sadly, Robert suffered a debilitating stroke soon after the wedding, and Rene was named as her husband's temporary guardian. Enter then a troublesome estranged son who surreptitiously and successfully petitioned the court to nullify his stepmother's standing and name a professional guardian. At the beginning of what would be a yearslong legal battle, the newly appointed guardian in charge of Robert aligned himself with the wayward son and got the court to agree to annul the marriage. This action ensured that the estate would stay in Robert's name and be fully available for liquidation by the guardian, the attorneys, and others the court had attached to the case. Of course, the son would be in line to financially benefit from his father's substantial estate as well. During an emotional interview conducted early in my research for this book, Rene told me, "My husband passed on April 23, 2015, holding my hand, and not before he apologized to me for his son's actions and for what I was going through trying to protect him from the jackals."

In Lorain County, Ohio, Fourough Bakhtiar, an eighty-one-year-old Iranian-born woman suffering from dementia, had to be rescued several times after wandering away from home. She was once found in a neighbor's flower bed in her nightgown pounding on a window and screaming for help. Her five adult children, including an estranged daughter, convened to discuss the situation, and it was decided they would all pitch in to keep their mother in her home with her husband of fifty-five years. Shortly thereafter, in April 2013, the sons reported that their sister picked up their mother for a supposed outing and then refused to return her, isolating the elderly woman from the rest of the family.[2] The daughter maintained that she had "rescued" her mother from a domineering patriarchal household. The rest of the family didn't see it that way. The older woman's wealthy husband, Dr. Mehdi Saghafi, and their four sons called it a "kidnapping." They accused the financially strapped daughter of trying to get control of her dementia-addled mother's half of the lucrative marital estate, which was valued at a reported $5 million. They pointed out that the daughter had taken swift and surreptitious action to erase her brother as the mother's power of attorney designee and to insert her own name on a notarized POA document. The mother's credit union account soon began to hemorrhage money, and with her newfound control, the daughter initiated both a guardianship proceeding and a divorce of her mother from her father.

Even though the law declared the guardianized woman to be "incompetent," probate judge James Walther found her to be "very bright, articulate and determined." He was convinced the elderly woman did want a divorce and he granted one. This action automatically split the estate between the wife and her former husband, leaving the mother's share under the management of her POA-designated daughter. Every attempt by the brothers to fight the guardianship was dismissed by the court as being "frivolous." It is important to note that in March 2015 the daughter was indicted on multiple felony criminal counts of kidnapping, abduction, theft, and telecommunications fraud. Ultimately, those charges were dropped. In the spring of 2016, a grand jury indicted the daughter and her husband on charges of theft, forgery, and tampering with records. Detectives in Amherst, Ohio, reported the couple had stolen tens of thousands of dollars from the local school system, money that was supposed to have gone to tutoring for their son with special needs. The couple pleaded guilty and were sentenced to two years community service and ordered to pay a fine of more than $36,000. Dr. Saghafi continued his long fight to reverse the divorce and bring his wife home. In 2019 his attorney, Charles Longo, filed a racketeering claim against nearly a dozen court appointees, alleging, among other things, that the guardianship was unnecessary, the forced divorce illegal, and that one of the attorneys fraudulently received $194,896.78 in guardian fees from the Saghafi/Bakhtiar estate.[3] Longo's brief to the court read in part, "If [the attorney] has transferred Saghafi assets to his personal account then it will bring into play the criminal RICO statute as well as other state and federal crimes." As an April 14, 2022, article in the Association of Certified Fraud Examiners newsletter put it, "The suit claims the guardians acted as financial predators by creating a maze of legal and financial problems and then billing the victim for dealing with the problems that they had created."[4] If the court were to find that guardianship appointees acted in concert to improperly defraud a ward, that could be interpreted as a "criminal enterprise" and could be declared a violation of the Racketeer Influenced and Corrupt Organization Act (RICO). Many in the guardianship reform movement hold out hope that successful use of the RICO statute will be the catalyst that brings the worst systemic abuses to an end.

Dr. Saghafi died in September 2020. At this writing, his sons continue to press their father's claim even though their mother, Furlough, died in a nursing home in the spring of 2022.

GUARDIANSHIP WAS NEVER DESIGNED to be a tool to use demolish a marriage, yet judges have allowed it to be used for precisely that. Further investigation reveals even more sinister applications of guardianship or conservatorship. In several cases, originating in different states, crafty divorce attorneys have counseled clients involved in contentious situations that by weaponizing the guardianship process they can render their spouse defenseless. What better way to get rid of an unwanted partner than to have the court strip them of their civil rights by declaring they are incapacitated and no longer capable of managing their own affairs? That said, make no mistake, this tactic is primarily aimed at legally silencing female spouses, and it usually begins by painting them as obsessed, hysterical, or otherwise mentally unstable.

It happened to Michelle of Coraopolis, Pennsylvania, and she says it nearly destroyed her.[5] Her story is recounted here in detail to emphasize the tragic human toll that can result at the hands of those who use guardianship vindictively.

Michelle was in her early forties and residing with her lawyer husband on a bucolic five-acre plot with a beautiful four-bedroom, five-bathroom home. Michelle's husband made sure she had a specially built kennel for the many rescue animals she volunteered to care for. The couple had no children and had been married about fifteen years. Right before Christmas 1994, her husband unexpectedly filed for divorce. During a series of phone interviews that took place in late 2021 and early 2022, she told me, "I was blindsided. Of course, I didn't want to get a divorce." Speaking from her current home in Beaver County, Pennsylvania, she said, "I didn't want to believe he had a girlfriend. But he did. . . . and she had been a law clerk for a local judge." According to Michelle, the girlfriend had also worked with the state police for a time in her capacity as a probation officer. At first, Michelle fought the divorce, but at the time she was also battling multiple health issues, most seriously her insulin-dependent juvenile diabetes. Michelle confessed that she became seriously depressed over her situation. She admits she was angry with her husband's betrayal.

Michelle's ex-husband would later tell a local reporter with the *Times/ Beaver* newspaper that in February 1995, at five thirty in the morning Michelle broke into the house in which he was staying, demanding to speak to him. Michelle says it was her birthday. According to her, "He called me to come up to his parents' house where he said he was staying while they were in Florida. And it wasn't five thirty in the morning." In the newspaper article, Michelle's ex would also accuse her of once attacking him in their kitchen and trying to start a fire, and, on another occasion, of confronting him in a store, punching him in the groin, and stalking him for months on end. Michelle denied all the accusations, saying, "Defending his nonsense is unnecessary once you understand his agenda."

In September 1995 Michelle was pulled over by local police for failure to use her headlights while driving on a "darkened" street. Michelle maintained it was close to seven o'clock on a sunny morning, and she went to the address because a private detective she had hired told her that was where her husband was living. She said she was simply planning to deliver an anniversary card to her estranged husband, unaware at the time that he was living in that house with a girlfriend. The officer who stopped her charged Michelle with stalking and harassment based on an affidavit of probable cause filed by a Pennsylvania state trooper named Dan Nelson.[6] The trooper alleged that Michelle had "repeatedly driven" around that neighborhood with no headlights, a charge she denied. There was no trial as Michelle accepted a one-year probationary period, and the charge was eventually expunged from the record. Michelle always wondered why a state trooper would involve himself in such a minor local case. Who was he, and what jurisdiction did he have, anyway?

For a while, Michelle said of her husband's infidelity, "I was open to forgiving him. But once you finally know what's going on, with a girlfriend and everything, well, I woke up and smelled the coffee." Michelle began to realize that the breakup was going to be permanent and likely ugly. The long, drawn-out divorce proceeding took place in the court of commons pleas in Allegheny County, Pennsylvania. The husband was finally granted the divorce he sought on December 10, 1996, and all that remained was to hammer out the financial issues. The newly single ex-husband married his mistress thirteen days later.

Michelle remained in the marital home as long as she could, operating in a swirl of anxious emotions, diabetes-related health issues, and a determination to get her equitable distribution of the marital estate. She felt overwhelmed being up against a former spouse who was a well-known local attorney, a man whose new wife was also a lawyer. Suddenly the word "guardian" was being mentioned in the Court of Common Pleas, which, under Pennsylvania law, is not the proper court to take up such a matter. Guardianships in that state are only established in the orphan's court. Nonetheless, the process suspiciously proceeded in the court of common pleas under the watchful eye of Judge Ronald Folino.

A review of court documents reveals that after the husband sought to conscript Michelle, Pennsylvania guardianship law was ignored every required step of the way. Judge Folino failed to require that a mandatory petition for guardianship be filed. He held no compulsory competency hearing to determine Michelle's state of mind. No evidence was presented to establish that Michelle was an incapacitated person in need of a guardian. All of this is required by the state's Rules of Civil Procedure.[7] Instead, the record only mentions that the judge denied Michelle's request for a health-related continuance of the divorce proceedings, and on April 8, 1997, Judge Folino wrote that "after telephone conciliation with counsel," he was issuing a brief order. It was short and life-changing for Michelle.

"It appearing that Wife is no longer able to effectively handle her affairs, counsel for Wife shall, within five (5) days of the date of this order, take immediate steps to have guardian ad litem appointed."[8]

Was the judge ordering Michelle's own lawyer to take immediate steps to guardianize her? That is unclear, but there is no record of Michelle's attorney ever submitting a petition to orphan's court. And perhaps most important, it is unheard of that a divorce lawyer would ever seek to guardianize his or her own client, so why would a judge order such an action? This is simply not the way guardianship is supposed to work. So, how was the guardianship of Michelle, a person with no history of mental illness or incapacity, allowed to happen? Was the judge ignorant of the proper legal process or did he simply choose to ignore it? Had Michelle's ex-husband or his new wife called in favors from the legal community to help erroneously paint her as incapacitated and in need of court control?

On April 29, 1997, Judge Folino simply appointed a guardian ad litem for Michelle. And other legal statutes were disregarded. Pennsylvania state law is very clear—a guardian or guardian ad litem must be a duly licensed lawyer. Curiously, the woman the judge anointed was not an attorney, and she had absolutely no legal training.

In the fall of 1997, Michelle was ordered out of the marital home. Her selected half of the material goods were removed and put in storage and her beloved animals taken away to kennels. "The court made me homeless, then I had to move to a Motel 6 for a month," Michelle said during one of our several interviews. "It's all just so stressful, you feel like you're in a rat's maze. You get so you don't even talk to people because nothing you do matters." While division of the marital finances was still pending, Michelle did receive support payments from her ex, but she said the money went directly to pay her legal bills. Michelle said she was forced to apply for welfare and got $195 a month.

More questionable legal machinations followed. Three weeks before the final financial settlement agreement was to be ratified, Michelle's attorney suddenly withdrew from the case. That left only the unqualified guardian to represent Michelle's best interests. Michelle said that on the day before the hearing, which was set for October 14, 1997, her guardian, unbeknownst to her, negotiated and signed an outrageous settlement agreement that gave away her portion of the marital estate. Court documents show that at the settlement hearing, the judge was presented with this consent agreement and automatically approved it. Just how a non-attorney was allowed to negotiate such an important contract on behalf of a ward—and why a judge would ratify it—remains a mystery.

This guardian also arranged the purchase of a new home for Michelle, and she was moved there in the late fall of 1997. It was a much smaller house in an adjacent county, and Michelle worried about how she would pay the mortgage since she had no job or guaranteed income. In addition, she felt unsafe in this new place. She said her mailbox was destroyed, so she missed important court notices. A friend said there were "people banging on the side of the house at night," noises that seemed designed to scare Michelle.

As with any combative divorce proceedings, there can be clarity in hindsight. In retrospect, Michelle came to believe that her husband and his then girlfriend deliberately orchestrated a predivorce series of contacts with police that would saddle her with a dubious-looking record and paint her as unstable. There was the early allegation that she had broken into a house demanding to speak to him, the stalking charge alleging she was skulking outside his house in the early morning hours, and she had told many friends how utterly frustrated and livid she was with her former husband. There were times she wished he was dead—and his girlfriend too! Once installed in her new house, Michelle knew that reporting any complaints about vandalism or nocturnal noises would make her appear to be even more irrational. She began to feel disoriented, like the beleaguered Ingrid Bergman in the classic movie *Gaslight* (1944) who is mentally manipulated by a spouse and made to question her own reality. Michelle's mind was further muddled by the private detective she had hired. He had insinuated himself into her life and repeatedly suggested she should buy a gun to protect herself.[9]

In late October 1997 Michelle's unnerving situation made her do something she would come to regret. She went to a local sporting goods store to buy a handgun. "I really just wanted to get [the PI] off my back," Michelle told me. "For months he kept pressuring me, saying, 'You ought to have one so whoever is scaring you will know you have a gun.' I thought to myself, 'Well, I'll let everyone think I have a gun and they will leave me alone.'" But at the store, Michelle was refused a purchase. The clerk told her the store was instructed to contact State Trooper Nelson if she ever came in to buy a weapon. There was that name again: Nelson. What was going on?

Michelle now believes the private investigator—a questionable character who would later testify in court that he also worked for Michelle's unqualified guardian—was actually spying on her and trying to set her up for serious charges. Was her guardian cooperating with this double-dealing PI or in cahoots with her ex-husband? Michelle now suspects that the guardian had gone to local law enforcement and falsely reported that Michelle was plotting to kill her ex and his wife. Michelle steadfastly denies that she was considering any such thing. "I am simply not a violent person and never have been," she said. Michelle also recalled that she considered buying a gun because she just didn't want to be a victim anymore. She had decided that if no one would stand up for her, she would stand up for herself.[10]

On November 3, 1997, the shady private investigator called to say he wanted to take Michelle to dinner. Not yet understanding his disloyalty, she accepted the invitation. Inside the local King's restaurant, he renewed his argument for why she should buy a gun, and he told her he could arrange for a private purchase. He even convinced Michelle to immediately withdraw a hundred dollars, and he drove her to a nearby Mellon Bank ATM to get the money. Upon returning to the restaurant, they were met by a man who they followed outside. "Turns out he was an undercover state police officer," Michelle said. "I had just taken my insulin shot and I just wanted to get back to eat my meal." Instead, she got into the man's car, a nondescript two-door Buick, for a quick lesson on how to use the "untraceable" Browning semiautomatic pistol. Michelle did not realize who this seller really was or that he was recording their conversation. The instant she extended the hundred dollars, all hell broke loose. "Suddenly there were all these cops and TV cameras swamped in," she recalled, "It was on the eleven o'clock news and, oh my God, my poor parents saw it." Michelle was taken to the local jail, booked on two charges of criminal attempt to commit homicide and possession of a firearm without a license, stripped of her clothing, given a paper gown to wear, and put into a chilly solitary cell under suicide watch. She says she stayed there for about ten days. Her mother and terminally ill father put up their house as bond. Upon her release, Michelle was put under strict supervision until her trial the following year. Michelle would later learn that her arrest was accompanied by another affidavit of probable cause written by the mysterious Trooper Nelson. It was revealed that it was Nelson who had enlisted the help of his undercover state police colleague to act as the gun seller.

The next thirteen months were a nightmare, according to Michelle. First, back in Allegheny County, her guardian was asking the trial judge to be released from her position. There was an awful financial tangle to clean up, in part resulting from real estate transactions the guardian had shepherded, and it was expected the issue wouldn't be finally resolved until the court appointee agreed to sign certain papers. The guardian had made it clear she wouldn't sign anything until she received tens of thousands of dollars more in fees and expenses. On September 11, 1998, the judge agreed to the guardian's termination and gave her thirty days to submit her final invoice.

Meanwhile, back in Beaver County, the ex-husband's new wife was relentless, according to Michelle. "Every time she saw a green Jeep like mine, she would call the cops and make a report, saying it was me following her. They'd check it out and it wasn't me," Michelle said. "She kept saying, 'Oh! There are so many police reports!' And, yes, they were the ones she had filed. They were making a paper trail against me." Michelle recalled one such report that was filed after the new Mrs. ran into the ex-wife at a local grocery store in December 1997. In-store surveillance video proved the wife's complaint of threats and harassment were unfounded. "It was obvious," Michelle said, "they were trying to prove I was in violation of my bond so I would be arrested again."

While she waited for her trial, and tried to keep her head down, the aforementioned article appeared in the local *Times/Beaver* newspaper on November 11, 1997. The article began by describing a christening ceremony for the new daughter born to Michelle's ex-husband and his wife. One of the happy couple's guests that day was Trooper Nelson, and according to the article he was in attendance because the new parents "were fearful that [his] ex-wife . . . would attend the ceremony and cause havoc." The article quoted the couple as saying that Michelle was "reportedly telling people she was going to buy a gun to murder her ex-husband and his new wife." To those following Michelle's story, she must have seemed like the psychotically obsessed Glenn Close character in the 1987 movie *Fatal Attraction*, the woman who just couldn't let go of her lover.

Michelle's criminal trial commenced in mid-December 1998, and several people were called to testify about angry and even threatening comments she had allegedly made about her ex-husband and his second wife. But as her lawyer, Paul Boas, explained to the judge in chambers one day, "At the time Michelle is making these statements . . . 'I'd like to kill that bastard, I've gotten screwed a million times' . . . it was an emotional [and] bothered time. A lot of people make statements like that. That doesn't mean she is going to go out and kill somebody." That argument convinced the judge to disallow testimony from those who had heard such comments from Michelle years earlier. Of course, it was that audiotape the undercover officer recorded during the November 1997 gun buy that provided the Perry Mason moment in the courtroom. Curiously, no complete transcript of that tape exists in the court record, even though jurors had been handed a paper copy of the text. However, attorney Boas did read exact quotes from the audiotaped conversation during his cross examination of the undercover officer. The following is from a section of the court transcript from that day.

Boas: You're trying to get her to say, "Yes, I am going to kill my husband with the gun," because that would make your case better?

Trooper: That is not correct. No.

Boas: So, when you said things like, "Now this gun, it's not traceable. It comes down from the south" . . . you talk about her husband. "You got a problem with your husband." You said that for a reason?

Trooper: Correct.

Boas: And if her answers were, "Yes. I want to do in my husband," that would make the case better?

Trooper: Correct.

Boas: I notice from the tape when it says, "I mean, you know, you want to take him out . . ." in the middle of that sentence, you don't even finish that, [and] she says, "Believe me, I'm using this for protection." Right?

Trooper: Correct.

Boas: Okay. And then she says, "I had some vandalism at my house. I just moved. I live by myself." But you keep going on, "Well, I don't care what you're using it for. Obviously, if you wanted it legal you would have bought it someplace else." That is your statement, isn't it?

Trooper: Yes.

Boas: Then you go on explaining how to use it and so forth, and you again go into this thing about, "Just like I said, whatever you're going to do with [it], you know, your ex or whatever, you do it. That's up to you, but make sure that you get rid of the gun." She says, "Well, hopefully it's just going to be for decoration," meaning she wouldn't even have to use it?

Trooper: Right.

Boas: So, at every point, you tried to get her to say something that would be helpful to you, and she doesn't say it?

Trooper: Right.

The tape would later be described as "a big nothing burger" by one of Michelle's supporters. On December 16, 1998, Michelle was acquitted on all charges. Perhaps buoyed by the victory of being cleared of the charges that could have sent her to prison for thirty years, Michelle's fight for justice continued. The financial settlement her non-attorney guardian had negotiated left Michelle in a perilous financial condition. And it had always bothered her that a court appointee could act in such a reckless manner. Michelle appealed the judge's approval of the settlement agreement based primarily on the improper appointment of a non-attorney guardian. On April 20, 1999, the Pennsylvania Superior Court issued a blistering finding that blasted the lower court judge. "Proper procedure was not followed," the ruling read in part. Specifically mentioned were the absence of an actual petition for guardianship, the failure by the judge to hold a hearing to determine incapacity, and the judge's one-sentence order for Michelle's attorney to take steps to have her guardianized. The lower court judge had stated that there was a consent decree presented to the judge that was signed by both the husband and the wife's guardian. The appeals court seemed aghast. "If wife was one of the parties consenting to this order, we are hard-pressed to understand why the court would have accepted her consent, since she was contemporaneously being adjudged incapacitated. If, in the alternative, consent on the part of Wife was merely that of her counsel, we disapprove of that practice." The appeals court ruling did not make mention of the fact that the state statute plainly states that a guardian must be a licensed attorney and Michelle's guardian was not a lawyer, but it made it clear that the guardian had been "appointed without a hearing," in violation of law. Surprisingly, the court of common pleas chose to ignore the higher court ruling, and on March 13, 2001, the guardian was awarded $50,000 as a final payment. During the seventeen months this woman acted as a court appointee, according to Michelle, "I believe, in total, [the guardian] got approximately two hundred thousand dollars." The scattershot of available court documents available to the public makes that figure impossible to confirm.

After the divorce, Michelle survived on government disability checks until she turned sixty-two and was then transferred to the Social Security rolls. Today, she also gets by with the help of food stamps, which is, in her words, "embarrassing every time you go to the grocery store." She said, "The court isn't supposed to make you a burden to everyone else. And you don't have someone who has means dump a spouse on the public dole. It's just not fair to all the people paying into Medicaid and Medicare."

Michelle's saga may seem to be a one of a kind, but unfortunately it isn't.

OTHER COMBATIVE DIVORCE CASES in which guardianship of the wife was either seriously attempted or actually established have been identified across several states, including Florida, Ohio, New York, Connecticut, and Pennsylvania. In fact, there were multiple divorce guardianship cases identified in Pennsylvania. Many of the victims chose not to have their stories related here for various reasons—for fear of further retribution, out of sheer weariness or embarrassment, or the desire to put it all behind them. One divorcing woman described her husband's attempt to guardianize her and isolate her from their three children as "the nuclear option for our legal system." Each of the women interviewed for this book, those who went on the record and those who did not, had a similar story to tell and an understandably traumatized way of telling it. They spoke quickly, interrupting their own train of thought to add in extra details about their victimization. Conversations became easily sidetracked. Sometimes they became breathless or cried as they recalled the brutal guardianship-related tactics their former spouses unleashed on them and that the court endorsed. It is safe to say that injecting the idea of guardianship into a divorce proceeding has been more common than the public realizes. Any divorce lawyer who would unnecessarily utilize a legal system that strips an opponent of their civil rights is a chilling development that should alarm all fair-minded people.

Elaine Mickman appears to be the bravest and most quotable participant in one of these guardianship-via-ugly-divorce cases. Her story stretches over more than a decade and is full of all sorts of legal twists and turns. This divorce was sought by Elaine's husband in April 2003 in Montgomery County, Pennsylvania. The final divorce decree wasn't reached until 2011 and the legal skirmishes continued until as late as 2019, all revolving around disputed financial matters. Elaine's full name is used here because she went public, writing a very detailed self-published book about her ordeal. Elaine and her spouse had been married twenty-one years. Her husband, who she described as "a multimillionaire professional money lender," abandoned her and their five children to live with another woman in London. Even though Elaine was listed as half owner of the family business when the divorce was filed, she said she and her children "went from millionaire to welfare" in the blink of an eye. Elaine is not the type of woman to go down without a fight, and she proceeded to vigorously battle for her half of the marital estate, along with alimony payments and child support.

Years into their dispute, on November 19, 2013, her husband's divorce attorney filed an "Emergency Petition for Appointment of a Guardian" to conscript Elaine and disarm her by stripping her of her civil rights. Court documents reveal that the husband's attorney became annoyed with Elaine's continued claims that her husband had committed major business fraud and had dodged the IRS. With no money for a lawyer, Elaine had to write her own court filings and her husband's attorney demeaned her so-called pro se motions. "Obviously she can't read English, and if she can't read English she needs a guardian," he declared to the judge at one point. It is absurd, of course, to think that illiteracy is a viable reason to guardianize someone. Elaine dodged a bullet when the judge rejected the emergency petition. Nonetheless, in July 2014, the estranged husband's divorce attorney attempted to guardianize this pesky and determined ex-wife a second time.

In her 2021 book *Court-Gate . . . The Courts "Divorced from the Law,"* Elaine correctly points out that Pennsylvania courts hearing divorce cases are distinctly separate from courts that entertain guardianship requests.[11] "My husband's ruthless and malicious attorney filed guardianship against me in the family court twice, but was denied," she wrote. "Guardianship is an Orphan's Court legal proceeding, but 'shady' divorce attorneys sometimes sneak it thought the family court. My husband's lawyer was a blatant liar."[12]

One of the most astounding tactics used against Elaine came during the second attempt to guardianize her. A local psychiatrist was hired by the husband's legal team to write an "assessment" of her mental state. This doctor was careful not to call his report an official "evaluation," but its conclusion was that Elaine had a personality that signaled the need for a guardian. This doctor also got a mention in Elaine's book. "My husband's attorney even tried getting guardianship on me by hiring a 'for-sale' psychiatrist, rather what I call a 'quackiatrist', Dr. K.W., MD, to unethically craft an assessment of me without him evaluating me, nor ever meeting or speaking to me." Elaine declined to share the psychiatrist's report out of embarrassment, but she said it was obviously written after "this quackiatrist merely reviewed cherry-picked court filings and orders provided to him by my ex-husband's attorney." The court record of the Mickman divorce proceedings had been sealed by the judge, so the attorney sharing such information with an outsider, even a medical professional, would seem to defy that confidentiality order.

On December 28, 2016, Elaine wrote up an official complaint about the doctor who never met her, spoke to her, yet had judged her and sent it to the Pennsylvania State Licensing Board. "Dr. [K.W.] wrote a slanderous, libelous, and defamatory 'fairy-tale' assessment falsely portraying me as a mentally ill person in exchange for money so that my ex-husband could obfuscate and obstruct my legal recourse to settle economic claims." Both the licensing board and local prosecutors declined to hold the doctor accountable; the board concluded that Dr. K.W. had clearly called his report an "assessment" so "no violation of the Medical Practice Act has occurred." This second attempt to guardianize Elaine also failed, but not without causing her much anguish and many sleepless nights during a time in her life when she was already down and out.

Elaine Mickman did receive some temporary monthly alimony for a while, but she said she has never received one penny in a divorce settlement, and she failed in her attempt to recover her half-share of the family business. As for child support, she said her ex-husband did pay beginning May 2003 through July 2011. After that, as their five children aged out of the system, the monthly amount was greatly reduced by amounts as high as 54 percent. The child support was completely terminated in December 2018 when their youngest child, a son with special needs, was still a minor.

Pennsylvania uses a computer system called PACSES, short for Pennsylvania Automated Child Support Enforcement System. This is the database that the state of Pennsylvania uses to keep track of all child support payments so they can receive federal matching funds. This Title IV-D program is Uncle Sam's contribution to help children and the custodial parent stay off the welfare rolls. In July 2011, as the final divorce papers were filed, Elaine said, the judge in their case suddenly and inexplicably decided to grant her ex-husband "a $550,000 PACSES credit for all the money he had spent putting our children through college." First of all, Elaine said, only the two oldest had been in college. Second, their actual university costs were nowhere near $550,000. "Here's the punchline," Elaine wrote in one of the many emails she exchanged with me in the spring of 2022, "All of the child support [I got] from August 2011 through December 2018, totaling just less than $297,000 was owed back. Therefore, the money I received through the child support computer system operated as a deferred loan" of sorts.

On January 28, 2019, Elaine's ex-husband filed a recovery petition with the court, and Elaine was ordered to bring a repayment check to the court's Domestic Relations Department for $313,000. She had one week to comply. Elaine has long believed that the $550,000 credit was issued after some sort of backroom deal was struck, and so this indomitable woman decided to fight on. She quickly filed an appeal citing several federal Title IV-D regulations and codes that, in her opinion, showed the judge's randomly awarded $550,000 credit had been illegally added to the PACSES system. Elaine specifically mentioned a regulation that read, in part, "The State plan shall provide that any payment required to be made under §§ 302.32 and 302.51 to a family will be made directly to the resident parent . . . having custody of or responsibility for the child or children."[13] As Elaine pointed out in her appeal, she, as the resident parent, hadn't received any part of a $550,000 college payment.

The state of Pennsylvania was facing a considerable financial penalty and a federal audit if Elaine's appeal prevailed. In addition, her ex-husband ran the risk of having their divorce case reopened if he continued with his recovery petition. Elaine took the matter to the Pennsylvania Supreme Court, which ultimately declined to hear the case, but the demand for her repayment of $313,000 was quietly dropped. She continued to try to fight for child support for her autistic son based on a Change of Circumstances motion she filed, but she was denied a hearing. The Pennsylvania Superior Court of Appeals quashed her final attempt, calling it "vexatious," and on May 27, 2021, entered an order that enjoined her from ever filing for back child support again. "Elaine Mickman's failure to adhere to these prohibitions shall result in the impositions of sanctions," the court wrote in its final ruling. This ruling flies in the face of Pennsylvania child support rules and regulations.[14]

While all states employ an online system like Pennsylvania's to track child support payments,[15] it is obvious that the system is really only as good as the human beings who enter the data into it.

When asked in 2022 to look back on and evaluate her court experience, Elaine wrote to me, "Just know that guardianship in divorce is a legal instrument to swindle and defraud a dependent spouse and leave them penniless, destitute, and homeless. Guardianship is a last-ditch-effort attack if other legal attempts . . . are not successful. It is tragic what they are doing to people." Elaine rightfully points out that in almost all divorce cases where guardianship is introduced, the guardian is ultimately dismissed, but only after extensive damage is done. Splitting an estate often means the marital house must be sold, sometimes leaving the dependent spouse temporarily homeless. And even if the guardianized person is allowed to remain in their own home, they are powerless to stop their half of the settlement from being tapped to pay court costs and the fees of various lawyers, caretakers, and, of course, their guardian. They can only stand by and watch as their nest egg shrinks with every transaction a professional guardian puts in motion. "After the money is all gone then they leave you alone," Elaine said during our final conversation. "They want to beat you down until they know you can't fight anymore." On December 14, 2022, Elaine Mickman filed a seventeen-page petition for Writ of Mandamus with the US Supreme Court that she compiled herself. She asked the high court to compel the Pennsylvania state court to restore her constitutional rights to pursue legal action against her ex-husband.[16]

10

Every Citizen Has Civil Rights—
No Matter Their Ability

The United States prides itself on embracing laws that ensure equality for all. This sets the US apart from many other countries, and that ideal was the bedrock of America's turbulent civil rights movement in the 1950s and '60s. Numerous federal civil rights laws were passed declaring that discrimination based on race, color, religion, sex, or national origin was illegal. It wasn't until passage of the Americans with Disabilities Act (ADA) that individuals with physical and intellectual disabilities were also specifically recognized for protection against discrimination.

The ADA is widely considered to be one of America's most comprehensive pieces of civil rights legislation and one that ensures both protection from discrimination and equal opportunity for citizens with disabilities. Signed into law by President George H. W. Bush in July 1990, the Act guarantees people with disabilities will "have the same opportunities as everyone else to participate in the mainstream of American life—to enjoy employment opportunities, to purchase goods and services, and to participate in State and local government programs and services." Those who gathered on the South Lawn of the White House to watch President Bush announce the bill that warm summer day were Americans representing a myriad of disabilities: the hearing and visually impaired; those with physical, cognitive, and varying degrees of intellectual disabilities. "I now lift my pen to sign this Americans with Disabilities Act, and to say: let the shameful wall of exclusion finally come tumbling down," the president told the crowd. "God Bless you all." [1]

Decades have passed, and both the Government Accountability Office and the National Council on Disability have reported that federal civil rights violations continue to plague undeserving wards conscripted into guardianship and conservatorship cases nationwide. The California-based nonprofit Spectrum Institute, which engages in research projects and educational programs on behalf of those with physical and intellectual challenges, concludes that "state courts act as though the ADA does not apply to conservatorship and guardianship proceedings." According to the institute's founder and executive legal director, Thomas Coleman, "Nothing could be further from the truth." During one of many conversations with Coleman, he said, "ADA laws do, most certainly, apply." Coleman, and other advocates for the vulnerable, believe that the minute a citizen is declared to be incapacitated, they are automatically protected by the federal ADA law and "they are entitled to due process of law like any other American." Coleman's influential group has asked Congress to prod the Department of Justice to get its nationwide team of US attorneys to investigate "violations of federal laws, civil rights statutes as well as criminal statutes being perpetrated by state courts, appointed attorneys, and professional fiduciaries operating within the guardianship system." So far, few meaningful results have occurred.

There has been a glut of ADA/guardianship-related complaints lodged since that day at the White House.[2] With such an inspiring proclamation from the president, and with such a precisely worded ADA law in place, how is it that each year reveals more examples of involuntary and abusive guardianships involving at-risk adults?

MICHAEL LIGUORI'S LIFE CHANGED shortly after his premature birth on May 5, 1998. A hospital-administered IV inserted into his tiny hand damaged it forever. After the botched IV, the two-pound infant was given morphine, which, according to his mother, caused cardiac arrest and deprived his brain of oxygen for a time. Court papers reveal Michael was subsequently diagnosed with a "mild case of cerebral palsy." The family filed a medical malpractice suit, which was settled for a reported $1.9 million. Because Michael was a minor, a mandatory guardianship was established to manage the funds during his childhood. Most of the money was put into an annuity designed to provide Michael with a monthly income once he became an adult.

When Michael turned eighteen, in May 2016, his for-profit guardian ad litem didn't want to let go and he petitioned the court to continue the guardianship arrangement. The GAL hinted that Michael's money might be in danger of being tapped by his family, but as his mother, Danielle Liguori, said during an interview for this book, "There was nothing to touch. The money was safely tied up in bonds and in an annuity." Even so, the GAL persisted. He claimed to the court that the now-adult Michael was incapacitated due to his cerebral palsy and unable to manage his own money. No specifics about Michael's alleged incapacitation were provided, it was simply the word of the court-appointed guardian that the arrangement should continue. The petition also made false claims against Michael's mother, alleging she had, in the past, violated a court order by accessing her son's money to buy a home in Staten Island, New York, following her divorce from Michael's father. That was more proof, the judge was told, that the young adult man needed help protecting his estate and should remain under guardianship. No witnesses testified that Michael had a habit of giving away or otherwise squandering his money, yet Richmond County New York judge Thomas P. Aliotta approved continuing the guardianship.

Court documents provided by a Liguori family supporter show that the GAL lawyer later admitted that before he prepared the adult guardianship document, he had not spoken to Michael or his mother, never been to their residence, never visited Michael's school or contacted any of his doctors, and didn't even know the Liguoris' religion or whether they attended church or not. So, on what basis did the GAL pursue continuing the guardianship? In a sworn written statement obtained from a source, the attorney curtly told the court, "I commenced this proceeding because in my experience and expertise Michael is incapacitated . . . and he has poor judgment, such that he was, or could be, taken advantage of by his parents." The attorney repeated the questionable allegation that "$303,000 of Michael's money had been used to purchase a house that was in foreclosure and this asset was in danger of waste." (It should be noted that as of December 2022 the Zillow estimate for the Liguoris' home was $1,230,400. Evidently, the mother's investment was not a "waste.")

Michael walks and speaks a little differently than others, but that does not equate to mental incapacity or any evidence of "poor judgment." Cerebral palsy affects the part of the brain that directs muscle movement, not intellect. Michael is a high school graduate and was a good and studious graduate of the prestigious Fusion Academy on Park Avenue in New York City. When Judge Aliotta was presented with Michael's straight-A grade transcripts, as a means of proving his mental capability, the document was ignored. Earlier, one of the court's appointees had erroneously reported that Michael attended a "special needs" school, so perhaps the judge looked past Michael's stellar performance as coming from an institution with less than top-notch standards. Perhaps the judge was simply in the habit of routinely approving all guardianship requests that came before him and ignoring submissions from the ward.

Michael is now an adult. Like any other adult, he should enjoy the due process and civil rights we all have. Even though he is forced to continue to fight for his freedoms, he seems to enjoy life. He often stays with his grandmother in Brooklyn and visits his mother and siblings in in the same Staten Island home where he grew up—a tidy, detached, multistory house with a Virgin Mary statue in the front yard. Michael loves the New York Yankees, is active on social media, where he embraces his Italian heritage by posting photos and recipes of his favorite Italian foods. According to his mother, he talks about attending college and studying to be a lawyer just as soon as his long battle against guardianship is over. Michael also faces the daunting prospect of additional surgeries on his damaged hand and he said he has been patiently waiting for his money to be freed up so he can pay for those procedures. Michael's Facebook page reveals he is vitally interested in the accomplishments of other people with physical disabilities, especially those who make beautiful music. He frequently posts messages from the evangelical motivational speaker Nick Vujicic, a man who was born without limbs and is happily married with four children.[3] Michael also stays informed about the nationwide issue of abusive guardianships. On November 12, 2021, the day the California court finally dissolved Britney Spears's long-running conservatorship, Michael posted a photo of the smiling singer with the caption "Hooray, woo-hoo! About time!"

During a series of personal texts Michael sent, he wrote, "It's terrible how they can strip you of your constitutional rights as an American and as a human being. They hijack your life." He wrote that he has two favorite quotes. "Martin Luther King junior said injustice anywhere is a threat to justice everywhere and president John f Kennedy said man will be what he was born to be free and independent." No, he didn't get all the punctuation and capitalization correct, but this was clearly not a text thread from a so-called uneducated, unaware, or incapacitated person.

Danielle Liguori is a passionate person who says it has "torn her heart out," to watch what the system has done to her son over the years. "I raised my son giving him the tools to go on without me, and for them to knock him down all the time. [They say,] in effect, that he's a 'retard' . . . They have so demeaned him. It's been so much pressure for so many years," and at this point in the conversation her voice falters. "I go to church; I give it to God. I cry," she said. "I've tried so much to protect him, and I can't. He's thrown into the fire with these vultures." In the meantime, Danielle has younger children to raise. "My girls are traumatized by this," she told me. "I have them in therapy. They don't even want to put their money in the bank because they say, 'What if they take it like they took Michael's money?'"

As for Michael's intransigent guardian ad litem—he, chillingly, boasts online as having been involved as a "GAL, Referee and Court Evaluator" in "several hundred" cases in New York. He has conducted multiple presentations and seminars instructing other lawyers how to become actively involved in the guardianship system.

As the year 2022 came to a close, Michael, then almost twenty-five years old, was still waiting for New York Supreme Court judge Thomas P. Aliotta to make good on a promise he had made months earlier to terminate the Liguori guardianship. Michael had almost given up hope as the case had dragged on far past his eighteenth birthday. By his own admission the guardianship stranglehold had been drawn out in the end because Michael fought against paying his unwanted court appointees some $100,000 in additional fees, and he balked at their collective demand that he be forever gagged from speaking publicly about his case. Michael told me he saw the gag order as taking away his constitutional right to freedom of speech. Also, Michael had found it difficult to find an attorney willing to represent him in the difficult area of guardianship, and that also caused delays. But on Christmas Day 2022, a jubilant Michael telephoned to tell me it was all over. He kept repeating, "I'm so happy!" And then a torrent of feelings spilled out. "The guardianship has been removed! At least I'm free! I don't have a guardian anymore! It's over!" Yet his freedoms had been restored only after he had capitulated and agreed to pay the outstanding fees. During our call Michael said he had no idea how much of his money was still left because the court-appointed accountant had apparently failed to file the required updated financial reports for several years. But the money didn't seem to be Michael's focus. He said he planned to take a month or two to try to figure out his finances and the rest of his life would follow. "I feel awesome," he said. "And I've learned that nothing is permanent in life. I'm just so relieved." Michael agreed it was the best Christmas present ever.

DAVID RECTOR WAS SITTING at the breakfast table one bright sunny March morning in 2009, coffee and newspaper at hand, chatting with his fiancée, Roz Alexander-Kasparik. He had recently wrapped up a twenty-eight-year career as a producer at National Public Radio in Washington, DC, and moved across the country to start a new career and make Roz his wife. The two had met at NPR in the early 1980s. She was an entry-level assistant, and he was a senior producer for NPR's *All Things Considered* and other programs. Life took them in different directions for a while, but these two friends had always stayed in touch, and then they fell in love.

During their familiar morning routine at the breakfast table, David suddenly grabbed his chest and doubled over. "David was laughing and talking, and then he wasn't," Roz recalled during a phone interview from her home in San Diego. "He stumbled as he tried to rise from the chair, and I just knew. I immediately called 911." Rector, fifty-eight, a tall, slim, physically fit African American man, walked painfully outside and sat on the curb to wait for the ambulance. Roz was at his side.

Because they weren't married, Roz was kept out of the ambulance and the hospital's emergency room at UC San Diego Health Hospital. After an agonizing wait, Roz was at David's bedside learning that he had had suffered a spontaneous aortic dissection, a serious condition in which a tear develops in the inner layer of the main artery to the heart. Testing would show that a tumor on David's kidney was likely responsible for his chronic high blood pressure, and the beta blockers he had been taking for that condition could have negatively affected blood flow to the heart, causing the cardiac emergency.

"The next day, in intensive care, David was all smiles," Roz said. "He was, like, 'Hey! What's happening?'" One of the staff told the couple, "You might have dodged a bullet." They were sure David would be coming home soon. But he didn't. David's condition suddenly worsened and he lapsed into a coma. A few days later, Roz can't recall the exact day because all the time spent at the hospital became a blur, David woke up and couldn't move any part of his body. Even though he was hooked up to an external oxygen supply, something had tricked his brain into thinking he wasn't getting enough oxygen. A frantic round of examinations and testing followed. Doctors then informed Roz that David had sustained a serious brain injury. Not only did he appear to be paralyzed, but David was also unable to speak. More days passed, and finally a most devastating diagnosis was delivered. David had developed a rare condition called Locked-in Syndrome.

It was an especially cruel fate for a man as creative and active as David, a widely respected radio producer, photographer, jazz aficionado, and devotee of comedy and comic books. He was a man eagerly looking forward to getting married once his next career path was settled.

"The one thing he could still move was his right thumb and forefinger," Roz explained. She devised a set of prewritten notes with the words "yes," "no," and other basic messages. With his finger, David could point to the note that answered her questions. This was proof to Roz, and the doctors, that David was aware of his surroundings and in command of his mental faculties. The only thing that didn't work properly was his body. "David was still there," Roz said. "Even though he wasn't able to speak, he was still David. His expressions were the same, his reactions were the same. He was my dearest friend, and I knew he understood exactly what was happening."

During this time, Roz reached out to David's extended family back in DC to alert them to the situation. She even offered to pay the airfare for a male cousin to come visit. Surprisingly, none of David's family ever came. David remained at UCSD for six months. He was then transferred to acute care for another three months. Roz put her marketing business on hold and constantly remained at David's side. One day at the acute care facility, security guards informed her that "next of kin" had called from DC, deleted her name from the visitor's list, and requested she be removed from the premises. Roz tried to explain that she was David's only advocate. "David was still intubated, unable to speak and they, literally, tore me away from his bedside," Roz recounted. "I was in tears, David was in tears," and suddenly she was out on the street, baffled as to why his family would take such a step.

The next day, Roz hired a family attorney to regain her access to David. He told her he would draw up the papers to present to the court. "He told me the emergency [conservatorship] petition was the only way I could get back into the rehab hospital to be with David," Roz said. "Had I known how life-ruining the petition would be for us, I would never have allowed [the attorney] to file it. He just kept telling me this was the only way the law allowed." Like so many other unsuspecting loved ones, Roz was not educated in the ways of conservatorship and therefore didn't even know the questions to ask about the consequences of such an action. Roz's petition asked that she be named conservator. After superior court judge Julia Kelety determined that David had about $80,000 in the bank, money that could be tapped to pay court appointees, she named a professional conservator and a guardian ad litem to represent David. While Roz could visit her fiancé, Judge Kelety inexplicably issued a six-point list of restrictions. Roz was shut out of any decisions when it came to David's location or medical care. Further, in an order dated February 1, 2011, Roz was instructed by the judge to write a weekly report, "of Mr. Rector's status and progress" for the family in Washington, DC.

Roz said she called more than fifty California lawyers trying to find one who would agree to take her case and fight to reverse the conservatorship. She finally found two willing attorneys and spent every penny she had trying to extricate David from what she called a series of "horrible . . . draconian nursing homes" the conservator had sent him to. Nothing seemed to work. Roz desperately wanted to take David home and care for him herself. The court appointees fought her every step of the way—until some eighteen months later, when David's confiscated bank account ran dry.

"Since there was no more money to pay these people who had caused David and me nothing but misery, they asked to be removed from his case," Roz explained during one of our many conversations in 2021. "I was now good enough, despite legal depositions, accusations, and all manner of cruelty to David and me, to become David's temporary conservator-of-the-person." At that point, of course, David had no "estate" left. The court continued to pay the guardian ad litem out of public funds, and Roz said the GAL spent another two years refusing to permit David to leave the nursing home system and go home with his devoted fiancée. Sadly, Judge Kelety took no action to change the situation.

Roz ultimately got her wish to remove David from his institutional setting, but there were enormous challenges. She had to find a suitable, wide-open living space to accommodate David's special wheelchair, the Hoyer lift used to move him from place to place, his computerized eye-tracking gear that translated his eye-activated keystrokes into audio and allowed him verbal communication, and other medical equipment vital to his survival. Roz was forced to borrow money from her family to meet monthly bills. Kind relatives got the couple a used van with a handicapped ramp so Roz could ferry her love, David, to and from doctor's appointments.

Roz Alexander-Kasparik was one of the featured speakers during a 2021 Commonwealth Club of California webcast entitled "Fee for All: How Judges Are Raiding Assets of Seniors & Lining Pockets of Conservatorship Attorneys."[4] She gave a passionate summary of her journey through the legal morass and ended by saying, "Thanks to the guardianship system, we were broke most of the time and struggling the rest. Things could have been very different if the conservatorship system hadn't so completely cost every asset we had, just when we needed those assets the most. We could have bought more therapy, gotten David's specialized wheelchair faster. These legal vultures stole all of our dollars. Shame on them."

David Rector lived ten years as a locked-in patient. During that time, he devoured his beloved newspapers by blinking his eyes when he wanted Roz to turn the page. He watched countless hours of television news to stay updated on current events. He fervently wanted to regain his right to vote, which the court had taken away from him. The Spectrum Institute joined David in that fight, asserting that people with disabilities shouldn't automatically be stripped of their right to vote. Ultimately, David was successful and got to cast a ballot in the 2016 general election.

When David died on October 15, 2019, Roz was taking him to a chemotherapy appointment. She had wheeled him to their van, turned to lower the ramp, and when she faced him again, he was slumped in the chair and had stopped breathing. David died of complications from cancer and respiratory failure. He was sixty-eight years old.[5]

Asked whether she felt the court system had kidnapped David, Roz answered, "I feel like the system swallowed us up. David had this terrible thing happen to him—to us. I always said to him, 'All you have to do is try.' And he agreed. People who try that hard every day for ten years should be helped. It's not a kidnapping—it's a swallowing us up. The system has to change."

THE CALIFORNIA CONSERVATORSHIP SYSTEM that was supposed to help Michael "Mikey" Parisio failed him over and over again. It forced this severely disabled young man, with a mental capacity of a three-year-old, back into the arms of the parent-guardians who reportedly beat him, starved him, and left him locked in a room to die.

When Michael was born, he was diagnosed with intellectual disabilities, and as he grew, his ability to communicate was limited. Despite his disabilities, he went to school for many years, made friends, and had a loving protector in his little brother. When Mikey, as he was nicknamed, turned eighteen, and Joe was sixteen, their parents went to court and were named legal conservators of their oldest son. State and federal subsidies came to them to help defray the costs of caring for their disabled child.

Joe would go off to college at Cal State Bakersfield when he was eighteen. He would return to what he called his "evil home" occasionally during his college career, and Mikey would always be thrilled with his presence. "He was always so happy to see me," Joe said during a phone interview. Speaking from his home in Ventura County, California, Joe remembered, "When Mikey saw people coming in, he would want you to rub his head, pat him on the head. The way [the parents] described him as being violent is just totally different than what everyone else saw."[6]

Joe would marry and have a child, and his visits back to his childhood home became infrequent. Today, Joe describes his mother as having had "a problem with alcohol and meds," and his father simply as a brutal, uncaring man. Authorities were aware of the situation with Mikey, according to Joe, because neighbors had phoned authorities about trouble inside the house, and there was an altercation between the parents and Mikey at a drugstore. It was such a serious event that eyewitnesses had called police. There was no intervention, and Mikey was sent home with his court-appointed conservators.

Years went by, during which Joe suspected his brother was being abused, but he just didn't have any concrete evidence. Finally, during a visit with his wife, Gabby, Joe saw his thirty-six-year-old brother's health was in obvious decline. There were bruises on his body, and the couple saw his father hosing down a naked and emaciated Mikey in the backyard instead of giving him a proper shower or bath. His mother restrained Mikey with police-grade handcuffs, which, she later claimed, was done on doctor's orders. Joe took several graphic photographs of the abuse his brother was suffering as proof.

"In 2011 I started calling the sheriff and Adult Protective Services," Joe said. He sent them the disturbing photos of a battered, handcuffed, naked, and painfully thin Mikey, photographs that Joe shared with me during my research for this book. Joe now refuses to recognize the elder Parisios as his parents and he refers to them dispassionately. "The father had a stick in Mikey's room he would hit him with. The mother would bite him. She would say, 'He's biting me, I'm just biting him back.'" Joe's conclusion? "They didn't want Mikey, they just kept him for the money" they got from government disability checks. Inexplicably, neither the local Lancaster, California, Sheriff's Department nor caseworkers at APS, an organization tasked with protecting vulnerable adults, took action to protect Mikey after Joe's complaints.

On June 25, 2012, Joe's wife wrote an urgent email to local law enforcement asking for help. It was shocking in its description. "We noticed that he was in his room without food and water for two days handcuffed," it read.

"He had underwear on but he had urinated and poop[ed] on himself." Referring to the photographs her husband had taken of his brother, Gabby continued, "Nobody seems to care. We have proved that this is really happening. We called to make a report twice and both times they just question the parents, and of course they denied it. We feel that if Mickey [sic] does not get removed from the home he might end up dying of starvation."[7]

The case of Mikey Parisio would be a first for attorney Tom Coleman. He had long worked with the Spectrum Institute on issues of abuse of people with developmental disabilities, but he had never encountered the confusing maze of the state's conservatorship system. Once Gabby's email crossed his desk, the ever-resourceful Coleman sprang into action. He said he went over the heads of APS and the Sheriff's office, called top-level state authorities, and warned them, "You are responsible for what happens to this young man. If you do not have him removed within twenty-four hours, I'm going to the media." The threat worked. The next day, July 2, 2012, authorities finally took steps to rescue Mikey.

When sheriffs' deputies and APS employees moved in to the Parisio house, they found Mikey profoundly ill and in an airless room where the temperature topped ninety degrees. He was prone on the floor in a fetal position, dehydrated and hungry, and he immediately grabbed the arm of a deputy and said, "Help, help. Water. Food." Once at the hospital, it was discovered that Mikey had a raging MRSA infection, various bruises and cuts on his body and head, a gash on his right side, and bruising to his groin area and buttocks. Mikey remained at the Antelope Valley Hospital for ten days, during which time his brother was allowed one short visit. "He was so happy to see me," Joe recalled. "He high-fived me and gave me that smile." During the abuse and neglect investigation, the hospital was so concerned about parental intervention they issued a "Do Not Announce" order, so if the elder Parisios called looking for Mikey they would not know he was there. Ultimately, the district attorney refused to press charges against the parents.

Once alerted to the rescue, the court appointed an attorney to look into the case and a separate court investigator. One of the appointees conducted a fairly thorough investigation and recommended the conservatorship be immediately revoked. The other court appointee's probe was lackluster, to say the least, since the investigator didn't bother to talk to brother Joe or his wife, Mikey's doctors, or any neighbors who reported they had heard screams for help coming from the Parisio home over the years. The second appointee concluded that Mikey should stay with the parents. After all, it was explained, there was really no other place to put him. The court was apparently not told, or didn't care, that Joe had readily volunteered to take his brother home with him. The judge approved the recommendation to send Mikey back to the parents on July 12, 2012.

On September 1, 2012, just weeks after being returned to his childhood home, Mikey was dead. The coroner's autopsy report lists his end-of-life ailments as pneumonia, dehydration, and renal insufficiency. Who within the conservatorship system was looking out for Mikey? The judge? His conservator? His guardian ad litem? The answer appeared to be no one, and the safety net responders couldn't save him either. Attorney Coleman would conduct his own probe and learn that the mandated annual reports on Mikey's welfare hadn't been submitted for years.

After their son died, Antonina Parisio and her husband, Michael Sr., sued the County of Los Angeles for removing Mikey from their home without their consent and for keeping his whereabouts hidden for ten days, in violation of state and federal law. They lost the suit and their appeal.[8] At last report, they left California and may have moved to Pennsylvania. They could not be located for comment.

11

Turning a Blind Eye: Where's the Legal Community?

If ever someone needed a guardian, it was former NFL quarterback Erik Kramer. So where was the legal community when he desperately needed protection? What happened to Kramer, following a suicide attempt that left him with a traumatic brain injury, perfectly illustrates the destructive legal practices so often found in the guardianship system. Kramer so obviously required a court-appointed guardian but was denied one through a series of legal machinations that can only be described as dystopian.

Beginning in 1987 Erik Kramer spent eleven seasons in the NFL and two more seasons with the Canadian Football League. In October 2011 Kramer's teenage son, Griffen, died of a heroin overdose. Six months later his mother died, he was going through a divorce, and his father was terminally ill. This quadruple tragedy plunged Kramer into years of despair.

In August 2015 Kramer checked into a Los Angeles–area hotel so his surviving son wouldn't be the one to discover his body—and shot himself in the head. He sustained a massive traumatic brain injury and severe injuries to his face and brain, but miraculously survived after being placed in a medically induced coma for several weeks. Erik underwent extensive lifesaving surgeries, and then endured years of rehabilitation to learn to walk, talk, and write again.

During his rehab in Las Vegas, and while living with his sister, an old girlfriend suddenly reappeared in Erik's life. She urged Erik to return to California for treatment. She moved herself, her young daughter, and their dog into Erik's Agoura Hills, California, home upon his return.

Kramer's family and a longtime friend came to suspect that the girl-friend, Cortney Baird, was stealing from Erik and even siphoning money from his dead son's memorial fund. By October 2016, with investigative help from a Los Angeles Sheriff's Department detective, evidence was gathered proving Baird had diverted more than $50,000 from Kramer's accounts. According to the former quarterback, Baird admitted to the detective in late November 2016 that she had transferred moneys from Erik's bank accounts, used his credit cards, and had taken thousands of dollars in unauthorized ATM cash advances.[1] Baird was not taken into custody, nor was she criminally charged, in part because at the time Erik simply could not comprehend enough of his situation to be a suitable witness against her.

Kramer's sister, his aunt, and his longtime friend Anna Dergan say they never gave up in their quest to convince the California court to place their debilitated loved one under conservatorship. In fact, they had even convinced Erik to go to his estate attorney's office to sign the volunteer application to become a ward of the court. On that very day, December 13, 2016, Cortney surreptitiously applied for a marriage license in nearby Santa Barbara County and secured a wedding date. Without telling anyone, she and Erik drove north and exchanged vows on December 22, 2016. Now the new bride had legal spousal protection. Kramer's family believed he was still not able to comprehend the true nature of the relationship.

The Los Angeles prosecutor assigned to the case could have filed criminal charges against Cortney at any time using Erik's bank records and Cortney's confession to the detective as proof. But that didn't happen. The assistant district attorney assigned to the Baird case simply dropped the investigation, citing Erik's inability to testify as he continued struggling to regain his mental capacity, and Cortney's newly acquired marital protection. Undeterred, Kramer's distraught family forged ahead and filed an official petition for conservatorship with superior court judge David Cowan on December 30, 2016.[2] The document clearly stated that Erik was incapacitated by a traumatic brain injury, that he had recently been duped into a sham marriage, that the new wife had been stealing funds from Erik, and that Cortney was still the subject of an active investigation by the Los Angeles Sheriff's Department.

None of that was enough to convince Judge Cowan to grant the petition. Instead, he appointed a so-called Probate Volunteer Panel (PVP) attorney named Michael Harrison to represent Kramer and determine whether a permanent conservatorship was warranted.[3] At this point, Kramer was still undergoing thrice-weekly rehab treatments, yet as time passed his court-appointed attorney did not press for conservatorship protection. Team Kramer began to realize that the more Harrison resisted requesting a conservatorship arrangement, and the more they argued for the court to establish one, the more hourly fees Harrison could charge to Kramer's estate.

In emails purported to have been written by PVP attorney Harrison, he refers separately to both Erik and Cortney as "my client," even though it would be highly unethical for a lawyer to represent both an incapacitated person with a traumatic brain injury, and the wife who was under active investigation for stealing from him. In other emails, Harrison threatened to pursue legal remedies for "elder abuse" against Kramer's family and friends, who continued to urge the court to establish permanent conservatorship protection for the fifty-year-old Erik. Court transcripts also show that attorney Harrison asked the judge to approve a $10,000 to $15,000 monthly allowance from Erik's estate to pay for "living expenses" for the Kramers, who were still residing in the same home together. According to Erik, Harrison did not mention to the court that the Erik Kramer Trust was already paying for all his major bills, including rent, utilities, medical services, and premiums for health and automobile insurance.

This case, as presented here so far, is what could be learned from Erik Kramer, his friend Anna Dergan, and scattered court documents. Since there are two sides to every story, specific questions were emailed to PVP attorney Harrison (i.e., Did you ever specifically ask the court to establish a conservatorship for Erik Kramer? If not, why not? In emails, you refer to both Mr. Kramer and Cortney Baird Kramer as "my client." Did you, in fact, feel you represented both of them? Were you unaware that the Erik Kramer Trust fund already paid rent/mortgage, utilities, medical services, and premiums for automobile and health insurance?). Michael Harrison did not answer any questions; instead, his attorney Howard Smith wrote, "We have had this matter reviewed by several expert probate/conservatorship attorneys who have all confirmed Mr. Harrison acted completely appropriate and within the standard of care in his representation of Mr. Kramer. In fact, four (4) probate judges, including two (2) supervising probate judges, approved all of Kramer's attorney fees and costs and time spent in his representation of Mr. Kramer."[4] Endorsements from court insiders did not answer the specific questions posed, and when pressed to address the outstanding queries, lawyer Smith subsequently wrote: "Mr. Kramer adamantly and clearly opposed a conservatorship, which is exactly what

Mr. Harrison advocated, as required by law. Significantly, neither the treating physician nor the probate referee supported a conservatorship either. Mr. Kramer was indisputably able to communicate his wishes opposing the conservatorship . . ." Court secrecy and federal HIPAA laws prohibit a journalist from accessing the final reports written by the probate investigator and the physician determining mental capacity to confirm that statement. But this begs more questions. Just how much weight should be given to a brain-damaged person's wishes about their future? Is it the court's responsibility—or the attorney chosen for the potential ward—to insist on at least a temporary conservatorship? If the system was designed to protect at-risk citizens, who should decide who needs protection—the person with the traumatic brain injury, or the court?

In response to the allegation that Harrison might have felt he represented both Kramer and his wife as his "clients," the answer was, "Mr. Harrison represented only Mr. Kramer, although Mr. Kramer insisted that his wife be present and together with him." This tussle over whether Erik Kramer needed to be declared incapacitated dragged on for nearly two years and the timetable of events was not made clear in these responses. Was Kramer asking that his wife be with him while he was still in the throes of mental instability, or later when he began to recover more fully? As for attorney Harrison asking the court for that generous monthly allowance, the explanation as put forth in attorney Smith's follow-up email was as follows: "Mr. Kramer didn't even have the cash to park his car at the courthouse. The trustee of his trust had stopped paying all of Mr. Kramer's credit card bills and had stopped transferring cash to his bank account."[5]

It appears that if Judge Cowan had simply approved the conservatorship Kramer's family sought from the very beginning, it could have spared Erik the multitude of complications that would come to plague his life, his relationships, and his finances. Interesting to note how so many guardianships and conservatorships are so quickly established, some for people who insist they are not incapacitated, yet when an obviously impaired citizen like Erik Kramer is presented, the court repeatedly hesitated.

One thing was for certain: Erik's estate was continuing to be tapped to pay the ever-mounting legal bills. During one phone interview Kramer said that every four to six weeks a court hearing was held on his case, with three and sometimes four attorneys attending. For every appearance, he said, he had to pay between $7,000 and $8,000 in legal fees. These events were described by Kramer as nothing more than "status conferences" to inform Judge Cowan of the latest developments. Erik said the main update always seemed to be that Cortney was no longer stealing from him.

Kramer's supporters believe the PVP lawyer assigned to represent Erik simply did not act in the best interest of his client during his eighteen-month tenure, and if ever someone needed protection from outside exploitation and help navigating life while he recovered, it was Erik Kramer. If attorney Harrison had acted solely on Erik's behalf during this time, the former NFL player believes, he would have saved hundreds of thousands of dollars. He also would have been able to spend more time with his loved ones instead of being isolated from them by his legal minder. Most importantly, Erik would have been protected from the continued manipulations of his wife. And he never would have faced the criminal charges Cortney would later file against him.

In June 2018, some three years after his near fatal injury, Erik Kramer's mind finally began to regain clarity. He came to realize the depth of Cortney's treachery and what he called "the financial crimes" against him. He told her he wanted a divorce, and that she needed to find another place to live. In response, he said, Cortney called 911 and falsely reported her husband as a violent domestic abuser. Erik was arrested, and Cortney quickly filed for divorce and told reporters she was "terrified" of him. The fact that he had used a gun in a suicide attempt, she told the *Daily Mail,* was "evidence that he has access to firearms and is willing to use them."[6] More court appearances followed, and Kramer's estate was again tapped to pay the mounting legal fees.

Through sheer persistence, Kramer convinced a family law judge to annul his marriage on January 28, 2019. With his critical thinking restored, Erik was able to assist authorities in reopening the criminal case against Cortney Baird. It took more than a year, but on February 10, 2020, Baird was finally arrested and charged with twelve felony counts of grand theft, forgery, dependent adult abuse, and identity theft.[7] The very next day, a criminal court judge dismissed the domestic violence charges against Erik. Despite being charged with a dozen serious felonies, Cortney Baird remained free. Her criminal trial was postponed several times because of Covid-19 court closures, but also due to her repeated changes of attorney, and her insistence that she receive only probation—no jail time and no order to pay restitution to Erik. As 2022 came to a close, there was still no definitive trial date set. Kramer estimates his estate was drained of about $700,000 during the duration of the court process. He said Cortney si-

phoned off some $300,000, and the rest was consumed by his forced pay-
ments to court appointees and lawyers.[8] "The system did more to abuse
me than the thief herself," Kramer said during a follow-up phone interview
conducted in February 2022. "When you are in it, you aren't protected. You
are further victimized."

As for Harrison, the court-appointed attorney, Kramer filed a professional negligence/legal malpractice suit against him in June 2019.[9] The
court shutdown during the coronavirus pandemic delayed the case, and
although the trial was scheduled to begin on October 31, 2022, as of late
December 2022 the court docket listed the trial status as "continued [with]
stipulation."[10] If Kramer's civil action against his former PVP lawyer were
to be successful, it could send major shock waves through the same California conservatorship community that was so starkly exposed during the
Britney Spears battle and other recent headline-grabbing cases. Lisa Mac-
Carley, the attorney who filed the explosive amicus brief in the Spears case
calling the genesis of that conservatorship into question, is scheduled to
be an expert witness on behalf of Kramer. In an email she wrote, "My hope
is that my testimony at trial will send a message [to] our legislators in
Sacramento. The judges . . . arrive without any experience and training,
and it's the legislators who woefully underfunded the courtrooms so that
these inexperienced judges do not have sufficient resources to know what
to do."[11] Several lawyers experienced with the guardianship system and
consulted for this book agree. They believe lawmakers simply do not understand what the system has devolved into. It has become a process where
judges, who either don't know or don't care about the real-life hardships
caused by their rulings often take their marching orders from predatory
and duplicitous lawyers with dollar signs in their eyes. In the meantime,
the lives of countless wards are affected.

If the public is to believe participants in the conservatorship and guardianship system when they say they are there "to protect the ward," then
what are we to make of the case of Erik Kramer? He so clearly needed to
be shielded from exploitation, but the court and its appointees did not provide that protection for him. And Judge Cowan, the overseer of Kramer's
welfare, allowed the process to stretch out for nearly two years, bankrolled
by a man struggling mightily to heal his injuries. Only after profound financial and emotional damage was done to Erik Kramer did the justice
system decide it would try to do something to punish Cortney Baird. Why
is there no swift punishment for those within the system who inflict so
much harm?

When there is a bad apple within an organization, astute executives know it is best to remove them as soon as possible, lest the rot spread. That's just common sense. Many family members of those who have gotten caught up in a predatory guardianship wonder why the legal community doesn't do more to police its own rogue actors. Why don't judges take time to truly listen to knowledgeable family members' complaints? Why don't they act more often act to rein in appointees who behave more like dictators than caregivers to the vulnerable? Why are there no statements of condemnation from professional associations representing the players within the system? To be sure, exploitation of wards couldn't happen if it weren't for the lawyers who write the petitions and the judges who approve them. Absent those two groups, there would be no need to name a court visitor, psychological evaluator, guardian or guardian ad litem, and no court clerk to keep the docket and handle the documents. But all those positions do, in fact, play prominent roles in the system. So, what do the organizations most identified with those primary players have to say about guardianships and conservatorships?

The American Bar Association (ABA), the nation's largest voluntary organization for lawyers and law school students, has as its motto: "Our mission is to serve equally our members, our profession and the public by defending liberty and delivering justice as the national representative of the legal profession."[12] The ABA has published reams of articles and position papers about guardianship and conservatorship over the years. They have financially backed countless educational presentations, conferences, and webinars on the topic. And the group has been one of the primary forces behind promoting and expanding state chapters of WINGS, the acronym for "Working Interdisciplinary Networks of Guardianship Stakeholders." WINGS is a project designed to bring together concerned citizens (called stakeholders) from all groups affected by guardianship and conservatorship—family members, guardians, judges, lawyers, nursing home administrators, home healthcare aides, and others—to discuss flaws in the system and come up with legislative recommendations to fix it.[13] The American Bar Association openly acknowledges that guardianships constitute "drastic intervention in which the guardian is given substantial and often complete authority over the lives of vulnerable wards," so it openly endorses alternatives like limited protective orders for at-risk citizens.[14] The ABA website also offers a four-page guide called the "Practical Tool for Lawyers" who want to offer clients the alternative of Supported Decision-Making.[15]

But what is glaringly absent from the group's voluminous record on the issue is any form of disciplinary recommendations for their members who are caught acting in a predatory or criminal manner in a guardianship or conservatorship case. There are no suggestions from this most prominent organization, for example, that such an offender should be publicly chastised, stripped of their ABA membership, or suspended from the practice of law if they are found guilty of a guardianship-related crime. If the ABA creed is that they equally serve their members, their profession, "and the public by defending liberty and delivering justice," then why no comment from the organization when one of their members is caught red-handed? It cannot possibly be acceptable that a licensed lawyer can double-bill a ward's estate or submit a petition for guardianship to the court that contains lies, or seek court approval to ignore carefully executed wills, trusts, and estate plans. Silence from an organization as reputable as the ABA purports to be does no good for their membership, the legal community as a whole, or the public trust. Silence does nothing to erase the tarnished reputation of lawyers that has developed over the years. In the words of reform activist Dr. Sam Sugar, "The ABA should consider . . . [that] there is now an army of victim-advocates hell bent on ending this awful stain on our democracy. The ABA would be wise to endorse and support them."

Likewise, there has been no official denunciation of bad actors from other associated legal organizations like the National Academy of Elder Law Attorneys, which declares that its members are "the premier providers of legal advocacy, guidance, and services to enhance the lives of people with special needs and people as they age."[16] There have been no specific cautions against judicial malfeasance from the National College of Probate Judges to their members who routinely make quick work of authorizing life-altering guardianships, tap the same uncaring appointees to oversee wards' needs, or fail to follow up on legitimate family complaints about guardians and conservators.

Another organization that could help prompt true and lasting change in the current system is the National Guardianship Association (NGA). Like the ABA, the NGA has developed a vast number of educational reports, presentations, training, and certification webinars, and has held annual conferences to facilitate networking of interested parties. Their website, guardianship.org, tells the public that the organization is "leading the way to excellence by establishing and promoting nationally recognized standards [and] encouraging the highest levels of integrity and competence through guardianship education." No doubt the NGA's promise to protect the "interests of guardians and people in their care" has inspired many benevolent caregivers to undergo training and receive certification to become a compassionate professional guardian. But just as certain is the fact that there are members of this brother/sisterhood who go on to do less than noble work, and the NGA has never issued a specific ethics caution or condemnation of a discredited or convicted member. It should also be noted that the NGA encourages a formidable grassroots lobbying effort, via its state chapters, that is well known to lawmakers who serve on committees considering legislation that would reform guardianship procedures. Insiders have said the NGA lobbyists vigorously buttonhole legislators to maintain the status quo.

A 2020 survey by the National Center for State Courts entitled "Adult Guardianship Monitoring: A National Survey of Court Practices" could have been highly informative and a catalyst for reform.[17] However, when the emailed questionnaire was tallied and released in May 2021, authors of the study had to admit that "the majority of responses came from a handful of states, making this report informative but not nationally representative." The report concluded that while most courts demand that a guardian file an annual accounting for each ward, there are no fines or other penalties when the reports are missing or delinquent. Many respondents said they knew that *someone* was responsible to review those reports, but they didn't know who that person might be. Others said that if an appointee's noncompliance became a habit, the guardian "might be replaced." As for what happened to complaints about a particular guardian or a protected person's circumstance, only 19 percent said their court had an established procedure to deal with that. Most of the judges who answered that question said that upon receiving a complaint, they would enter a show cause order and have a hearing. Family members who register such complaints report that those hearings rarely go against the court appointee, in part because family members are often not allowed to speak. One more finding from the survey: It was rare that a judge would hold periodic hearings to assess whether continuation of a guardianship was necessary. That is one more indication that once a guardianship is put in place, it most often stays in place.

The general public has likely never heard about the Uniform Law Commission (ULC), but it too can play a role in how the current guardianship and conservatorship system operates.[18] Based in Chicago, the ULC has been around since 1892 and was created to attract the nation's most prominent legal scholars to work together to devise uniform laws that every state can adopt. The commission's membership is populated by specially nom-inated lawyers, judges, law professors, and legislators and their staffs, all of whom are qualified to practice law. Members are appointed from each state, the District of Columbia, Puerto Rico, and the US Virgin Islands. The idea is to bring together the country's brightest legal minds to provide the states with premiere, standardized laws where "uniformity is desirable and practical."[19] Way back in 1997—a full decade after Chairman Claude Pepper held his highly publicized hearings on predatory guardianships—the commission began working on a law to govern the application of guard-ianships and conservatorships. It eventually became known as the Uni-form Guardianship, Conservatorship, and Other Protective Arrangements Act (UGCOPAA). Ten years later, in 2017, the commission released an up-date to the act and recommended that every state enact the legislation.[20] To date, only two states have agreed to do so—Maine and Washington.[21] This is puzzling, as the UGCOPAA calls for—among many other sensible things—due process for the proposed ward; advance notice of a guardian-ship hearing and the right to an attorney; a guardian who is free of crimi-nal convictions or debtor actions; a path to levy fines on anyone who files a petition for guardianship in bad faith; a streamlined complaint-to-the-court procedure if "physical or financial abuse, neglect, exploitation, or abandonment by the guardian or conservator or a person acting for or with the guardian or conservator"[22] is suspected; and a definitive section that states, "The court may not establish a full guardianship if a limited guard-ianship, protective arrangement instead of guardianship, or other less re-strictive alternatives would meet the needs of the respondent." The very mention of these proposed changes to the system seemed to be an admis-sion that in its current form, guardianships and conservatorships are sim-ply too ripe for corruption.[23]

Make no mistake, the Uniform Law Commission is an august and highly reputable body, and appointment to its ranks is a high honor. So why doesn't the UGCOPAA include a mandated code of ethics for lawyers who are appointed as guardians or conservators? Why hasn't this organization, which acknowledges the failings in the guardianship system, offered up a strongly worded statement condemning their fellow attorneys who prey on wards of the court and denigrate their profession? After all, there are abun-dant examples on record of guardians and/or conservators acting in ques-tionable and even criminal ways. Perhaps a more important question is: why haven't these prominent ULC members been able to convince lawmak-ers in their home states to enact this long-contemplated legislation? After all, this legally sanctioned system operates in every state of the union, and it affects millions of citizens and their family members. Is it because the fissures in guardianships and conservatorships seem too complex to comprehend? Have lobbyists from the legal, healthcare, nursing home, financial, and guardian communities quietly convinced lawmakers everything is fine? Are favors or money changing hands to keep the system as it is? There are many questions for which there are no definitive answers.

Elaine Renoire, founder of the National Association to Stop Guardianship Abuse, worked with the ULC on its latest update to the UGCOPAA. She thinks the reason few states have adopted the uniform legislation is due more to the nationwide lockdown during the pandemic. "I think Covid had a lot to do with that. I believe the experts will now be much more likely to travel and promote UGCOPAA in person to interested states. UGCOPAA turns guardianship as it is now practiced on its head, and so there is a lot of behind the scenes work to change the mindset and direction," Renoire said.

To be fair, none of the organizations mentioned in this chapter make the laws. They can only make suggestions. Their membership can only operate under the laws and judicial orders of their individual state. It is up to legislators to come up with statutes that can help ensure deliberately fair—not potentially destructive—application of guardianships and conservatorships. Several states have begun to consider—and sometimes enact—proposals regulating certain aspects of the system.[24] These ever-evolving bills are too numerous and varied to list here. But as an example, in New Mexico the legislature approved several new pieces of legislation in recent years that include opening up court records and hearings that were previously closed to the public;[25] preventing guardians from arbitrarily limiting visitation with the protected person; establishing a new grievance pathway so families have a one-stop complaint department to file complaints about abusive guardians or conservators; requirements that guardians consider the least restrictive options for the ward; and creation of a new court division that will review all mandatory annual reports filed by guardians and conservators.[26] During the 2022 legislative session, New Mexico's legislature also passed a multipurpose bill that will restrict attorneys from arbitrarily filing for fast-track emergency guardianships and requires judges who approve emergency petitions to hold full hearings within ten days. In the past, some judges failed to hold timely hearings on whether a temporary "emergency" guardianship should be made permanent, thus sometimes leaving the ward and their family in temporary limbo for months. Before the final vote on that bill, New Mexico Supreme Court Justice Shannon Bacon informed law-makers that the annual number of emergency guardianships in the state is "in excess of 800. It should be about eight."[27] Another key section of the bill prohibits temporary guardians from selling any of the ward's belongings or property or moving them out of their home without specific permission from the judge. Reformers in New Mexico applaud the changes, but they also report that some court appointees are still finding ways to get around the new regulations and judges are doing little to stop them. These advocates continue to work on more legislative ideas to present to lawmakers in the future.

The popular retirement state of Florida has long grappled with ways to keep up with a mountain of grievances against guardians. Its Office of Public and Professional Guardians, established in 2016, is supposed to follow up on public complaints, but from the get-go it seemed to be an impossible task since the office has been consistently flooded with accusations of guardian wrongdoing.[28] Since 2016, every session of the state legislature has seen proposals introduced to try to better manage the ever-increasing number of problematic guardianship cases, primarily those involving elderly retirees. In June 2020, for example, Florida governor Ron DeSantis signed multiple bills that promised to curb guardian abuses. Among other things, the new laws restrict guardians from being able to petition the court for appointment to specific cases unless they are related to the proposed ward; make it mandatory that guardians report detailed spending information to the court; expand the required reporting the guardian must file in each case; and mandate that a guardian get permission from the court before signing a Do Not Resuscitate order for a ward. Sadly, that statute was made necessary after a guardian defied a family's wishes and put a DNR order on a ward's medical chart—a military veteran who was not suffering from a fatal illness—and he died a short time later as medical staff stood by helplessly.[29] For all the legislative remedies the state of Florida has enacted over the years, the number of guardian complaints from the public continues to swell. New and stricter laws can be enacted, but if judges and the court system fail to adequately supervise appointees and demand compliance, nothing much will change.

In Michigan, WXYZ television began exposing a series of abusive guardianships in 2017, and the state's attorney general was forced into action.[30] Attorney general Dana Nessel headed up an elder abuse task force, and in the spring of 2019, after more than two years of work, the panel issued their recommendations. Later, Nessel was front and center with a bipartisan group of Michigan lawmakers announcing the introduction of nearly a dozen guardianship-related bills to be considered during the 2021–22 legislative session.[31] Four new statutes were introduced in the state House of Representatives and five in the Senate. Among the proposed changes: a requirement that judges explain on the record why they appointed a professional guardian rather than a family member; better medical information to be provided to the court so a judge has the most up-to-date information before approving a guardianship; an obligation for guardians to spend a certain amount of face-to-face time with each ward; and mandatory certification of all for-profit guardians.

At a hearing of the Michigan State Senate Judiciary Committee on June 10, 2021, attorney Bradley Geller—a man who wrote the Michigan guardianship reform act, has worked in state probate courts for ten years, and has decades of experience with the administration of guardianships—gave a very frank assessment of the pending legislation. As director of the Michigan Center for Law and Aging, Geller said, "These bills are meaningless and would change nothing if they were passed by the legislature today and signed into law by the governor." Geller's voice periodically and passionately rose during his testimony. "The basic problem in our guardian system is that *judges. don't. follow. the. law!*" he said, deliberately punctuating each word and sparking a round of applause from spectators. "And it is magical thinking to believe that if judges don't follow the law now, that if we pass new provisions, then suddenly the judges will comply!" A citizen in the audience offered a hearty "Amen!"[32]

Geller later wrote to me about the fate of the proposed package of legislation that had been so publicly endorsed by the attorney general and other local politicians. "[The] bills were wholly inadequate as introduced and they got worse as they went through the House Judiciary Committee," Geller said. "Luckily the bills only made it as far as the House floor. They all died at the end of the year."[33]

Absent any federal legislation, each state is left to cobble together its own solutions for dealing with their at-risk populations. But is the Band-Aid state-by-state approach the right solution? Randy Asplund, a crusader for change in Michigan, doesn't think so. He's seen the problematic system up close. His mother was conscripted into guardianship after he and his siblings disagreed on what was best for their mother following her stroke. During an interview from his home in Ann Arbor, Michigan, Asplund said, "I call it 'the leaky boat syndrome,' where you can make a few patches and hope the boat holds up, or you can just junk the boat. But if you do the latter, people drown, and you can't have that." Now, he said, "We need to think outside the boat."

First and foremost, lawmakers need to realize that stopgap solutions slapped on a systemically troublesome process like guardianship or conservatorship are useless without meaningful changes to the system itself. Many family members caught up in exploitative or unwanted guardianships believe the first legislative step should be to do away with the ease with which a person can fall under court control. Perhaps just as important, they say, is the need for all parties to rally around the idea that those who cheat, abuse, neglect, isolate, or otherwise heartlessly manipulate a ward must be publicly identified and shamed, officially disciplined, and criminally charged if warranted. Without the threat of swift and meaningful punishment, bad actors in the shadowy world of guardianship and conservatorship will simply continue to victimize the vulnerable.

12

The Cowgirl vs. the Conservator

There is much discussion in this book about the way vulnerable citizens are treated by unethical guardians. But truth be told, it is the court-appointed conservator who often wields the most control. They hold the purse strings, and as everyone knows, money is power. This type of financial power is easily misused in a setting where supervision is sparse or nonexistent. Some conservators act spitefully after concerned family members question or complain about their financial decisions. As shown in this book, there are multiple cases where conservators have asserted their control over a ward's estate to line their own pockets or those of others involved in the system. Some conservators have been known to operate out of sheer ego and arrogance. As one aggrieved daughter of a conservatee related, "When I asked the conservator why in the world he would do such a thing to my elderly mother, he answered, 'Because I can, that's why.'" The case of Blair Darnell illustrates just how uncaring and vindictive a conservator can be. This case was first reported by me in late 2016, in a multipart series in the *Albuquerque Journal*.[1]

Jane Blair Bunting Darnell became the quintessential cowgirl. She was a handsome, vibrant, former Mardi Gras queen from New Orleans whose passion for the study of anthropology drew her to the great American Southwest. She and her two-year-old daughter moved to New Mexico in the late 1950s. It was there that Blair met the love of her life: a former World War II bomber pilot named Clarence "Casey" Darnell. He owned a seventeen-acre ranch, nestled along the Rio Grande outside of Albuquerque, where he raised and trained champion quarter horses. Shortly after arriving in the state, Blair bought a horse from Casey, but after the animal bucked her off, she took it back to the ranch and crisply demanded Casey either break the horse or refund her money. Casey was captivated by this feisty little woman and smitten by her spirit, and on January 27, 1957, they got married. He would soon adopt Blair's toddler daughter, Kris. The couple went on to add three more children to their happy family: Cliff, Emily, and Mary, in that order. They had a wonderful horse-centric life together. Blair was almost always outfitted in a classic western shirt, blue jeans, dusty western boots and hat, and she was more at home in the outdoors than in the kitchen. Through her volunteer work with the local 4-H club, Blair welcomed underprivileged children to the property. She believed working the land and learning to care for animals was an important part of teaching kids responsibility. Casey became well known within the national equestrian community as vice president of the American Quarter Horse Association. He was inducted into the Quarter Horse Hall of Fame in 2009. The couple made sure all four of their children learned to ride, and both parents helped the children prepare for equestrian competitions.

Casey Darnell died on August 10, 2001. A short time later, while going about her daily ranch routine, Blair was kicked by a horse, and when she fell, she hit her head on a railroad tie. She was unconscious for about thirty minutes, but in her tough cowgirl fashion, Blair shook it off and refused medical treatment. In later years, daughter Mary came to believe her mother's forgetfulness was a delayed byproduct of that accident. In the fall of 2008, Mary became her mom's primary caregiver after the Darnell siblings realized their mother's health was failing and someone needed to live on the property with her. Mary, her longtime partner, Dick, and their infant son, Casey Jr., were available. They returned to the ranch and lived in a small house on the property, one that afforded them a line of sight to Blair's home. By then, Blair's memory loss had developed into a diagnosed case of mild dementia.

On an icy January afternoon in 2010, Mary looked out her kitchen widow and spotted several unfamiliar cars parked near her mother's house. She walked over, and upon entering, she was met by a baffling group of strangers who identified themselves as being from a local elder care company called Decades.[2] "All these people were walking around [Mother's] house looking at everything, and I thought, 'This is weird,'" Mary said. "They hand me a stack of papers. A woman named Nancy Oriola from Decades told me there had been a court hearing and Mother was being put under temporary guardianship and conservatorship."[3] Mary had no idea what the words meant. A court hearing? When? Mary knew neither she nor her mother had been in any courtroom. Then she spotted a familiar face standing in the corner of the kitchen. "My older sister, Kris, was there, and I was, like, 'What have you done?'" It is likely that neither sister realized at that moment all of their lives had just changed forever, and that their mother suddenly had fewer civil rights than a convicted murderer. "Everyone was being very quiet and hush-hush and scurrying around," Mary remembered of that January afternoon in her mother's home. "And then they whisked Mother off because they thought my sister and I were going to get into an argument, and they didn't want her to be affected by our conversations. I'm, like, 'Where are you taking her?' And they said, 'We don't have to disclose that.'"[4]

As frequently happens in so many of these cases, the four adult Darnell children had been meeting—and often disagreeing—about their mother's situation and her future. Mary, a licensed real estate agent, had helped her mother with a couple of land transactions, with an eye toward tying up loose ends and solidifying Blair's affairs. One deal involved a property in North Carolina that was sold to a cousin (who had had the right of first refusal) for $156,000. Some of that money was then invested in a parcel of land Mary owned a few miles away, with Blair's name being added to the title. After the family agreed, Mary also listed her mother's ranch to see what the market might bear should Blair decide to sell. These two deals would soon be used against Mary by an attorney representing her stepsister, Kris.

Kris has steadfastly refused to be interviewed about her mother's guardianship case. But conversations with others, and court documents, reveal that Kris was the instigator of the petition for guardianship and conservatorship that conscripted her mother into the system. Because it was presented as an "emergency," the proceeding was fast-tracked though the court without a due process hearing, or the fourteen-day written notice to the proposed ward and any adult children, as is required by state law.[5] Kris's lawyer, Gregory MacKenzie, filed the paperwork on January 6, 2010, and he painted a dire picture of what was happening to the seventy-eight-year-old Mrs. Darnell at the hands of her children.

The petition read in part: "These children have been wholly ineffective in managing their mother's affairs, have failed to exercise proper supervision over her medical situation and living arrangements, have self-dealt with assets entrusted to them, and have persistently borrowed money from her to such a degree that her ability to pay for long-term care is now in question." While MacKenzie complained about all three youngest Darnell children, he really zeroed in on caretaker Mary, demonizing her and accusing her of seriously neglecting her mother's medical needs and of "self-dealing" by directing her mother into questionable financial deals. MacKenzie specifically mentioned the two real estate transactions Mary had shepherded, claiming they were detrimental to Blair's financial well-being and were instigated by Mary "acting as a realtor" so as to get herself a big commission. Without so much as checking the facts of the situation or hearing from witnesses, judge Beatrice Brickhouse took the "emergency" at face value.[6] She signed an order the next day putting the guardianship into motion. Technically, it was a temporary guardianship until competency was established, but the court record shows the judge immediately referred to Blair as "an incapacitated person."

"Mary had the power of attorney," Cliff Darnell said about the real estate transactions his "baby sister" had conducted. "It wasn't a hidden thing . . . it wasn't a crooked thing," he said. "She had all the authority to do what she did. We all knew what was happening." Speaking from his home in Arkansas, Cliff maintained that all the siblings, including Kris and their mother, had fully discussed both land deals and had unanimously agreed to proceed. According to all three younger Darnell siblings, sister Kris was miffed that they had not agreed to liquidate their mother's possessions to create a $850,000 fund allocated for Blair's future medical needs. That amount simply seemed arbitrarily high according to Cliff, Emily, and Mary. The stalemate apparently spurred Kris to hire a lawyer and take the dispute to court. "I guess the first one that gets to the courthouse, that's the one they listen to," Emily said.

As for the charge that Mary had ignored her mother's medical needs, she maintained that Blair had always been private about her health and was "never much of a medical person . . . she kept to herself about things like that, and I had no idea she was missing doctor's appointments." At a hearing to make the temporary guardianship permanent, convened by Judge Brickhouse six weeks after the "emergency" petition was filed, Mary hoped to fully explain her side of the story. There are no available transcripts of this closed-door session, but Mary said Judge Brickhouse did not allow her to speak, and neither of her supportive siblings got the opportunity to address the court either. The trio felt completely helpless. "They say you did all these horrible things and then say, 'Now we have to come in and hire all these people to help your mom,'" Emily said during an interview at her home in a suburb of Albuquerque. "They make it all about the money, which it never was. It was a trauma, like torture, watching what they did to Mother."

Try as they might, the three Darnell siblings could not undo the damage. The guardianship was firmly in place. Total strangers would be in charge of their intensely independent mother for the rest of her life. Blair was allowed to stay on the ranch, and a rotating cadre of home health aides were hired to watch her twenty-four hours a day, seven days a week. It was a crushing development to this strong-willed woman. Blair would sometimes find ways to sneak away from inattentive caretakers and walk over to the home of her closest neighbors, Denny and Connie Gentry. The Gentrys were also well known in the horse world; Denny was the founder of the World Series of Team Roping. Denny said Blair would visit their home just to snatch a few minutes of freedom from her court-ordered minders.

As restricted as this free spirit felt under guardianship, Blair would get boot-kicking, fist-slugging angry once a man named Darryl Millet entered the picture. He was a familiar face in the courtrooms that controlled guardianships, frequently being appointed as a conservator or trustee for a protected person. (For more about attorney Millet, see chapter 1.) In April 2010 attorney Gregory MacKenzie recommended Millet be appointed as conservator to handle Blair Darnell's estate, estimated then to be worth about $5 million. Judge Brickhouse readily agreed with the recommendation.

Blair lived a simple, comfortable life on her monthly Social Security pension of $968, as well as two family trusts administered in South Carolina and Louisiana that routinely provided her between $60,000 and $80,000 a year. There was no need, according to Blair's three youngest children, for her to ever touch the two trusts established with her late husband. But that was not what happened after conservator Millet was added to the number of people already being paid out of Blair's estate.

Attorney Millet presented as an intimidating, large man who, at the time, drove an equally imposing red Hummer. During research on the guardianship situation in New Mexico, Millet's name repeatedly popped up in multiple allegedly abusive cases. One family member who also had dealings with him said, "Millet goes after people like a pit bull," and other relatives of the conscripted echoed that conclusion. They accused Millet of sloppy accounting, questionable business and real estate practices, and arrogant tactics, including threats of arrest against those who disagreed with him. In a written statement, Millet insisted that was an unfair characterization. "I have worked very hard all my life as an attorney to be honest and straightforward," Millet said. "I have a great reputation with the judges and other attorneys in town. When I am appointed as conservator, the reason . . . is because the family members have shown they are untrustworthy with respect to their parent's money."[7]

To that point, the most outlandish charge against Mary Darnell, which apparently began as a whispered rumor among the original caretakers hired by the Decades guardianship firm, was that she had stolen $1 million from her mother's accounts. When the rumor made its way to loyal ranch hands, the jig was up, and the aide who spread the false gossip was fired. But the claim stuck like glue to the already beleaguered Mary. During a telephone interview about the Darnell case in June 2016, conservator Millet voluntarily brought up to me a cryptically similar charge. "There were allegations . . . substantial allegations that family members had taken substantial financial advantage of their mother," Millet said. "When I looked at the numbers the first conservator [Decades] came up with after their investigation, it appeared to me that there was well over $1 million missing from Mom's estate." The three youngest Darnell siblings say that any such theft was impossible because Blair had no major liquid cash reserves. The Darnell estate largely consisted of Blair Darnell's irrevocable "Trust A," which held the two-acre homestead parcel with the main house and outbuildings and her investment accounts. The late Casey Darnell's irrevocable "Trust B," which included fifteen acres of the ranch, the horses, cattle, farm equipment, and some undeveloped land in North Carolina that had been bequeathed to the couple. In defense of his sister, Cliff astutely mentioned that if a conservator-attorney had information that someone had stolen a million dollars from one of his wards, especially an incapacitated elderly person, "They should have been going after an indictment, but no one did."

Millet always correctly asserted that his job as conservator is not to focus on what the family of a guardianized person wants but, rather, on what is in the best interest of the ward. However, his words and deeds—as detailed by eyewitnesses and in his own abrasive emails—demonstrate just how a conservator can use their power to bully, overpower, and marginalize a protected person and their family.

Neighbor Denny Gentry remembers the day he drove by the Darnell property on the way home and spotted something suspicious. He and his wife had vowed to keep an eye on Blair after Casey's death, and on this spring day in 2010, Denny noticed a security guard posted outside the Darnell home. When he stopped to inquire, another man appeared and identified himself as Darryl Millet, a court-appointed lawyer. "He asked what

I wanted, so I explained I was a longtime neighbor and [was] checking up on Blair," Gentry said. "He informed me that he was now in charge and I had one minute to get off the property or he would call the law." The isolation of Blair was now coming at her from two sides—from her guardian and her conservator. The guardian had denied Blair permission to travel to Arkansas for the funeral of her granddaughter, Cliff's daughter who had died in a tragic car accident. And conservator Millet had ordered Mary, Dick, and young Casey to move off the Darnell ranch property, leaving Blair in the care of an ever-changing group of caretaker strangers.

The Gentrys had nothing good to say about their dear friend's plight under this court-ordered set up. The process made Blair's life "a living hell," according to Denny. They could only watch in sorrow, he said, as bit by bit the Darnells' horses and ranch equipment were sold off by conservator Millet. "The image I will always have in my mind," Gentry said, "is Millet with his hand on the lever, loading up her worn-out old car onto a trailer, pushing Blair away with his other hand as she was kicking him in the shins." Blair hadn't driven her old Jeep in quite a while at that point, but Gentry said it had to have been a symbol of mobility and freedom to her. Watching it be towed away to be sold was heartbreaking and yet another blow to Blair's independence and dignity.

At one point in the conservatorship, the mostly confined Blair requested a dog door be installed for her beloved terrier. Millet hired a company to do the work, but for some reason the door was placed in an inconvenient part of the house that was sealed off in the winter. It fell to Mary to ask Millet if they could add a $100 thermostat in that room so it could be heated and left open during the coldest months. Millet's email response to her was curt. "If you cannot get the dog outside to relieve herself, she must go."[8] It was a strange denial, according to Mary, given that after Millet was told the Decades caretakers had complained that the Darnells' television didn't get enough channels, he approved the installation of satellite TV. That amenity cost Blair's estate nearly $90 each month.

Mary's inquiry to Millet about replacing a thirty-year-old gas line in the house was met with another snarky reply. He insisted there was no gas leak and asserted that Blair couldn't afford to replace the whole mechanism. Eventually, Millet did schedule the work, but he emailed out a stern caution to all involved. "Mary is not to talk to the workers or to the inspector about the work being done at all. If I find out that Mary . . . has in any way interfered with the plumbers or said anything that causes additional expense, I will take swift action to make certain it never happens again."

After the work was done, a visiting uncle reported that he smelled gas in the house. And Mary noticed the required inspection tag was missing. She informed conservator Millet. He wrote back an angry email: "We have now had a county inspection, in addition to the two contractor pressure checks done previously, and as I have repeatedly stated, THERE IS NO LEAK in the gas system." But Mary was inside her mother's house and she was sure she smelled gas, so just to be safe she took her mother and the dog, Jack, to her nearby house for the evening. In the morning, the dog was dead.

"If there was an antagonistic route to take," brother Cliff said, "That is the route Millet took. He's one way in front of the court, he is another way in front of men . . . and he can't handle a woman who's got backbone."

On March 20, 2013, Millet filed a motion with Judge Brickhouse outlining his plan to sell the bulk of the Darnell ranch, about fifteen acres. This was the acreage contained in the irrevocable Casey Darnell "Trust B." That trust was established with the idea that the contents would be passed on to the Darnell children. Millet was under no legal obligation to inform the siblings about his pending transaction, but Mary, Emily, and Cliff soon found out through the grapevine that he was seriously entertaining a $1.5 million offer for the property. As an experienced real estate agent, Mary believed that price was too low. She came to learn that Denny Gentry had a standing offer, reached years earlier with Blair, to buy the fifteen acres adjoining his land for $1.7 million. After a flurry of back-and-forth pleadings and affidavits, Judge Brickhouse inexplicably approved the lower $1.5 million sale on June 25, 2013. Since guardianship court proceedings are kept from the public, there is no way to learn the judge's logic for this decision. However, for some reason, the sale didn't go through.

In the meantime, Mary got an expert opinion on conservator Millet's fiduciary responsibility to her family. After reviewing all the information he had been sent, real estate lawyer John Lieuwen wrote to say he considered the sale proposal Millet had submitted to the court to be "suspect." First, Lieuwen opined, a third-party independent realtor should have been engaged to handle the transaction. Second, he wrote, "It is blackletter law that a trustee owes a fiduciary duty to both the present income beneficiary (Blair Darnell) and the remaindermen (the heirs). Even if the trustee's primary charge is the current beneficiary, he cannot do anything which will compromise the remaindermen's interest."[9] Breaking an irrevocable trust and deliberately selling a property for hundreds of thousands of dollars less than was on the table surely compromised the Darnell heirs' inheritance. And why, Mary wondered, would Millet want to go through with such a substandard sale? Maybe there was some under-the-table benefit waiting for her mother's conservator? That was impossible to prove.

Questions lingered, time elapsed, and on October 29, 2013, Mary, supported by brother Cliff and sister Emily, filed a motion asking Judge Brickhouse to force Millet to produce financial information on the proposed sale, or, alternately, to remove him as conservator/trustee. The very next day, before the judge ruled on their motion, Millet closed on a deal to sell the Darnell ranch—now the entire seventeen acres—for the even lower price of $1.4 million.[10] Included in this jaw-dropping all-cash deal was a stipulation that allowed Blair to remain in her home—on a fenced-in, one-acre lot—until she died. After her passing, the land and the house would automatically revert to the buyer. Again, the Darnell children felt steamrolled, and wondered how this could happen with irrevocable trusts in place.

Their childhood ranch was lost. Their parents' dreams destroyed. Their ranch was prime property once described by the New Mexico Game and Fish Department as representing "one of the largest underdeveloped parcels of land fronting the Rio Grande River in this area.[11] It provides prime access to the river and Albuquerque's Cottonwood Bosque, supports multiple species of migratory waterfowl including many duck species, Canada geese, and sandhill crane." In 2010, when the Blair Darnell guardianship case was first presented in court, attorney Gregory MacKenzie's emergency petition declared the Darnell ranch land was worth some $300,000 per acre, for a total of more than $5 million. Just three years later—in a decidedly improved real estate market—conservator Millet inexplicitly sold the property for approximately $82,000 an acre, settling for a bottom-line price of just $1.4 million.[12] The question of why a court-sanctioned fiduciary would enter into such a questionable deal, and why a judge presumably preapproved the sale, still persists. Because the players in this state's judicial system enjoy a blanket of legalized secrecy, it is likely their reasonings will never be known.

Blair would survive another two years on her shrunken parcel, surrounded by an ugly eight-foot-tall chain-link fence conservator Millet erected as a formidable demarcation zone. Undaunted, the feisty Blair, then in her eighties, once steered a wheelbarrow over to a remote corner of the fence and boosted herself up and over and into freedom. "She walked over to the gas station and sat down to have a coke," Mary later recalled. Meantime, a couple of hours ticked by and the inattentive caretakers suddenly noticed Blair's absence and were "freaking out," according to Mary.

"My sister Emily used to teach at a school nearby the gas station and the staff recognized Mom. They called Emily and she came to get her." Some time after that, a tragic photograph of Blair was taken as she sat under a tree in her fenced-in plot of land. She had dragged a lawn chair close to the spot where she had once escaped and was captured staring forlornly at the chain-link barrier that kept her from the outside world. One of her caretakers hovers nearby. Mary took that photo and said she can never forget "what they reduced my mother to."

Blair Darnell lived the last five years of her life confined to an isolated lifestyle she surely would never have chosen for herself. More than seventy different caretakers had been assigned to watch her day and night. Working from what were described as jumbled and incomplete accounting sheets from conservator Millet—Peter Brunson, a CPA hired by the Darnell family, filed a sworn affidavit with the court that read in part: "The documents submitted by Mr. Millet, if they are to be a financial accounting, are inaccurate and substantively deficient." This professional accountant went on to declare, "These pages are nothing more than a printout of a register, similar to a checkbook register."[13] Working off the conservator's financial filings, Mary said she calculated that over the years their mother's estate paid out at least $497,464 for the in-home aides. Darrel Millet was found to have written checks to his own Albuquerque Advocates firm totaling more than $175,000, but since the record is incomplete, the total was likely higher. Then there were the fees paid to a rotating set of guardians, attorneys, and other court appointees. The Darnell estate, estimated at more than $5 million when the court first stepped in, dwindled to less than $750,000. "The professionals should not be allowed to feast off your whole estate until the ward dies," Mary said. "It is barbaric and corrupt."

Blair Darnell died at home, surrounded by her family and friends, on November 18, 2015. Had she lived five more weeks, she would have celebrated her eighty-fourth birthday.

Mary Darnell was a brave pioneer in refusing to be silenced by the court system she saw as brimming with injustice. Her sister, Emily, and brother, Cliff, would also become fearless whistleblowers as well. The judge's gag order requiring strict secrecy was explicit; threats of contempt of court charges and hefty fines were very real and had been levied against other people Mary knew. So why did she take on the thankless leadership role of revealing the totality of her mother's plight to this journalist? Mary said she kept fighting the system, despite her battle with breast cancer along the way, because in quiet conversations toward the end of her mother's life, Blair had told her "not to let the bastards win."

"My mother told me, 'Get these laws changed so this doesn't happen to another family,'" Mary said. "And I intend to do that." To this day, Mary Darnell and her sister, Emily, continue to work toward passage of new laws that will force the New Mexico courts to reject bogus "emergency" petitions; provide more due process; honor preplanned documents like wills, irrevocable trusts, and end-of-life wishes; be more transparent in their decision-making; and more willing to listen to family members who know the incapacitated person's deepest desires in life. Most of all, the Darnells want the system to recognize and respect the constitutional rights of vulnerable citizens and promote policies that keep families together instead of tearing them apart.

More than seven years after their beloved mother's death, Mary, Emily, and Cliff Darnell continued their legal battle with conservator Millet in both state probate court and the US District Court of New Mexico. The probate court fight is over the ownership of a valuable piece of art by renowned French artist Antonio de la Gandara. Blair's children say the portrait of Madame Pierre Gautreau (1897) was given to their mother by their maternal grandmother, Ethel Jane Bunting, decades ago and well before Grandma Bunting died. "It's spelled out in my grandmother's papers, she clearly left [the painting] to my mother," Mary Darnell said. "It isn't even mentioned in her will because she had already given it to Mother." Yet in court papers that conservator Millet filed months after Blair Darnell's death, he claimed that Blair had just a half-interest in the painting, with her sister, Amy, owning the remaining 50 percent. Millet told the court his investigation discovered the dual ownership, and that the painting, which insurance valued at $234,000, was on loan to the Gibbes Museum of Art in Charlestown, South Carolina. In an email Millet sent out in early 2016 and obtained for this book, he wrote, "I talked to the attorney who handled the probate, and he sent me the court filed pleading attached. It is the probate attorney's opinion that the painting is equally owned by Amy and Blair's (now) estate. I agree."

Mary said she learned long ago to fact-check Darryl Millet, and she discovered that effort can be a full-time job. She took great pains to contact the South Carolina lawyer whose name appeared on Millet's court filing as the attorney of record on her grandmother's final distribution papers. On February 1, 2016, that lawyer, Tom Rutledge of Charleston, wrote back to

Mary to declare he had not spoken to Darryl Millet, and there had never been a probate lawyer involved as he, the estate lawyer, had handled the final arrangements. "No," Rutledge wrote, "This Proposal for Distribution has nothing to do with Madame [Pierre Gautreau]. I have never told anything to Darryl about this." Further, when one analyzes the content of the court filing on Grandma Bunting's inventory that Millet sent out, it only says that her daughters, Blair and Amy, were to split "miscellaneous personal property" along with proceeds from the sale of Grandma's Charleston, South Carolina, home. The painting at the center of the dispute isn't even mentioned.

"See, that's the kind of thing you're up against. They can flat-out lie to the courts," Mary said during an interview in spring 2022. "I have all the evidence about the painting, but we can't get into court. We can't get a judge to hear it." The probate proceeding has been frozen until the US District Court case is over.

The Darnells' federal lawsuit alleges fraud, breach of fiduciary duty, deceit, and collusion on the part of conservator Millet. Also named in the suit is Zia Trust Company, which was the firm Millet used to transfer the Darnell property deeds. The Darnell siblings' goal was to hold conservator Millet accountable for an accurate final accounting of their mother's estate (including full ownership of the Antonio de la Gandara painting), and for what they consider to be a fraudulent land deal that cost them their family ranch. It is worth noting that the Darnells' federal suit sat dormant on the desk of US district judge James O. Browning for nearly six months, and on October 7, 2021, he finally revealed that "Darryl Millet . . . has done some personal real estate work for me in New Mexico and Texas," and that Millet had "for many years" been the attorney of record for three landholding companies held by the judge and his late wife. In addition, Judge Browning's recusal, a copy of which is part of the research collected for this book, revealed that Millet's wife, Lori, "is [Judge Browning's] estate lawyer." Why it took Judge Browning so many months to declare his recusal wasn't explained.[14] Perhaps it had something to do with court closures during the coronavirus pandemic. But the Darnells feel that the interpersonal dynamics within the familiar community surrounding guardianship—from lawyers, guardians, and conservators to probate judges and jurists sitting on the bench in higher courts—have worked against them every step of the way.

Chief United States district judge William Johnson took over the federal case, and the Darnell siblings were hopeful. However, on January 12, 2022,

Judge Johnson ordered conservator Millet dropped from the lawsuit and ruled the Darnells were responsible for paying his legal fees. The judge pointed to the settlement agreement the family had signed back in September 2016, which legally terminated the conservatorship and included a so-called waiver of liability that protected Millet from any future lawsuits.[15] It's unclear whether Judge Johnson was informed that at the time of the settlement signing, Millet's lawyers had warned the Darnell siblings that if they didn't agree to settle, Millet would hold back $100,000 to pay for his continued services and other anticipated legal expenses. The threat was clear: agree to stop all legal action immediately or lose another $100,000 of the inheritance. Cliff and Emily signed the settlement agreement first, and finally Mary gave in, realizing that the more they fought, the more of their mother's money would be lost to her nemesis, Darryl Millet. "That document was signed under duress, with the extortion of $100,000 hanging over our heads," Mary said. She still seethes about Millet's unorthodox tactics and how the courts let him get away with so much. "He's not held to any standards whatsoever—but they hold our feet to the fire at every step," she said. Blair Darnell's three youngest children vow to keep fighting, led by valiant sister Mary.

13

The Richer the Better

The more money a person has, the more tantalizing a target they become to the unscrupulous actors operating within the guardianship system. That is a fact. And those with the most money have been legally victimized for more than one hundred years under this process. The US government's authorized practice of subjugating those thought to be "lesser than" can be traced back to before the turn of the twentieth century.

In 1894 oil was discovered on Osage Indian territory in what is now known as north-central Oklahoma.[1] The tribe, which the US government had forcibly moved to the area from their homes in Kansas, became incredibly rich after their new land began to reveal its treasure. Once the oil started flowing, tens of millions of dollars were suddenly available, and tribal leaders shared the wealth among all members of the Osage community. This did not sit well with whites in Oklahoma and elsewhere. Many became resentful that people they saw as being ethnically inferior would reap such a bounty simply because they had the good luck to live above a vast oil reserve. The popular press at the time began to exploit the hostile relationship by writing scathing articles about tribe members' excesses and luxurious lifestyles. They had built mansions, they rode in fancy cars driven by chauffeurs, and they sent their children to schools in Europe. For this the Osage were portrayed as being undeserving, ignorant, and wasteful with their windfall. Much was made of the shocking idea that tribal members had become so wealthy and lazy that they had dared to hire white servants. Ugly sentiments about the tribe mutated across the country, and outside speculators flocked to the quarterly oil lease auctions overseen by the Department of the Interior. The department distributed royalties to the tribe, and by the early 1920s those annual payments would swell to $27 million.[2]

The tribe legally owned their land and what laid underneath, thanks to the congressionally approved 1906 Osage Allotment Act, so there seemed little that the Caucasian chattering class could do to significantly elbow their way into the tent of riches.[3] A solution was arrived upon when it was decided that the Osage must be mentally incapacitated, given the seemingly flamboyant ways they acted, and in 1921 Congress passed a law requiring any full- or half-blooded Osage member to be appointed a guardian until they could prove their own "competency."[4] Minors who were heirs to the land were also required to have guardians, even if their parents were still living. The appointed guardians were, of course, white attorneys and businessmen who were supposedly "protecting" the Osage from their own foolish spending. There was little government oversight of this guardianship process and little record keeping of exactly how guardians doled out monthly allowances and invested the rest of their ward's wealth. Corruption among guardians, and outsiders hoping to get their hands on lucrative oil leases, lead to what the Osage called the "Reign of Terror." Many tribespeople were mysteriously murdered, according to written histories of the time. In the book *Bloodland: A Family Story of Oil, Greed and Murder on the Osage Reservation* (1999), author Dennis MacAuliffe reopens his own family's wounds to recount the murder of his Osage grandmother, and in the process he exposes the widespread murder conspiracy against the tribe.[5] This shameful period of American history is also painstakingly recorded in another nonfiction book, *Killers of the Flower Moon: The Osage Murders and the Birth of the* FBI (2017) by David Grann.[6] After more than twenty-four murders of both Osage tribespeople, and those who dared to investigate the spate of deaths, the FBI began its first-ever major homicide investigation. As Gann writes, "the bureau badly bungled the case," until director J. Edgar Hoover brought in a former Texas ranger, who teamed up with the only American Indian agent in the FBI, and together they began to expose the awful truth about the murders. Thus, at the dawn of the twentieth century, the Osage tribe became the earliest and largest group to fall victim to the US guardianship system. The program that was supposedly designed to protect the neediest had been inhumanely hijacked by greedy outsiders.

Since money is the motivator, it should come as no surprise that the ultra-wealthy of more modern times have also been victimized by greedy predators. After Brooke Astor, the New York socialite and philanthropist with a $200 million estate, fell victim to physical and psychological abuse and fraud at the hands of her only son, Anthony Marshall, a court-ordered guardianship saved the day. Anthony's son, Phillip, filed the guardian petition in 2006, as a way to protect his 104-year-old grandmother. Phillip's report to the court was graphic: Mrs. Astor, who had been diagnosed with Alzheimer's several years earlier, was living in "dirty and dilapidated" conditions in her Park Avenue apartment and was living that way at the discretion of Phillip's father. According to the grandson, Brooke Astor was neglected, underfed, and "forced to sleep in the TV room in torn nightgowns on a filthy couch."[7] Phillip also mentioned several instances of financial improprieties, including his father's sale of one of his grandmother's prized pieces of art for $10 million. Shortly after that transaction, Anthony and his wife, Charlene (a woman Brooke Astor detested), bought a mansion in New Jersey. The court approved the guardianship petition, and the media immediately picked up on the high-society scandal. The *New York Daily News* headline proclaiming "Disaster for Mrs. Astor!" helped launch a yearlong criminal investigation. At the trial in November 2009, Anthony Marshall's sons, Phillip and his twin brother, Alec, testified against their father. Marshall and his accomplice, attorney Francis X. Morrissey Jr., were found guilty of fourteen counts of conspiracy, financial exploitation (resulting in the loss of millions), fraud, grand larceny, and other charges.[8] Marshall, at age eighty-five, was sentenced to one to three years in prison. His frail health was invoked shortly after he was imprisoned, and Marshall would serve only eight weeks behind bars. Brooke Astor did not live to see her son be brought to justice. She died on August 13, 2007, at the age of 105.

Seeking a protective guardianship can be a positive step. In the case of Mrs. Astor, court intervention allowed her to live out the final months of life peacefully and under excellent care. But not all prospective wards from the super-rich segment of society see the court's intervention as necessary. Bradford Lund, fifty-two, grandson of the legendary Walt Disney, has been fighting against guardianship and for his rightful inheritance for fifteen long years.

The battle revolves around Brad's share of several trusts,[9] including those his late mother, Sharon (one of Walt Disney's two children), established to provide for her three children.[10] The beneficiaries were Victoria, a daughter adopted during Sharon's first marriage, and twins Brad and Michelle, born to Sharon and her second husband, Bill Lund. Each child, already living very comfortably thanks to their Grandpa Disney's success and generosity, were to receive $20 million on their thirty-fifth, fortieth, and forty-fifth birthdays. However, there was one stipulation that allowed a small group of trustees to withhold the money if the children did not demonstrate "maturity and financial ability to manage and utilize such funds in a prudent and responsible manner."[11]

According to the *Hollywood Reporter* and other sources, half sisters Victoria and Michelle had long battled the demons of substance abuse. Victoria lived an especially erratic lifestyle. She would splurge on charter planes and fancy hotel suites in Vegas, and during one Disney cruise she so destroyed her luxury suite that the trustees were called upon to pony up considerable money to restore it. There were reports that Victoria's drug addiction had advanced to the point that her hands were "blackened from heroin use." Nonetheless, when Victoria turned thirty-five the trustees released her first $20 million birthday distribution. A short time later, in September 2002, she died of liver failure at age thirty-six. Victoria's portion of the Disney/Lund estate, which was then estimated to be as much as $400 million, would be split between her two half siblings.

As for sister Michelle, she and her twin brother, Brad, were educated in private schools for children with learning disabilities. While Michelle was reportedly diagnosed as having dyslexia, the exact nature of any other learning differences she may have had has not been made public. But her past wild-child ways have been widely publicized. Media reports published in 2014 revealed Michelle's substance abuse became so acute that on Labor Day 2009, after a raucous night partying with pals, she was rushed to an Orange County, California, hospital.[12] She had suffered a brain aneurysm, likely caused by too many drugs and too much alcohol, and was close to death. To this day, there are family members who say Michelle still suffers from brain damage caused by the episode. Like her sister, Victoria, there is no evidence Michelle ever had a job or pursued a career. Yet, on June 5, 2005, when her thirty-fifth birthday bequeathment came due, the trustees dutifully transferred over her $20 million present. They did not do the same for Brad.

The trustees believed Brad did not have adequate maturity or the financial wisdom to be handed millions of dollars. In rebuttal, attorneys for Brad have long argued he was much more stable and accomplished than his sister and half sister. Brad graduated from Cape Cod Community College with a certificate in culinary preparation. He had worked at several different jobs in restaurants, in the mailroom of an insurance company, and he once owned a UPS store where he regularly worked behind the counter serving the public. Brad led an independent, sober life, and in

2003 he made the choice to move from California to Arizona to be closer to his father, Bill Lund, and his stepmother, Sherry.

People close to the case, and close to Brad, have indicated he may be on the autism spectrum, but they deny he would be unable to adequately safeguard the funds left in his name. In the past, his late father had been quoted describing Brad variously as having Down syndrome, fetal alcohol syndrome, or some "learning issues." [13] At one point a DNA test provided to the court proved Brad did not have Down syndrome. Over the years, no argument would sway the trustees. They stood firm and consistently denied Brad his birthday distributions. Michelle, on the other hand, continued to get her birthday millions every five years.

It should be noted that those in charge of the trust funds are handsomely rewarded, reportedly earning between $500,000 and $1 million apiece every year. The amount of their annual pay depends on how much money is in the trust fund, so as long as Brad's millions remain held back, the trustees are assured a more lucrative paycheck. Administration of the fund is also highly profitable for the bank handling the money and for the bevy of lawyers who have been hired on in various capacities over the years. In other words, the status quo arrangement that keeps the distribution conflict brewing benefits everyone—except the named heir, Bradford Lund.

Naturally, in a case where so much money is at stake, the players wound up in court. Brad Lund's lawyers have had to fight several battles, in several different courts, in two states—California and Arizona. In October 2009 Brad's aunt (his mother's sister, Diane) and two of his other half sisters filed papers in Arizona Superior Court's probate division asking that a guardian and a conservator be appointed for him. The trustees and their legal team are alleged to have urged Aunt Diane to file the petition to reinforce their conclusion that Brad was not capable of handling his own inheritance. This surprise battle was launched, according to Brad's stepmother, Sherry, at the same time sister Michelle was in the hospital fighting for her life with that brain aneurysm. "It was pure evil," Sherry said during a phone interview in early 2022. "The trustees paid for [Diane's] legal action. While Michelle is in the ICU in a coma fighting for her life, they used her money to fight her brother!"

The lengthy trial record shows a statement by Brad acknowledging that he has developmental disabilities, and later a court-appointed neuropsychologist concluded Brad suffered "significant cognitive deterioration from 2003 to 2011." Aunt Diane's petition would hang in limbo for several years and was punctuated by much drama. At one point, Arizona Superior

Court judge Gary Donahoe became so angry at Brad's attorneys fighting against guardianship that he ordered one of them to be briefly detained and handcuffed in open court. The lawyer had refused to answer questions under oath about who or what was behind a certain discovery subpoena because, he said, it would reveal confidential attorney-client privileged information. Judge Donahoe ordered the man restrained, and then turned to the other pro–Brad Lund lawyers demanding they answer questions about whether the subpoena was written to "harass or delay the proceedings." After those attorneys also asserted attorney-client privilege, the judge dropped the threat of jail and found the group in contempt of court. Each was sanctioned thousands of dollars. The team challenged Judge Donahoe's decision before the Arizona Court of Appeals and won. In July 2011 the higher court concluded, "No attorney should fear that the assertion of privilege will result in the deprivation of his or her liberty until the full measure of due process has been afforded. The conduct of the [Donahoe] court in this case represented a clear abuse of discretion." [14]

This dispute was just one of numerous legal sidetracks Lund's lawyers were forced to take over the years in an effort to keep Brad's fight for independence and his inheritance on track. Aunt Diane's petition for guardianship of her nephew would linger, unresolved, for nearly eight years, consuming untold millions in legal fees—all paid for by the Disney/Lund trust. In December 2010 Brad's legal team also initiated a trust proceeding in the California court in an effort to force the trustees to give him his thirty-fifth and fortieth birthday distributions. That case would also remain unresolved for years, creating a blizzard of petitions and motions and all manner of legal maneuverings.

In December 2013 Brad's lawyers were in the probate division of Los Angeles Superior Court with judge Mitchell Beckloff presiding. They hoped for three things: to dispel the notion that Brad was not mentally capable of handling money; to win an order forcing the trustees to disperse his birthday distributions; and to remove First Republic Trust Company (FRTC) from being the business entity that administered the trusts. The attorneys argued that the trustees were less interested in doing right by a recognized beneficiary and more interested in collecting a continuing stream of sizable fees. As the *Hollywood Reporter*'s Eriq Gardner wrote, "Among other contentions, Brad's legal team asked why, in light of granting drug addict Victoria her $20 million, the trustees refused to hand down money to Brad, known for his frugality. They asserted that the trustees did this for their own gain." [15] In hopes of bolstering his position, Brad took the stand

and was asked whether his condition had improved since 2006 when he had taken the ill-advised step of filing and then withdrawing a request for the Arizona court to assign his father, stepmother, and stepsister, Rachel, as his guardians. Seven years later, Brad testified he had much improved. "Well, there are several reasons," he told the court. "Number one, I've got glasses. Number two, new hearing aids. Number three, I'm on no medication. And number [four], I don't get as flustered as easy. I have a much better memory." Exactly what had caused this vast improvement in Brad—be it a specific therapy, eliminating medication, or simple attention to his personal needs—was not revealed.

One of the trustees testified at the Beckloff trial that "Brad had considerable disabilities that were evident," and he raised suspicions about the undue influence Brad's father, Bill, had over him. It was alleged that the elder Lund had engaged in past questionable financial dealings.[16] Another trustee testified that Brad did not understand the value of money. He told a story about a trip to a gift shop in Sweden and Brad's indecision over which of three $15 train sets to buy. Brad allegedly told the trustee he "couldn't afford" to buy all three. However, the next day, according to the witness, Brad bought three $500 decorative Russian eggs.

On June 3, 2014, after a lengthy trial, Judge Beckloff ruled that he was not convinced that the trustees were withholding the birthday money "for fee-generation purposes." In his final order, Beckloff wrote, "The Trustees sincerely believe that Mr. Lund does not have the maturity and financial ability to manage and utilize a substantial trust distribution . . . [they] are legitimately concerned about Mr. Lund's ability to protect himself from those around him who may wish to take financial advantage of him." But Beckloff handed Brad two victories. First, he agreed that confidence had been irrevocably broken between beneficiary Lund and First Republic Trust Company, and FRTC was removed from administering the trusts. Second, Beckloff ruled that, after hearing Lund testify, he concluded Brad had not fallen victim to any undue outside influence and he "had the capacity to remove and replace his trustees" on two specific trusts. It was the first time a court had used the words "capacity" and "Bradford Lund" together.[17]

With that positive court decision in hand, the attention of Lund's legal team shifted back to the Arizona court and the still unresolved petition for guardianship and conservatorship that Brad's aunt had filed. After a new judge was assigned to handle the case, a verdict was finally reached in July 2016. Arizona Superior Court judge Robert Oberbillig, an experienced jurist known for his ability to settle complex legal issues, stepped in and commenced a ten-day bench trial. Among the witnesses were Brad, his estranged sister Michelle, one of the trustees, and medical professionals who had evaluated Brad. At the conclusion, Judge Oberbillig ruled that Bradford Lund "consistently demonstrated that he makes mature, appropriate financial decisions" and can "manage effectively his medical care, estate, and other affairs." The most important line in the ruling from Brad's perspective was this: "Presently, in 2016, he is not incapacitated [and] an appointment of a guardian is not necessary."[18] Perhaps the most poignant line from Judge Oberbillig's ruling found that "although not his burden of proof, Bradford Lund has proven that he deserves the freedom in life to make his own choices."[19] Sherry Lund told me, "Two states and five doctors have found Brad to be competent. How much more do you put a person through? How much embarrassment and humiliation? I ask myself all the time, how can the [trustees] sleep at night? How can they look at themselves in the mirror? They have no conscience at all."[20]

In December 2018, back in Los Angeles, probate court judge David Cowan was in charge of the long-standing proceeding focused on releasing Brad's inheritance, which now included three missed birthday payments totaling $60 million. The controversial Judge Cowan, apparently choosing to adopt fluid equity court rules, took a surprising action and issued a "sua sponte" order that led to the appointment of a temporary guardian ad litem for Brad, an action Team Lund had strenuously argued against.[21] A few months later, perhaps influenced by the two capacity rulings in favor of Brad, all parties in the Disney/Lund Trust dispute appeared to have come to what is called a "global settlement agreement." That included all the trustees, twin sister, Michelle, and Brad. Sherry Lund, who remains so close to her stepson that they live in side-by-side homes in Arizona, revealed that Brad had agreed "to give the trustees $14.5 million" in walk-away money. But when the parties brought their plan to the courtroom, Judge Cowan refused to approve the settlement. In quashing the agreement, Cowan said, "Do I want to give two hundred million dollars, effectively, to someone who may suffer on some level, from Down syndrome? The answer is no." Brad's attorney, Sandra Slaton, immediately corrected the judge and reminded him that an Arizona court had already established, via a DNA test, that Bradford Lund did not have Down syndrome. She asked Cowan to retract the statement and strike it from the public record. Slaton told me during a phone conversation in the spring of 2022 that Judge Cowan responded with a curt one-word answer: "Denied." Judge Cowan appeared to act capriciously when he zeroed in on Slaton, falsely accusing her of bias and misconduct. He issued an inflammatory order to show cause why she shouldn't be removed from the case, a highly unusual move and one Cowan has employed previously in other conservatorship cases.[22] In addition, Cowan would preside over a heated fight on Brad's request to seal certain court documents, specifically those dealing with his private, personal medical information. The Lund legal team was making no headway in front of this particular California judge. Thus, more side-tracking legal issues were born and had to be litigated in still other courts.

Lund's lawyers sued Judge Cowan in federal court for violating Brad's civil rights, citing the judge's failure to hold a due process hearing before appointing the guardian ad litem. They asked that Cowan be removed from the case for his "judicial bias" against people with Down syndrome, and they would later add the claim that Cowan had violated the Americans with Disabilities Act. But by the time the case wound its way through the appeals process, Judge Cowan had dismissed his guardian ad litem appointee and removed himself from the case. Therefore, on July 15, 2021, the US Court of Appeals, Ninth Circuit, ruled much of the Lund complaint to be moot.[23] The appellate court's final opinion, written by Judge Kenneth K. Lee, begins with this: "For over a decade, Bradford Lund—the grandson of Walt Disney—has languished in perhaps the Unhappiest Place on Earth: probate court. Lund has yet to claim a fortune estimated to be worth $200 million." Judge Lee took the opportunity to publicly scold the lower court judge. "Judge Cowan did not comment on Lund's perceived disability out of the blue in the courtroom or (thankfully) on Twitter," Judge Lee wrote. "To be clear, we find Judge Cowan's comment troubling. That someone has Down syndrome does not necessarily preclude the ability to manage one's own financial affairs."[24] However, the opinion concluded that punishment for Judge Cowan was not warranted since he was protected by judicial immunity. In addition, it was noted that Cowan had already taken a preemptive step by withdrawing from the Lund case.

The global settlement agreement crumbled. As Sherry Lund put it, "Brad was ready to give them [more than] $14 million to get them to go away. But after everything happened, he said to me, 'You know, forget about it. Money doesn't matter. They all need to be in jail.'" Sherry said the saddest part of their long ordeal has been the forced separation from Michelle. "I miss my [step]daughter," she said. "They've ruined our family. Michelle has a conservator who gives her money, but they have people living with her, bodyguards and such. She is in total isolation from the rest of the family." Asked how Brad is holding up, his stepmother said, "Brad is devastated. He hates the trustees, he's lost his mother, his father, his sister Victoria, and he's estranged from his twin.[25] When I got Covid . . . Brad wrote me from next door to say, 'Please don't go anywhere, Sherry. I need you.'"

In March 2021, after members of the House Judiciary Committee eagerly stepped into the spotlight of the Britney Spears conservatorship case by announcing their intention to hold public hearings, Brad Lund (via his attorney) wrote to the head of the committee. He asked chairman Jerrold Nadler, and every other member of the committee, to broaden the investigation and look into his case as well. He informed them how long he had been fighting, of the abusive and hostile way he had been treated at the hands of the courts, about the trustees who were holding his birthday distributions hostage, and about the court findings of his capacity in not one but two states. To date, no one from the House Judiciary Committee has responded to Bradford Lund. And he still hasn't gotten any part of his thirty-fifth, fortieth, or forty-fifth birthday money. His fight continues.

OLIVER WILSON BIVINS of Amarillo, Texas, came from a pioneer ranching family. At the turn of the twentieth century, his grandfather, Lee Bivins, had astutely bought up as much land as he could in the north Texas panhandle, and then branched out into areas of New Mexico as well. At one point it was said that the Bivins enterprise was the biggest cattle ranch in America. In the early 1920s, oil and natural gas deposits were discovered under the Bivins land, and, reminiscent of the Osage tribe's storyline, the family's wealth skyrocketed, providing the means for succeeding generations to live extremely comfortable lives.[26] When it came time, Oliver took charge of the vast family business, nurturing it, collecting mounds of royalties, and investing wisely in real estate. Oliver's first marriage ended when his young son, Julian, was just six years old, and his ex-wife, Dorothy, relocated to New York. Oliver would visit the little boy frequently, and Oliver ultimately bought the five-story Scribner House mansion[27] on the tony Upper East Side of Manhattan, as well as a retail building on Lexington Avenue.

In 1961 Oliver married a New Yorker named Lorna, a woman his ex-wife had introduced him to at a party. They led rather separate lives, Oliver preferring his home in Amarillo above all others, and Lorna remaining in the New York mansion, attracted by the nightlife and social scene. At some point in 1990, when Oliver was about seventy years old, Lorna adopted an infant boy, unbeknownst to her husband at first, and named him

Oliver Bivins Jr. The Bivinses also enjoyed a luxury apartment in London and an upscale condo in Palm Beach, Florida. As 2010 ended and 2011 began, the well-traveled Oliver and Lorna agreed to meet in Palm Beach for a vacation. All these years later, it is impossible to say for certain how this wealthy couple was targeted for guardianship. During a phone call with *Palm Beach Post*, investigative reporter John Pacenti, who covered the Bivins story as it unfolded, "They were corralled by a spotter, as I recall."[28] The term "spotter," interchangeable with the word "troll" in guardianship circles, is used to describe someone who scouts out and identifies potential wards of the court for a fee that is paid by lawyers, guardians, elder care companies, and other for-profit entities connected to the guardianship system.

In an article published in August 2017, Pacenti referred to an unidentified "social worker who became concerned," about the Bivins couple, but no more details were offered.[29] What is known for certain is the name of the person who filed the petitions for emergency temporary guardianship of both Oliver and Lorna Bivins. Court documents show that the petitioner was Sonja Kobrin and her business address was listed as V.I.P. Care Management in Lantana, Florida.[30] According to her LinkedIn, Kobrin is a "senior citizen counselor" and the president of her company, which she started with her husband in 1993. Another online source advertises Kobrin's firm as offering a wide array of services. "We arrange, coordinate supervise services provided by other professionals such as Attorneys, Physicians, Financial Planners, Home Health Care Services and Movers. Through Our Real Estate Company, South Florida Real Estate Connection We Offer Real Estate Sales and Rental, Property Management As Well As Estate Liquidation And Property Clean Out / Staging The Property For Sale." Note that this guardianship firm operates several other businesses that can also benefit financially from their court appointment to guardianship cases.[31] Just how Kobrin became the official petitioner in the Bivins case, how long she stayed involved, or what she might have charged for her services could not be ascertained. But almost immediately after the petitions were filed, Lorna and Oliver were declared wards of the court. At that point in time, the estate of Oliver Wilson Bivins was conservatively estimated to be worth "multiple tens of millions," according to a family attorney.

Oliver's son, Julian, was living in Arizona when the petition was presented. "When I first heard about a temporary guardian, I thought it was a good thing since Dad was getting up there in age," Julian said during a

FaceTime interview from his current home in the South of France. But Julian said it didn't take long for him to change his opinion. He had been regularly communicating with the temporary guardian and soon heard about ominous developments. "[The temporary guardian] warned me, he said, 'Julian, you need to hire an attorney here. You won't believe what they are saying about you. And they want to undo your father's will.'" According to Oliver's up-to-date last will and testament, Julian was the sole heir to his father's fortune and was listed as executor of Oliver's estate. Julian, an independently wealthy man in his own right, did hire a Florida law firm, and the fight to protect his father, and defend himself against claims that he was trying to steal his dad's estate, was on.

It was an uphill battle. The original petition filed with the court made all sorts of erroneous allegations against Julian, including the charge that he had "financially exploited" the couple and that he had "with the help of an attorney, apparently dissolved Lorna and Oliver's fifty-one-year marriage and transferred all of Oliver's assets to himself without their permission." The petition goes on to claim that the couple was "devastated to learn they were divorced," and that because Julian had diverted all their money, their phones, their cable TV, and their electric bills had gone unpaid, as had their Florida-based caregivers.

Julian told a completely different story during interviews for this book. He said his father discovered that Lorna, who he described as a calculating and materialistic woman, had been surreptitiously fiddling with their assets over the years, secretly commingling holdings via a joint trust and adding both her name and Oliver Jr.'s name to certain holdings. When Oliver Sr. discovered this, according to Julian, he was angry and sought legal advice. He was told the best way to unravel the mess was to divorce his wife, reclaim his marital holdings, and execute a whole new will. The divorce was finalized, on July 28, 2010, and it was a mechanism for the elder Bivins to dissolve the joint trust and recapture all his holdings, including the family's Texas-based oil and gas leases. Oliver Sr. then transferred to Julian several parcels of real property, the oil and mineral rights in Amarillo, and as well as his Amarillo condominium. Julian insisted he'd had absolutely nothing to do with the divorce proceeding.

"Lorna wasn't happy with this," Julian said, "but they continued to live the same kind of lifestyle. They visited back and forth and vacationed together, and they probably would have gotten married again," he said. Julian denied all the ugly assertions made in the petition. It should be noted that the Palm Beach County judge overseeing the case never sought to explore the validity of the criminal claims made about Julian before immediately granting the temporary emergency guardianship.

Sadly, about six weeks into the guardianship, Lorna died of a heart attack. Oliver Jr., twenty-one, was appointed to handle his mother's substantial estate, and he was her sole beneficiary. Oliver Sr. just wanted to return to his beloved Amarillo, but his court-appointed minder wouldn't allow it, and neither would the court. Controversial probate court judge Martin Colin had signed an order prohibiting Oliver Sr. from leaving the state of Florida.[32] Julian quickly realized he had two fights on his hands: defending himself against false charges of estate grabbing, and trying to free his father from the grip of guardianship so he could get him back home to Texas. Julian said he also quickly came to see his primary adversary was young Oliver, with whom he had no relationship. Oliver Jr.'s lawyers were clearly trying to corral not only Lorna's far-flung holdings but to grab control of half of Oliver Sr.'s estate as well. "They tried to convince everyone that I was trying to steal everything, when in fact they were doing that," Julian said.

The sheer size of Oliver Bivins's estate made it a most attractive target. It was a sure bet that opposing lawyers would fight to keep Oliver Sr., and therefore his money, under Florida control. That definitive step occurred on May 10, 2011, when Judge Colin officially declared Oliver to be incapacitated and his temporary guardianship was made permanent. Bivins was allowed to continue to live in his condo on South Ocean Boulevard, and a group of home healthcare aides were on hand to watch him 24/7, not because he needed medical attention, according to Julian, but because the lawyers didn't want Oliver to leave the state. The first guardian stepped aside, and on the recommendation of Oliver Jr.'s legal team, he was replaced with a man named Curtis Rogers. Julian said his first meeting with his dad's new guardian was not pleasant. "The greeting I got from Rogers was, 'You are restricted to one mile of the condo [with your dad]. Your visits will be supervised by nurses at all times. If you try to take him out of town or to the airport, I will have you arrested.'"

Julian says he and his legal team were sure it would only take a short while to dismiss the guardianship and free Oliver. But that was not the case. The divorce had left a confusing tangle of property ownership, and the opposition lawyers took their time trying to straighten it all out. Judge Colin allowed their slow-walk tactics and seemed to entertain their every request. After all, the guardian maintained, these lawyers were Oliver Sr.'s first line of defense against his conniving oldest son, Julian. "The other side dragged things out and dragged things out," Julian said. "Every roadblock they could put up, they did. We really thought we'd get him out fairly quickly, but they kept going back and back to court to ensure they got more fees." The guardian hired his own attorney. There were additional lawyers hired on in Florida, and then in New York to handle matters relating to the property holdings in Manhattan. And of course, all fees were being paid out of the Bivins's family fortune, fueled by all those oil and gas royalties and a worldwide portfolio of wise investments and expensive real estate holdings.

Julian visited his father's condo frequently, and Julian's son, Jude, moved in with his Grandpa Oliver for nearly two years, but he finally left under the crushing 24/7 surveillance and conflicts with nitpicking nurses. Oliver Sr. fell into a deep depression. "He had a little bag that he traveled with, and he kept that bag at the front door every day, ready to go home to Texas," Julian said. For nearly four years, Oliver Bivins was confined to live a life he did not want. This was not the way he had planned to spend his last years.

Julian's legal team, led by experienced litigator Ron Denman, never gave up the fight to get the state of Florida to loosen its grip on Oliver Bivins Sr. Finally, in February 2015, they won. Julian remembers his father was "on his deathbed" when he was loaded onto a private plane and flown home to Amarillo. Oliver went to live in the Bivins Memorial Nursing Home, a facility his charitable-minded grandmother, Mary Elizabeth, had established in 1949.[33] He died there just a month after his arrival, on March 2, 2015. Oliver Wilson Bivins was ninety-seven years old.

Julian Bivins was determined not to let the personal and financial indignities done to his father go unpunished. On January 8, 2016, he filed a federal lawsuit suit against the two guardians, three law firms, and every lawyer who played a part in forcing his father to stay in Florida.[34] Among the allegations: breach of fiduciary responsibility and professional negligence including "reckless and negligent" behavior, charging of excessive fees and retainers, and failure to look out for the best interests of Oliver Bivins and his estate. Each defendant would rely on the argument that they could not be held liable or guilty of malfeasance because all their actions had been approved by the guardian court, namely Judge Martin Colin.[35] In early August 2017 the jury reached its verdict and awarded Julian an eye-popping $16.4 million. "It's really kind of a landmark case," Julian told the *Palm Beach Post* after court. "It sends a message to the unscrupulous lawyers and guardians that they are not going to be able to get away with it anymore." Several years later, Julian would tell me he knew it was going to be difficult to actually collect on his award. His lawyers warned him the defendants could drag their feet, appeal to a higher court, or even declare bankruptcy. The opposing sides eventually reached an out-of-court settlement. "I'm not allowed to disclose the amount," Julian said. "But when you figure the amount of money I spent on lawyers and all the rest, I don't think it even covered all my legal bills."

During an intercontinental FaceTime call in March 2022, Julian reflected on the most tragic and painful part of the long ordeal: the guardian had filled his father's head with false tales. "He convinced Dad that I was gallivanting around Europe, spending and stealing his money . . . [and that] I didn't care about him. I would visit Dad and try to explain to him what was really going on. He had no dementia, but at that age he was very vulnerable to what they were saying." At one point during our conversation, Julian's voice cracked and it appeared he was fighting back tears. No matter his legal victory, he said, "You can't put a price tag on the torment my father endured the last years of his life, the pain and suffering they put him through. The last four years of his life were pure hell."

FOLKS IN ALABAMA called her the Potato Chip Queen. Joann Bashinsky, widow of Sloan Bashinsky, the founder of Golden Flake Foods, was the richest woman in Mountain Brook, an upscale suburb southeast of Birmingham. She was probably the richest woman in all of Alabama, with an estate worth nearly $220 million dollars. Golden Flake, founded in 1923, didn't just make plain potato chips. They expanded over the years to offer chips with flavors like Sweet Heat, and cheese curls and puffs, snack crackers, fried pork skins, popcorn, and tortilla chips. Golden Flake's most popular spokesmen was Paul "Bear" Bryant, the revered football coach of the University of Alabama's Crimson Tide. Bryant endorsed the chips, along with Coca-Cola, for years, with the slogan, "Great pair says 'the Bear!'" The company became so successful that Utz Quality Foods bought them out in 2016 for a reported $141 million.

Joann and Sloan were married for thirty-seven years before his death in 2005. Joann's only daughter also passed away, leaving her with only one heir, her grandson, Landon Ash, whom she adored. Joann, known around town as Mama B. or Mrs. B., did not live a flashy life. She was a faithful churchgoer. She loved to read books, and play bridge and Scrabble with friends. She collected frogs, and frog-themed doodads were scattered throughout her tidy home. But it was her charity work, at the Big Oak Ranch for Boys and through the Bashinsky Foundation, that gave Joann the most joy. The foundation had been started to help send the children of Golden Flake employees to private schools and colleges. She later expanded her largess to others, and it was estimated that over the years Mrs. B. contributed some $17 million to fund scholarships and provide school supplies. Due to her wealth, and her involvement in so many outside endeavors, Joann employed a lawyer, John McKleroy, to whom she had given power of attorney, and a longtime bookkeeper and finance manager named Patty Townsend. Both had worked for Golden Flake for years, and after the Utz takeover they continued to work for Joann.

Court records show that in late summer 2018 Mrs. B. asked McKleroy and Townsend to execute a transfer of a some of her funds from one financial adviser to another. They did not follow her instructions. On September 26 Joann emailed the adviser herself and asked that the transfer be made. Several days went by, and on October 1 she sent a follow-up email firmly directing the adviser that the transaction should be made immediately. The quick answer from her investment firm left Joann stunned. "It is our understanding that immediately prior to this request that you were diagnosed with dementia. It is our responsibility to ensure that the account and the assets with it continue to be managed in your best interests." Mrs. B. had not been diagnosed with dementia, and she wondered who would have told the investment adviser that. Joann Bashinsky, then eighty-six years old, put two and two together and promptly fired McKleroy and Townsend. But the guardianship wheels were already in motion. On that very day, October 1, 2018, the once-trusted pair of employees filed an emergency petition for temporary guardianship and conservatorship for Joann Fulghum Bashinsky. Jefferson County Probate Court judge Alan King promptly accepted the petition and assigned a guardian ad litem to determine whether a permanent guardianship was necessary. In their petition, McKleroy and Townsend claimed that they had witnessed "a decline in Mrs. Bashinsky's mental faculties in their discussions with Mrs. Bashinsky about financial matters." They also told the court that since 2012 she had loaned over $23 million to her grandson. The petitioners presented themselves as simply worried and protective of Joann and her deteriorating mental state. Judge King held no due process hearing, and Mrs. B. was not allowed to explain her side of the story to the court. Outside court, Joann questioned why it was anyone's business what she did with her money and why anyone would question gifts she gave to her only blood relative. "I love him and I'd do anything for him," she said of her grandson. "I wanted to help him in his businesses. I loaned him whatever he needed because I could afford it." Joann was clear about her final wishes. When she died, Landon would inherit everything she owned. Naturally, this devoted grandmother wanted to see her grandson enjoy at least some of her riches while she waited for the Good Lord to take her home.

During the long, grueling legal fight that followed her conscription, Bashinsky's team would do their homework. Court documents reveal that when lawyer McKleroy prepared an updated version of Joann's last will and testament, a section was inserted that named him and Ms. Townend as coexecutors of the estate. Bashinsky's lawyers also claimed that without Mrs. B.'s knowledge or consent, McKleroy had included language in the new will spelling out how he and Townsend would each be paid almost 4 percent of the entire Bashinsky estate as final compensation, totaling an extra $600,000 apiece.

When the guardian ad litem's report was presented to probate court judge Alan King, it stated that the GAL "did not observe any level of significant confusion by Mrs. Bashinsky, nor did she appear to be out of touch with reality. "[She] did acknowledge that her loans to her grandson were excessive, but she focused on the fact that [he] is her only grandson" and that she wished to help him in his business endeavors.[36] The court appointee also noted that when interviewing Bashinsky, she was "pleasant and cooperative" and answered all his questions "in an appropriate manner." Judge King either ignored or overlooked this positive report, and the court-ordered temporary control of ward Bashinsky continued.

During an interview with a local reporter, Joann spoke of the guardianship imposed upon her and her inability to access any of her money. "It feels like I'm nobody, like all my rights have been taken away. I feel like I'm a prisoner in my own home."[37]

But Mrs. B. was not the type to give up. She instructed her lawyers to take her case all the way to the Alabama Supreme Court.

On July 2, 2020, Alabama's highest court issued a scathing rebuke of Judge King's actions.[38] The justices found that Joann Bashinsky's constitutionally protected due process rights were "egregiously" violated. They made it a point to note that "Ms. Bashinsky was admittedly deprived of proper notice of the hearing and, more egregiously, not given the opportunity at that hearing to present her own explanations for her behavior." The high court ruling also said the petitioners and the probate judge "may all firmly believe that Ms. Bashinsky's generosity to her grandson is financially unwise, and they may be correct in that judgment. But such a concern is not an occasion for invoking the emergency procedures."[39] While the state Supreme Court's decision erased the temporary guardianship, the petition asking for permanent guardianship remained in play.

For the last six months of her life, Joann Bashinsky was free to spend her money—or give it away—if she wanted to. But she lived under the shadow of possibly having to return to court to fight being permanently placed into the guardianship system. On January 3, 2021, at the age of eighty-nine, she died from complications of a heart attack. Her grandson, Landon Ash, issued a heartfelt statement, "Words can't describe my sorrow for my grandmother's passing, though I take comfort in knowing she was one of Alabama's finest women to ever live and that she is now with the rest of her family in heaven." Ash took time to remind the state how much his "Nonny" had contributed to others. "My grandmother was a champion for those in need for decades, and her passing will be felt by countless people whose lives were touched by her kindness and incredible compassion for humanity."[40]

IT IS EASY FOR SOME to pooh-pooh the trials and tribulations of the super wealthy. It's tempting to say, "Well, at least they had the money to fight it." But that is not the underlying point. In the case of a system as life-altering as guardianship, extra care should be taken to ensure that everyone is afforded their constitutionally protected civil rights no matter their social standing. It is about expecting and receiving due process, and not being blindsided by those who wrap themselves in a false cloak of caring. When any citizen turns to the courts for help, it is supposed to be about finding true justice. Even in equity courts, we have the right to expect truth, judicial integrity, and justice.

As the stories in this chapter—and in many other chapters in this book —reveal, that is simply not happening. Judges are often more accommodating to the regulars in their courtrooms than to the citizens who are brought before them in guardianship or conservatorship cases. Those who appear hoping for impartiality are frequently left feeling as though they've been flattened by an out-of-control steamroller. And so do their worried families, who come to realize there is nowhere to turn for help. Some readers might also shrug and think that, well . . . at age 105, like Brooke Astor, or at 97, like Oliver Bivins, these wards had lived a good and long life.

That is also beside the point. It doesn't matter if one is old, middle aged, or young—nearly all of us have a plan in mind for how we want to live the rest of our lives. When an outside force disrupts those plans—even if it is said to be for someone's own good—it feels unjust. And when it happens in a secretive, ramrod fashion, in a court setting that is supposed to be deliberative and focused on the integrity of the process, it feels criminal.

14

Desperate Is as Desperate Does

When a relative finds they are helpless to change the course of events in a loved one's guardianship, profound frustration can cloak their better judgment. Many who are caught on the outside looking in at the system believe if they just keep fighting, they can loosen guardianship's grip. In reality, the continued court battle only depletes their cherished family member's finances and fills the wallets of court appointees who charge fees for every appearance before the judge. The system leaves challengers broken.

Next of kin who refuse to stand down are often portrayed in court as money grubbers, unstable or unworthy to even visit the ward. Merciless guardians and conservators have been known to combine a group of slight transgressions by a relative—from being a few minutes late for a ward's doctor appointment to questioning how the guardianized person's money is being spent—and present it as something sinister. Overworked or uncaring judges frequently accept the opinion of their own appointee over an explanation from an outsider. Faced with a hopeless situation, some family members begin to doubt their own motives, and serious depression and desperation can take hold. And there have been cases where guardians have filed criminal complaints against interfering family or friends. After tempers cool, some of those charges are later dropped, but some family members have been convicted and sentenced to serve time in jail.

Roger Hillygus, fifty-two, a firefighter in the Reno, Nevada, area, hit a breaking point in the fight to care for his guardianized and Alzheimer's-stricken mother. Roger and his sister had long argued about administration of the million-dollar family trust, and how to care for their widowed eighty-year-old mom, Susan. Roger tried mightily to undo both the guardianship and his mother's 2016 placement at the Stone Valley Assisted Living and Memory Care facility in Reno. Roger decided to try to fight the legal system on its turf. Acting as his own attorney, he filed multiple motions and lawsuits against state lawyers and judges alleging financial collusion. He also prepared a federal racketeering and corruption lawsuit that named forty defendants. So frequent were his legal filings that his mother's case file swelled to multiple thousands of pages.[1] All of Roger's legal attempts failed. One family court judge called the mounting number of motions filed by this anxious son "frivolous, repetitive and not based in fact." Roger was ultimately labeled a "vexatious litigant," and his mental health was questioned.

At some point in 2016, the assigned guardian petitioned the court to sell Susan Hillygus's house, presumably to help pay her expenses at the memory care facility. The judge granted the request. According to court documents, Roger refused to leave the home, and the visiting guardian who had come to inventory Susan's belongings felt so threatened she filed a temporary restraining order against her ward's son.

The situation continued to simmer, and so did Roger's determination. The sale of the Hillygus home was stalled until August 9, 2019. On that day, a hearing was held to approve the final transaction but, curiously, Roger was not present. The day before, on August 8, 2019, Roger and a friend, retired Nevada sheriff Stewart Handte, walked into the Stone Valley facility and presented the staff with what looked like an official court document. It proclaimed that a "unanimous jury verdict" had been reached and that "the State has not met the standard of Clear and Convincing evidence that the Son is dangerous or abusive to his parents such that the State is compelled to intervene in this Family. This verdict is effective immediately."[2] To a legally unschooled healthcare provider, this notarized document must have appeared to be genuine, and its conclusion that "all orders contrary to the Trust Documents are void and unenforceable" seemed like an official court finding. The paperwork also declared that since "Roger Hillygus is the sole Successor Trustee of the Hillygus Family Trust," his wishes should be honored. Actually, the documents presented to the facility that day had been generated by a firm called We the People Court Services based in Arizona. The papers were meaningless, and the company had no legal authority in Nevada or any other state. The ploy worked. Roger and former sheriff Handte walked out of the facility with Susan Hillygus within minutes of presenting the worthless documents to the staff. Roger, placing his mother in the car seat beside him, likely felt victorious at that moment. Soon, the state of Nevada would call this a kidnapping and issue arrest warrants.

At two in the morning on August 16, 2019, more than a week after Roger removed his mother from the facility, and after an hour-long standoff at an apartment complex in Bellflower, California, a Los Angeles County sheriff's SWAT team moved in and arrested Roger Hillygus. He was charged with second-degree kidnapping and conspiracy to kidnap.[3] His noncommunicative mother appeared to be in good health and was not hurt during the capture of her son. Back in Nevada, Stewart Handte, fifty-nine, had been arrested almost immediately after Susan was taken from the facility. Handte was charged with felony kidnapping, kidnapping of an elderly victim, and providing false information to the facility's staff. Later those charges would be reduced to a sole count of "conspiracy."[4]

Both Hillygus and Handte were released on bail while awaiting trial. The judge presiding over Handte's case ordered him to be fitted with an ankle monitor, but the former sheriff refused. He was jailed for nearly ninety days.[5] Roger Hillygus stopped communicating with his lawyers; he failed to appear at a court hearing in late April 2022, and there were reports that he may have fled the United States. At the beginning of October 2022, agents with the US Marshals service located and arrested Hillygus in Kansas City, Missouri, and he was extradited back to Nevada.[6] As of early 2023 both Hillygus and former sheriff Handte were awaiting trial on charges of removing Mrs. Hillygus from assisted living.

Susan Hillygus died on October 16, 2019, two months after her "adventure" to California where she, briefly, hid out at her brother's Bellflower apartment with the son who desperately didn't want her to live in a nursing home.

YOU MIGHT SAY CARL DEBRODIE was also kidnapped—both in life and in death. The desperation in his case came not just from the intellectually disabled Carl, but also from his court-approved caretakers who took reckless and even criminal steps to cover up their crimes against him.

The Missouri-born Carl came into the world on November 18, 1985, with multiple disabilities, born to a mother the court would declare was "severely intellectually, psychologically, socially, and occupationally impaired." She was found to be so unfit that a judge revoked her parental rights. Carl was diagnosed with autism at an early age and was unable to read, write, or speak. But as he grew, so did his cheerful disposition. By all accounts Carl loved being outside, fishing, and baseball. He became fascinated by go-karts and the fire trucks he encountered at the local fire station. He hugged just about everyone he met, and he loved eating coleslaw.

Mary Martin still remembers the first time she saw Carl. She was driving a school bus for the Jefferson City School District when she spotted the ten-year-old with his broken arm in a sling and a huge smile on his face. Mary would later become Carl's "Big Sister" in the Big Brothers Big Sisters program. She and her husband came to adore Carl, and he was readily accepted into their bustling family home. In September 1999, when Carl was thirteen, a Cole County Circuit Court appointed Mary Martin to be Carl's legal guardian, and he moved in with the kindhearted Martins full time.[7] Mary was quoted as saying, "We had a blast, he just loved us. We loved him. It was a family, just like anybody else's. He was our child." The Martins made sure Carl continued to have contact with his mother and various other family members. But Carl ate, played, slept, lived, and was truly loved at the Martin's home.

In 2003, after Carl reached legal adulthood at eighteen, he was adjudged to be an incapacitated and disabled adult and was designated as a ward of the court.[8] He was given a court-appointed guardian ad litem and a co-guardian. Carl remained with the Martins until he turned twenty-one, and then he moved to the Brady Independent Living Community in Fulton, Missouri. It was an attempt to have Carl learn how to live on his own. For a while he seemed to be doing well, and he got a job at a nonprofit organization that employed adults with disabilities. The Kingdom Project was (and still is) part of the Callaway County, Missouri, effort to train special-needs individuals in various jobs such as lawn care, commercial janitorial and laundry services, and industrial sorting and packaging. The situation lasted less than a year.

It is unknown why Carl decided to move back in with his troubled mother. Perhaps it was that most human need for motherly love and attention. A report from his GAL concluded that his mother's home was an unhealthy place for Carl. During one of her visits there, the GAL reported she found Carl chain-smoking and "just pacing and pacing and pacing" around the house. Yet Carl stayed with his mother for several years, his disabilities worsening. Mary Martin must have sensed how bad the situation was, and in 2009 she again petitioned the court to be named as Carl's legal guardian. While the proceeding lingered, Carl moved out of his mother's house and into another group home called Second Chance. It was a new opportunity for him to try to learn independent-living skills. In 2010 the court officially rejected Mary's guardianship petition.

In 2011, when Carl was twenty-five, the determined Martins filed papers for an adult adoption of Carl. The GAL prepared another report informing the judge that the Martin home was "very chaotic" with too many family members coming and going. She recommended against the adoption and concluded that the Second Home facility was a better fit because Carl had quit smoking there and had learned to "feed cows." She described finding "tremendous positive change" in Carl since he moved to Second Chance.

However, another court appointee, one who took pains to visit the Martin home and spend time with Carl and the couple as they interacted, reported that the young man seemed at ease with them. She observed that Carl had access to the entire house, got his own drinks, let the dogs out, and visited comfortably with various family members. Carl was also warmly greeted by neighbors and friends who dropped by. She noted that Carl hugged Mr. Martin and indicated he wanted to stay in the home. This appointee recommended that the judge approve the adoption request. In the end, the judge rejected the Martins' application. Leaving Carl in the care of the Second Chance organization would turn out to be a deadly decision.

Mary would later tell a local newspaper, "He was at my house for Christmas one year and he had bruised ears, bruised body, a bruised eye, and that wasn't the end of his bruises." Martin said she took photos of Carl's injuries and promptly phoned a local hotline to report suspected abuse at Second Chance. "After my hotline call, and me taking this to the guardianship, I wasn't allowed to talk to [Carl] on the phone," Martin said. Operators at the Second Chance facility "would hang up on me or they wouldn't answer," she said. When confronted with the photos of Carl's bruises, his GAL dismissed them, saying they probably happened after Carl was "bumping into things outdoors." When Carl lived with the Martins, he was able to go to the toilet independently. But Mary noticed that after living at the Second Chance facility, Carl had started wearing adult diapers. He appeared to be heavily medicated and "sad and lonely and lost," according to Mary. Because of his speech limitations, the Martins couldn't simply ask Carl what was happening at the group home, but they feared the worst.

The Second Chance facility in Fulton, Missouri, the group home where Carl spent his longest period of time, was run by Sherry Paulo and her husband, Anthony Flores. "Sadistic" doesn't adequately describe this couple. At some point Carl's weight dropped alarmingly, and a doctor prescribed meal supplements to help him return to a heathy weight. Sherry Paulo was listed as Carl's home care manager, and as such she was responsible for his medical care. That included monitoring his medications, scheduling and providing transportation to and from his doctor's appointments, and making sure Carl ingested the newly prescribed supplements to regain weight. By all accounts, she completely failed as a caregiver. As court papers revealed, Paulo had fabricated doctor's notes about Carl's medical care long after she had stopped taking him to see any of his physicians. Husband Flores, who also worked at Second Chance, noted that Carl's weight, health, and mobility continued to decline. When Carl did get out of bed, Flores observed, he moved very slowly.

According to prosecutors, this heartless couple ignored Carl's deteriorating health and began taking him home with them, effectively kidnapping him, and forcing this ward of the court to perform manual labor. After his unpaid work around their house was done, Carl was relegated to the unfinished, windowless basement, where he slept on the concrete floor with no access to running water or fresh air. They not only used this young man for their own personal benefit, but they also forced him to physically fight with another Second Chance housemate for their amusement. It was during one of these fights that Carl sustained serious injuries, including six broken ribs. A federal lawsuit filed by Carl's family alleged that Flores found Carl screaming and having a seizure in the basement one evening, presumably after one of his forced fights. No emergency medical care was summoned. Instead of calling for help, the couple asked the housemate to carry Carl upstairs and put him in a bathtub with the shower running in hopes it would stop the seizure. It must have been a terribly painful way to die.

Carl's exact date of death is not known because Paulo and Flores never reported it. Law enforcement concluded that Carl died in the bathtub and his body lay there for two or three days. The couple then stuffed Carl's body into a large trash can, filled it with concrete, and took it to a remote storage unit. They had already made sure Carl's contact with the outside world was nonexistent, so there was no one left to notice over the ensuing months that he had disappeared. It was easy, then, for the couple to continue to submit invoices for Carl's care to Medicaid, and the checks kept arriving. Paulo fraudulently collected federal funds of more than $106,000 for services never rendered. Rudy Viet, a local attorney who represented Carl's mother, said during an interview that for at least six months the young man went unaccounted for.

On April 17, 2017, a new company was set to take ownership of the Second Chance facility. On the day of the final transaction to close the sale, Paulo and Flores suddenly contacted authorities to report that Carl had gone missing that morning at about seven thirty. The couple apparently took the action because the new owners of the home would surely notice that one of the residents wasn't there. A widespread weeklong search was launched for the lost, disabled man, which was, of course, unsuccessful. It wasn't until police interviewed Carl's housemate that they learned about the large trash can, the cement, and the storage unit. On April 24, 2017, Carl's badly decomposed remains were discovered. It was determined that he had been dead for months, perhaps having died as early as September 2016. Carl DeBrodie lived to be thirty-one, victimized first by an unstable mother, then neglected and abused by the very system that took him away from her and was supposed to protect him.

The judge, several state agencies and their employees, as well as the numerous court appointees who were paid to make sure Carl was safe shared responsibility for Carl's care. Carl DeBrodie's safety net didn't just have holes in it; it was nonexistent. Or as attorney Viet said during a telephone interview in the summer of 2022, "It broke down in just about every way it could have broken down."

A Callaway County case manager should have been visiting Carl monthly, but that didn't happen. Her records claiming that she had seen the ward every thirty days were discovered to have been falsified. The state had a contract with a registered nurse who was supposed to conduct face-to-face visits with Carl every month. She didn't. She pleaded guilty to federal healthcare fraud and lying to investigators. Most shocking, it was discovered that this licensed nurse had signed seven months' worth of false medical reports claiming she had examined Carl—after he was already dead. Adding to those who failed Carl was the Missouri Department of Mental Health. That agency should have been auditing Second Chance's operations, as the facility reapplied for licensing every two years. That procedure requires the state to evaluate a facility's care plans and monthly notes for each resident. Carl lived at Second Chance for several years, so how did state auditors miss his dire situation? (It was only after Carl was reported missing that DMH moved to terminate all contracts with Second Chance.) The only people who unconditionally cared about Carl during his lifetime were Mary Martin and her husband. But the courts had effectively shut them out of his life by denying their attempts to become Carl's guardians or adoptive parents.

It turns out this particular guardian nightmare was a family affair. Paulo and Flores were assisted in their cruelties by their daughter, Mary Flores, and son, Anthony R.K. Flores, both of whom worked at Second Chance. Mary admitted having a mostly no-show, salaried job at the facility, and to taking another Second Chance resident to one of Carl's doctor's appointments to get a prescription in the deceased man's name. In addition, Mary confessed to lying to investigators about Carl's whereabouts and helping her mother place Carl's body into the trash can, which was then loaded into a crate and filled with concrete. Their son, Anthony R.K., revealed that he then helped his parents transport the crate to the storage unit. Anthony R.K. also admitted to obstructing the investigation. Every member of this family pleaded guilty to federal criminal charges associated with the death of Carl Brodie. One other Second Chance caretaker, who was charged with a state misdemeanor offense, also admitted guilt.

Sherry Paulo, described by federal prosecutors as the "matriarch" and "the most culpable person" was sentenced to seventeen and a half years in prison. She owes the federal government $106,795 for the illegal moneys she collected from Medicaid using Carl's name. Anthony Flores was sentenced to serve fifteen and a half years. Their adult children got off far easier with either probation or only a few months behind bars. In July 2019 attorney Rudy Viet filed a federal wrongful death lawsuit on behalf of Carl's mother and another relative. It was reportedly settled by the state of Missouri for more than $1 million.

THOSE WHO DARE to try to interfere with court-ordered control of a ward, insisting that they know what their loved one truly wants in life, are almost always confronted with the same response: only the court-appointed guardian or conservator can make decisions for the ward because they are there to "protect" them. Often there is no compassionate consideration given to any life plans a ward might have made. They are simply considered no longer capable of expressing their own wishes or of giving permission to be taken away. Any disruption to this arrangement is automatically considered to be criminal in nature. It is ironic that a family cannot count on law enforcement to help them fight a disputed guardianship because it is considered to be a civil matter. But police can be used to arrest a family member defying a court order because that is seen as a criminal offense. There is no empathy clause in the law for an adult son who frantically tries to do what he believes is best for his mother after the courts closed all legal avenues to him, as in the case of Roger Hillygus. There is no compassion in the law to help those who have been trapped in an egregiously flawed guardianship and subjected to abuse, as was the fate of Carl DeBrodie. His tragic death was needless, senseless, and criminal.

The loving Mary Martin and her husband tried every available avenue to try to extricate Carl and were rebuffed, perhaps because if they had been given responsibility for the young man, no state and federal money would have been available to split among the court appointees. This leads some reformers to suggest that if the profit motive of guardianship could somehow be eliminated—or at least reduced—those with greedy intentions would go elsewhere, and wards would be less apt to fall victim to exploitation.

15

The Sad Stories of Theresa and Susan

Spending a career in the service of your country should count for something more than just a paycheck and a pension. Members of the military, for example, receive all sorts of lifetime perks—from free medical care and home loan guarantees to educational opportunities and special job training. They also enjoy the respect and special recognition of their peers and the nation. While many federal employees never have to face physical danger on the job, the decision to devote their life's work to the operational security and safety of the nation—often at an hourly rate below the private sector—should afford them a level of special admiration from the rest of us. Yet when it comes to fighting off an unwanted guardianship, dedicated federal workers (or retirees) should not expect any particular intervention from Uncle Sam.

Theresa Jankowski spent her entire career working for the Federal Bureau of Investigation. Her sister, who was fifteen years older, worked for the Detroit office of the FBI as a Polish translator during World War II, and when seventeen-year-old Theresa was fresh out of high school, her sibling helped her secure an entry-level job at the bureau. The sisters craved an escape from Detroit's harsh winters, and so they decamped for the warmth of California, both transferring to the FBI's Los Angeles office. There, Theresa, a woman raised in a strict patriarchal Polish family, worked diligently over the years to climb the ladder. She never married, and at the end of her career, Theresa was a top staff supervisor and a well-loved member of the FBI community. She owned her own home and lived life as an independent woman long before that was fashionable. Theresa was known for her sharp analytical intellect, ready smile, the gift of conversation, and an almost flirty, wisecracking wit. Theresa Jankowski hardly ever met a person she didn't like, and everyone liked her. But nothing in her life experience would prepare her for what would happen beginning in August 2016, when she was eighty-two years old.

After Theresa retired, she sold the home she had shared with her late sister and decided to move to a senior independent-living facility called Brookdale in Monrovia, California. Being the strategic and organized thinker that she was, Theresa had planned ahead. She had a longtime Wells Fargo financial adviser named Kevin Mahserejian, who at the time was a vice president within Wells Fargo's Wealth Management division. He and Theresa got along famously, and he had even invited her to his home where she was introduced to his family. Their cordial relationship changed, according to a close friend of Theresa's, the day the retiree informed Mahserejian that she wanted to draw up a new will and leave all her money to two dog charities.

"Theresa told me he literally yelled at her, and it was the first time he had ever raised his voice," Sharon Holmes said during one of several phone interviews from her home in California. Theresa tried to explain to Mahserejian that she had no living family and her deep love of animals drove her decision, but he allegedly berated her for wanting to leave her estate "to the dogs?!" Theresa later told her good friend Sharon that shortly after that contentious meeting, she was presented with several documents to sign. "Theresa said Kevin didn't give her time to read the papers. He said he was in a hurry, and he held his hand over the top of the papers and kept saying, 'Just sign here, and here, and here . . .'" Holmes recalled. Mahserejian had been Theresa's financial guru for a long time, and apparently she had no reason not to trust him at that point. Mahserejian did not respond to multiple written requests for comment.

Court documents reveal that the papers Theresa signed on August 23, 2016, designated a stranger named Jodi Montgomery,[1] "a private professional fiduciary, as successor trustee" to the Jankowski estate, which was estimated to be more than $600,000.[2] The documents also gave Montgomery powers of attorney for both the financial and health care of Theresa Jankowski. Theresa had no way of knowing that Montgomery, along with her then husband, ran a professional fiduciary firm called Pais Montgomery, which specialized in creating conservatorships and handling trusts and probate estates.[3] If Theresa checked the company's website, she would have learned that Montgomery's top billing listed her as a "National Certified Guardian."[4]

How did Montgomery, a familiar face in Los Angeles courtrooms, suddenly come into Theresa's life? Court documents answer that question. Motions filed in the Los Angeles County court that hears conservatorship cases read in part, "Montgomery was introduced to Jankowski by Kevin Mahserejian, Jankowski's longtime financial advisor." It is unknown whether it was standard operating procedure within Wells Fargo for someone of Mahserejian's standing to orchestrate a meeting between a well-to-do client and someone with a history of filing conservatorship petitions. Financial advisers consulted for this book said such action would be "highly suspect." As of August 2016, and despite the fact that the two women were strangers, Jodi Montgomery suddenly had the legal authority to control all of Theresa's money and her healthcare decisions.

It is important to understand that during this time, Wells Fargo Bank was publicly embroiled in multiple financial scandals.[5] It was reported that bank staff had created millions of new savings, checking, and credit card accounts for customers without their knowledge, all in an effort to satisfy strict sales goals imposed by upper management.[6] It was a blow to the reputation of the once-esteemed organization's brand and would ultimately result in Wells Fargo paying federal regulatory fines of more than $185 million.[7] Other controversies erupted, including the revelation that the bank overcharged military veterans to refinance their mortgages. That discovery resulted in the institution paying a federal fine of $108 million.[8] Perhaps the most internally serious scandal to engulf the organization centered on the Los Angeles office of Wells Fargo's Wealth Management division. A top manager from that office, a man named Christopher Lewis, turned whistleblower and had gone to federal investigators with specific "bank fraud" complaints against several Wells Fargo Wealth Management advisers.[9] The same month Theresa's wealth management adviser had her sign papers relinquishing control of her life, Lewis filed a wrongful termination suit against Wells Fargo. Eight months later, federal officials ordered Wells Fargo to pay a whistleblower award to Lewis of $5.4 million. The bank foolishly fought the award, and according to *FinancialPlanning.com*, Wells Fargo wound up paying Lewis an out-of-court settlement believed to be close to $10 million. In March 2018 Wells Fargo told the Securities and Exchange Commission it had ordered up an independent investigation of its renamed Wealth and Investment Management division, with an eye toward "whether there have been inappropriate referrals or recommendations" made by advisers. Four months later, the bank refunded $114 million to customers of that division who had been overcharged.[10] The bottom line: there was a rogue element within Wells Fargo's California offices where Kevin Mahserejian operated and where Theresa Jankowski had signed away her freedom. It is important to note that no official complaints of wrongdoing against Mahserejian could be found.

Theresa Jankowski would tell several people—including Sharon Holmes, her attorney, Albert Rasch, and a friend and neighbor at Brookdale Senior Living named Daisy—that at their first meeting, Montgomery explained she was there to help Theresa pay her bills on time. Theresa was left with the surprising impression that Montgomery believed she had been derelict or late in paying what she owed, specifically her monthly apartment rental at Brookdale. "Nothing was further from the truth," Sharon Holmes said during one of many phone interviews. "I went through boxes of Theresa's financial records and, in fact, she always, always paid Brookdale early."

Sharon Holmes has been in the business of serving the needs of seniors as an eldercare consultant for sixteen years. She first met Theresa Jankowski in April 2017, eight months after Theresa signed those documents at the Wells Fargo office. Theresa had confided to Daisy that she was having trouble accessing her money and admitted she didn't know what to do. Daisy called a friend who knew Sharon and brought them together. Sharon was advised that the woman she was about to meet was suffering from dementia or Alzheimer's. "I went to a three-hour lunch with Daisy and Theresa," Sharon said. "I found Theresa to be alert, charming, and she had a great sense of humor. She was able to carry on detailed conversations, remember topics mentioned earlier, and did not present like someone with dementia." Having worked with dementia and Alzheimer's patients, Sharon had come to know the telltale signs of diminished capacity, and she insisted Theresa was mentally alert and totally aware of what was happening around her.

"I fell in love with Theresa," Holmes said, "I took care of her like I would have taken care of my own mother." In May 2017 estate attorney Albert Rasch first met Jankowski and took an immediate interest in her case. At the lunch, and in multiple conversations later, Theresa told Sharon and Albert that in addition to the restrictions on accessing her money, her mail delivery had mysteriously stopped, and the staff at Brookdale was suddenly making life uncomfortable for her—following her, trying to monitor and restrict her movements. Theresa said she desperately wanted to move away from Brookdale. For expressing these feelings, she would be labeled "delusional and paranoid" by her new fiduciary, Jodi Montgomery.

"She wasn't being paranoid about not having control of her money and mail," Sharon said, "She absolutely did not have control of her money and her mail! I saw it firsthand." Holmes related a story about arriving to take Theresa out to lunch one day and a Brookdale staffer running after them into the car park, yelling at them to stop and threatening to call the police if Sharon removed Theresa from the property. "Now, understand, this is a woman who had an independent-living arrangement with Brookdale," Sharon explained. Theresa's independent-living status at Brookdale was much like someone staying a hotel. Employees at a hotel would never have the right to restrict a guest's movements in and out of the building. "I've been in the business of helping seniors a long time," Sharon said. "They had no right to tell her when she could and could not go." Sharon said the Brookdale staff reported her to Adult Protective Services more than once, claiming she was exerting undue influence over the older woman and trying to "kidnap" Theresa. Attorney Rasch confirmed those Brookdale staffers' actions. After that, Monrovia police detective Gerald DeHart became involved in his capacity as an elder crimes investigator. He took a personal interest in Theresa Jankowski's fate and warned the administrators at Brookdale that their staff was out of bounds. Detective DeHart, along with Sharon Holmes, and lawyer Rasch would become Theresa's fiercest advocates. And as is common in so many conservatorship and guardianship arrangements, they were demonized in court for their loyalty. In contested cases there always has to be a "good" versus an "evil" side.

Court documents provide a summary of the events that followed.

In February 2017, Jodi Montgomery reported to the court that she had "met with the Health and Wellness Director at Brookdale to discuss staff members' concerns about Jankowski's confusion, paranoia and refusal to follow doctor's orders." There was no explanation how Montgomery was acquainted with this staff person, nor was there a reason given why the staff would be monitoring an independent-living guest's interaction with a doctor. No doctor's name was provided.

On May 18, 2017, Jodi Montgomery told the court that an employee at another senior facility—the Meridian at Anaheim Hills some forty miles away—was "concerned that Sharon Holmes is pushing [Jankowski] to move to Orange County." While Theresa had expressed interest in moving to the Meridian, in part because it would cost her $2,000 less per month for a similar apartment, there is no explanation why this decision should be viewed as so concerning, or how an unnamed Meridian employee would know to contact Montgomery to discuss Theresa's intentions. These developments led Team Theresa—Holmes and Rasch in particular—to believe that Montgomery might have had some sort of preexisting arrangement with staffers at the two senior living facilities to pass her information. They wondered why Montgomery appeared to be so adamantly against Theresa moving away from Brookdale.[11]

With Albert Rasch on the scene, and perhaps fearing a hostile takeover of her client by another lawyer, Jodi Montgomery hired clinical psychiatrist Dr. Allan P. Hess to conduct a mental evaluation of Theresa, apparently with an eye toward applying for full conservatorship. On June 8, 2017, Hess reported that after observing Jankowski over five sessions he concluded that Theresa was "delusional, suffers from dementia and needs a trustee to look after her affairs." It would soon be learned that Hess had a dark past. A 1988 Statement of Fact filed with the court concluded Hess had "sexually molested three minor plaintiffs contemporaneous with the psychological treatment of them. This molestation occurred both at Dr. Hess's office . . . and elsewhere. The molestation of these children went on for approximately two years before it was discovered by the mothers of the children."[12] Dr. Hess had his license suspended for a period of time, but he was later allowed to resume his clinical psychology practice—treating only adult patients. His evaluation of Theresa was rarely mentioned in court after his past troubles surfaced.

Attorneys Rasch and Montgomery agreed upon an unknown-to-them geriatric psychologist, Dr. Stephanie Moore, to conduct a neuropsychological assessment of Theresa. In early 2022, during a telephone interview from her home in southern California, Dr. Moore remembered that she had been approached by Montgomery before ever meeting or evaluating Theresa and was told that "she is a paranoid, delusional, elderly woman. So, I found it could be plausible." Moore conducted an evaluation of Theresa, and in her initial report to the court on June 21, 2017, Dr. Moore concluded that Theresa lacked capacity. But Dr. Moore told me that a short time later she was serendipitously introduced to Sharon Holmes at a random social event. She chose not to elaborate on details of their conversation except to say it had to do with Theresa Jankowski. "I got new insight, new information," Dr. Moore said, and she came to realize that "Jodi Montgomery lied to me. Theresa was right. She wasn't being paranoid. She truly hated Brookdale and she felt like a prisoner there." Just three weeks later, on July 15, 2017, Dr. Moore delivered an updated report on Theresa's competency. It concluded that while the eighty-two-year-old had "mild cognitive impairment . . . her verbal reasoning was in the superior range of function. Her only deficits are in memory and slowed processing speed. She has the capacity to give informed consent to any form of medical treatment. *She does not need to be conserved*" (emphasis added). Dr. Moore also found no delusional thinking and reported Theresa's short- and long-term memory was just fine, as was her ability to reason using abstract concepts. Asked whether she now believes Montgomery had been trying to influence her evaluation by offering the upfront opinion that Theresa suffered from mental deficiencies, Dr. Moore said, "Without a doubt. She had the POA, she had total control over Theresa."

Five days later, on July 20, 2017, and despite the latest neurological report of Theresa's competency, Jodi Montgomery and her attorney, Lauriann Wright, filed a petition for conservatorship of Theresa Jankowski in Los Angeles Superior Court. Montgomery assertedly proclaimed, "Proposed Conservatee is diagnosed with senile dementia with paranoid delusions. As a result of her current condition, Proposed Conservatee is highly subject to undue influence." Montgomery claimed, under penalty of perjury, that Theresa "lack[ed] the capacity to give informed consent for medical treatment" and "is unable to properly provide for her personal needs for physical health, food, clothing, or shelter."[13] A box on the petition form was checked asking the court to give Montgomery permission "to authorize the administration of medications appropriate for the care and treatment of dementia." Judge Mary Thornton House did not approve the petition and expressly did not approve Montgomery's follow-up request for a temporary conservatorship.

On July 24, 2017, Theresa's lawyer filed documents revoking the durable power of attorney and trustee appointment given to Jodi Montgomery — effectively terminating Montgomery's role in the case. Attorney Rasch wrote that Theresa wanted a new professional fiduciary named Elaine Watrous to handle her finances. He pointed out that no court had found Theresa Jankowski to be incapacitated and, therefore, her request should immediately be honored. Like any other citizen, Theresa had every right to name who she wanted to represent her and decide where she wanted to live. Rasch would later offer an amendment in which Theresa named him as trustee of her estate upon her passing, but he made it clear in that filing that he was not, and never would be, a beneficiary to the Jankowski estate.

On July 30, 2017, Theresa got her wish and moved to the independent-living section at the Meridian at Anaheim Hills. She was assisted by her friend Sharon Holmes, Albert Rasch, and Elaine Watrous. Detective DeHart made sure that aggressive Brookdale personnel were made to step aside to allow the movers in to transport Theresa's property. DeHart stayed in touch with Theresa and would later write to the court, "I have spoken to Theresa Jankowski since the move and she states she could not be happier." By all accounts, Theresa quickly acclimated to her new home, made new friends, and eagerly engaged in outings and events. Meridian's administrator offered a sworn statement that Jankowski showed no signs of needing a conservatorship.

On August 2, 2017, with the petition still pending and no legal determination made as to Theresa's competency, there was another court hearing. Controversial judge David Cowan was now in charge of the case.

Even though there was no conservatorship in place, Cowan dipped into the Probate Volunteer Panel (PVP), a pool of California lawyers who agree to represent the interests of potential conservatees, and appointed a man named Robert Risley.[14] Risley appeared to be in his eighties, about the same age as Theresa. His demeanor in court has been described by those who have watched him as "appearing befuddled and confused." Cowan showed a marked favoritism toward Risley, and the judge repeated for the record the Montgomery/Risley allegation that Holmes, Rasch, and Watrous had conspired to move Theresa from Brookdale, "despite an opinion of Dr. Shephane [sic] Moore that Jankowski should not be moved . . . and that Jankowski lacked capacity." Judge Cowan had obviously overlooked or ignored Dr. Moore's updated report declaring exactly the opposite. When Dr. Moore traveled north to Los Angeles to testify as to exactly why she changed her opinion, and to reiterate that Theresa Jankowski did not need to be conserved, she was joined by Detective DeHart. He was also on hand to testify on behalf of Theresa. However, Judge Cowan refused to allow either of them to take the stand. "I was stymied," Dr. Moore said. "I couldn't believe a judge wouldn't listen to the expert witnesses. It blew me away." Jodi Montgomery's attorney consistently painted Team Theresa in a conspiratorial light, negatively focusing on Dr. Moore's "contradictory reports" and blaming Holmes, Rasch, and Watrous for all sorts of questionable actions and for exerting "undue influence" over Theresa. As for the move from Brookdale to the Meridian, Judge Cowan inserted into the record that "under the pre-existing medical directive, all medical decisions . . . should have been made by Montgomery." With that pronouncement, Cowan made it clear he had chosen to ignore Theresa's updated power of attorney directive removing Montgomery.

Judge Cowan issued a show cause order as to why he shouldn't "disqualify" Theresa's lawyers after they filed papers in early June 2018, asking for PVP lawyer Robert Risley to be dismissed for failing to adequately represent Theresa Jankowski. Their request was denied. On September 10, 2017, they also filed a motion for Judge Cowan to recuse himself. The team of Albert Rasch and Brook Changala argued that Cowan's behavior in the case had a "chilling effect" on their ability to represent Theresa. They cited public speeches the judge had delivered, in which Cowan consistently referred to PVP lawyers, like Risley, as "the eyes and ears of the court," as if they worked for him and not the prospective ward.[15] A PVP lawyer should be no such thing, they argued, and they took great exception to Risley's pronouncement to the court that he believed Theresa should be conserved. They argued that such a stance was unethical, and that Risley's real duty was to zealously advocate for his client's wishes and not to act in what he might interpret to be "the best interests" of his client.[16] Judge Cowan denied the motion, and Rasch and Changala realized the deck was stacked against them in that courtroom. By then, Theresa had moved to the Meridian facility in Orange County, so they filed a Hail Mary motion to transfer her case to that county's probate court. On November 3, 2017, an unyielding Judge Cowan denied that request as well.

Judge Cowan's next step was to appoint Dr. David Trader, whom he called "a well-regarded geriatric psychiatrist commonly used by the Probate Bar in Los Angeles," to examine Theresa to access her mental capacity and susceptibility to undue influence. In other words, Trader was a familiar face around conservatorship courtrooms and was well known to the judge. Attorney Rasch revealed that invoices showed Trader charged $600 an hour and "that included his drive time." In addition, the court-appointed Mr. Risley submitted phone records that showed he had called Dr. Trader after the doctor's second and final evaluation session with Theresa—and before the doctor's report was filed—six separate times. Those calls were an indication, Rasch said, that there was some sort of collusion. "It goes to impeach both of them," he said. "Ex parte conversations are not allowed."

On April 17, 2018, Dr. Trader filed a twenty-three-page report saying Theresa met the criteria for major neurocognitive disorder/dementia and had serious medical problems that rendered her dependent on others for her care. Theresa Jankowski, the report read in part, "lacks sufficient capacity to provide properly for her personal needs for physical health, food, clothing, and shelter," and is "substantially unable to manage her own financial resources and resist fraud or undue influence." He recommended the court appoint a conservator. During an interview for this book, attorney Rasch explained that by the time Dr. Trader entered the picture, Theresa had suffered through a fall, a hematoma, a broken back, and two heart attacks, "due in part to the stress of the court action. So, of course, she had to depend on others to help her for a while." She had also been in hospital isolation for several weeks due to a C-Difficile infection of the large intestine. Rasch maintained his client was evaluated by Dr. Trader while under the effects of medication, at a particularly vulnerable time, and that she was never incapacitated. The doctor treating Theresa after her heart attack agreed, according to a sworn statement Rasch filed with the court. "Dr. Patel concurred, saying she was of sound mind and perfectly capable of making good decisions. In fact, every one [of] Ms. Jankowski's treating physicians has opined that she has capacity to make her own decisions," Rasch wrote. In a carefully crafted objection to Judge Cowan's insistence on continuing the case, attorney Brook Changala wrote, "The proponents of Jankowski's autonomy are significant: two disability rights advocates, two attorneys with impeccable records, a clinical neuropsychologist, a senior care advisor, a private professional fiduciary, a police detective, and every treating physician Jankowski has ever had. In fact, the people that say she does not need to be conserved outnumber those that say she does. Certainly, her supporters cannot all be dead wrong and/or acting in bad faith."

The courtroom machinations went on and on. Theresa Jankowski was not under conservatorship, yet the legal system had her in a chokehold as if she was already conscripted. Every maneuver her attorneys tried on her behalf was stonewalled either by Judge Cowan or by the court insider Jodi Montgomery, who refused to acknowledge that she was not wanted. This was not a grade school game of "first dibs" on a playground mate. This was a battle over a dedicated public servant's right to live out her life the way she had so carefully planned.

Ultimately, the judge took the unusual step of officially disqualifying and removing Rasch and Changala from the case. It is an example of the unorthodox tactics that can occur in an equity court proceeding. If lawyers for a proposed ward fight too diligently, a judge can simply fire them. The action was reminiscent of what happened to Britney Spears after she hired attorney Adam Streisand to try to prevent her conservatorship from being established. The judge in that case summarily dismissed him, and Spears was immediately conserved.

As one legal practitioner who has experience in both Los Angeles and Orange County conservatorship courts said, "Everyone who deals with this will tell you the L.A. probate court is a black hole. It's just terrible. First of all, in Orange County every [potential ward] can hire their own attorney. And if they can't afford one, then and only then the court steps in." This California-based lawyer defined Los Angeles Probate Court's operational creed this way: "It's based on a business model, not a caring model."

As swiftly as Jodi Montgomery entered Theresa's life, she was suddenly gone. Toward the end of 2018, Montgomery informed Judge Cowan that she wanted to be recused, and he granted the request. Perhaps she became tired of the unexpected fight, maybe she came to see that her involvement was truly not in the best interests of Theresa Jankowski, or maybe Montgomery had found a more lucrative conservatorship client to concentrate upon. Her next client was superstar Britney Spears. Research for this book uncovered court documents in which Montgomery stated she was assigned as "case manager" for the pop star in August 2018.[17] This would seem to indicate that Montgomery was active in both the Jankowski and Spears cases simultaneously. Documents were uncovered listing Montgomery's charges to Spears's estate during the fall of 2018 totaling multiple thousands of dollars, certainly more than she was making trying to conserve Theresa Jankowski. As it happened, Montgomery was elevated to the role of Britney's co-conservator in September 2019, replacing the star's controversial father, Jamie Spears.

The Jankowski court case did not go away when Montgomery did. And Judge Cowan reluctantly accepted the resignation of Robert Risley as well. He appointed a new fiduciary named Alexandra Matejic, and another PVP lawyer, Lawrence Lebowski. Court watchers reported a sudden new attitude in the courtroom, one with a decidedly conciliatory tone. As one observer noted, it was as if Judge Cowan wanted to move this case toward settlement and away from any possible involvement of the appellate court. Finally, after a two-year nightmare, Theresa won the right to live her life without the threat of conservatorship. She got to choose where she would live, who she could visit with, and who would help her manage her money. The conclusion gave Theresa everything she had been asking for since the very beginning of her battle, and it made her supporters wonder why Judge Cowan had let the case drag on for so long, robbing the elderly woman of her peace of mind in the final years of her life. After the settlement, Theresa and Sharon Holmes spent considerable time together shopping, going to lunches and church, and spending quality time together.

Holmes said she has always believed there was a specific preplanned plot to conserve Theresa Jankowski that was hatched, at least in part, in the offices of Wells Fargo. As Sharon rightly points out, it was Theresa's longtime wealth management adviser, Kevin Mahserejian, who first introduced the elderly woman to fiduciary Jodi Montgomery. It was Mahserejian who got Theresa's signature on the POA papers. Holmes said she suspects Mahserejian and Montgomery already had some sort of cooperative side-relationship, but that could not be ascertained. Sharon also wonders whether other vulnerable and wealthy Wells Fargo clients were exposed to similar introductions. Her theory cannot be corroborated or debunked since both Mahserejian and Montgomery declined to respond to repeated requests to be interviewed for this book. And, certainly, there is no law against introducing one person to another. But it is clear that both the financial adviser and the fiduciary knew that Theresa had no living relatives who might complain if outsiders stepped in to take control of her life. And with Theresa's unusual pronouncement that she wanted to leave her considerable estate to animal charities, well . . . Sharon thinks the pair figured it wouldn't be hard to convince the court that Theresa was not of sound mind. After all, who leaves all their money to dogs? Further, it is Sharon's belief that with the myriad of scandalous headlines swirling around Wells Fargo back in late 2016 and 2017, time was of the essence to try to get Theresa officially declared incapacitated so she could not be called as a witness should federal prosecutors come knocking at her door.

These suspicions led Sharon Holmes to research which FBI office was investigating the Wealth Management division of Wells Fargo. Sharon revealed during one of several phone interviews that she found the FBI special agent in charge of the probe in the San Francisco office, and she poured out details of Theresa's involvement with Wells Fargo and how it had led to her winding up in conservatorship court. The agent seemed attentive, asked good questions, and at the end of the conversation Sharon finally said, "I'm glad you are interested, because Theresa is one of yours." After the agent learned that Jankowski had worked for the FBI her entire professional life, he said something to the effect of, "You should have led with that information!" Sharon was buoyed by the idea that someone high up the judicial food chain appeared interested in helping her friend. According to Sharon, the agent asked her to continue to report in about what was happening with the court case, and she regularly complied. "I felt I was in a third-world country when I was in court and saw the lying and conniving," she said. "I was ashamed of my country. That was not justice." However, in the end, the FBI did not become actively involved. There was no federal case brought against anyone in the Wells Fargo Wealth Management division in connection with Jankowski's situation. The bureau did not intervene in the case of their longtime employee in any way.

In the early morning of October 18, 2021, Sharon was on her way to her regular visit with Theresa when she got the call that her dear friend had died. "I got to spend time talking to her alone until [the coroner] got there," Sharon said. "I told her that the fight for justice was not over, we would fight so other seniors would not have to go through years of being scared that their freedoms would be taken away." The selfless character traits that steered Theresa to dedicate her life to the FBI and public service remained with her until the end, according to Sharon. "Theresa always said it would all be worth it if what she went through helped others."

SUSAN TERRANOVA loved her job in Washington, DC, but she always clung to the dream that when she retired, she would return to her native Massachusetts, buy a beach house, and spend the rest of her life surrounded by her loving extended family and friends. Susan has always been especially close to her namesake niece, Suzanne Terranova Whelan, and she was the maid of honor at Suzanne's wedding in September 1991. Susan doted on Suzanne's boys and she cherished the idea of spending more time with them. The relationship between the two women was always more like sisters than aunt and niece. When they are together, the family refers to them as Suzy and little Suzy, a nod to the sixteen-year age difference.

When Susan went off to university, and then to New England School of Law, the Suzys stayed in constant touch. Immediately after graduating from law school in 1976, Susan took a job in Washington as a lawyer in the US Customs and Border Protection Department. When that was absorbed into the newly formed Department of Homeland Security (DHS) in 2002, Susan remained. She would travel the world, including trips across Europe, Macedonia, and Greece. Her entire career—nearly thirty-four years—was spent in service to the security of her country.

"My aunt Susan is so sweet, highly intelligent . . . a big reader who seldom watched television unless it was Masterpiece Theater sometimes," Suzanne said during a series of interviews for this book. "She was always smiling, very athletic . . . and frugal, but generous with money [gifts] to her family. Everyone loved Susan, she didn't have a mean bone in her body." But Suzanne said her aunt was also someone who "guarded herself, and she didn't trust men." Specifically, Susan did not get along with her brother, Joe; they had ceased to have any meaningful communication years earlier.

During frequent get togethers, Susan and Suzanne would swim, hike, or go ice skating in the winter. While Susan had bought herself a lovely three-bedroom, three-bathroom red brick home on a cul-de-sac in Arlington, Virginia, she was frequently up and out of the house, either to travel the fifteen minutes to her office or to engage in her passion for swimming, Zumba classes, or some other sort of physical activity. Susan Terranova always seemed to be a woman on the go!

Susan retired from the DHS in 2012. Since she was unmarried with no children, she had been able to save a considerable amount of money—more than $2 million according to 2017 bank records obtained for this book. In addition, Suzanne said her aunt's home had been appraised by the town at nearly $759,000, and court documents show Susan collected an estimated $86,000 a year from a government pension and about $12,000 per year from IRA distributions. Taken together, those incoming funds were more than enough to cover monthly expenses. The idea that Susan could buy a beach house on Cape Cod or some other Massachusetts seaside town was more than a pipe dream; it was exactly what the retired government worker had carefully planned for. Susan, still vibrant in her early sixties, had enough money to make it a reality. But for some reason, Susan hesitated to make the move north after her retirement. Maybe she was simply enjoying her free time, or perhaps she found it hard to leave her friends and the life she had built in Virginia. Suzanne said, "She was trying to figure out what to do next. Her house had some mold in the basement and she knew she needed to do something. But then she didn't take the initiative to do anything about it." Suzanne said her aunt was so sharp that she had to have noticed her own declining mental state. But Susan was always an intensely private person, and she may have found it difficult to seek medical attention for fear the diagnosis would not be good news. "Denial. I think Susan was in denial," Suzanne said during one of our many conversations.

In the late summer of 2016, Susan's sister, Mary, tried calling her but discovered the phone in Arlington, Virginia, had been disconnected. Later it would be determined that Susan had forgotten to pay the phone bill and her service had been terminated, but at this point in time, Mary apparently already sensed there was something wrong with her sister. When she couldn't reach Susan, Mary called police and Adult Protective Services in Virginia and asked that they conduct a welfare check. Mary lives in California, and she sent concerned emails to her twin brother, Joe, in Alabama.[18] On August 1 Mary wrote to Joe, "I just got off the phone with Adult Protective Services. A social working [sic] will be going to Sues' [sic] house tomorrow, she will call me so I can ease Suzy into accepting help. She said we need to either have an elder law attorney be legal conservative [sic] or have Power of Attorney of a family member." The next day, Mary wrote again to Joe, "The woman from APS just called me. Suzy is not answering the door and her car is not in the driveway or garage. She will try back in a couple of hours. I'm worried." Niece Suzanne, who lives in Connecticut, believes Susan was simply out and about as usual, and to this day she remains piqued that her aunt Mary would "call in the law," as she put it. "I would have driven down there to check on her in a heartbeat, it's only less than five hours from my house to Aunt Susan's. But no . . . Mary had already called Adult Protective Services on her," she said. Sister Mary's phone call to authorities was the spark that lit the guardianship fire that ultimately stripped Susan Terranova of her freedoms.

Suzanne is also still angry that her aunt and uncle didn't notify her of their concerns about Susan's well-being until it was too late for her to do anything about it. She would remain in the dark until Aunt Mary wrote her on August 6, 2016. "I need to up-date you on some things about Aunt Suzy. I had to have her admitted to a hospital. Uncle Joey is there and will take her to a facility in Alabame [sic]. She has Dementia/acute. I didn't want to tell u until after your BD. Very hard stuff."

Susan was hospitalized for a week and evaluated at Virginia Hospital Center in Arlington, Virginia. By all accounts, the diagnosis was dementia. As any professional will attest, dementia is not a specific disease. It's a catchall term that describes a group of symptoms like memory loss, problems communicating, and personality changes that can become worse as the person ages.[19] And about 20 percent of dementia patients never go on to develop Alzheimer's—which is a specific disease. Yet according to Dementia.org, "Dementia is a real health condition that can, in some cases, be stopped or even reversed. Early intervention is more likely to result in better response to treatment."[20] Not so with Alzheimer's.

Sister Mary described Theresa's diagnosis as "acute" dementia. But there is no way to know for sure just how far Susan's particular condition had advanced at that point. On August 9, 2017, believed to be the same day she was released from the Virginia hospital, Joe Terranova took his sister to a local attorney where she signed a power of attorney and an advanced healthcare directive giving her brother control of her life. If Susan's condition was, in fact, acute dementia, those documents might easily be declared null and void, but no one challenged them in court. Susan quickly found herself on the way to Alabama, a state in which she knew no one except for Joe and his wife. Once there, she was not taken to her brother's home; rather, she was immediately institutionalized in the Elmcroft of Halcyon assisted-living facility in Montgomery, Alabama. Within days, Mary wrote on what she called her "Time Line of Susan Terranova," a copy of which was obtained for this book, that she had spoken to her sister and Susan was pleading for help, expressing regret about her choice of POA. "[Susan] says she made a mistake about JT . . . was adamant in removing JT from POA, and consistently remains lucid in knowing this is what she wants." Mary also wrote that she and Elaine Harmon, a lifelong friend of Susan's in Massachusetts "try to calm her down" over the phone. By mid-August Mary made a note that her brother "shows disdain for Susan" and he complains about "how his life has been affected by her 'wanting attention and high maintenance.'" On August 18 Mary indicated that Joe had sent an email stating, "If Susan is not happy by 3 weeks, move her and give up POA, [he] cannot put up with her much longer." The very next day, the incarcerated Susan told her sister, Mary, that she wanted to fire Joe as her POA. Mary quoted Susan as saying, "Joey doesn't like me and he talks meanly to me and hurts my thinking. He is also trying to tell me what to do with my will even though I told him it was none of his business." And in phone conversations with Suzanne, Susan repeatedly begged her niece to come rescue her from Elmcroft and take her to Massachusetts. She also complained that she was not being allowed to hire her own attorney, a fundamental civil right in the United States. Most important to note: no court had determined that Susan Terranova was incapacitated, yet this resident of Virginia was being held in Alabama against her will. There was no lawyer conveying her wishes to a court of law.

Joe Terranova sold his sister's home in Arlington for $535,000, well below the assessed value, according to Suzanne, and most of Susan's furniture and belongings went to the Salvation Army. As the story goes, Susan Terranova, a conscientious attorney who urged several relatives to execute a last will and testament and then helped them write one, did not have a will of her own. At least brother Joe told the family he couldn't find a will among Susan's papers. Once Susan was moved to Alabama, he distributed a document that he had titled, "Letter of Agreement on the Susan Terranova's [sic] Financial Assets After Death," a copy of which I have in my research file. That Joe would assume to decide the distribution of his still living sister's wealth did not sit well with Aunt Mary in California. In late

October 2016 she engaged a lawyer in Montgomery, Alabama, to write a stern letter to her twin brother. "You cannot effectuate an estate plan for Susan by circulating an agreement among Susan's siblings," wrote attorney April D. Wise. "Notwithstanding that, this agreement is contrary to the expressed desires of Susan, this agreement is not an effective estate planning tool and will not control the disposition of Susan's assets at her death. We understand that you have repeatedly requested that Susan sign certain estate planning documents this past month and Susan has refused." Absent any court proceeding on the matter, Susan clearly retained the right to determine her own advanced directives.

"As stated in our Petition, we further understand that you, against the advice of financial professionals, have improperly used your power of attorney to assume joint ownership of Susan's financial accounts by adding your name as a joint owner to these accounts," lawyer Wise's letter to Joe Terranova continued. "We demand that the ownership of these financial accounts be restored to Susan's individual ownership." Joe was also requested to provide a detailed accounting of all financial transactions he had initiated. Copies of multiple checks written by Joe Terranova on his sister's accounts were made available for this book. Some of the checks he wrote to himself were for a few thousand dollars. One was in the amount of $30,000. Lawyer Wise also informed Joe in that letter that she was filing a petition with the court to appoint someone else to be in charge of Susan—one Mr. J. Ed Parish Jr., the Montgomery County guardian and conservator. That replacement request was ultimately approved by the court. But Suzanne said the swap of Joe Terranova for Parish was like exchanging one nightmare for another. Life did not get better for Aunt Susan.

Those who work within the guardianship and conservatorship field frequently speak out to dispel the notion that court appointees are the only bad actors in the system. And they are right. A large percentage of the financial problems vulnerable citizens face originate within their own families. An adult child may siphon off money from their elderly parent's account, or a parent might illegally dip into their child's conservator-protected medical malpractice award. There is a significant body of evidence that shows many financial frauds are perpetrated by close relatives or family friends and not a for-profit court appointee. However, the difference in how they are treated when their crimes are discovered is stark. A friend or family member can be prosecuted much more easily than those persons appointed by a judge. Professional guardians and conservators enjoy a significant blanket of protection from the court.

Suzanne wrote to her aunt Mary on November 4, 2016, to report a disturbing phone call she'd had with a very determined Susan. "I saw Aunt Susan six weeks ago, and the conversation I just had with her is the same person I saw and spoke to six weeks ago. She is not in advanced dementia and she knows it." Suzy and little Suzy had spent considerable time on the telephone talking about Joe's controlling tactics as he still held the power of attorney authority. Suzanne reported more about her conversation with her distraught aunt Susan to her aunt Mary. "She said to me, 'Does he have my money?' I said, 'Yes, he does.' She said, 'He cannot have my money, it's mine and I earned it not him. All he cares about is my money and not me.' I said, 'What do you want? She said she wants to come to Massachusetts to the place Elaine found, and she wants Elaine and I [sic] to take care of her." Suzanne added that during their conversation, Susan had asked her niece at least two dozen times, "Please, come get me out of here," and they made plans for Suzanne to travel to Alabama to rescue her. After all, there was no court order keeping Susan there, only the stern orders from brother Joe. From the very beginning of her Alabama odyssey, Susan Terranova was consistent in her desires. She wanted to eliminate her brother's involvement, and she wanted to live her life in Massachusetts. She, like any other American, should have been free to enjoy all her constitutional rights.

The two Suzys had no way of knowing then that their phone calls were being recorded and were apparently monitored by both Joe and guardian Parish. Court documents show that others also heard parts of the calls, including staff at Elmcroft and the court representative who wrote about listening to phone call tapes in his competency report to the judge. These recordings were also immortalized in a letter to the guardian from Susan's best friend, Elaine Harmon. She wrote, "Ed, please step up and discontinue the monitoring and recording of Susan's phone calls. Why was Joe allowed to remove her landline without her consent, and given approval to actually monitor and record all her phone calls? Why was Joe personally allowed to install a $10 phone recording app on Susan's iPhone which gives him access to all of her cell phone calls? Again, this upsets Susan greatly as she feels that her rights are being violated." According to Suzanne, once guardian Parish learned of her plan to fly to Atlanta, rent a car, and drive to Montgomery to liberate Susan, he reported to the judge that he had heard about the plot by listening to a tape recording of their phone call. This cannot be independently verified, as Alabama probate courts do not provide a transcript of such hearings.

Shortly after the two women spoke on the phone about rescuing Susan and taking her to Massachusetts, Ed Parish went before probate judge Steven L. Reed with an emergency petition for guardianship of Susan Terranova. Case number 16-00641 was filed on November 23, 2016. Susan's loved ones believe it was a preemptive move taken by the county guardian before the proposed ward could leave the jurisdiction and take control of her money with her. Attached to the petition was a short letter from a Dr. Larry Epperson, a local Montgomery neurologist, written the day before the hearing. "I write on behalf of Ms. Susan Terranova, who is a 64-year-old female with presumed Alzheimer's disease. Her symptoms began several years ago. She has had a thorough workup in the past, and present. Recent PET scan of the brain revealed advanced Alzheimer's disease. J. Ed Parish should be appointed legal guardian."[21] Judge Reed promptly established the emergency guardianship and appointed Parish without seeing or speaking with Susan or her family. He would make the arrangement permanent soon after.

"Wait just a minute," Suzanne said emphatically during one of our many phone conversations, "Aunt Susan's symptoms did *not* begin several years ago. I don't know where this doctor got that information. She had only been diagnosed in Virginia three months earlier. And the diagnosis was dementia—not Alzheimer's! Suddenly she has full-blown Alzheimer's? I don't buy it." And as Aunt Mary's lawyer wrote in that cautionary letter to Joe, "It is surprising that Susan was competent to sign legal (POA) documents in August of this year [in Virginia] but several months later she is conveniently not competent to meet with her own legal counsel or sign legal documents." Judge Reed's approval of the guardianship effectively stranded Susan in a state in which she was not a resident, in a situation she did not want, and with no control over her own body, living arrangements, or finances.

When Suzanne visited Elmcroft in June 2017, she was able to take her aunt on an outing, and she took the opportunity to sneak Susan into a nearby walk-in health clinic with the goal of getting an independent mental evaluation. During an examination by a Dr. Jesse Austin, Suzanne said the door to the private examination room suddenly swung open. "It was Ed Parish. He just barged right in! I had no idea who he was. But he was demanding that whatever the doctor was writing down be given to him. The doctor looked at him and just said, 'No.'" The Clinical Summary Report the Suzys got that day notes that the patient, Susan Terranova, "Comes in today for a[n] altered mental status" check. The doctor noted that Susan's blood pressure, pulse, breathing, and temperature were all normal. She was listed as taking a drug called Namzaric, which is used to treat moderate to severe confusion. After speaking with Susan for about thirty minutes, the doctor's conclusion was that she was in very good health but had "unspecific dementia without behavioral disturbance." He referred her to a neurological specialist named Dr. Bell. Suzanne remembered telling Dr. Austin that her aunt had been diagnosed with advanced Alzheimer's, and he said he thought that was an "over evaluation," based on the way Susan functioned and her ability to readily answer his questions. Dr. Austin, a Tulane-educated emergency and family medicine doctor with decades of experience, cautioned that Susan should not be left alone for any length of time, nor should she drive. Guardian Parish, who had been alerted to the scene by the sitter who had been waiting in the car, did not get a copy of the doctor's report, although Suzanne said he waited until the doctor had finished typing it up. His last attempt to get a copy failed. "Then," Suzanne said, "He stormed out in a huff."

A short time later, on June 20, 2017, the guardian sent a letter on Parish Law Firm letterhead to the family of Susan Terranova. "Interfering with the care of an Alzheimer's patient is an incredibly serious offense. This type of behavior will no longer be tolerated," he wrote. Parish ended the letter with a threat. "I would like to put you all on official notice that Susan Terranova is not to leave Montgomery County. If she is taken, criminal charges will be pursed." By writing such a letter, Parish continued to advance the potentially false narrative that Susan had Alzheimer's. He did not explain how this resident of Virginia, who wanted nothing more than to go back to her native Massachusetts, was being "protected" by being held in the remote state of Alabama.

Copies of spreadsheets kept by the guardian and in my possession reveal just how guardian Parish was spending Susan's money beginning March 3, 2017, and extending through February 11, 2019. The attorney Joe Terranova had hired to keep his sister in Alabama billed $24,795 to the estate during that time period. The lawyer who Susan's sister Mary engaged invoiced for a little more than $10,420. Guardian Ed Parish charged annual retainers as high as $55,785.46, and during the nearly two-year time span covered by the spreadsheets, checks were written to him in the amount of $109,378.09. The Elmcroft facility cost Susan nearly $5,000 a month, and the company the guardian hired to supply sitters to supervise her were paid upward of $8,000 some months. Most mysterious was the list of "authorized electronic debit card transactions" processed via a Best Buy Visa credit card. There was a steady flow of purchases using that card—totaling more than $7,300—that go unexplained on the spreadsheet. A guardian might authorize a ward to buy a television set, a microwave, or a small piece of furniture for their private room, but the price of those items wouldn't add up to anywhere close to $7,300. Upon further investigation it was learned that the Visa card in question was issued in Susan's name and her signature is seen on the back. She may have used it to buy things for herself—like clothes, undergarments, or an occasional visit to a hair salon—but guardianized wards are not usually allowed to make purchases on their own, and Susan was known as a frugal person. With Elmcroft providing for her daily needs, it seems out of character for Susan to have spent that much on incidentals over the course of twenty-three months. Others in Susan's guardianized sphere likely would have also had access to that account number, but just who might have used the card could not be determined. "So, how do you draw the line?" Suzanne Terranova Whelan asked. "How do we stop those who are using our loved ones as human ATMs? This is estate trafficking. It is human trafficking."

No one involved in this case denies that Susan Terranova was experiencing diminished capacity when her phone bill went unpaid and Virginia APS stepped in. It is what happened next that perplexes and angers those who love Susan the most. How can a state conscript someone who is a legal resident of another state—and then hold them indefinitely? How can someone as intelligent and accomplished as Susan become so ensnared in a system and have absolutely no rights to fight her way out? The answer may lie in something she once said to her favorite niece. "She told me we should just burn all her money," Suzanne said. "Aunt Susan was right when she told me, 'It's all about the money. If I was a pauper I wouldn't be going through this crap.'"

In late summer 2018 a third party who had heard about Susan's plight got the Montgomery County district attorney's office to contact Suzanne in Connecticut. When Suzanne spoke to the DA investigator, she went through the whole long saga of Susan Terranova. She asked whether anything could be done to help her aunt leave the state of Alabama. She wondered whether criminal charges could be pursued against brother Joe for, say, kidnapping his sister or illegally spending her money. Might the guardian be in violation of state law, or could the family somehow have his power over Susan and her money curbed? Did Judge Reed really have the authority to place Susan Terranova into a permanent guardianship?

Research for this book revealed that a confidential grand jury subpoena was issued on August 17, 2018, and it was presented to the custodian of records at the Montgomery Probate Court. It ordered the official "to bring and produce at the time and place aforesaid, to be used as evidence, the following: A certified copy of any and all documents pertaining [to] Susan Terranova . . . from 01/01/2015 to the present date and time." Those records were ordered to be in the Grand Jury room on September 4, 2018. Since this type of proceeding is highly secretive, it is next to impossible for a journalist to discover what the DA might have been looking for. Why did the prosecutor want evidence about Susan dating back to a year and a half before she ever set foot in Alabama? Did they question how Susan's diagnosis could so quickly go from dementia to debilitating Alzheimer's? Were they looking for something in particular that might indicate criminal activity like financial fraud or perjury?

The DA's investigator stayed in touch with Suzanne, and from her home in Connecticut, the devoted niece provided as much information and as many documents as she could. Suzanne said she felt certain that her aunt Susan had an existing will. She was positive that the Alabama-based diagnosis of advanced Alzheimer's was a ruse to keep Susan and her money under the state's control, and she provided a family history to the DA's office, including the fact that her aunt Susan and uncle Joe had a history of estrangement. Suzanne also offered to return to Alabama to testify if need be. She was excited when she got a call from the Montgomery DA's office in October 2018 telling her, in her words, "that they had all the evidence they needed and they were headed to the grand jury." Suzanne was told to stand by to come testify. Her subpoena didn't arrive for a full nine months. She was ordered to appear May 2, 2019.

"It didn't seem real when I got there," Suzanne said when asked to describe what happened. "The prosecutor just asked me basic questions like, 'How old is Susan?' and 'How much was her Virginia home worth?' And that was about it." Suzanne said she had followed the prosecutor's instruction to prepare a short statement to present to the Grand Jurors, but she was never allowed to read it. Frustrated and confused, Suzanne returned home to wait. "A week went by and [the prosecutor] called and she said, 'We decided not to indict—we didn't find any evidence.'" The final sting, according to Suzanne, was when this deputy district attorney curtly told her, "You know, Suzanne, if you think your aunt is competent, get her before the judge, get her declared competent, and get her out of here." And then she hung up.

Suzanne simply refused to give up on her beloved aunt. She continued to regularly FaceTime with her, and she traveled to Alabama to visit in person. "My aunt hated being there every day. She was bored, and the sitters would not let her get the exercise she wanted. The guardian canceled her swim club membership at one point. They did not provide her with the foods she liked . . . they gave her bacon and meat daily even though she does not eat meat." For the first time in her life, Susan became overweight. Her niece estimates Susan gained about sixty pounds. When Suzanne would say goodbye and explain that it was time for her to go back home to her family, Susan would cling to her and they would both cry in anguish. These heart-wrenching moments were later described as Suzanne "upsetting" Susan, and their face-to-face visiting time was drastically restricted by guardian Parish. To travel all that way and be allowed just a thirty-minute visit didn't make much sense. And then the Covid-19 pandemic hit in March 2020. No visitors, period. Susan's Covid isolation extended well into 2022.

As she entered her seventh year of involuntary residence in Alabama, Susan appears to be bedridden much of the time. "I do get to FaceTime with her once a week," Suzanne said in May of 2022. "Mostly she's in bed. She stares at me sometimes, other times she talks a bit." Given her debilitating condition now, perhaps Susan does have advanced Alzheimer's disease. However, it is clear that back in 2016 when her ordeal began, Susan Terranova knew precisely what she wanted and how she wanted to live her life. She has now lost years that could have been spent living close to her loving family in Massachusetts and nearby Connecticut. At this writing, Susan Terranova is seventy-one years old. She remains in an institution in Alabama, and none of the retirement plans she so carefully saved up for and dreamed about have come to pass.

No, it doesn't matter if someone is a celebrity, a multimillionaire, or has dedicated their life in service to the country. Whether they worked for the FBI, the DHS, or some other government agency, they should not expect assistance should an unwanted guardianship overtake them in ways they find impossible to escape. If a person with ill intent and a hidden agenda wants to control someone else's life, the guardianship courts are ready, willing, and able to accept the petitioner's claim that they are really only there to help.

16

Guarding against Guardianship

It is a fact that the imposition of a court-ordered guardianship most often stems from a breakdown of the family. When families are absent from an at-risk relative's life, or if they fail to agree on a workable plan to care for their vulnerable family members, the way is paved for the legal system to step in. This is a bitter pill to swallow for the kin of a protected person who see the injustices of an abusive guardianship and feel compelled to lay blame for the situation on the courts, guardians, conservators, or hired caretakers. As those who operate within the court-appointed sphere are fond of saying, "We wouldn't be involved if the families took care of their own."

As this book has outlined, there are many ways a citizen can suddenly find themselves overcome by a surprise guardianship proceeding. Their name can be passed on to an eager petitioning attorney by any number of outsiders, many of whom receive a finder's fee for referrals. Among those who can get the guardianship ball rolling, unbeknownst to the family, are people who work in hospitals or nursing homes, financial advisers, social workers, real estate agents, business partners, estate planners, bank or credit union personnel, neighbors, or even someone who is owed money from the potential ward. Once again, there are no firm statistics, but the harsh reality is that too often it is a member of a bickering family who instigates the guardianship process.

When adult brothers and sisters disagree on what's best for their aging mom or dad, for example, they create a scenario that encourages one of their family to seek legal advice, usually from an elder law or estate attorney. That can be all it takes. That lawyer might push guardianship as a panacea and suggest that a petition be drawn up to file with the court. After an initial consultation, and after learning the basic facts of the case, the attorney can surreptitiously approach the court alone to ask for a guardianship. This officer of the court may even tell a client that, as a concerned relative, *they* can be named as the guardian when, in fact, conflicted family members are frequently labeled as "dysfunctional," and judges name a stranger to the post. Years of research for this book unearthed a multitude of family members who initiated the guardianship process only to be consumed by guilt over the spiderweb of trouble it caused. Beware. As the American population ages, it is likely the number of family conflicts over elderly parents will increase. The best way to prevent a guardianship is to make sure family members realize what is at stake, namely the freedom and civil rights of their loved one, as well as their own peace of mind.

If there could be only one suggestion offered for how to try to avoid a guardianship, it would be to turn to professional family mediation before involving the courts.[1] It is far less expensive than litigation. If there is any family quarrel over the guardianship, it will often result in lengthy and very costly court hearings that will deplete both the estate and the contesting party's bank account. It is a lose-lose proposition. Mediation with an experienced and neutral person can heal both old and new disputes by facilitating purposeful discussions. As the Massachusetts Council on Family Mediation explains, "Family mediation is transformative: Using family mediation services can result in sound decision-making, reconciliation of divergent views, clearing the air, lessening resentment, greater understanding, improved communication, and transformation of relationships. Family mediation reduces pain."[2]

In his book *Guardianships and the Elderly: The Perfect Crime*, Dr. Sam Sugar devotes many pages to preventing guardianship.[3] He also suggests mediation as a first step to head off possible court action. "Unless you have absolutely no other choice . . . never ask a lawyer to solve family disputes," he writes. "Do not believe that facts and truth always succeed in court."[4] He also suggests that if there is even a hint of an unwanted, unnecessary guardianship, concerned relatives should take immediate action and, among other things, take the following steps.

* "Obtain a notarized, comprehensive Medical Certificate of Capacity for your loved one from a physician, preferably a specialist in

neuroscience." This will act as a baseline of competency should the matter proceed to court.

* Whenever possible "place your loved one's assets in joint tenancy accounts. It is much harder for the court to seize these accounts." However, understand that a guardianized person's accounts may not be touched by a nonguardian. In addition, if a new joint account is established just prior to court action, the judge can declare it null and void.

* Advise loved ones that banks have a duty to report suspicious transactions, especially those of elderly or disabled people. Sugar suggests warning the targeted person "to limit her visits to financial personnel, such as banks, brokerages, or credit unions, to avoid overeager employees" who might report their financial activities in a misguided effort to "protect" them.

* Make a list of "at least six individuals who would be acceptable if the absolute need for guardianship should arise. They need not be family members." This increases the chances that a judge might — just might — pick one of those names to appoint as guardian.

* Sugar also offers this controversial advice — "Because guardianships are often sprung on naïve, unsuspecting families and seniors when they least expect them, should anyone even offhandedly mention the possibility of guardianship . . . *recognize this as an emergency.* Remove your loved one to another state . . . [and] establish residency quickly." He then offers multiple suggestions for how to implement such a move.[5]

A drastic step like immediate relocation may not be necessary if the potential target has prepared the proper advanced directives. Yes, some guardians and conservators have been known to act in ways that contradict a ward's written wishes, and judges have given them permission to do so. But it is still highly advisable for everyone to prepare a last will and testament, and it should include your thoughts on guardianship or conservatorship. For uncomplicated estates, you can find online templates that can be used, and if properly notarized they are legally binding. It is also important to designate someone to be the executor of the estate and another person to have power of attorney. Just be sure that the chosen candidates are willing to perform the necessary tasks should they be called upon. It is always a good idea to name successors, since there is no guarantee that the primary executor or POA choices will still be alive when they are needed. You may want to include a section that specifically forbids a for-profit professional from being appointed under any circumstances. In addition, prepare a final health directive with end-of-life instructions. Should heroic actions be taken to maintain your life in every instance, or is a Do Not Resuscitate order preferred? Is the choice a public funeral and burial or a private cremation? If it is the latter, who should receive the cremains? These are very personal decisions that need to be carefully documented. For more complicated estates, it is highly recommended that these documents be prepared by a trustworthy professional. In the case of wealthy individuals, there may be trusts (aka irrevocable trusts) involved. If you have substantial amounts of money and/or property, forming a group of three or more trustees might be a wise choice. If an abusive guardianship materializes, a knowledgeable panel of trustees can present a united front against a hostile guardian or conservator's attempts to undo the ward's stated desires.

To underscore the fact that no safeguards listed in this chapter are foolproof, take the case of former attorney-trustee Mark Avery. He was one of three trustees appointed to administer the California-based trusts left by Stanley Smith, a multimillionaire who amassed great wealth selling iron ore to Japan after World War II.[6] When he died in 1968, Smith left an estate worth close to half a billion dollars. True to his philanthropic ways, three-quarters of Smith's wealth went to a foundation helping the homeless, veterans, and people with disabilities. That left his widow, May Wong Smith, with some $100 million. When she developed advanced dementia, trustee Avery, then in his fifties, went on an unprecedented spending spree, according to federal prosecutors. Before the other two elderly trustees realized it, and over the course of just six months, Avery drained Mrs. Smith's trust of an astounding $52 million. According to the indictment handed down in Anchorage, Alaska, Avery spent the money on various "pie-in-the-sky" purchases, including two World War II–era fighters, a P-51D Mustang, an F4U-4 Corsair, other antique aircraft, real estate, a personal mortgage payoff, a forty-seven-foot Carver Yacht, and a thirty-seven-foot heavy-duty patrol boat.[7] Mark Avery was found guilty of a massive wire fraud and money laundering scheme that allowed him to quickly siphon off that $52 million. On May 23, 2016, he was sentenced to more than thirteen years in federal prison. Most of us will not have anywhere near this kind of wealth, but it is a cautionary tale that reminds us to be ever vigilant about who should be trusted to handle our money.

As we age, we tend to imagine the way we want the rest of our lives to play out. Travel, new hobbies, home or garden renovations, or moving to a new location. All these hopes and dreams should be openly shared with loved ones so they fully understand your intentions. If you are a parent of warring children, you especially want to make sure all your wishes are crystal clear. It is suggested that a family meeting be convened. Using a cell phone or other camera, record the session. Begin by displaying that day's newspaper to establish the date and declare that you are of sound mind and body. Pass out a copy of your will to each person in attendance, but if the schism in the family is so deep that no one attends, speak directly to the camera. Briefly go through the main points of your estate plan, and explain who will inherit what material goods, investment accounts, and property. Fully describe any trusts that have been established, and be advised that you don't have to reveal any dollar amounts. Designate who you want to take care of you should you need assistance in the future. Do you want to stay in the family home forever, regardless of the cost? Do you have an assisted-living facility in mind? If the idea of a guardian is acceptable, who might you want to fill that position? Before concluding the session, make sure the family understands that anyone who contests any part of the estate plan—or anyone who initiates a contested guardianship against you—will automatically be disinherited. Finally, be sure to make copies of the videotape or digital file, keeping at least one at home and one in a safety-deposit box or other secure location. Stating your well-reasoned intentions, coupled with your preplanned documents, establishes an irrefutable evidentiary record that can be used in court later should the need arise. Any judge confronted with this kind of indisputable evidence of a person's intention would be less likely to allow their wishes to be violated.

But what do you do if someone in your family is suddenly conscripted into an unwanted guardianship, even a temporary one? As soon as possible, have a recorded conversation with your loved one. Even if the targeted person has memory loss, immortalize their condition, because mere forgetfulness does not necessarily mean incapacitation. Ask them about any legal documents they have prepared, prompt them to talk about their dreams for their future, ask them where they see themselves living in two, three, or five years. Discuss who they want to inherit their worldly possessions. If a family disagreement led to the filing of a guardianship petition, spend some time asking about the personalities involved, and urge the ward to be honest about who they feel is trustworthy and who is not. A coherent, recorded conversation with a ward could go a long way toward convincing a judge to not appoint an undesirable relative. If the judge refuses to view the recording or make it part of the court record, don't despair. Local television or newspaper reporters may find it quite compelling should you decide to go to the media with the story. If that is the course taken, understand that for the story to be considered newsworthy, the reporter will also need as much documentation as possible, including court documents, medical records, brief family testimonials, and at least one relative who is willing to go on the record. History has proven that responsible media coverage can change the course of a guardianship or conservatorship case.

As Dr. Sugar writes about the early days of guardianship, "Time is your enemy. Each day that passes reduces the odds of reversing course."[8] Realize that there is a well-oiled machine at play that will throw up costly roadblocks to nearly everything you try. Phone messages left for the guardian may go unanswered, letters written to the judge could be ignored, and contacting police with complaints of being isolated from your relative will likely amount to nothing, since law enforcement only investigate criminal matters. One might try to involve their local district attorney, state attorney general, or the regional office of the FBI. Good luck with that, as each of those agencies has a dismal record of investigating complaints stemming from guardianship and conservatorship cases.

You will probably come to the conclusion that you need a lawyer, and you do. But which kind of legal expert do you choose in this age of specialties? Depending on your loved one's situation, intuition might guide you to a civil rights lawyer or maybe a disability rights attorney. But they are probably not trained in the various intricacies of equity courts. You could spend considerable money as they work hour upon hour struggling to understand the machinations of guardianship. If the ward is a senior citizen with some money, you might think an estate attorney or elder law lawyer is the way to go. Understand that those two groups of counselors have historically provided the most questionable players in the guardianship racket. Your choice of a particular elder law or estate attorney may be a fine, upstanding person who operates in an honorable way, but the very fact that some of their peers are among the worst predators should cause concern. They may agree to take up your fight, but they face the possibility of seeing their livelihood diminish as they are later shunned by their colleagues. In short, locating a knowledgeable attorney who is not already connected to the guardianship cabal will be difficult.

Some of the few civilians who have successfully challenged a guardianship or conservatorship, as Britney Spears did, emerged victorious after hiring a litigator. This type of lawyer is different from, say, a trial attorney who seeks to file multiple motions, develop a case, and then argue it before a judge and jury. That is a lengthy and costly proposition. A litigator's goal is to come up with the best negotiating strategy in difficult situations and choreograph a settlement. In Spears's case, litigator Mathew Rosengart refused to play the typical guardianship games and went right to the human heart of the matter. His client, he told the court, had been held a virtual prisoner by her father and others approved by the court, forced to work while being denied the freedom to make her own decisions. As Rosengart told the court, she had been placed under illegal surveillance, institutionalized, overmedicated at times, and denied her basic civil rights, like the right to choose her own doctor or have a baby. And Britney's attorney hammered home the most obvious point: During her lengthy conservatorship, Britney earned millions of dollars and employed multiple dozens of people, certainly not typical achievements for someone who is incapacitated. Rosengart's strategy worked.

This book is not intended to offer any sort of legal advice. Rather, the observational information offered here is based on years of research. If my loved one was swept up into an unwanted guardianship, I'd be looking to hire the best bulldog litigator in town. Naturally, top legal expertise doesn't come cheap. This is one of the most insidious realities of the system. A worried relative can spend their entire life savings trying to fight what they see as a cruel and abusive guardianship. But the battle only generates more face time with the judge who established the guardianship in the first place, and more fees for the for-profit professionals the judge appointed. One could fight back by hiring extra lawyers to appeal distasteful rulings to a higher court. But history shows these skirmishes can cause bankruptcy for those who challenge the system, and proceedings can last until all the protected person's money is gone. At that point, the ward is put on the public dole and faces placement in a less than satisfactory Medicare-funded assisted-living facility or group home. Fight the system, and you run the risk of leaving your loved one destitute and alone. Continue the battle and you also ensure any inheritance will be diminished. It's quite the conundrum.

These are just some of the reasons why maintaining family harmony and preparing advanced directives are so vitally important. In countless cases, in states across the country, adult siblings and other relatives are paying the emotional price for failing to come to agreement about the best course of action for their vulnerable loved ones. Brothers and sisters don't grow up believing they will be betrayed by their own blood. They don't stop to think that childhood rivalries can fester over the years and result in irreparable family divisions. But it happens all the time. And unfortunately, while the opposing sides lose themselves in the battle, it is the ward of the court who is damaged the most. Here are three illustrative cases.

New York fashion design team David and Frances Rappaport were married for seventy-two years. They had three sons—Michael, Errol, and Richard—and a spectacular penthouse apartment in a landmark building at 200 Central Park South. A few years before David died, the couple asked Errol to leave his publicist job in Los Angeles and return to New York to care for them. Errol, a Vietnam veteran and trained medic who wears fashionable designer eyeglasses and his graying hair in a ponytail, agreed to return. He moved into the sprawling twenty-fifth floor apartment where his parents had lived for more than four decades.

At the pinnacle of their success, the elder Rappaports are said to have amassed a fortune of between $9 and $10 million, thanks to the popularity of David's Italian knitwear line, and the elegant Frances's famous silk blouses (marketed under the name Francesca of Damon) favored by celebrities like Lucille Ball, Princess Aga Khan, and Manhattan fashion icon Iris Apfel. In keeping with their Jewish tradition of trusting the first-born son with the family business, brother Michael was groomed to take control. According to court documents uncovered during my research, after small bequeathments to their grandchildren, it was always the elder Rappaport's plan to split their estate equally between all three brothers. After patriarch David died in 2010, the ever-devoted Errol stayed on to care for his mother with help from two trusted healthcare assistants. He was paid $2,500 a month for his services, a payment that attorneys for brother Michael would criticize as "self-dealing."

Michael Rappaport initiated a guardianship petition in September 2011, which resulted in the court assigning a Park Avenue attorney named R. Demarest Duckworth III as guardian ad litem for Frances Rappaport.[9] Serious disagreements erupted, as Errol raised pointed questions about how brother Michael had handled his parents' finances over the years. Court documents show that in the late 1990s Michael had purchased the elder Rappaports' five-bedroom, five-and-a-half-bathroom lakeside home in New Milford, Connecticut, for $500,000, as part of a tax shelter move. That was $300,000 below the appraised value. In February 2012 the home sold for $2 million, and Errol maintains this older brother kept that money for himself instead of using it to care for their mother.[10]

In addition, court papers show that Michael had possession of some $450,000 in bearer bonds that he claimed were a "gift" from his father and therefore should not be included in the estate. There was also a question about why this oldest son was charging his parents to rent a home he owned in Florida long after they were too old to travel there. Michael asked the estate to reimburse him for $133,680 in unpaid rent. Guardian ad litem Duckworth III's report to the court concluded: "The administration of Decedent's estate brings to mind Marcellus in Shakespeare's play Hamlet stating, 'Something is rotten in the state of Denmark.'"[11] The GAL's conclusion was that there was not enough available money to continue to care for Frances Rappaport in the home she so loved. The apartment, appraised at about $3 million, would have to be sold. Michael Rappaport did not respond to my repeated requests for comment.

Errol fought against relocating their ninety-five-year-old mother, arguing that as her dementia worsened she should live out her life in familiar surroundings and in full view of her beloved Central Park. The apartment was, as the family liked to describe it, "overlooking God's television." During this time, Errol posted poignant videos of his mother on YouTube as they performed the traditional lighting of Saturday evening Shabbat candles and had long conversations during which Frances cried about the possibility of being sent to a nursing home. In one video, Frances is seen sitting at a table overlooking Central Park, with a porcelain mug of tea and a tissue box before her. She asks in a tearful voice, "Errol, would you ever put me in a nursing home?" Off camera her son is heard to say, "Mother, on my life, and on a stack of Jewish bibles, I will never put you in a nursing home." Even after Errol moves in to comfort her, Frances is not consoled. She relates the story of how a good friend's daughter has just sent her to a nursing home. "She put her there, and that's where you go to die," Frances laments. Errol sits next to her, gives her kisses, and says, "Mother, you are never going to a nursing home. Stop crying. You don't have to worry at all." And the old woman simply says, "Thank you." In another video, the pair discusses where several members of their family have gone to live outside of New York. Frances Rappaport holds her son's hand, looks intently into his eyes, and says, "I would be alone without you. Errol, you are wonderful. I love you so much." She refers to him as "my Errol-ah."

Errol alleged that brother Michael, as executor of the estate, stopped paying the monthly co-op fee of $4,500, and in January 2014 the building sued for nonpayment. Errol was served with a notice to vacate the home, and he was forced to leave his mother for the first time in seven years.[12] Soon the penthouse was listed for sale, and the guardian moved Frances Rappaport out of her cherished Manhattan home of forty-six years and into a small apartment miles away in Queens, New York. Errol, then in his early seventies, said he was left homeless after having exhausted his savings battling his older brother. At his age, he said, he had zero job prospects. "I have to take two different buses to get out to Queens just to visit with my mother, and right now I'm couch surfing with various friends." Errol said. He spoke to me in the courthouse hallway during a break in yet another guardianship-related proceeding he was summoned to attend in downtown Manhattan. This proceeding was called to take Errol to task for posting so many revelatory YouTube videos of his mother. On this day, the judge ordered Errol to remove the videos or face serious contempt of court charges. Many of those videos still remain online.

When asked at the time how frequently he is able to see his mother, he said, "I have to call forty-eight hours in advance for approval [of visits] so a paid monitor can be there to supervise, and I can only stay for two hours." After scheduled appointments to see his mother were canceled at the last minute, Errol became so angry and frustrated at his lack of access to her, he took to pacing outside her Queens apartment building with a large sign that read, "I want my mommy!" The guardian would not relent on the ironfisted visitation policy, and that included nixing a celebration Errol wanted to throw for his mother's hundredth birthday. "So, I got a hundred people to do short video messages for her birthday," he said. "That's all the guardian would allow." Frances Rappaport would live another year in near isolation inside that small Queens apartment, far from her familiar view of Central Park. She died in December 2018 at the age of 101. When contacted in December 2022, Errol Rappaport said his mother's case continued to linger in New York's surrogate court, and the remaining $1.4 million estate was still sitting in an escrow account.

FABIAN AND GENEVIEVE BUSH had five children and lived on a fifteen-acre parcel of forested land in Chester County, Pennsylvania. Fabian owned his own mechanical engineering business, handled all the company and personal finances, and over the years he made astute buys of stocks, bonds, and other profitable investments. This determined World War II veteran who had built the family home himself ultimately amassed an estate worth as much as $3 million. While the Bush patriarch had established individual accounts in the names of all his family members, when he suffered a debilitating stroke in February 2004 he had not yet executed a will or named a power of attorney designee. On Valentine's Day that year, the still-hospitalized Fabian and his wife signed wills that provided their adult children with equal shares of the couple's combined estate. They also named their oldest son, Joseph, as their POA and son Michael as the alternate. Fabian Bush died four months later. Genevieve had been almost completely dependent on her husband. She did not drive and had little social contact except for family members and a few close neighbors.

To say that the four surviving Bush children—Joseph, Mary, Michael, and Justin—didn't get along would be an understatement. During one of several phone interviews for this book, Mary accused one brother of attempting "to inappropriately touch" her when they were teens. She said all her brothers had victimized her with relentless childhood bullying, and after their father died, she insisted they were engaged in a money grab that would deprive their mother of her rightful estate. Once in court, the brothers denied any financial impropriety and would testify that Mary had long had irrational anger issues that would explode into acts of physical violence. In the summer of 2005, after Mary allegedly attacked brother Joseph (Mary claimed he started the fight), the brothers enlisted the help of the police to involuntarily commit their sister to an institution. Joseph testified in court that the goal was to get Mary some psychological help and to try to free their mother from the isolation their sister had engineered. Mary was released from the Chester County Hospital after one day.

Mary said her brothers hardly ever came to visit their mother and the burden of being the sole caretaker fell to her. Brothers Joseph and Michael testified that their sister had changed the locks on the family home on multiple occasions and installed surveillance cameras to keep them away from Genevieve. They also claimed that in 2006 and 2007 their sister had pressured their widowed mother into changing both the will and the POA to designate Mary as the controlling designee and sole beneficiary of the estate. Court records show that on March 11, 2008, Genevieve "sold" the fifteen-acre homestead to Mary for just ten dollars. Mrs. Bush then gave Mary $50,000 for renovations on the house that she had put in her daughter's name.

During a conversation in March 2022, Mary told me that after her father's death and during the ensuing years of turbulent family relationships, her still-grieving mother began seeing a psychiatrist. According to Mary,

Genevieve Bush then divulged her deepest secret: she had been a victim of sexual abuse that began when she was just four years old. Mary said her mother disclosed that she had been repeatedly raped by her own father, and he had ultimately been sentenced to prison for sex offenses. There is no way to independently confirm this account, and no mention of this sexual abuse was found in the court record reviewed for this book. "She was diagnosed with avoidance personality disorder," Mary said of her mother. "It's when life is too much and you shut down. The psychiatrist said that was what formed her way of dealing with life." Genevieve's habit of falling silent during times of stress, along with her deteriorating mental state, may account for her inability to put her foot down and referee her adult children's many grievances. Mary said once she learned of her mother's tortured past, it caused her to become an extra-protective daughter.

Mary maintains her brothers came up with a plan to guardianize Genevieve as a means to punish her and to solidify their control of the Bush estate. Brother Joseph testified that he and his siblings decided on an emergency guardianship in a last-ditch attempt to win visitation with their mother and to protect her from Mary's repeated threats to "commit suicide" if Genevieve didn't do what Mary wanted. This was an especially hurtful threat, according to the court record, because Jeff Bush, the youngest Bush brother, had taken his own life years earlier, and their mother had never gotten over that trauma.

When the emergency guardianship petition was filed in orphan's court on October 30, 2009, judge Katherine Platt did not immediately grant it. Instead, she ordered mental examinations of Genevieve Bush and scheduled a plenary guardianship hearing. After being evaluated by two doctors specializing in forensic and clinical psychology and personnel from a private for-profit guardianship service called IKOR, all participants agreed that Genevieve Bush suffered from aphasia and that significant memory loss caused her to be permanently incapacitated.[13] The incapacitation determination in 2011 was reached without the judge ever seeing or speaking to Mrs. Bush.[14] Judge Platt ultimately decided that the best thing for Mrs. Bush was to find a way to keep her children close to her. She appointed Joseph to be the guardian of the estate's finances, and Mary and Michael were tapped to be co-guardians of the person, meaning they would share the duties of taking care of their mother's daily personal needs. This arrangement would turn out to be a recipe for disaster. Mary and Michael had battled since childhood and were simply unable to set aside their simmering disputes long enough to come up with a unified way to minister to their mother. Adding to the tension was Judge Platt's review of Mrs. Bush's medical records, which indicated that she had suffered serious cognitive difficulties as far back as 2004. Because of that, the judge set Genevieve's date of incapacitation years earlier and thus voided the 2006 and 2007 legal documents Mrs. Bush signed that had given Mary her powerful sole beneficiary status.

After the co-guardianship was established, the steady stream of complaints to the court from both Mary and Michael seemed never-ending. They had been ordered not to be in their mother's home at the same time, but they sniped about the way each conducted themselves around their mother. There were squabbles over food, medicines, housekeeping, and the confrontational way Mary treated the home healthcare aides, including one documented incident in which an aide's arm was slammed in a door, resulting in a workers' compensation claim. It all came to a boiling point during a court hearing on May 6, 2013. Judge Platt declared, "Mary cannot continue as guardian of the person. As long as Mary is guardian of the person there will be war. . . . Mary is irrational, totally irrational about her brothers. Mary was not able to alter her behavior because she's stuck in the rut of the 10-year-old, 12-year-old, 13-year-old Mary Bush who believes she's [still] bullied by her brothers."[15] Mary was removed from her court-appointed position and ordered to move out of her mother's house. An outside professional, attorney Elizabeth Srinivasan, was named as co-guardian with Michael. Mary was still allowed to visit with her mother, and the brother and sister adopted a strained care routine. Michael was with their mother in the evenings, Mary would visit during the day, and there was always a home care aide on duty with them.

Then a particularly shocking allegation against Michael surfaced and was the subject of multiple court hearings. Mary accused her brother of sexually assaulting their mother by digitally penetrating her to apply an unnecessary vaginal cream. The charge was substantiated on September 17, 2013, when a disturbing email written by home healthcare aide Robin Raymond was sent to both co-guardian Srinivasan and Genevieve's court-appointed lawyer. The aide related an "uncomfortable situation" that occurred when Michael was helping her shower his mother that morning. Raymond reported watching Michael glove himself, apply cream to his fingers and, "He went from behind and inserted his finger inside of Genevieve's vagina. This was extremely uncomfortable to me. He shouldn't be sticking anything up inside of his mom," she wrote. A week earlier, a similar scenario had been observed between Michael and his mother, according to the sworn testimony of another caretaker. In both instances, the prescription cream involved was Estrace vaginal medication, and court transcripts revealed that Michael had previously been told not to use it on his elderly mother for fear it could cause cancer. During a hearing on January 9, 2014, Michael denied being warned not to use the cream, and when asked what he was thinking when he administered the medication the way he had, he cryptically testified, "I did it with the hopes that Mary would wake up the next day and be rational, and that didn't happen."[16] The notion that her mother may have once again been the victim of sexual abuse caused Mary to become hypervigilant about her mother's safety when in the care of her brother Michael. And it became clear that this brother/sister feud had festered to the point of seriously damaging their mother's well-being. "I think he went inside mom to get to me," Mary said to me on the telephone. "He wanted to show me he could do anything he wanted. He would not have been able to access mother if it weren't for guardianship."

On May 11, 2015, Mary noticed a deep bruise just above her mother's public bone. It looked as though Genevieve had been punched, and Mary took a photo, which she provided as research for this book. The emails this worried daughter sent out to the appropriate court appointees resulted in no action, according to Mary, even though she had attached photographs showing the bruise had spread over time, prompting fears that internal damage had been done. Finally, a frustrated Mary phoned the Pennsylvania Department of Aging, and on May 18 officials appeared to examine Genevieve. It was a fateful call. The eighty-four-year-old widow was removed from her home and taken directly to an elder care facility. That was the last time Genevieve would live in the house her devoted husband had built for her so many decades earlier. It was an arrangement that pleased the brothers, who had been urging such a move—especially Joseph, who said he had worried about the mounting home care costs and the drain on his mother's estate.

By August 2015 the situation surrounding Genevieve Bush had become so fraught that Judge Platt agreed to approve attorney Srinivasan's request to withdraw as co-guardian because she simply couldn't take the stress of the Bush siblings squabbling anymore. The judge also granted Mary's request to remove Michael from his post as co-guardian. The for-profit firm Guardian Services of Pennsylvania was immediately appointed as guardian for Mrs. Bush.[17] For her part, Mary was mightily displeased with the quality of care her mother was receiving at the care facility, and she made her feelings known to the administrators. At one point, Mary said, she was forced to telephone 911 to come get her mother from the care home and take her to the hospital. According to Mary, doctors discovered Genevieve had an untreated broken leg, cellulitis, and high blood pressure. It wasn't long before she was summoned by the facility's administrator and told, "You are no longer a daughter, you are a trespasser." Mary said that beginning January 27, 2016, she was banned from visitations there.

Layers and layers of perceived indignities, complaints, and countercomplaints occurred over the next several years, but the bottom line is that Mary said she was relegated to seeing her mother only once a month, for one hour, and only at a sterile Adult Protective Services building some twenty minutes away from Genevieve's nursing home. Mrs. Bush's estate had to pay for an ambulance to take her to these strained visitations, Mary said she had to pay for an aide to travel with her mother, and an APS supervisor and an armed deputy sheriff had to be present. "She [Mother] was in such a terrible state," Mary said during one interview. "But I was told I couldn't touch her, I couldn't take a photograph . . . [and] my brothers never visited her."

When contacted for comment about his mother's guardianship ordeal and his sister's allegations about his behavior, Michael Bush responded, "Thank you for your inquiry, issues about this matter are still being litigated and it would not be appropriate to comment until all litigation has ended."[18] He did not respond to follow-up emails containing specific questions, including how often he visited his mother and his courtroom admission about administering the Estrace cream.

Mary says the last time she was allowed to see her mother was February 19, 2019. Genevieve Bush lived another two years. On June 16, 2021, Mary said she got a two-word text from her brother Michael. It read simply: "Mom died." Apparently there was no funeral or memorial service, and Mary said she still has the dress her mother wanted to be buried in. Not knowing exactly when her mother would be interred, Mary said she went to the local cemetery every day. On the morning of July 1, she discovered her father's grave had been disturbed, apparently to place her mother's coffin on top.

Genevieve Bush lived under guardianship for a full decade. Never during that time did her adult children stop their incessant fighting. To this day, the brothers and their sister do not speak.

THE GUARDIANSHIP OF BERTHA KORNICKI lasted nearly thirteen years and involved two headstrong sisters, Marian and Terri. In 2005 their elderly father, Manny, filed a complaint with the Nassau County, New York District Attorney alleging that over the previous seven years, Terri had robbed the family accounts of approximately $3 million. The DA began an investigation. Manny and his daughter, Marian, then sought legal advice about how to safeguard their remaining assets, and how to protect the Alzheimer's-stricken Bertha should something happen to her husband. An estate attorney recommended the father and daughter petition for coguardianship. However, the judge did not appoint either Manny or Marian. Instead, without a due process hearing, the judge named two stranger attorneys as co-guardians to oversee the rest of Bertha's life. Manny and Marian were shocked and tried to withdraw the petition but were denied.

In an article Marian wrote in January 2022, entitled "Guardianship Destroyed My Family," she said that the court appointees who were supposed to look after the family money did nothing to secure it and Terri still had access to it.[19] They also did little to look after Bertha's personal needs, and according to Marian the guardians suggested at one point that she and her warring sister should share those duties, even though at that point Terri had been arrested for grand larceny. "Everything in my life and my parents' lives then became a nightmare," Marian wrote. After her father died in 2006, "Different court-appointed guardians, all private attorneys, cycled in and out of our lives. All the while they billed my mother hundreds in hourly rates." It has been reported that fees as high as $600 an hour were awarded by the court for menial tasks "like responding to e-mails or reviewing receipts."[20] In all, Marian said her family lost $1 million to the court appointees. "Our mistake was filing for guardianship, which others used to turn us into human ATM machines," Marian said, in a familiar refrain. She added that her late father's estate plan provided a lifetime trust for Bertha, but the judge allowed the guardians to ignore it. As Marian would attest, there is a lot more to this saga, including what she called years of harassment from her felony-charged sister.[21] "The court repeatedly sided with Terri whenever she tried to intervene," according to Marian. "She rarely visited our mother but did try to have her placed in a nursing home so she could take the house. All of this is an example of how guardianship can create chaos within families." This case also highlights the finality of the guardianship system. There is no allowance given to a petitioning family that changes its mind; no "do-overs" are entertained once a potential ward has been identified to the court.

Bertha Kornicki passed away on May 8, 2018. As 2022 came to a close, the guardian had still not turned over the deed to the family house to Marian, despite the fact that she has been made to pay for everything involved in the home's upkeep, including all the property taxes.[22] Four years after her mother's death, Marian continues to pay for a house she does not legally own. Today, Marian is active in a national coalition called Victims and Families Harmed by Guardianship, an organization of state groups that have joined together to demand reform from federal lawmakers.

THE VERY BEST WAY to defend against a guardianship that could exploit your loved one, cost them their life savings, and likely drain your savings and potential inheritance is to steer clear of the system altogether. Families must understand what the worst-case scenario of a guardianship or conservatorship looks like. And, most importantly, fractious family members need to realize that continuing to act on ego, childhood sibling rivalries, or perceived slights can only result in outcomes like those endured by the Rappaports, the Bush family, and the Kornickis.

It would be a mistake for readers to believe some of the stories here are "old news." The temptation might be to think that, surely, the situation for wards under guardianship or conservatorship has gotten better in recent years. That may be true in a handful of cases in which an enlightened judge passed on establishing a full guardianship and instead chose a less restrictive path for the proposed ward. However, one investigative analysis estimates some two hundred thousand new guardianships are sought in the United States every year.[23] The odds of nationwide, voluntary changes in this predatory system are extremely low.

17

Possible Solutions to Improve the System

Jenny Hatch is "the rock that started the avalanche," as her attorney Jonathan Martinis so aptly put it. Jenny's is the guardianship case that began a nationwide movement away from the oftentimes cruel realities of the system and moved it toward a more humane approach called Supported Decision-Making.

Jenny was born with Down syndrome. Her disability didn't stop her from getting a job, earning a paycheck, paying taxes, having an active church and social life, participating in Special Olympic events, and volunteering in political campaigns. In March 2012, when Jenny was twenty-nine years old, she was living in a Hampton, Virginia, apartment with a family friend, because Jenny, her mother, and stepfather simply did not get along. One rainy evening, Jenny was bicycling home, when the car behind her honked to indicate the driver intended to pass her. In the process, Jenny turned to look over her shoulder and accidentally veered into the passenger side of the car. She was thrown to the pavement and badly injured her back. After spending ten days in the hospital, Jenny was told her roommate was losing the apartment and she was, in effect, homeless.

Five years earlier, Jenny had walked into the Village Thrift Shop in Newport News, Virginia, laid an application on the counter, and explained to the owners, Kelly Morris and Jim Talbert, why they should hire her. She persisted until they gave her the job. Over the years, her employers came to love Jenny, and upon her release from the hospital they invited her into their home. Jenny and the couple's fifteen-year-old daughter, Jordon, who has cerebral palsy, became especially close.

In an effort to enroll Jenny for Medicaid services, it was learned she could become eligible faster if she were declared homeless. In May 2012 the couple explained to Jenny that if she would temporarily move to a group home, she would then receive all sorts of long-term government assistance. It was an emotional time, but Jenny was told she would always be welcomed back if she didn't like living at the group home. On Monday, August 6, 2012, the Medicaid waiver was approved and Jenny moved back in with Morris and Talbert. Two days later, Jenny's parents filed a petition with the court to place her under guardianship. They truly felt that Jenny would be best protected in a strictly supervised group home situation. Once again, Jenny was forced to leave her employer's home.

"When I met Jenny, she was under a guardianship order," disability rights attorney Martinis told the *Washington Post*.[1] "She was living in a group home she didn't want to live in. She wasn't allowed to go to her church. She wasn't allowed to go to work. Her laptop was taken away. Her phone was taken away. If you wanted to see Jenny, you had to fill out a permission slip. You had to say when you wanted to see her and what you would do, and you couldn't talk about her guardianship." Lucky for Jenny, Martinis took up her cause. He was able to demonstrate to the court that Jenny had a long history of making good decisions—like whether to have surgery after her bike accident and understanding a complex power of attorney document before she signed it.

Jenny made these good choices, he said, by instinctively employing a simple method called Supported Decision-Making (SDM). As Martinis wrote, "People who use Supported Decision-Making work with friends, family members, and professionals to give them the help they need and want so they can understand their situations and choices they face and make their own decisions." As attorney Martinis likes to point out, don't we all use this technique as we go through life? "Have you ever asked a doctor to talk to you 'in plain English?' Or gone to an accountant to help with your taxes? Or asked a mechanic to explain why you need repairs?" he asks. "When you do that, whenever you get help making a decision, you're using Supported Decision-Making, just like Jenny does." Martinis's presentation to the court requesting a Supported Decision-Making plan for Jenny resulted in a victory, not only for his client but also for countless other Americans with developmental disabilities. On August 2, 2013, the judge agreed to transfer the guardianship duties to Morris and Talbert. The ruling stipulated it was to be a one-year temporary guardianship, and if everything went well, Jenny would then be free to live the life she wanted.[2] And that is what she is doing today—supported, of course, by a trusted group of friends and outside supporters.

In a blog post Jonathan Martinis wrote for the National Resource Center for Supported Decision-Making, he urged people to look past superficial disabilities and see the person inside, struggling as we all do, to live their best life. "'Protecting' people by taking away their right to make choices, because they may make a bad choice, denies them the chance to learn and grow, to become better, wiser, more well-rounded adults," he wrote.[3] "In a Supported Decision-Making environment, we can all focus on what fellow citizens *can* do, instead of what they *can't* do."

As this book was being readied for publication, there were sixteen states that had adopted laws recognizing SDM as a viable alternative to guardianship. An online list of state-by-state guardianship laws is regularly updated with the latest information.[4] According to Sam Crane, legal director at the Quality Trust for Individuals with Disabilities group, "Many [other] states have a general provision in their guardianship code that SDM should be considered as a less restrictive alternative but not specifically providing for SDM agreements."[5] Each state has its own version of the SDM law,[6] but generally speaking, the statutes establish a formalized agreement whereby individuals with disabilities can call on trusted family and friends, volunteers from advocacy groups, or government social service agency employees to help them make good decisions about their life. The advisers in this support system determine the needs of the individual and carefully explain to them what their best available choices might be. Together they talk it through, discuss consequences, and reach a decision. This method does away with the wholesale cancellation of a person's civil rights. Perhaps more importantly, it removes the profit motive in helping at-risk citizens, thus eliminating from the equation the dishonest, fee-driven element. The latest annual National Guardianship Summit, held in May 2021, enthusiastically endorsed the idea of Supported Decision-Making[7] and lawmakers in several other states are contemplating passing their own version of SDM legislation.

Another alternative idea courts are beginning to consider is called Eldercaring Coordination.[8] It is a program that was born in Florida and has now spread to nearly a dozen other states. A judge can opt to institute this concept rather than establish a more binding guardianship or conservatorship. The premise of Eldercaring is to assign a qualified coordinating counselor to a two-year term to help families that have a history of conflict focus on their elder's need for relevance and independence. It is part mediation, part psychology, with a big of dose of preserving the dignity and desires of the elderly ward. Participants are prompted to focus their decisions on what their aging relative says they want (or what they've said they wanted in the past) instead of on adversarial retaliatory actions. The program is designed to emphasize the strengths of disagreeing family members instead of focusing on blame. The counselor's fees are shared by all, which saves the high cost of individual lawyer-led court actions.

A wise person once said that if there are lots of different things wrong with something—a business, a house, a relationship, or a government system—there is really only one thing wrong. In the case of guardianship and conservatorship that one thing is: *there are too many of them.* Currently there is no way to ascertain which of the estimated 1.5 to 2 million guardianships involve people with intellectual and/or physical disabilities, or those who had been conscripted while temporarily ill and should now be removed from the rolls. But if just 20 or 25 percent of guardianships could be replaced with alternative programs, like Jenny's Supported Decision-Making, think of the burden that would automatically be lifted off the court system, the healthcare industry, and the shoulders of anxious wards and their family members. But what else can be done?

First and foremost, we have to understand the size and scope of what we're dealing with. Any discussion about solutions to the defective guardianship system must begin with the admission that the general public really has no solid concept about how pervasive a problem it is. To fully grasp the issue, everyone seems to agree on the need for each state to establish a reliable, digitally accessible, and consistently updated database of guardianship and conservatorship cases. This would include a tally of each active case and particulars about the ward's age, health status, and prognosis; where they are located; the name of the judge assigned to the case and each of their appointees; and the ward's date of death, if applicable. Once this state tally is accomplished, compiling a national database would be a veritable breeze. That this has not already been done is curious since the nation has been able to keep an official state-by-state tally of children living in foster care—407,493 in 2022 according to Statistica .com—but no uniform effort has been made to count the number of adults conscripted to guardianship and conservatorship.[9]

There is also widespread agreement that the use of "emergency guardianship" petitions, frequently presented as a way to skirt due process hearings and quickly create a mostly binding temporary guardianship, must be seriously curbed. Yes, there are some instances where an at-risk person needs immediate protection, but most knowledgeable participants admit the practice has been grossly overused and abused. One state Supreme Court judge in New Mexico, for example, admitted in an open legislative hearing that of the more than eight hundred emergency petitions granted in that state annually, "It should be about eight." In addition, for too long judges have opted to approve full-blown guardianships simply because that's what the petition before them requested. For many judges, especially those who are primarily concerned with clearing their overburdened dockets quickly, routinely approving a permanent guardianship is seen as the most expedient way to go. Gavel down, next case, please. This fast-track approval practice needs to end. Each person who comes before the bench deserves a careful look before being stripped of their constitutionally protected civil rights. Judges who rule on guardianships and conservatorships need to take mandatory training courses on ways to better administer—and more fairly manage—their caseloads.

In recent years, other, less restrictive methods of helping vulnerable adults have begun to be sporadically employed. For example, a judge may choose to assist a person with a hearing disability by ordering appropriate technology be installed to help them communicate with the outside world. Similarly, other types of technological assistance have been provided for blind persons. Perhaps a potential ward cannot manage a checkbook and needs minimal help paying bills. Court appointment of a representative payee would fit the bill better than a far-reaching, all-encompassing guardianship. An elderly person of sound mind may not be able to travel to medical appointments or shop for groceries on their own. What they really need is transportation assistance, not a total usurpation of their freedoms via guardianship.

It is unclear whether attorneys can ever be convinced to voluntarily scale back their petitions to the court or to persuade judges to seriously consider less restrictive measures for each ward. Such actions would, of course, negate the need for so many crony colleagues to be appointed and would likely not sit well with the fee-driven industry that operates within this part of the justice system. But judges have the absolute power to step back from any guardianship request, to ask to see and speak with the targeted person and their family members, and to decide for themselves what level of care might be needed. So far, in the long history of guardianships, very few judges have been inclined to do that.

While some aggrieved participants believe the best thing to do is to entirely scrap the guardianship system, there are others who think the original altruistic idea that launched the process is sound, albeit in need of major correction. One most frequent recommendation to change the system is compulsory punishment for wrongdoers, including criminal convictions, if warranted. If bad actors are swiftly punished, it will send a signal to the entire professional community that misconduct and criminal activity will not be tolerated. After years of research and investigation into disputed guardianships, I can report that the process is plagued with court appointees who are repeat offenders. In case after case, the same names cropped up, along with the same core complaints: isolating the ward; unfairly demonizing family members; presenting the court with questionable psychological results; ignoring advanced directives; suspicions of overbilling and overmedication; inaccurate or nonexistent accounting reports; uncaring and even brutal behaviors by guardians, conservators, and other court appointees. The findings were similar in a wide-ranging number of states, including but not limited to Alabama, California, Florida, Maine, Michigan, Nevada, New Mexico, North Carolina, Ohio, Oregon, Pennsylvania, Texas, and Washington State. Punishment for offenders was uncommon, the culprits rarely even admonished by the court, and those appointees caught committing malfeasance were commonly allowed to continue offering their services, undaunted. Currently, there are so few punitive actions taken against exploitative guardians or conservators that it is considered a permission, of sorts, for predatory players to keep doing what they do. The lack of meaningful punishment is thought to actually attract characters with ill intent.

One suggested procedure to try to control rogue appointees would be for a regulatory agency to assign black-mark demerits to offenders for a wide variety of unacceptable actions. For example: failure to file the ward's annual financial report in a timely fashion would earn the court appointee a demerit. If careless overbilling or double-billing is proven, a mandatory demerit would be levied. If a ward was needlessly isolated from loved ones or their possessions disposed of without consulting the family, a demerit would be issued. It should be strictly forbidden for a guardian or conservator to hire one of their own family members to assume the role of a ward's caretaker, gardener, driver, or any other position. Discovery of such an infraction would merit a black mark. Under the umbrella of a three-strikes-and-you're-out policy, a trio of demerits would trigger an automatic suspension of the offender's ability to work for a period of time.

Any additional offense would result in permanent exclusion from the list of those available to be appointed by the court.

Family members who have been directly and negatively impacted by guardianship have their own list of suggested changes to improve the system. Many of them had originally sought to be appointed guardian of their loved one and were denied, and then they had to fight a stranger guardian for the right to remain meaningfully involved in the ward's life. First and foremost, they want judges to more seriously consider appointing loving family members to the role of guardian, and not just take a negative report from a petitioning attorney as gospel. They also want unfettered access to their guardianized loved one and the right to be heard in court should a guardian or conservator unjustly isolate the ward or misbehave in other ways. They want one dedicated state office they can approach to lodge complaints, with a staff that takes their grievances seriously and automatic involvement of law enforcement, if warranted. They would like a detailed and up-to-date accounting of how their relative's money is being spent, and access to automatic state-funded audits when serious questions of accountability arise. They believe they should be immediately informed when their loved one is moved to a new location, hospitalized, or when they are near death. And families would appreciate swift closure of the case after the ward dies. Restricting the length of time a case can remain open after death would eliminate the sometimes yearslong fee grab by guardians, lawyers, and conservators. It would also go a long way toward helping grieving family members heal more quickly.

Reformers believe each state should devise a strict certification program and a licensing procedure for guardians and conservators. Currently, only fourteen states require guardians to be officially certified as capable to carry out the necessary duties by either the Center for Guardianship Certification or a similar state-run entity.[10] Such accreditation is seen as a badge of professionalism among guardians, yet it is unclear how many active guardians have bothered to become certified. If a state requires someone to be specially trained and licensed before becoming, say, a plumber or electrician, then someone who assumes responsibility for another person's health, wealth, and well-being should also be a specialist. Licensing is thought to be of the utmost importance, because if a court appointee knows they risk having their license to operate revoked, they would likely think twice before engaging in questionable or criminal behavior. Also, why shouldn't guardians, conservators, and lawyers involved in the system be required take continuing education classes as other professionals are expected to do?[11]

Professor Pamela Teaster, an ethicist and gerontologist at Virginia Tech, has spent years studying the guardianship system. She was asked whether the Center for Guardianship Certification's "minimum standard" is enough to prepare a court appointee to take over the complex life decisions of an at-risk person. "Does it really do it? No. But does it help? Yeah, I think so," she said during an interview for this book. "I am a professor so I profess, and I teach, and I educate, so I've got to believe that people who are more knowledgeable than people who are less knowledgeable maybe stand a chance of doing a better job than people who don't." Professor Teaster has personally served as a guardian—twice—and she declares the current guardianship system in the United States to be "a mess." "I believe there is a percentage of people who are doing it poorly because they don't know what they are doing, and that's a problem," she said. "And then there are others who are doing it poorly because they mean to do it poorly."

To keep track of potential predators, it is recommended that a statewide, publicly available registry be kept of all those participating in the guardianship system—from lawyers and medical evaluators to guardians, conservators, court visitors, and clerks. Who are they, what is their certified expertise, have there been complaints lodged against them, and if so, what was the outcome of the mandatory investigation? Included in this registry would be the number of wards assigned to each appointee. In addition, some believe it would be instructive if each participant would reveal their hourly fee or salary in the name of transparency.

And since nothing can happen in a guardianship proceeding without a judge, it is suggested that a companion registry be established to track judicial actions. How many emergency petitions for guardianship has a judge approved? Is the judge assigning the bulk of their guardianship/conservatorship cases to just a handful of people or firms? How many times has the judge given permission to ignore a ward's preplanned estate documents like a will, irrevocable trust, or end-of-life directive? Has the judge (or a staff member) reviewed older guardianship cases to see if the ward could be moved to a less restrictive arrangement? What complaints have been filed against the judge, and what was done about them? And since there are a multitude of whispers about "lawyers and judges on the take," it would be helpful if all campaign contributions to judges were listed on this public registry. Perhaps such contributions from guardianship appointees and their firms should be outlawed. Maybe judges should have their tax returns confidentially reviewed by an independent panel, looking for unexplained loans or infusions of cash.

Critics of the current system also believe there should be a cap on fees that can be charged to a ward commensurate with the value of their estate, and a clear standard for billing. Opening a piece of mail for a ward or taking a quick phone call on their behalf should not result in a full hour fee. In short, reformers believe that instituting procedures that result in less secrecy, more transparency, and certain punishment for the bad actors will make for a much fairer system.

Criticisms of current procedures and suggestions for modifying the guardianship process are usually met with countercomplaints from insiders. They are quick to remind outsiders that guardianships exist because families are so dysfunctional that they cannot reach solutions for caring for their loved one on their own. They see little need to adjust the way the system works, and they frequently describe themselves as guardian angels of sorts, there to anticipate the ward's every need, and shelter them from every possible upset, as if that is ever achievable in life. The lawyers among the court appointees are often the most adamant champions for maintaining the status quo.

Naturally, new requirements and stepped-up oversight means the judicial system will need more money to fulfill its new role. Extra judges, support staff, auditors and law enforcement liaisons will have to be hired. A new and stronger commitment to service the nation's neediest population more compassionately will have to emerge. Therein lie two of the biggest impediments to reforming the way things currently work: finding the necessary money in tight state budgets, and opposition from those who financially benefit from the current system.

Flashback: A most interesting idea to significantly change the process was first mentioned decades ago during the 1987 congressional hearings held by Congressman Claude Pepper.[12] To wit: remove all for-profit players and replace them with paid staff. The notion came from Mrs. Etan Merrick, the widow of the once-conserved Broadway producer David Merrick. At the end of her testimony about living through contentious court control of her ex-husband, she offered two recommendations. First, limit all arrangements to just two years, as happened with Merrick after he suffered a debilitating stroke. The automatic review of his case helped Merrick win restoration of his rights and once again regain control of his entertainment empire. Mrs. Merrick told the House Subcommittee on Health and Long-Term Care:

> My second recommendation is a very strong objection to the patron-age system, which should be removed entirely from the administra-tion of the estates of the disabled and the elderly. Perhaps the Federal Government could construct an organization of salaried employees, whose only function would be the administration of conservator-ships, wherein the assistance and cooperation and advice of family and close friends would be sought, thus eliminating an arena of polit-ical machination often resulting in long-distance, impersonal care by functionaries who often view their wards as vehicles for fees. Again, to reiterate what I have already stated, if my husband could be vic-timized by the system as it now exists, I can only imagine what could happen to others, who do not have his resources.[13]

One can only imagine, too, the intense lobbying effort that might ensue if Mrs. Merrick's anti-patronage idea took hold today. Lobbyists from or-ganizations representing elder law and estate lawyers, courts, guardians, conservators, hospitals, nursing homes, financial institutions, and oth-ers would certainly not accept exclusion of all for-profit players without a fight. But Merrick's long-ago recommendation brings up another possi-ble solution that has been discussed for decades: federalizing the system. Despite all the hearings and political posturing on Capitol Hill, it seems unlikely that the federal government will step in to take command of the state-centric system anytime soon. Yet this is the very action many believe will be necessary to achieve meaningful change to this vital system. At the very least, reform activists wonder why there has been no move to di-rect the US Department of Justice to seriously investigate the ever-growing number of citizen complaints about the guardian and conservator system. For years now, the DOJ has dispatched teams to investigate suspected civil rights violations within state and local police and sheriff's departments. A DOJ statement posted in April 2021 proudly announced, "If we find that one of these law enforcement agencies systematically deprives people of their rights, we can act."[14] So, what's stopping the agency from using the same tactic to investigate and monitor civil rights complaints about the court-ordered system that purports to protect the vulnerable? Police are supposed to serve and protect the citizenry, and when they don't, the federal government can move in to make sure the offenders and their departments are punished. Why the double standard of enforcement for the nation's guardianship courts, their officers, and their appointees?

At this point, the closest thing the United States has to a nationwide guardianship and conservatorship law is the aforementioned Uniform Guardianship, Conservatorship, and Other Protective Arrangements Act.[15] Since state legislatures have found it so incredibly difficult to fully regulate guardianships and conservatorships, the UGCOPAA is presented as a comprehensive piece of legislation that can easily be passed, as is, and put to immediate use. At this writing it has only been ratified in two states, Washington and Maine, and a few other states have cherry-picked and passed portions of the proposal.[16] The UGCOPAA is a 258-page document, hammered out after years of studying guardianship practices in all fifty states. It was written by lawyers serving on the Uniform Law Commission, and that fact is enough to color the opinion of those involved in abusive guardianships who feel they've already been victimized by lawyers. They believe that it is the fee-driven legal community that is primarily responsible for keeping conflict alive within the system.[17] While the ULC is top heavy with lawyers, the organization did seek advice from grassroots reform groups, including the American Association of Retired Persons (AARP), the Association for Retarded Citizens (now formally known as simply the ARC), the National Disability Rights Network, and the National Association to Stop Guardianship Abuse (NASGA) before it issued its final legislative proposal.

NASGA has been active in trying to convince states to accept the UGCOPAA in full and pass it into law. Its director, Marcia Southwick, wrote a comprehensive white paper offering a list of reasons why the act should become the law of the land. First and foremost, Southwick wrote, "UGCOPAA requires the court to consider all possible alternatives to guardianship, such as Supported Decision-Making, before placing a guardianship on someone."[18] (She does not mention that this directive is already included in many states' guardianship laws and has been ignored by judges for years.)

Southwick points out that under the act, courts will no longer be allowed to establish a guardianship on the basis of hearsay evidence, as the proposal calls for the petition to be accompanied by "clear and convincing evidence" of the need for a guardianship. If there is absolutely no alternative to guardianship, UGCOPAA requires due process proceedings, including allowing the targeted person to speak in court and hire the attorney of their choice. Due process is, of course, part of every citizen's rights under the US Constitution, yet judges have routinely overlooked that process in guardianship and conservatorship cases.[19] If the proposed ward cannot attend the initial hearing for reasons beyond their control, the court is instructed to take the proceeding to the person's location. In addition, before a guardianship can be granted, the guardian must submit a detailed plan for care of the ward, along with their proposed fees, and a list of the ward's closest family members and friends who will act as the eyes and ears for the court. If there is any deviation from the care plan, members of the monitoring support group can report suspect activity to the judge. These family and friends are to be promptly notified anytime the protected person is relocated or hospitalized, or if the person dies. Also, the ward is to receive all bank and investment statements and can contest questionable transactions.

"Until now," Southwick wrote, "financial accountings have fallen into a black hole, creating secrecy and encouraging fraud." In addition, she notes that under the UGCOPAA guidelines, the guardian is not allowed to restrict visitation with a ward for more than a week without presenting clear evidence to the judge that the restriction is necessary. All complaints against a guardian must be fully addressed, and details of the grievance are to be placed in the guardian's permanent file to keep a record of their actions. The NASGA white paper also endorsed a section of the act that, if adopted, would be a chilling development for court appointees: if a guardian contests termination of a guardianship, and their efforts fail, they will be responsible for paying their own legal fees. As Southwick concluded, "This disincentivizes guardians from continuing to fight since they are restricted in the use of the protected person's funds." Last, Southwick pointed out, "UGCOPAA is a living document into which further reforms may be added." There have been hopes expressed elsewhere that if enough states adopt the act, it can be used as the template for federal legislation. Supporters of this route, like NASGA, firmly believe that since states have failed to get a firm grip on the problem, it is up to lawmakers on Capitol Hill to set a new nationwide standard.

NASGA's interpretation and support of the legislation appears persuasive, and the organization clearly believes the UGCOPAA proposal is a good place to start reforming a clearly imperfect system. But other reformers criticize the act and offer up compelling reasons not to endorse the UGCOPAA. "It's like putting lipstick on a pig," Rick Black of the Center for Estate Administration Reform said during one of our many conversations. "The UGCOPAA only gives more power to the predators." Black, who established CEAR with his wife, Terri, after her father was caught up in an abusive guardianship in Nevada, has counseled or investigated over four thousand suspect cases. His bottom-line conclusion is that the act's "feel-good" recommendations and vague language have no teeth and don't directly solve any of the current problems. That assessment of the UGCOPAA recommendations is echoed by others who have studied guardianship's weaknesses. After analyzing the act, Black offered his own interpretation of its potential effectiveness and cited the specific sections CEAR believes are lacking.[20]

* The act continues the practice of allowing judges the right to create, modify, or dismiss a trust, life insurance policy, or last will and testament of a ward upon the petitioning of a guardian or conservator. It also fails to require duly executed estate documents (durable power of attorney, healthcare advance directive, trust, or will) to be protected as sacred contracts. (Section 414)

* The act continues to expose proposed wards to known abuses by allowing judges to issue orders for temporary guardianship or conservatorship without notice to the targeted person and without conducting a due process hearing. (Sections 312 and 413)

* The act allows conservators to sell off a ward's property, including their homes and other real estate, without prior court approval. (Section 421) This is frequently described as the "Don't ask for permission first, ask for forgiveness later" play.

* The act fails to recognize the importance of assigning an independent, fully trained, and zealous attorney to represent the proposed ward *prior* to any judicial guardianship or conservatorship order being issued. (Section 406) Every American is entitled to legal counsel when they enter the judicial system, even if they are involuntarily conscripted. It is CEAR's position that there is *never* an emergency that justifies an order for guardianship or conservatorship without this constitutionally protected right being honored.

* The act fails to mandate specific penalties or disciplinary action against bad actors, including but not limited to those who commit constructive fraud during a guardianship proceeding.[21]

* The act continues to embrace a lack of transparency in guardianship proceedings by allowing the court to seal records and ignore petitions from interested parties (e.g., family members) seeking access to those records. (Sections 308 and 409)

* The act further exposes wards to financial exploitation by the shallowness of financial reporting "recommendations." CEAR's position is that mere recommendations are meaningless in an equity court setting. Plus, the only possible penalty for an offending court appointee who fails to file regular reports or presents inaccurate reports is their *potential* removal and a reduction in their fees. (Sections 317)

* One of the first requirements for any guardian is to make a complete inventory of a ward's assets, from every investment and bank account they have to every vehicle, home furnishing, and piece of silverware they own. Many families have complained that expensive items were left off their loved one's inventory sheet and suddenly disappeared. Yet the UGCOPAA sets forth no penalties for missing items in the initial inventory, and no requirement for trust holdings to be included in the inventory if the judge has modified the trust in any way.

* As proposed, the act fails to set forth any requirement for the guardian to supply receipts or to reconcile the ward's accounts from one filing to the next. (Section 420) The act carries no specific obligation for the court to order an independent audit should the guardian's annual accounting be challenged, nor does it mention any penalties for a guardian who fails to list all of a ward's assets on the initial inventory sheet.

* Finally, states that ratify the UGCOPAA enjoy "exclusive jurisdiction globally." This means the court that originates a guardianship or conservatorship would retain perpetual control of both the ward and their wealth. If the protected person happened to be an out-of-state resident, they can be forced to stay put. If some, or all, of their money is held in another jurisdiction, the act allows the originating state to retain full control of all the ward's assets for the duration of the guardianship.[22] The act also allows the initiating court to ignore orders from all other jurisdictions. (Sections 104, 105, 106, 309)

The final analysis from Rick Black is that the UGCOPAA is toothless because it "*suggests*" or "*encourages*" judges and court appointees to behave in certain ways. The act "*recommends*" and "*urges*" changes in the status quo. It "relies on the honor system" and does not address the realities of today's often out-of-control guardianship proceedings. During one of many interviews for this book, Black said that simply because the ULC has bundled up all these "so-called protections" and put them into one document, that does not guarantee predatory players in the system will suddenly follow them.

"Too many equity courts are dysfunctional," Black maintains. "Too many judges have poor judgment. Too many predatory attorneys prevail in this perverted reality." And nothing seems to ever change within the system, he said, because "every attorney makes more money from . . . fraudulent adult guardianships. Fraud ensures conflict, and conflict ensures litigation and [ever-increasing] fees." Asked why one activist reform group could so heartily endorse the UGCPOAA while another does not, Black said, "It's not a surprise. They want to be loved by those in power. I want a more equitable system."

Two additional points about the UGCOPAA. First, many family members say they are put off by language changes in the act that they interpret as an attempt to soft-pedal what has happened to victims of the system. The authors of the proposed legislation decided that the historically used words "ward," "ward of the court," and "protected person," have become too pejorative, so they replaced them with what they see as the odiously generic phrases such as "adult subject to conservatorship" or "individual subject to guardianship." Those who watched loved ones suffer under the system see the wordplay as a way for the legal community to try to disinfect the past with a linguistic sleight of hand. To guardianship reformists it is rather like suddenly deciding to refer to the orphaned Oliver Twist as "an individual without parentage."

Second, the UGCOPAA makes no mention of the core need for states to establish a database of guardianship information or registries to keep track of wards, family members' complaints, and caseloads of court appointees and judges. This kind of record keeping is seen by many involved in guardianship reform as mandatory precursors to enactment of any meaningful changes, yet the act ignores the need for an often-recommended database. The fact that the ULC, a group made up entirely of lawyers, did not recommend a means to keep track of a system that is largely populated by lawyers is not lost on those educated in the sometimes-destructive tactics used in the guardianship and conservatorship system.

The most often heard argument against establishing a publicly available database or registry may have been most succinctly expressed by Florida state representative Linda Chaney. She sponsored a bill to create a statewide database, but to keep it closed to everyone except court insiders. She said excluding the public was necessary to protect the wards. "The reason for that is there are times when family members have good intentions, and family members have bad intentions," she said. "So, we didn't want them to have full access to the ward's information, and maybe be[come] part of a problem."[23] Representative Chaney's comment outraged Florida's most outspoken reform activist, Dr. Sam Sugar. On his now-deactivated website, he responded by saying he's tired of families being blamed for what's wrong with the system. "If the information from this proposed database were ever allowed to be examined openly by the public and professionals, the Bar fears that their perfidy would be far too obvious," he said. Dr. Sugar has gathered and analyzed thousands of guardianship cases over the last decade. He concludes that the benefits to society could be enormous if state databases were completely transparent and available for serious study. "Real statistics on guardianships could be developed, evidence of court bias revealed, financial records studied, paper trails followed, and actual evidence gathered. Instead, they use the hackneyed excuse that revealing personal information about a ward would be deleterious to the ward, as if destroying their entire life, making them helpless and dead in the [eyes of the] law, taking away all their rights, stealing their life savings and work *isn't* deleterious to the ward."

As discussed elsewhere in this book, several state legislatures have passed new laws to try to refashion the guardianship and conservatorship process into a less autocratic system. Sponsoring lawmakers insist the modifications have made the process more responsive to wards and their families. After studying the new legislation, many reformers have called the changes mere Band-Aid solutions that determined predators will either regularly ignore or find a workaround to thwart the intent. What follows is a brief summary of some of the latest statutory fixes. Readers may wonder why these most recently adopted steps weren't standard operating procedure in the first place.

* Before appointment, all guardians and conservators must be positively cleared via checks of a national criminal history database, the National Sex Offender Registry, the Abuse and Neglect Registry, and a full credit check. (Nebraska)[24]
* Wards or potential wards have the right to choose their own lawyer, and any "interested party" may petition the court to investigate allegations of elder abuse. (California)[25]

* Every potential adult ward must first be provided with an independent government-paid legal aid lawyer whose sole purpose is to
represent their client's wishes, and to make sure the client is fully
informed about the guardianship system and told that a guardianship petition has been filed in their name (Nevada: adopted in
2017). In the past, targeted individuals and their families frequently
had no idea a court action had been initiated. This new Nevada law
remedied that and is seen as a possible model for other states. The
Legal Aid Center of Southern Nevada reported that in 2021 they
were able to defeat 25 percent of the petitions presented in Clark
County by acting on behalf of targeted citizens. The annual cost of
this program: $3.2 million.

One of the most recent positive developments cited by reform activists comes from the state of Minnesota. Lawmakers there passed a
seventeen-point "Bill of Rights for Persons Subject to Guardianship or
Conservatorship." Among its provisions is the directive that all wards be
treated with "dignity and respect," that they have the right to participate
in decision-making regarding their abode, health care, and religious practices, that they have a path to communicate directly with the court and
to petition for an end to their guardianship, that they be consulted before
their personal property is disposed of, and that they have the right to communicate with whomever they want, to procreate, and to vote unless a
court has ruled otherwise.[26]

It should also be noted that in 2019 Mississippi passed an omnibus bill—
called the GAP Act (for Guard and Protect)—which substantially updated
much of the state's thirty-year-old guardianship and conservatorship
laws.[27] A year earlier, Missouri adopted massive changes to its outdated
guardianship and conservatorship statutes, the first major alteration since
the laws were enacted in 1983. In April 2022 the state of Michigan announced it had received a federal grant to construct and administer a website called Guardian Compare that will track the state's guardians and rate
them on quality of performance standards. One stated goal of the effort is
to weed out the bad apples in the system.

Curiously, Nebraska was the last state to enact an official state-funded
guardianship system.[28] It wasn't until 2015 that the state legislature finally
approved a public guardianship agency, and it was established after a major scandal. Judith Widener, seventy-one, owner of a supposed nonprofit
organization providing services to the elderly and those with disabilities,

was discovered to have stashed at least $600,000 of her ward's money in more than forty different bank accounts.[29] Widener was charged with nine felonies and two misdemeanors. In October 2014 she accepted a plea deal and was sentenced to six months in prison.[30]

No matter what solutions are proposed, or ultimately enacted into law, activists in the field of guardianship and conservatorship reform believe nothing will change unless and until judges practice better case control. Michigan attorney Bradley Geller, a man with thirty-five years of experience in the field of guardianship, has welcomed the nationwide spate of new reform legislation in recent years, but he doubts it will make any difference. Geller believes there are probably enough laws already on the books, and suggests the real power to change things is in the hands of each state's highest court. "All that a state Supreme Court need do is write a one-sentence order to the lower court saying, 'From this date forward, probate judges in guardianship proceedings will follow the law.' Period. End of story. And you know what it would cost for them to do this? Nothing." Geller continued, "It's not like we don't know there's a problem. It's not like we don't know what the solutions are. We just can't get the powers that be to change things."[31]

Of course, the best solution to prevent a potentially fraught guardianship is to take every possible precaution to avoid one in the first place. Make the time to prepare a will that is carefully thought out, to establish a power of attorney, and to gather other end-of-life documents. Inform the family about your plans, and record a video in which you clearly articulate your wishes, specifically in regard to potential guardianship. And above all else, make it clear that anyone who seeks to circumvent your plans will automatically be disinherited.

EPILOGUE

For as many individual stories that have been told here, there are count-less more that could have been included. Each case represents palpa-ble heartache endured not only by the ward but also by their loved ones who were rendered helpless in the face of a compassionless, uncompromis-ing system. Some of the people caught up in painful guardianships shared their stories with me as a way to temporarily ease their burden, but then they did not want to go public for fear of retribution—from estranged fam-ily members, the court, or court appointees. Others said it was just too painful to go over what happened in all the detail a journalist needs. It was like prodding an open wound for them to remember how they came to feel victimized by a system that supposedly helped families, but then destroyed theirs.

Two sisters in the heartland told me how they battled against the guard-ianship and institutionalization of their mother. They wanted desperately to care for her, but they were up against their heavy-handed brother who initiated the guardianship petition. He was their small town's chief of po-lice, and they felt there was no way they were going to prevail and bring their mother home. They suspected their brother had tapped their phones and strong-armed the nursing home staff to keep them at bay with a strictly enforced visitation policy.

A heartsick son in Pennsylvania told me how he'd taken his mother to a senior-care center "spa day" to, among other things, get her hair done in preparation for Easter. When he arrived to pick her up, he discovered his weeping and unattended mother in an isolated side room, and he was informed that a staffer had called Adult Protective Services claiming the elderly woman had fleas. It wasn't true. But after APS got involved, the widow was so quickly enlisted into the guardianship system that her son was unable to stop it. Did her quick conscription have anything to do with the fact that she was the widow of a wealthy owner of a local construction company? Her son told me he believed that was the case.

There are so many stories from across the nation that deserve a mention, and I ask for forgiveness for not including each and every abusive or exploitative guardianship story told to me, but there is simply not enough space in one book to relate them all. While a disproportionate number of cases seem to originate in sunny retirement areas in California, Nevada, New Mexico, Texas, Alabama, and especially Florida, abusive guardianships and conservatorships have occurred in nearly every state of the union—*and they continue to occur as you read this.* Michigan is a hot spot, for example. And I discovered cases in Arkansas, Idaho, Maine, Ohio, Oregon, Tennessee, and Washington state, to name a few others.

While Florida has made some strides in holding predatory players accountable, that does nothing to erase the damage that has already been done. And currently this state continues to have an unusually high number of scandalous guardianship cases. Floridian Lesa Martino became so distraught about what she saw as the poor medical care of her elderly guardianized father that she took to Facebook to express her opinion about his guardian, Traci Samuel Hudson, calling her a "liar," "exploiter," "vulture," and a "witch." Hudson then filed a successful libel lawsuit against Martino and won a sizable judgment, which ultimately resulted in Lesa losing her $480,000 house in a court-ordered sale. Lesa's complaints to state regulatory agencies about court appointee Hudson were routinely ignored. In 2019 Tampa Bay Police detectives finally investigated complaints about this guardian and arrested her for exploitation of a ninety-two-year-old man in her care. In June 2021 police arrested Hudson again and charged her with twenty felony counts of perjury, exploitation, and stealing from four of her wards. At this writing, Hudson is awaiting trial.[1]

Gentye Dirse of Lithuania achieved the American dream after immigrating to Florida. She owned a modest but money-making roadside motel on St. Pete Beach. Her devoted grandnephew, Gedi Pakalnis, helped run the establishment for fifteen years. A local real estate agent, who those close to the case agree was not a friend, pushed Gentye to sell the motel. She repeatedly refused, and instead sold a portion of the property to Gedi at an under-market price. The agent enlisted a local attorney and together they filed a guardianship petition insisting that Gentye's real estate transaction was proof of her incapacitation. In January 2018 probate judge Pam Campbell agreed and appointed the aforementioned Traci Samuel Hudson as the guardian. Hudson relegated Gentye to a nursing home and cut off all contact with her beloved grandnephew, and Judge Campbell allowed it. Between Hudson and court-approved lawyers, Gentye's estate was charged nearly $290,000 in less than two years. Gentye died—alone—of Covid-19 on May 5, 2020.

Dr. Lillie Sykes White of Palm Coast, Florida, was plucked from a doctor's waiting room in August 2016 by a guardian who refused to tell her family where she had taken the widowed octogenarian. Lillie, a retired educator with $4 million in assets, was conscripted after an estranged granddaughter in Maryland successfully petitioned the Florida court for guardianship. After years of not knowing where Lillie was living, her sister and niece teamed up with a private investigator. He was able to finally locate Lillie in 2018. She was being held in a nursing home in another county. A brief surreptitious family reunion took place there, but soon after Lillie's guardian ordered extra security measures to make sure the family was permanently kept away. Four long years in isolation ended for Lillie on December 31, 2021, when she died from apparent complications of Covid-19. Two weeks passed before her family was notified of her death.[2]

Doug Franks fought tirelessly to help his mother, Ernestine, escape from an unwanted guardianship in Pensacola, Florida. He was finally successful in freeing her in November 2016. After just forty-five days of freedom, and after a joyous daylong outing that ended with her favorite ice cream cone, Ernestine had a massive heart attack and passed away in Doug's arms. Years earlier, brother Charles Franks, the person who sought the guardianship of his mother, was advised by a lawyer that court intervention via guardianship would be a positive step for Ernestine. Charles took that lawyer's recommendation, convinced it was a good idea. After his mother's death, Charles said, "I am tortured by that decision."[3] Doug Franks continues to be an outspoken and persuasive guardian reform advocate. He appears frequently to testify at public hearings and guardianship conferences and to lobby for changes in the system.

The judiciary system in the United States has changed as societal needs have evolved. When cases involving veterans or illegal drugs flooded the courts, new divisions were created. Veterans courts populated by staff who have military experience were established. Many states now have so-called drug courts dedicated to considering rehabilitation instead of incarceration. As the US population ages, and those with mental and physical disabilities are more frequently winding up in guardianship or conservatorship proceedings, it seems clear that dedicated, compassionate, and well-funded guardian courts should be seriously considered.

A handful of courageous state lawmakers have embraced the idea that the United States can and must do a better job of caring for the vulnerable. But unfortunately, what remains undone is legislation to get rid of the bad practices taking place *inside the courtroom*—at the very beginning of the process. That is where guardianships start and flourish, and for the most part new laws have not changed the way the insular court proceedings take place. Attempting to tourniquet a deeply traumatizing system after it has conscripted someone does nothing to stop the wounds that will be inflicted going forward. Proposed legislation that fails to address the very creation of questionable guardianships allows the unscrupulous to establish an intractable advantage.

When one analyzes the flock of recently passed state reform laws, it is easy to see that none stop the predatory process at its inception. There has been no legislation to ensure punishment for lawyers who present petitions to the court that contain exaggerations or outright lies. There has been no movement toward laws to rein in rogue judges who routinely approve emergency petitions without much consideration, or judges who ignore due process as if it were a mere inconvenience and allow their appointees to ignore thoughtfully constructed wills, estate plans, irrevocable trusts, and power of attorney appointments. There are no suggestions for statutes that would outlaw plea deals for court appointees who are caught overcharging or stealing from a ward, thus allowing them to be prosecuted for *all* their crimes. The lack of meaningful response to these systemic flaws only serves to further erode public confidence in both the justice system and the legal community. And for all the grand talk about "fixing" the guardianship and conservatorship process, it is plain to see that the problems baked into the current system are still occurring nationwide.

Dorris Hamilton was the first African American principal in the state of New Mexico.[4] She is a revered figure in her Las Cruces, New Mexico, community where she has lived for fifty years. As she aged, Dorris realized it was time to pass on her power of attorney to her only child, Rio. On July 20, 2019, the pair visited a local attorney named CaraLyn Banks to put the plan in motion. As Rio tells it, nothing was settled during that initial meeting, and neither he nor his mother signed papers engaging Banks's services. (In published reports, Banks seemed to dispute this, but she did

not respond to multiple requests for further comment or clarification.[5])
Within days, lawyer Banks filed an emergency petition for "a Full Temporary Guardian and Conservator and Full Permanent Guardian and Conservator" of Dorris Hamilton. She listed the petitioner as Rio Hamilton and
herself as Rio's attorney. During an interview for this book, Rio said, "She
flat-out lied to the court. She said I was okay with her using my name. I absolutely wasn't. We never hired her." Nonetheless, in August 2019 district
court judge Manuel Arrieta approved the guardianship petition. There was
no notice to the family, no due process hearing, and no medical evaluation of the proposed ward attached to the petition. Ninety-one-year-old
Doris was unceremoniously deposited in a nursing home, often isolated
and overmedicated, according to Rio. "Oh my God, she got whatever the
drug cocktail was that they give all of them," he said during one telephone
conversation. "And it was worse on the weekends when they had reduced
staff. It was so depressing!"

Rio kept up a steady fight to undue the arrangement, and with the help
of pro bono lawyers from Disability Rights New Mexico, Rio finally won
the battle to be his mother's guardian in May 2021. He located another
assisted-living facility for his mother, "a lovely place . . . a paradise," as
he described it. And Rio frequently ferries Dorris back to her home to
have special lunches or entertainment time with "her lady friends." For
some inexplicable reason, after Rio became guardian, Judge Arrieta allowed attorney CaraLyn Banks to remain attached to the case as a self-ap-
pointed lawyer. As of April 2022 she was still submitting invoices for her
fees. According to Rio, Banks continued to "throw a wrench into things,
constantly making it necessary to have another and then another hearing.
We've had nine hearings in three years," he said. Typically, each court proceeding costs a ward's estate thousands of dollars in legal bills. So far, Rio
estimates his mother's $400,000 in savings have been depleted by about
$250,000.

In Harbor Springs, Michigan, World War II veteran George Pappas admitted to a social worker at the Veterans Administration that he needed
help with everyday chores. Pappas, ninety-five, was referred to the Em-
met County Probate Court, which assigned Elise Page to be his conservator. According to the *Record-Eagle* newspaper, the sheriff's department
ran a criminal background check on Page but did not discover her history of bad debts, bounced checks, and unpaid medical bills going back
to 2004.[6] Shortly after she was appointed, Page moved all $63,665 of Pap-
pas's money to a credit union and attached a debit card in her own name.

Within weeks this court-appointed conservator withdrew $10,300 in cash from her ward's account and racked up debit card purchases for more than $3,600 at vape shops, fast-food restaurants, and a Victoria's Secret store. In July 2021 Elise Page pleaded guilty to various embezzlement charges.[7] She served five months of an eleven-month sentence and was ordered to pay court costs and restitution to George Pappas. Court documents show she only needs to pay back thirty dollars per month. At that rate, the *Record-Eagle* reported, Mr. Pappas wouldn't be made whole until he turned 138 years old.

Ginger Franklin died in July 2017 at the age of fifty-eight, and her guardianship case sparked both outrage and changes to Tennessee law.[8] When Ginger was in her late forties, she sustained a traumatic brain injury after a fall and was conscripted into an emergency conservatorship. After weeks of hospitalization, Ginger was placed in a small group home costing $850 a month. Then the conservator sold Ginger's car and condominium in Hendersonville, Tennessee. According to a longtime friend, at the group home Ginger encountered residents living with severe mental illness, including sometimes violent "paranoid/schizophrenic, manic people." The home's owners not only collected a monthly fee from Ginger, but they also used her as an unpaid worker to do chores that no truly incapacitated person could ever perform. Ginger did all the grocery shopping, cooked meals for the patients, dispensed their medications, and kept track of doses in a computerized database. Every time Ginger appealed to probate judge Randy Kennedy to terminate her guardianship on the grounds that she had recovered, her conservator objected. Ginger was finally freed from court control in 2010, and she successfully sued the operators of the home. In 2014 a circuit court judge awarded her $23,050 and ruled that she had been the victim of "egregious and intentional abuse." The conservator was forced to resign after *The Tennessean* newspaper raised serious questions about her billing practices.[9] This court appointee was not prosecuted.

Those diagnosed with certain psychiatric disorders are also known to have come under court control, even though they might have been able to lead independent lives had their path in life been different. Two such cases researched for this book were most compelling: a young woman in Virginia diagnosed with ADHD, depression, and borderline personality disorder; and a bipolar Missouri man with a master's degree in business. Both were placed into guardianship. The woman was guardianized in 2016 at age eighteen. She submitted her story to the National Association to Stop

Guardianship Abuse website, writing, "There are people out there living with the mental conditions that I have and do not have a guardian. I am currently enrolled in college and I have a GPA of 3.143. I do not think I need a guardian."[10] The brother of the Missouri man also submitted a summary to NASGA about his then forty-seven-year-old brother's confinement in a nursing home.[11] He said no one in their family had been given notice about the guardianship hearing that claimed his brother decades earlier. "[He] is bipolar. This is an inherited illness . . . mother was bipolar and she lived a normal life with occasional hospital stays do [sic] to the illness. However, the court-appointed guardian will not allow [my brother] to have a life, family, or friends . . . his illness has worsened."[12] To be sure, both of these testimonials are only one side of likely complex personal stories, but one can only wonder whether these two citizens could have lived very different lives if kept out of the court system and treated by a qualified mental health specialist in a closely monitored program of medicines and therapy. It is impossible to ascertain how many people with the same diagnoses as these two wards have successfully lived their lives in freedom. Another point: do we want to be a society that essentially imprisons and then strips away the civil rights of citizens who suffer from mental illness?

When things go wrong, it is human nature to want to find out who is responsible. In the case of guardianships and conservatorships, there seems to be little or no accountability. Yet the facts are clear. It is the person who sits on the bench that initiates the guardianship process. Every judge is sworn to uphold the law and represent the integrity of the judicial system. If they create a situation that harms—rather than helps—a ward, who else should the public hold responsible? When conscripted citizens are hidden away from loved ones by heartless guardians—sometimes for years—leaving them to die alone believing their family abandoned them, who should stand accused of wrongdoing? When someone who suffered a temporary infirmity is forced to remain in the system permanently or long after they have recovered, who should be held accountable? And when unwanted divorce decrees are issued, or longtime marriages are annulled so the marital estate can be split and spent to pay court appointees, who should be held liable for tearing apart a legal union? Again, the judge is the final arbiter, and his or her offending officers of the court will always say that "the judge gave me permission to do what I did."

In many of the cases mentioned here, human beings have had their lives destroyed by a system that finds it easier to warehouse people than to give thoughtful consideration to humane alternatives. Perhaps the most baffling aspect of the current situation is the lack of action from law enforcement and regulatory boards and agencies. The former insists that despite evidence of potential criminality—like conspiracy to defraud, theft, embezzlement, forced isolation and overmedication, or physical abuse—they cannot investigate because a civil judge has already ruled. The latter, like state judicial or lawyer disciplinary boards or state watchdog groups, seem to routinely file away complaints without much, or any, investigation and next to no recommendations for punishment.

When Congressman Claude Pepper held his groundbreaking hearings in 1987, nearly all targets of the unscrupulous were elderly, and a majority were women who had outlived their husbands. Today, the victim pool has expanded as predators have figured out ways to entrap people with physical and intellectual disabilities who receive malpractice trust annuities or generous government subsidies; young people who have earned or inherited sizable amounts of money; women caught up in contentious divorce proceedings; those who have suffered workplace injuries and received substantial workers' compensation settlements; or people who own valuable property that can be bought and then sold for a tidy profit. It is likely that few of these conscripts had ever heard of guardianship or conservatorship, and many had absolutely no warning about what the system could do to them until it was too late.

As the *New York Times* wrote in December 2018, "Guardianship [is] where the breakdown of modern life—broken families, broken health, broken finances and broken bureaucracy—tumbled together in a system that appeared to bring out the worst in people: secretive, confusing and run by lawyers, with extraordinary powers over vulnerable individuals. It was also the last defense for lives that had come undone." This is the state of our modern-day guardianship and conservatorship system. In civilized society, where every person possesses indisputable human rights and civil liberties, no right-thinking person can argue that the status quo should be allowed to stand unchecked. The judges, lawyers, guardians, conservators, medical evaluators, and others who populate the system know full well about the activities of the deceitful and money-driven element within. Those who perform their duties honorably—and there are countless well-meaning players in the system—should understand that their dishonest colleagues corrupt the entire process and taint everyone in it. Those who act in good faith but remain silent about the corruption provide cover for the predators and condone the inhumanity inherent in stealing money and freedom from the vulnerable.

Could an unexpected guardianship or conservatorship happen to you or someone you love? You bet it could. In a very real sense, this is the most under-discussed civil rights issue of our time. It is way past time for a serious overhaul of this corrupted system.

NOTES

INTRODUCTION

1. Procedures for emergency guardianship petitions vary from state to state. A quick online search offers a summarized guideline. Some states include checklists for private citizens who want to file for an emergency judgment on their own. See, for example, California's instructions, "How to Ask for an Emergency Guardianship," www.courts.ca.gov/partners/documents/ask_for_emergency_ guardianship.pdf.

2. The case of Dr. Mike Reichert. National Association to STOP Guardian Abuse, "Investigation: Guarding the Guardians," *NASGA* (blog), May 19, 2015, nasga-stopguardianabuse.blogspot.com/2015/05/investigation-guarding -guardians.html.

3. In Texas, not all judges are trained lawyers. In the case that guardianized Dr. Mike Reichert, the Titus County judge was not a member of the Texas bar association.

4. Brenda K. Uekert and Richard Van Duizend, "Adult Guardianships: A 'Best Guess' National Estimate and the Momentum for Reform," *Future Trends in State Courts* (2011): 106–13. At the time of this writing, this report is available at the following website under the section "Guardianship Data," subsection "A 'Best Guess' Estimate of Guardianship Cases," www.eldersandcourts.org /guardianship-old/guardianship-basics-old. A 2018 estimate from the National Council on Disability set the number of guardianized Americans at 1.3 million. See "Beyond Guardianship: Toward Alternatives That Promote Greater Self-Determination for People with Disabilities," March 22, 2018, https://ncd.gov /publications/2018/beyond-guardianship-toward-alternatives.

5. Katie J. M. Baker and Heidi Blake, "8 Important Findings From BuzzFeed News' Investigation Into Guardianships," *BuzzFeed News*, December 29, 2021, available online at buzzfeednews.com.

6. Dennis Thompson, "How 1.3 Million Americans Became Controlled by Conservatorships," *PressNewsAgency*, October 19, 2021, https://pressnewsagency.org/how-1-3-million-americans-became-controlled-by-conservatorships/.

7. Alisa Partlan, "They Say Legal Guardians Ripped Them Off—and the State AG Let Them Down," *City Limits*, June 5, 2018, available online at citylimits.org.

8. See chapter 12: "The Cowgirl vs. the Conservator."

9. Public guardians, those hired by the state to take care of indigent individuals, are held to a more stringent and well-defined set of fees, though state laws vary. See the Standard Fee Schedule detailed by Guardian Finance and Advocacy Services, www.yourguardian.org/services/guardian/schedule-of-fees/.

10. The National Center for Law and Elder Rights, an agency within the Department of Health and Human Services, warns in its online Elder Justice Toolkit of the "immense" power of unchecked guardians. "Guardianship & Elder Abuse," available online at ncler.acl.gov. Eleanor Bader declared that guardianship can be "a feeding frenzy for unscrupulous professionals and for a growing number of non-profit corporations." Eleanor J. Bader, "The Power to End a Person's Life," *The Progressive*, March 7, 2022, available online at progressive.org.

11. National Guardianship Association, *Standards of Practice*, 4th ed. (National Guardianship Association, 2013), 8, 23, www.guardianship.org/wp-content/uploads/2017/07/NGA-Standards-with-Summit-Revisions-2017.pdf.

12. Léonie Rosenstiel, *Protecting Mama: Surviving the Legal Guardianship Swamp* (Minneapolis: Calumet Editions, 2021), 158.

13. Carol Kuruvilla, "Hospice Overdosed Patients to 'Hasten Their Deaths,' Former Health Care Executive Admits," *Huffington Post*, May 18, 2018, available online at huffpost.com.

14. See the case of guardian April Parks in Tom George, "Disgraced Former Nevada Guardian Sentenced to Serve up to 40 Years," *KTNV Las Vegas*, January 4, 2019, available online at ktnv.com.

15. See also chapter 6: "Guardians from Hell—and Lawyers and Judges Too." For more on the case of guardian Rebecca Fierle, see Danielle DaRos, "I-Team: Florida's Most Notorious Guardian," *CBS12 News* (Gainesville, FL), November 5, 2021, available online at cbs12.com.

16. See quote from Dr. Sam Sugar in Eleanor J. Bader, "The Power to End a Person's Life," *The Progressive*, March 7, 2022, available online at progressive.org.

17. See the case of Paul Kormanik in "Convicted Guardianship Lawyer Died of Suicide, Attorney Says," *Columbus Dispatch*, October 5, 2015, available online at dispatch.com.

18. See the case of Patience Bristol in Colton Lochhead, "Court-Appointed Guardian Accused of Stealing from the Vulnerable Sentenced to Prison," *Las Vegas Review-Journal*, May 28, 2014, available online at reviewjournal.com.

19. A state-by-state list of criminal and credit background checks is available from the Center for Guardianship Certification at guardianshipcert.org.

20. Catherine Anne Seal and Pamela B. Teaster, "The Time Has Finally Come: An Argument and a Roadmap for Regulating the Court-Appointed Professional

Fiduciary," *Syracuse Law Review* 72, no. 469 (2022): 470, 488, https://lawreview
.syr.edu/wp-content/uploads/2022/09/469-494-Seal-2.pdf.

CHAPTER 1. THE FLOODGATES OPEN

1. Judge Brickhouse is also mentioned in chapter 12: "The Cowgirl vs. the
Conservator."

2. Attorney Millet is also mentioned in chapter 12: The Cowgirl vs. the
Conservator."

3. Mr. Millet disputes this conclusion on his website, saying that derogatory
statements made about him have been advanced by "two disturbed persons"
posting on the internet. He concludes: "I value my reputation as an honest and
fair attorney. That opinion is shared by the vast majority of attorneys who have
been on the other side of cases from me, and the judges who heard those cases."
See albuquerqueadvocates.com/.

4. According to the American Bar Association, when a lawyer receives large
sums on behalf of a client, they are required to deposit the funds in trust accounts so the earned interest goes to the client.

5. In the Matter of the Jack A. Herrmann Revocable Trust, Notice of Filing
of Final Accounting and Motion to Terminate Trust, relevant sections: 7–10,
presented by Albuquerque Advocates //s// Darryl W. Millet, Attorney at Law,
undated.

6. Diane Dimond, "Elder Guardianships: A Shameful 'Racket,'" *Creators Syndicate*, February 20, 2016, available online at creators.com.

7. The facility refused to respond to multiple requests for comment on the
Winstanley case.

8. Richard Winstanley refused numerous requests for comment.

9. See the Health Insurance Portability and Accountability Act of 1996
(HIPAA), available at www.cdc.gov/phlp/publications/topic/hipaa.html.

10. Diane Dimond, "Plundering Grandma's Estate Via Court Ordered Guardianships," *Creators Syndicate*, May 7, 2016, available online at creators.com.

11. "Betty Winstanley RIP July 2018 after having her assets and her life stolen
from her by Judge Jay J. Hoberg & Judge James P. Cullen," *Judicialpedia*, July
17, 2014, available online at judicialpedia.com.

CHAPTER 2. THE CASE HEARD 'ROUND THE WORLD

1. Ronan Farrow and Jia Tolentino, "Britney Spears's Conservatorship Nightmare," *New Yorker*, July 3, 2021, available online at newyorker.com.

2. Liz Day, Samantha Stark, and Joe Coscarelli, "Britney Spears Quietly
Pushed for Years to End Her Conservatorship," *New York Times*, June 22, 2021,
available online at nytimes.com.

3. Madeline Berg, "Britney Spears' Net Worth Revealed—And It's Shockingly
Low Compared To Her Pop Peers," *Forbes*, February 17, 2021, available online at
forbes.com.

4. Day, Stark, and Coscarelli, "Britney Spears Quietly Pushed for Years to End
Her Conservatorship."

5. Farrow and Tolentino, "Britney Spears's Conservatorship Nightmare"; Nicholas Hautman, "Who Is Lou Taylor? Meet Britney Spears' Embattled Former Business Manager," *Page Six*, July 6, 2022, available online at pagesix.com.

6. Lynne Spears, *Through the Storm: A Real Story of Fame and Family in a Tabloid World* (Nashville: Thomas Nelson, 2008).

7. Farrow and Tolentino, "Britney Spears's Conservatorship Nightmare."

8. Marissa Martinelli, "Why Did Britney Spears Have to Confirm She's Not Being Held Hostage?," *Slate*, April 24, 2019, available online at slate.com.

9. Liz Day (@LizDDay), "5. Specifically, an email from Lou to Jamie two weeks before they applied for the conservatorship," Twitter, July 5, 2021, 1:01 p.m., https://twitter.com/LizDDay/status/1544365784096333826.

10. "Michael Lohan to Fight Dina & Lou Taylor for Lindsay Conservatorship," *X17 Online*, September 2010, available online at x17online.com.

11. Cameron Frew, "Courtney Love Says Britney Spears' Manager 'Almost Killed' Her and Kurt Cobain's Daughter," *UNILAD*, December 17, 2020, available online at unilad.co.uk.

12. BreatheHeavy.com, "My Apology to Britney Spears' Former Business Manager Lou Taylor (By Demand)," Facebook, December 19, 2020, www.facebook.com/watch/?v=706406550300300.

13. Farrow and Tolentino, "Britney Spears's Conservatorship Nightmare."

14. Dana Kennedy, "Britney Spears' Family Has a Long, Dark History of Locking Women Up," *New York Post*, October 9, 2021, available online at nypost.com.

15. Joe Coscarelli, "Britney Spears Announces 'Indefinite Work Hiatus,' Cancels Las Vegas Residency," *New York Times*, January 4, 2019, available online at nytimes.com.

16. Karen Mizoguchi, "Everything to Know About Britney Spears' Father Jamie's Health Battle: He 'Almost Died,'" *People*, April 4, 2019, available online at people.com.

17. Jason Pham, "Judge Approves Britney Spears' New Conservator after Kevin Federline Files Restraining Order against Dad Jamie," *US Weekly*, September 9, 2019, available online at usmagazine.com.

18. Tufayel Ahmed, "Who Is Jamie Spears? Britney Spears' Sons File Restraining Order against Their Grandfather," *Newsweek*, September 4, 2019, available online at newsweek.com.

19. Elizabeth Wagmeister, "Britney Spears' Father Jamie Spears Agrees to Step Down from Conservatorship," *Variety*, August 12, 2021, available online at variety.com.

20. For more about attorney Jodi Montgomery and the conservatorship case of Theresa Jankowski, see also chapter 15: "The Sad Stories of Theresa and Susan."

21. Day, Stark, and Coscarelli, "Britney Spears Quietly Pushed for Years to End Her Conservatorship."

22. Farrow and Tolentino, "Britney Spears's Conservatorship Nightmare."

23. California Code, Probate Code—PROB § 2601, https://codes.findlaw.com/ca/probate-code/prob-sect-2601.html.

24. Alexander Kacala and Diana Dasrath, "Britney Spears Fiercely Addresses Court in Controversial Conservatorship Case," *Today*, June 23, 2021, available online at today.com.

25. Cheri Mossburg, "Read the Full Transcript of Britney Spears' Court Hearing Statement," *CNN*, June 24, 2021, available online at cnn.com.

26. Ma'ayan Anafi, Senior Counsel for Health, Equity and Justice, National Women's Law Center, Newsweek, February 3, 2022. In addition, see a state-by-state list indicating which states allow guardians to pursue sterilization of a ward: https://en.wikipedia.org/wiki/Sterilization_law_in_the_United_States.

27. Liz Day and Samantha Stark, "The Surveillance Apparatus That Surrounded Britney Spears," *New York Times*, September 24, 2021, available online at nytimes.com.

28. Jenna Ryu and Cydney Henderson, "Britney Spears: Judge Grants Bessemer Trust's Request to Withdraw from Conservatorship," *USA Today*, July 1, 2021, available online at usatoday.com.

29. Tomás Mier, "Britney Spears' Attorney Sam Ingham Asks to Resign Following Bombshell Court Hearing," *People*, July 6, 2021, available online at people.com.

30. Reuters, "Britney Spears' Longtime Manager Resigns over Her Intention to Stop Singing, Reports," *NewsNation*, July 6, 2021, available online at newsnationnow.com.

31. Video with ABC News anchor Linsey Davis, "Britney Spears' Conservatorship 'Is a Sinking Ship' at This Point: Legal Expert," July 13, 2021, available online at abcnews.go.com.

32. ACLU Southern California, "ACLU, Disability Rights Orgs File Amicus Brief in Britney Spears Case," July 13, 2021, available online at aclusocal.org.

33. Zoe Brennan-Krohn, email message to author, August 3, 2022. Ms. Brennan-Krohn chose not to reply to the specific question about whether the ACLU, or any of its chapters, had ever been involved in a guardianship or conservatorship case prior to the one involving Britney Spears.

34. Andrew Dalton, "Judge Allows Britney Spears to Hire Her Own Lawyer in Conservatorship Case," *Los Angeles Times*, July 14, 2021, available online at latimes.com.

35. Madeline Berg, "Britney Spears' Net Worth Revealed—And It's Shockingly Low Compared To Her Pop Peers," *Forbes*, February 17, 2021, available online at forbes.com.

36. Ashley Cullins, "Britney Spears Taps CPA to Take Over as Conservator of Her Estate," *Hollywood Reporter*, July 26, 2021, available online at hollywoodreporter.com.

37. Tom Pattinson, "Everyone Loves Britney - III. Toxic," March 11, 2021, in *Defiance*, produced by Peter McCormack, podcast, 53:52, at 49:30, www.stitcher.com/show/defiance/episode/everyone-loves-britney-iii-toxic-82308300.

38. Zoe Christen Jones and Mandy Aracena, "Britney Spears' Conservatorship Is Terminated after More Than 13 Years," *CBS News*, November 12, 2021, available online at cbsnews.com.

39. Cole Delbyck, "Britney Spears Announces Engagement to Sam Asghari," *Huffington Post*, September 12, 2021, available at huffpost.com.

40. Amici curiae document entitled "Supplement to: petition to terminate conservatorship of the person and estate; Declaration of Lisa MacCarley," pages 1–28, including various exhibits from commencement of original conservatorship in 2006, filed in Superior Court of Los Angeles, Central District, September 13, 2021; emphasis included in original.

41. "Dr. James E. Spar," *US News & World Report*, available online at health.usnews.com.

42. Lisa Richwine, "Sumner Redstone Has Capacity to Make Trust Decisions, Says Doctor," *MarketScreener*, June 3, 2016, available online at marketscreener.com.

43. Chris Gardner, "Netflix's Britney Spears Doc: 12 Revelations from 'Britney vs Spears,'" *Hollywood Reporter*, September 28, 2021, available online at hollywoodreporter.com.

44. Pattinson, "Everyone Loves Britney: III. Toxic," at 13:00.

45. See chapter 12: "The Cowgirl vs. the Conservator" for a detailed explanation of how a waiver of liability thwarted the Darnell family when they attempted to take legal action against conservator Darryl Millet.

CHAPTER 3. THE PLAYERS

1. "What Is Probate Court? 8 Steps to Probating a Will," Executor.org, https://executor.org/probate-court/.

2. See, for example, Rhode Island, in "What Is Probate Court?," FindLaw, last updated June 30, 2022, available online at findlaw.com.

3. Mary McMahon, "What Is a Court of Equity?," MyLawQuestions, September 11, 2022, available online at mylawquestions.com.

4. Julie Garber, "What Is a Probate Judge?: Probate Judges Explained," *The Balance*, January 14, 2022, available online at thebalance.com.

5. See the Health Insurance Portability and Accountability Act of 1996 (HIPAA), available online at cdc.gov.

CHAPTER 4. BRITNEY IS NOT ALONE

1. Rosamund Park's character was said to be based on April Parks, a notorious convicted guardian in Nevada. See chapter 6: "Guardians from Hell—and Lawyers and Judges Too."

2. Andy and Danielle Mayoras, "Judges Order Conservatorship Over Peter Falk," The Probate Lawyer Blog, June 2, 2009, available at probatelawyerblog.com.

3. Victoria Kim, "Family Fights for Control of Sick Actor," *Los Angeles Times*, May 29, 2009, available at latimes.com.

4. Ester NJeri, "Falk Had 'Very Loving Relationship' with Daughters Yet Stepmom Did Not Let Them Visit Him before Death," August 29, 2022, AmoMama.

5. WENN, "Falk's Wife Awarded Conservatorship," June 2, 2009, available online at contactmusic.com.

6. CBC Arts, "Judge Imposes Conditions to Ensure Daughter Can Visit Ailing Peter Falk," CBC, June 2, 2009, available at cbc.ca.

7. "Judge Considers Conservatorship Over Actor Peter Falk," May 18, 2009, updated January 7, 2010, available online at nbclosangeles.com.

8. "Peter Falk's Daughter Says She Was Banned from His Funeral," July 11, 2011, updated July 12, 2011, available online at insideedition.com.

9. https://catherinefalkorganization.org/.

10. Diane Dimond, "'Columbo' Bill Seeks to Curb Guardian Power," March 13, 2017, available online at abqjournal.com.

11. Rachel Sharp, "'I Hope It Ruffles Some Feathers': Casey Kasem's Daughter Speaks Out About His Death in New Podcast and Insists Bitter Legal Battles with His Widow Were NOT Over His Wealth," *Daily Mail*, June 26, 2021, updated June 27, 2021, available online at dailymail.co.uk.

12. Stephanie Nolasco, "Casey Kasem's Daughter Kerri Hopes New Podcast on Star's Controversial Death 'Ruffles Some Feathers,'" June 26, 2021, available online at foxnews.com.

13. "Jean Kasem Refuses to Let Friends & Family See Casey Kasem," Rumor-Fix, video, 2:44, October 3, 2013, available online at youtube.com.

14. Alan Duke, "Judge Rejects Conservatorship for Casey Kasem; Finds Wife Taking Good Care of Him," *CNN*, November 19, 2013, available online at cnn.com.

15. "Casey Kasem: Daughters to Pull Life Support," June 11, 2014, available online at tmz.com. Includes video of Jean Kasem.

16. Stephanie Nolasco, "Casey Kasem's Daughter Wants to Bring Star's Body Back from Norway, Stepmother Denies Elder Abuse Allegations," *FoxNews*, June 18, 2019, available online at foxnews.com.

17. Nancy Dillon, "Casey Kasem Could Have Died from Wife Disconnecting His Feeding Tube, Snatching Him From Nursing Home: EXCLUSIVE," June 12, 2014, available at nydailynews.com.

18. "Jean Kasem Throws Raw Meat after Casey Kasem Taken Away in," Lindsay Cohen, video, 0:09, June 2, 2014, available online at youtube.com.

19. Kerri Kasem and Aliza Rosen, "Ep. 366, Kerri Kasem Bitter Blood: Kasem vs. Kasem," June 11, 2021, in *Reality Life with Kate Casey*, produced by Aliza Rosen, podcast, 43:00, available at podcasts.apple.com.

20. http://kasemwrightcoalition.org/.

21. "Glen Campbell's Final Interview - 02-10-12 - KTVT/CBS-11," Daniel Penz, video, 3:52, August 9, 2017, available online at youtube.com.

22. Jennifer Ruby, "Moving on: Country Star Glen Campbell Sells His Malibu Mansion for $4.5 Million after Farewell Tour due to Alzheimer's Diagnosis," *Daily Mail*, January 6, 2013, available at dailymail.co.uk.

23. Jane Warren, "Glen Campbell's Family at War: Singer in Alzheimer's Home as Wife and Children Battle," *Daily Express*, March 7, 2015, available online at express.co.uk.

24. "Documentary Shares Glen Campbell's Alzheimer's Journey," Mayo Clinic, video, 4:22, January 15, 2015, available online at youtube.com.

25. "*Glen Campbell: I'll Be Me*, Official Movie Trailer," Gwenaëlle Gobé, video, 3:00, August 21, 2014, available online at vimeo.com.

26. Christie D'Zurilla, "Glen Campbell's Kids Fighting Singer's Wife for Control of His Affairs," *Los Angeles Times*, March 4, 2015, available online at latimes .com.

27. Stephanie Nolasco, "Mickey Rooney's Daughter Recalls Close Bond With Star After Her Mother's Tragic passing: 'We Cherished Him,'" April 6, 2019, available at foxnews.com.

28. Judge Goetz was the presiding judge who originally established the Britney Spears conservatorship.

29. Testimony of Mickey Rooney before the Senate Special Committee on Aging, March 2, 2011, www.aging.senate.gov/imo/media/doc/hr230mr.pdf.

CHAPTER 6. GUARDIANS FROM HELL—AND LAWYERS AND JUDGES TOO

1. "Who We Are," National Guardianship Association, available online at guardianship.org.

2. www.floridaguardians.com/.

3. Brenda K. Uekert and Richard Van Duizend, "Adult Guardianships: A 'Best Guess' National Estimate and the Momentum for Reform," *Future Trends in State Courts* (2011): 106–13. At the time of this writing, this report is available at the following website under the section "Guardianship Data," subsection "A 'Best Guess' Estimate of Guardianship Cases," www.eldersandcourts.org /guardianship-old/guardianship-basics-old. A 2018 estimate from the National Council on Disability set the number of guardianized Americans at 1.3 million. See "Beyond Guardianship: Toward Alternatives That Promote Greater Self-Determination for People with Disabilities," March 22, 2018, available online at ncd.gov.

4. Colton Lochhead, "Clark County's Private Guardians May Protect—or Just Steal and Abuse," *Las Vegas Review-Journal*, April 13, 2015, available online at reviewjournal.com.

5. Diane Dimond, "Where Is Accountability for Guardians' Actions?," *Albuquerque Journal*, March 25, 2017, available online at abqjournal.com.

6. The guardianship of Del Mencarelli, the father-in-law of Rick Black, founder of the Center for Estate Administration Reform (CEAR), began in the summer of 2013. Black and his wife, Terri, immediately started to enlist the help of state officials and then, in frustration, the media.

7. Jon Norheim was removed from guardianship court in 2015. He was transferred to preside over cases involving neglected children. "EDITORIAL: Victims of Guardianship Travesty Finally Receive Justice," *Las Vegas Review-Journal*, January 8, 2019, available online at reviewjournal.com.

8. Matthew Hoffman, "Breaking Down the Law: Elder Abuse and the Case of April Parks," *NBC3 News* (Las Vegas, NV), December 18, 2019, available online at news3lv.com.

9. Rachel Aviv, "How the Elderly Lose Their Rights," *New Yorker*, October 2, 2017, available online at newyorker.com.

10. Marvin Clemons, "Four Plead Guilty to 270 Counts in Nevada's Largest Elder Exploitation Case," *NBC3 News* (Las Vegas, NV), November 5, 2018, available online at news3lv.com.

11. Colton Lochhead, "Grand Jury Indicts Nevada Guardian on More Than 200 Charges," *Las Vegas Review-Journal*, March 8, 2017, available online at review journal.com.

12. Sean Kelly, "Man Makes Shocking Discovery in Storage Unit (Photo)," *Opposing Views*, March 6, 2018, available online at opposingviews.com.

13. Parks and her codefendants agreed to what is called an Alford plea, an arrangement that means the defendant decided it would be better to be sentenced than to take their chances in a criminal trial, which could lead to a maximum sentence. John Devendorf, Esq., "What Is an Alford Plea?," LawInfo, last updated June 8, 2021, available online at lawinfo.com.

14. David Ferrara, "Ex-Nevada Guardian to Serve up to 40 Years behind Bars," *Las Vegas Review-Journal*, January 4, 2019, available online at reviewjournal .com.

15. David Ferrara, "Ex-Nevada Guardian to Serve Up to 40 Years Behind Bars," *Las Vegas Review Journal*, January 4, 2019, available online at reviewjournal. com.

16. Colton Lochhead, "Grand Jury Indicts Nevada Guardian on More Than 200 Charges," *Las Vegas Review-Journal*, March 8, 2017, available online at reviewjournal.com.

17. Associated Press, "Ex-Appointed Guardian Gets Prison in Nevada Elder Abuse Case," *Washington Times*, January 4, 2019, available online at washing tontimes.com.

18. Bennett Loudon, "Fourth Department Disbars Lawyer," *The Daily Record*, November 19, 2019, available online at nydailyrecord.com.

19. Greg Angel, "Watchdog: County Probe Raises More Questions About Embattled Florida Guardian," *Spectrum News13*, July 26, 2019, available online at mynews13.com.

20. Monivette Cordeiro, "Man Died After Orlando Guardian Filed 'Do Not Resuscitate' Order against His Wishes, Investigation Finds—Exclusive," July 15, 2019, available at orlandosentinel.com.

21. Monivette Cordeiro, "Judge Dismisses AdventHealth from Lawsuit by Family of Man at Center of Guardianship Scandal—For Now," September 2, 2020, available at orlandosentinel.com.

22. Cordeiro, "Man Died After Orlando Legal Guardians Filed 'Do Not Resuscitate' Order."

23. At a closed hearing before Judge Thorpe in late July 2019, a transcript of which was obtained by the media, Lori Loftis of the Office of Criminal Conflict and Civil Regional Counsel said, "Almost every [Fierle] case had a DNR." Monivette Cordeiro and Jeff Weiner, "Florida Elder Affairs Chief Announces 'Immediate' Changes as Embattled Orlando Guardian Rebecca Fierle Resigns from All Cases," *Orlando Sentinel*, July 26, 2019, available at orlandosentinel .com.

24. "Cremated Remains of 9 People Found in Office of Embattled Central Florida Guardian," *NBC WESH2* (Orlando, FL), last updated August 7, 2019, available at wesh.com.

25. Adam Walser, "New Audit Shows AdventHealth Paid Embattled Guardian Rebecca Fierle Nearly $4 Million," *ABC Action News WFTS* (Tampa Bay, FL), September 12, 2019, available at abcactionnews.com.

26. Mike Schneider, "Audit: Florida Guardian Had Wards with No Court Supervision," *The Ledger*, September 12, 2019, available at theledger.com.

27. Phil Diamond, CPA, Orange County Comptroller, "Investigation of Payments Made to Professional Guardian—Rebecca Fierle by AdventHealth," September 2019, www.occompt.com/download/Audit%20Reports/rpt479.pdf, pages 14–15, September 2019.

28. The clerk's offices that participate must be, among other requirements, accredited by the Florida Commission for Law Enforcement, accreditation for Inspectors General.

29. Available online at orlandosentinel.com.

30. Greg Angel and Curtis McCloud, "Watchdog: Guardian Removed from 98 Seniors' Care After Man's Death," July 19, 2019, available at mynews13.com.

31. Monivette Cordeiro, "Rebecca Fierle Trial: Judge Declares Mistrial in Orlando Guardian's Case," September 15, 2022, available online at msn.com.

32. It is not entirely clear, but it appears Mr. Stryker was found urinating in public at one point and that was the offense that earned him his sex offender designation. A Brevard County, Florida, arrest record reveals that in April 2000 Stryker was charged with one felony count of "exposure of sexual organs/lewd or lascivious exhibition." He was found guilty on September 6, 2001, and ordered to be placed on the state's sexual offender registry. Supporters of Stryker describe the offense as "taking a whiz at the beach," but that cannot be independently confirmed.

33. Monivette Cordeiro, "Man Died after Orlando Legal Guardian Filed 'Do Not Resuscitate' Order against His Wishes, Investigation Finds | Exclusive," *Orlando Sentinel*, July 26, 2019, available online at orlandosentinel.com.

34. Monivette Cordeiro, "Expert's Complaint Against Florida Guardian Rebecca Fierle Was Ignore For Years Before Scandal Erupted—Exclusive," available online at orlandosentinel.com.

35. Emails exchanged and telephone interviews conducted between the author and Angela Woodhall beginning in early March 2022 and concluding on July 31, 2022.

36. Diane Chau et al., "Opiates and Elderly: Use and Side Effects," *Clinical Interventions in Aging* 3, no. 2 (2008): 273–78.

37. Robert J. Young, "Dextropropoxyphene Overdosage," *Drugs* 26 (1983): 70–79; Lawson, A. A. H. Lawson and D. B. Northridge, "Dextropropoxyphene Overdose," *Med Toxicol Adverse Drug Exp* 2 (1987): 430–44; R. Afshari et al., "ECG Abnormalities in Co-Proxamol (Paracetamol/Dextropropoxyphene) Poisoning," *Clinical Toxicology* 43, no. 4 (2005): 255–59; S. Simkin et al., "Co-Proxamol and

Suicide: Preventing the Continuing Toll of Overdose Deaths," *QJM: An International Journal of Medicine* 98, no. 3 (2005): 159–70.

38. "Bodycam Video Shows Guardian Was Calm during Arrest," *Ocala Post*, February 15, 2020, available online at ocalapost.com.

39. More on Judge Colin in chapter 13: "The Richer the Better"; see the case of Oliver Bivins.

40. The 2016 *Palm Beach Post* series was entitled "Guardianship: A Broken Trust."

41. Judge Colin earned $146,000 a year as a circuit court judge.

42. John Pacenti, "Professional Guardian Elizabeth Savitt Accused of Taking Fees Before Court Oks Them," *Palm Beach Post*, January 13, 2016, updated October 3, 2018, available online at palmbeachpost.com.

43. Code of Judicial Conduct for the State of Florida, as amended through July 3, 2008, 22–24, https://2ndcircuit.leoncountyfl.gov/resources/judicial Conduct.pdf.

44. Holly Baltz and John Pacenti, "Did Judge, Wife Commit a Crime? State Attorney Says No, But Probe Had Glaring Deficiencies," June 30, 2019, www .ccfj.net/CORRJudgeWifeCrime.htm.

45. Anthony Palmieri, Investigation Report, Case Number OPPG Guardian INV 2016-003, Division of Inspector General, West Palm Beach, FL, March 10, 2017, reissued December 8, 2017, www.documentcloud.org/documents/4839961 -Savitt-IR-Redacted.html.

46. "Report: Savitt Involved with 'Corruption, Collusion of judges,'" *Palm Beach Post*, September 8, 2018, available at palmbeachpost.com.

47. See page 8 of Palmieri, Investigation Report, Case Number OPPG Guardian INV 2016-003. The inspector general's twenty-five-page report concluded: "The Clerk's IG traced the source of funds used to satisfy the large debt of mortgage" and determined any connection with a guardianship case was "unfounded."

48. See pages 4 and 5 of Palmieri, Investigative Report, Case Number OPPG guardian INV-2016-003, www.documentcloud.org/documents/4839961-Savitt -IR-Redacted.html.

49. John Pacenti, "Report: Savitt Involved with 'Corruption, Collusion of Judges,'" *Palm Beach Post*, September 8, 2018, available online at palmbeach post.com.

50. Holly Baltz and John Pacenti, "State Attorney Didn't Turn Over Colin Probe Records Until Post Threatened to Sue," *Palm Beach Post*, May 9, 2019, available online at palmbeachpost.com.

51. Holly Baltz and John Pacenti, "Did Judge, Wife Commit a Crime? State Attorney Says No, But Probe Had Glaring Deficiencies," *Palm Beach Post*, republished June 30, 2019, http://www.ccfj.net/CORRJudgeWifeCrime.htm.

52. John Pacenti, "Judge Martin Colin, Wife Elizabeth Savitt Benefit from Frail Seniors' Money," *Palm Beach Post*, January 13, 2016, updated October 3, 2018, available online at palmbeachpost.com.

53. John Pacenti, "State Revokes Guardianship Registration for Savitt," *Palm Beach Post*, March 21, 2019, updated March 22, 2019, available online at palm beachpost.com.

54. See https://colinmediation.com.

55. Staff Writer, "Ohio Doesn't Require Guardian to Meet with Wards, and Many Don't," May 19, 2014, available online at dispatch.com.

56. Staff Writer, "Investigations Launched into Billing by Lawyers Appointed as Guardians," May 18, 2014, updated May 18, 2014, available online at dispatch .com.

57. "Rico Indictment Filed against Columbus Attorney," Franklin County Prosecuting Attorney, January 28, 2015, available online at prosecutor.franklin countyohio.gov.

58. Lucas Sullivan, "Restitution for Wards May Be Long Fight," *The Columbus Dispatch*, November 28, 2015, available at dispatch.com.

59. Jan Goodwin, "Antipsychotics in Nursing Homes," *AARP Bulletin*, July/ August 2014, available online at aarp.org.

60. Email from attorney to author, April 8, 2022, 11:05 a.m.

61. See Rita Cole's obituary at tributearchive.com/obituaries.

62. Colleen Heild, "Former Ayudando CFO Sentenced to 20 Years for Bilking Clients," *Albuquerque Journal*, March 2, 2020, available online at abqjournal.com.

63. "Albuquerque Couple Sentenced to Federal Prison in Ayudando Guardians Case," Department of Justice, US Attorney's Office, District of New Mexico, July 15, 2021, available at justice.gov; Carol A. Clark, "FBI: Albuquerque Couple Sentenced to Prison for Crimes Committed in Connection with Ayudando Guardians Case," *Los Alamos Daily Post*, July 19, 2021, available at ladailypost.com.

64. This hearing was set to pass sentence on Susan and William Harris and their CFO, Sharon Moore. Craig Young's sentencing hearing was held in June 2020. "Craig M. Young Sentenced to 71 Months in Prison in $11 Million Ayudando Guardians Financial Fraud Scheme," Internal Revenue Service, June 11, 2020, available at irs.gov.

65. Colleen Heild, "Ayudando Fugitives Arrested in Oklahoma," *Albuquerque Journal*, April 15, 2020, available online at abqjournal.com.

66. Colleen Heild, "Accountant: Ayudando Served As a 'Family ATM,'" July 17, 2021, available online at abqjournal.com.

CHAPTER 7. HOW DO THE BAD ACTORS GET AWAY WITH IT?

1. Colton Lochhead, "Clark County's Private Guardians May Protect—or Just Steal and Abuse," *Las Vegas Review-Journal*, October 13, 2017, available online at reviewjournal.com.

2. In 1982 the Food and Drug Administration banned Gerovital H3 saying research revealed no evidence that it had any antiaging or health benefits. Thomas Perls, "The Reappearance of Procaine Hydrochloride (Gerovital H3) for Antiaging," *Journal of the American Geriatrics Society* 61, no. 6 (2013): 1024–25.

3. Steve Miller, "Speculation on Why Jared Shafer Has Not Yet Been Indicted," *The PPJ Gazette*, November 6, 2017, available online at ppjg.me.

4. Lochhead, "Clark County's Private Guardians."

5. Steve Miller, "Private 'Guardians' Jared E. Shafer and Patience Bristol Sue Blind Man for Libel, now Ask Taxpayers to Pay the Bill," *American Mafia*, June 30, 2014, available online at americanmafia.com.

6. Lachlan Markay, "Families of Abused Nevada Seniors Blame Politics for Senate Hopeful's Inaction," *Washington Free Beacon*, September 21, 2016, available online at freebeacon.com.

7. At the time of this writing, the search results on "Jared E. Shafer" at RipOffReport.com return fifty-one reports.

8. See the search results on "Guardian Jared Shafer" at RipOffReport.com.

9. RipOffReport.com, Report: #901541, reported by Molita, Saint George, UT, submitted June 22, 2012.

10. John Taylor, "Court-Appointed Guardian Used Wards' Funds to Stoke Gambling Addictions, Authorities Say," *Las Vegas Sun*, October 8, 2013, available at LasVegasSun.com/.

11. Colton Lochhead, "Court-Appointed Guardian Faces Charges of Stealing from Clients," *Las Vegas Review-Journal*, October 8, 2013, available online at reviewjournal.com.

12. "How a California Woman Got Her Father out of a Dangerously Financial Conservatorship," *NBC News*, video, 5:44, September 13, 2021, available at nbcnews.com.

13. Rachel Aviv, "How the Elderly Lose Their Rights," *New Yorker*, October 2, 2017, available online at newyorker.com.

14. Aviv, "How the Elderly Lose Their Rights."

15. Case No.: 2:14-cv-01298-GMN-NJK, United States District Court, Southern District of Nevada, May 20, 2015, www.stevemiller4lasvegas.com/Olvera AmendedComplaint05-21-2015.html.

16. See page 4 of document Case No.: 2:14-cv-01298-GMN-NJK.

17. "Guardian Abuse of 93 Year Old WWII Vet by Las Vegas Corrupt Family Court System & Jared E. Shafer," court proceedings, SteveMiller4LV, September 8, 2010, video, 2:26, February 16, 2013, available online at youtube.com.

18. Steve Miller, "Guadalupe Olvera's War! Elder Abuse Likely—Under Color Of Law," *American Mafia*, February 25, 2013, www.americanmafia.com/Inside _Vegas/2-25-13_Inside_Vegas.html.

19. "In the Matter If the Guardianship of the Persona and Estate of Guadalupe Mena Olvera, Adult Ward," Case No. G28163, District Court, Family Division, Clark County, Nevada, January 19, 2011, www.stevemiller4lasvegas.com /OliveraArrestWarrant.jpg.

20. Steve Miller, "Las Vegas 'Guardian' Jared E. Shafer Sued for 'Embezzling' $420,000 from 95 Year Old Former 'Ward,'" AmericanMafia.com, August 11, 2014.

21. Miller, "Las Vegas 'Guardian' Jared E. Shafer Sued for 'Embezzling' $420,000.00 from 95 Year Old Former 'Ward.'"

22. Markay, "Families of Abused Nevada Seniors Blame Politics for Senate Hopeful's Inaction."

23. Emails exchanged between Becky Schultz and the author, July 2022.

24. Case No.: A-171758506-C, Dept. No.: 28, Eighth Judicial District Court, Clark Counter, Nevada, www.stevemiller4lasvegas.com/JasonsAmended ComplaintWithCorrectNRS1.pdf.

25. See page 9 of document Case No.: A-171758506-C.

26. "Guardian Jared E. Shafer Exploits Special Needs Trust—Part One," Steve-Miller4LV, video, 5:22 at 2:18, March 2, 2014, available online at youtube.com.

27. Steve Miller, "'Guardian' Jared Shafer's Political Signs Become a Public Nuisance," *Canada Free Press*, April 29, 2014, available online at canadafreepress .com.

28. For various annual reports, see the search results on "Signs of Nevada, llc" at the website for the Nevada Secretary of State, www.nvsos.gov.

29. "Private Guardian Jared E. Shafer Orders Judge to Close Court to Public," court proceedings, SteveMiller4LV, May 22, 2013, video 1:25 at 0:53, March 18, 2014, available online at youtube.com.

30. The signature appears to be an oft-used stamp of Judge Hoskin's signature. A lowercase *j* is seen on the far right of the signature and likely indicates Hoskin's judicial assistant approved the order. This calls into question whether there was a hearing held on Shafer's request or if it was simply signed ex-parte by the assistant.

31. See page 7, paragraph 22 of document Opinion No. 04-01, "In the Matter of the Request for Opinion Concerning the Conduct of Jared Shafer, former Public Administrator, Clark County," Before the Nevada Commission on Ethics, June 10, 2005, https://ethics.nv.gov/uploadedFiles/ethicsnvgov/content/Opinions /2004/Opinion_04-01C.pdf.

32. Colton Lochhead, "Clark County Judges Take Guardianship Oversight Away from Embattled Judge, Hearing Master," *Las Vegas Review-Journal*, May 21, 2015, available at reviewjournal.com.

33. Judge Steel specifically mentioned Nevada Revised Statutes Chapter 159 and its inventory requirements, which can be accessed at www.leg.state.nv.us /NRS/NRS-159.html.

CHAPTER 8. WASHINGTON COULD HELP—BUT IT HASN'T

1. Fred Bayles, "Guardians of the Elderly: An Ailing System Part I: Declared 'Legally Dead' by a Troubled System," *AP News*, September 19, 1987, available online at apnews.com.

2. See page 8 of "Abuses in Guardianship of the Elderly and Infirm: A National Disgrace. A Briefing by the Chairman of the Subcommittee on Health and Long-Term Care of the Select Committee on Aging House of Representatives, One Hundredth Congress, First Session," Comm. Pub. No. 100-641, September 25, 1987, https://files.eric.ed.gov/fulltext/ED297241.pdf.

3. "Abuses in Guardianship of the Elderly and Infirm," 8.

4. The first federal use of guardianship can be traced to the early 1900s when federally mandated Indian reservation lands were found to have vast stores of oil, gas, and valuable minerals. An early form of "protective guard-

ianship" was used to seize those below-ground assets. Matthew L. M. Fletcher, "Failed Protectors: The Indian Trust and Killers of the Flower Moon," *Michigan Law Review* 117, no. 6 (2019): 1253–69. See also David Grann, *Killers of the Flower Moon: The Osage Murders and the Birth of the FBI* (New York: Doubleday, 2017), and see chapter 13 in this book.

5. "Abuses in Guardianship of the Elderly and Infirm," 6.

6. "Abuses in Guardianship of the Elderly and Infirm," 6.

7. "Abuses in Guardianship of the Elderly and Infirm," 22–27.

8. "In a continuation of their efforts to protect seniors from exploitation, Aging Committee Chairman Collins and Ranking Member McCaskill Hold Hearing on Elder Financial Abuse: 'Trust Betrayed: Financial Abuse of Older Americans by Guardians and Others in Power,'" United States Senate Special Committee on Aging, press release, December 1, 2016, available online at aging.senate.gov/press-releases.

9. "Senate Aging Committee Examines Ways to Strengthen Guardianship Programs," United States Senate Special Committee on Aging, press release, November 28, 2018, available online at aging.senate.gov/press-releases.

10. Senator Collins was likely quoting the statistic found at the US Census Bureau website. See Table 2, Projected Age and Sex Composition of the Population, available online at census.gov.

11. "Senators Collins, Casey Introduce Bipartisan Bill to Protect Individuals Under the Care of Guardians," official website of US senator Susan Collins, press release, September 28, 2021, available online at collins.senate.gov.

12. "S. 2881—117th Congress: Guardianship Accountability Act of 2021," www.GovTrack.us, 2021, available online at govtrack.us.

13. Adam Walser, "Daughter of Artist Peter Max Says Guardianship Has Cost Her Father $16 Million: Guardians Aren't above Prosecution Act Introduced," *ABC Action News WFTS-TV* (Tampa Bay, FL), November 10, 2021, available online at abcactionnews.com.

14. Laura Snapes, "Britney Spears: Congressmen Demand Hearing on Use of Conservatorships," *Guardian*, March 10, 2021, available online at theguardian.com.

15. Snapes, "Britney Spears: Congressmen Demand Hearing on Use of Conservatorships."

16. "Toxic Conservatorships: The Need for Reform," US Senate Committee on the Judiciary, Subcommittee on the Constitution, subcommittee hearing, September 28, 2021, available online at judiciary.senate.gov.

17. Nicholas Clouse, "Toxic Conservatorships: The Need for Reform," US Senate Committee on the Judiciary, Subcommittee on the Constitution, written testimony, September 28, 2021, available online at judiciary.senate.gov.

18. Clouse, "Toxic Conservatorships: The Need for Reform," page 2.

19. "Guardianships: Collaboration Needed to Protect Incapacitated Elderly People," United States Government Accountability Office, a report to the Chairman, Special Committee on Aging, US Senate, Report No. GAO-04-655, July 13, 2004, available online at govinfo.gov.

20. "Guardianships: Cases of Financial Exploitation, Neglect, and Abuse of Seniors," United States Government Accountability Office, a report to the Chairman, Special Committee on Aging, US Senate, Report No. GAO-10-1046, September 30, 2010, available online at gao.gov.

21. "Guardianships: Cases of Financial Exploitation, Neglect, and Abuse of Seniors."

22. "Elder Justice: National Strategy Needed to Effectively Combat Elder Financial Exploitation," United States Government Accountability Office, Report to Congressional Requesters, November 2012, available online at gao.gov.

23. "Elder Justice," United States Government Accountability Office.

24. "Elder Abuse: The Extent of Abuse by Guardians Is Unknown, but Some Measures Exist to Help Protect Older Adults," United States Government Accountability Office, Report to Congressional Requesters, November 2016, available online at gao.gov.

25. "Elder Abuse," United States Government Accountability Office, 10–11.

26. Steve Duin, "A Veteran's Worst Nightmare," *The Oregonian*, June 3, 2016, available online at oregonlive.com.

27. Kean Bauman, "Contact 13: Guardian Sentenced to Probation," *ABC13 KTNV* (Las Vegas, NV), July 31, 2017, available online at ktnv.com.

28. Bauman, "Contact 13."

29. Senator Klobuchar first introduced the Guardian Accountability and Senior Protection Act in late 2011. It was never passed into law.

30. "S.178—115th Congress (2017-2018): Elder Abuse Prevention and Prosecution Act," October 18, 2017, available online at congress.gov.

31. "Antoinette T. Brown," https://docs.house.gov/meetings/JU/JU08 /20191017/110089/HHRG-116-JU08-Bio-BaconA-20191017.pdf.

32. See page 1 of the Introduction in "Annual Report to Congress on Department of Justice Activities to Combat Elder Fraud and Abuse," US Department of Justice, October 18, 2021, available online at justice.gov.

33. "Court-Appointed Pennsylvania Guardian and Virginia Co-conspirators Indicted for Stealing Over $1 Million from Elderly Wards," Department of Justice, US Attorney's Office, Eastern District of Pennsylvania, press release, June 30, 2021, available online at justice.gov. Julie Shaw, "She Went to Prison for Fraud and Bad Checks. Then Courts around Philly Let Her Manage the Finances for Elderly Residents," *Philadelphia Inquirer*, March 30, 2018, available online at inquirer.com. See also the Department of Justice, Eastern District of Pennsylvania, press release in the previous note.

34. Shaw, "She Went to Prison for Fraud and Bad Checks."

35. Julie Shaw, "3 Court-Appointed Guardians Embezzled More Than $1M from 108 Victims, Delco DA Says," *Philadelphia Inquirer*, October 21, 2019, available online at inquirer.com.

36. "Owner of Kitsap County Guardianship Business Pleads Guilty to Stealing from Disabled and Elderly Clients," Department of Justice, US Attorney's Office, Western District of Washington, press release, January 24, 2020, available online at justice.gov.

37. Andrew Binion, "Guardian for Vulnerable Adults Gets a Year for Stealing $250k from Clients," *Kitsap Sun*, October 8, 2020, available online at kitsapsun .com.

38. "Former State Attorney Indicted for Extortion as Part of Conspiracy with Defense Attorney, as Well as Bribery, Wire Fraud, and Filing False Tax Returns," Department of Justice, US Attorney's Office, Middle District of Florida, press release, February 26, 2021, available online at justice.gov. See also the Department of Justice, Middle District of Florida, February 26, 2021, press release.

39. See the Department of Justice, Middle District of Florida, February 23, 2022, press release in the previous note.

40. See page 12 in "Annual Report to Congress on Department of Justice Activities to Combat Elder Fraud and Abuse," US Department of Justice, October 18, 2021.

41. Elder Justice Initiative (EJI), The United State Department of Justice, www.justive.gov, https://www.justice.gov/elderjustice.

42. See page 84 in "Annual Report to Congress on Department of Justice Activities to Combat Elder Fraud and Abuse," US Department of Justice, October 18, 2021.

43. Telephone interview between Professor Teaster and the author conducted on May 23, 2022.

44. Telephone interview between Bradley Geller and the author conducted in March 2022.

CHAPTER 9. WEAPONIZING GUARDIANSHIP TO END A MARRIAGE

1. More on this in chapter 17: "Possible Solutions to Improve the System."

2. "Zachary Simonoff v. Mehdi Saghafi, No. 19-3001 (6th Cir. 2019)," https://law.justia.com/cases/federal/appellate-courts/ca6/19-3001/19-3001-2019-09-26.html.

3. Interestingly, that attorney is married to a Lorain County Domestic Relations Court judge. She is not a party to the Saghafi lawsuit. Juliette Fairley, "Heirs Find Ally in 6th Circuit Over Elder Guardianship Dispute," *PacerMonitor*, February 6, 2020, available online at pacemonitor.com.

4. Brett Darken, "When Caretakers Empty the Coffers: A Look at Guardianship Fraud," Association of Certified Fraud Examiners, April 13, 2022, available online at acfe.com.

5. This is a fictious name used here to protect this former ward's identity from further retaliation.

6. The name of this trooper has been changed.

7. "Appeal from the Order Entered October 16, 2017 In the Court of Common Pleas of Clinton County Civil Division at No(s): 1073-2013," Superior Court of Pennsylvania, No. 1766 MDA 2017, October 11, 2018, available online at pacourts.us.

8. Judge Folino's order and many other court documents pertaining to this case were obtained during research for this book. They will remain confidential here per agreement with Michelle to keep her identity confidential.

9. "Private Eye Aley Waives Hearing on Threat Charges," *The Herald*, May 31, 2021, available online at sharonherald.com.

10. Michelle's court-appointed guardian moved out of state and could not be located for comment.

11. Elaine Mickman, *Court-Gate . . . The Courts "Divorced from the Law": Without Liberty or Justice at All* (self-pub., Amazon Digital Services, 2021).

12. Mickman, *Court-Gate*. See chapter 6, which is entirely devoted to her fight against guardianship.

13. Office of Child Support Enforcement, "Final Rule: Title IV-D of the Social Security Act: Child Support Enforcement Program," June 26, 1975, see subheadline: 302.38 -Payments to the Family, www.acf.hhs.gov/archive/css/policy -guidance/final-rule-title-iv-d-social-security-act-child-support-enforcement.

14. Child Support is always modifiable per Pennsylvania Rule *1910.19 Change of Circumstance*, and the right to appeal is a PA constitutional right per Article V section 9. Further, the court does not have the authority to order-away rights per *210 PA 63.1*; see introduction.

15. The Child Support Enforcement program was established and signed into law by President Gerald Ford in 1975 as part of the Social Security Act. See the introduction to chapter 8, "Child Support Enforcement," at https:// greenbook-waysandmeans.house.gov/book/export/html/282.

16. "A Writ of Mandamus is a formal, legal document that commands a lower court or a government official to do something." See https://study.com/academy /lesson/writ-of-mandamus-definition-example.html. Also see SupremeCourt .gov/docket and search the name Elaine Mickman (docket for 22A71). Her Writ of Certiorari (docket for 22-5654) asking the Supreme Court to review her state court record was previously denied.

CHAPTER 10. EVERY CITIZEN HAS CIVIL RIGHTS—NO MATTER THEIR ABILITY

1. "Remarks of President George H. W. Bush at the Signing of the Americans with Disabilities Act," United States Department of Justice, Civil Rights Division, July 26, 1990, available online at ada.gov.

2. "Just the Facts: Americans with Disabilities Act," United States Courts, July 12, 2018, available online at uscourts.gov.

3. Wayne Kelly, "Nick Vujicic Life Story," *Affiliate Training Vault* (blog), September 3, 2016, https://thriveandachieve.wordpress.com/2016/09/03/nick -vujicic-life-story/.

4. "Fee for All: How Judges Are Raiding Assets of Seniors & Lining Pockets of Conservatorship Attorneys," virtual panel moderated by Thomas F. Coleman, Commonwealth Club, video, 1:04:01, December 8, 2021, available online at commonwealthclub.org.

5. "Remembering Former NPR Producer David Rector," obituary by Scott Simon, National Public Radio, *Weekend Edition Saturday*, audio, 1:17, November 9, 2019, available online at npr.org.

6. Telephone conversations and emails between Joe Parisio and the author took place beginning August 2022.

7. This email was provided to the author by Tom Coleman of the Spectrum Institute.

8. "Antonina Parisio, Individually and as Successor in Interest, etc. et al., Plaintiffs and Appellants," Docket No. B262108, Court of Appeals of the State of California, Second Appellate District, Division Seven, March 14, 2017, available online at casemine.com.

CHAPTER 11. TURNING A BLIND EYE: WHERE'S THE LEGAL COMMUNITY?

1. Cameron Buford, "The Complex Story of Erik Kramer," *News Observer*, March 30, 2021, available online at ognsc.com.

2. Judge David Cowan, the former supervising judge of the probate division of the Los Angeles Superior Court, is linked to multiple questionable conservatorship cases in California. See the Bradford Lund case in chapter 13: "The Richer the Better"; and the Theresa Jankowski case in chapter 15: "The Sad Stories of Theresa and Susan."

3. The use of the term "volunteer" is misleading as PVP attorneys are, indeed, paid by the ward's estate.

4. Attorney Howard Smith, email to the author, September 20, 2022.

5. Attorney Smith, email to the author, September 21, 2022.

6. Chris Pleasance, "Wife of Ex-NFL Quarterback Says She Is 'Terrified' That He Is Coming to Kill Her and Her Daughter after He 'Attacked Her at Their Home,'" *Daily Mail*, June 21, 2018, available online at dailymail.co.uk.

7. Michael David Smith, "Erik Kramer's Ex-Wife Charged with 12 Felonies for Abusing, Stealing from Him," *Pro Football Talk*, August 18, 2020, available online at profootballtalk.nbcsports.com.

8. Tyler Dunne, "The Fight for Erik Kramer's Life, Part II: Victimized," *Go Long*, June 26, 2021, available online at golongtd.com.

9. "Erik Kramer vs Michael Harrison," *UniCourt*, case summary, filed June 17, 2019, available online at unicourt.com.

10. Available online at docketalarm.com.

11. Email sent by attorney MacCarley to the author in February 2022.

12. See https://us-barassociation.org/.

13. "WINGS," American Bar Association, available online at americanbar.org.

14. Erica F. Wood, "State-Level Adult Guardianship Data: An Exploratory Survey," American Bar Association Commission on Law and Aging, August 16, 2006. For further discussion, see chapter 17: "Possible Solutions to Improve the System."

15. "Practical Tool for Lawyers: Steps in Supporting Decision-Making," American Bar Association, available online at americanbar.org. This Practical Tool document is a blueprint for lawyers to remain engaged even if less restrictive arrangements are approved by the court. For more on the ABA's position on Supported-Decision Making also see David Godfrey, "Challenges in Guardianship and Guardianship Abuse," American Bar Association Commission on Law and Aging, March 11, 2021, available online at americanbar .org.

16. "NAELA to Host Elder Law and Special Needs Planning Conference," National Academy of Elder Law Attorneys, press release, April 20, 2017, available online at naela.org.

17. Diane Robinson, Sarah Trescher, and Miriam Hamilton, "Adult Guardianship Monitoring: A National Survey of Court Practices," National Center for State Courts, May 2021, https://cdm16501.contentdm.oclc.org/digital/collection/famct/id/1690.

18. See their official website: http://uniformlaws.org/home.

19. See www.uniformlaws.org/aboutulc/overview.

20. The full text of the act can be retrieved at "Guardianship Conservatorship and Other Protective Arrangements Act," Uniform Law Commission, available online at uniformlaws.org.

21. A few states, like Alabama, have signaled they will consider adoption of the UGCOPAA in the future. A handful of other states have adopted certain sections of the act, including Nevada, New Mexico, Iowa, Mississippi, and South Carolina. See "A Few Facts about the Uniform Guardianship, Conservatorship, and Other Protective Arrangements Act," Uniform Law Commission, 2017, available online at uniformlaws.org.

22. See the latest version of UGCOPAA, page 32 (2), www.guardianship.org/wp-content/uploads/2018/09/UGCOPPAAct_UGPPAct.pdf.

23. For more specific information on the UGCOPAA, see chapter 17: "Possible Solutions to Improve the System."

24. A state-by-state list of guardianship law changes can be found at Morgan K. Whitlatch, "Guardianship Laws by State," The Jenny Hatch Justice Project, available online at jennyhatchjusticeproject.org.

25. "Access to Information in Adult Guardianship & Conservatorship Cases," New Mexico Courts, flow chart, https://adultguardianship.nmcourts.gov/wp-content/uploads/sites/9/2021/09/PQ-Flow-Chart-Access-to-Documents-1.pdf. As the chart at this link clarifies, there are important caveats attached to these laws. As for availability of court records, only the docket sheet (schedule of hearings) is accessible to the public. Distribution of pleadings or professional reports are strictly limited. Likewise, hearings are "open to anyone unless the judges issues an order for courtroom closure," but only "pre-adjudication" hearings.

26. "Guardians and Conservators," New Mexico Courts, https://adultguardianship.nmcourts.gov/. This is a full listing of all changes to New Mexico guardianship laws from 2018 to 2021.

27. Colleen Heild, "Lawmakers Close Loophole in Guardianship System," *Yahoo! News*, February 20, 2022, available online at news.yahoo.com.

28. Diane Dimond, "The Face of the Elder Guardian Trap," *RealClear Investigations*, February 22, 2019, available online at realclearinvestigations.com.

29. See the case against Rebecca Fierle in chapter 6: "Guardians from Hell—and Lawyers and Judges Too."

30. Heather Catallo, "Michigan Leaders Announce New Legislation Addressing Problems within State's Guardianship System," *ABC7 WXYZ* (Detroit, MI), June 9, 2021, available online at wxyz.com.

31. "Guardians and Conservators," House Fiscal Agency, State of Michigan, House Bill 4849, May 18, 2021, available online at trackbill.com.

32. www.facebook.com/watch/live/?ref=watch_permalink&v=2183402 63439268.

33. Email from Bradley Geller to author on December 16, 2022.

CHAPTER 12. THE COWGIRL VS. THE CONSERVATOR

1. Diane Dimond, "Who Guards the Guardians: A Series by Diane Dimond," *Albuquerque Journal*, November 30, 2016, available online at abqjournal.com.

2. Specific names of companies, guardians, lawyers, and conservators are mentioned here as they were previously made public in an *Albuquerque Journal* series published in late 2016.

3. Diane Dimond, "Who Guards the Guardians?," *Albuquerque Journal*, November 27, 2016, available online at abqjournal.com.

4. Mary Darnell first began speaking to the author about her mother's guardianship case, on the record and in defiance of a judge's gag order, in the spring of 2016. Shortly afterward her siblings, Emily and Cliff, followed suit and provided additional information. Over the ensuing years numerous phone conversations, face-to-face interviews, document exchanges, and emails have followed. The quotes in this chapter from Mary, Emily, and Cliff Darnell came from these contacts.

5. "2011 New Mexico Statutes Chapter 45: Uniform Probate Code Article 5: Protection of Persons Under Disability and Their Property, 45-5-101 through 45-5-617 Section 45-5-405: Notice in conservatorship proceedings," Justia: US Law, available online at law.justia.com.

6. Judge Brickhouse is the same judge who approved the guardianship of Dr. Jack Herrmann, as discussed in chapter 1: "The Floodgates Open."

7. Diane Dimond, "Family Members Feel Helpless When Court Takes Control," November 30, 2016, available online at abqjournal.com.

8. Diane Dimond, "Get Rid of the Dog," November 30, 2016, available online at abqjournal.com.

9. Colleen Heild, "Darnell Conservator Disputes Claims," May 6, 2017, available online at abqjournal.com.

10. The seventeen acres transaction included the smaller two-acre homestead parcel that was supposed to be protected by the Darnell Trust A.

11. Diane Dimond, "Families Feel Steamrolled as Estates Disappear," November 30, 2016, available online at abqjournal.com.

12. In the summer of 2015, Bernalillo County records show the land was resold to the New Mexico Game and Fish Department for $2.8 million, or about $165,000 an acre.

13. Original reporting, source document.

14. During this time period, many of the nation's court functions were seriously interrupted by the coronavirus pandemic lockdowns. However, that was not mentioned as a reason for the delay in Judge Browning's ultimate decision to recuse himself.

15. It is common practice among guardians and conservators to demand a so-called waiver of liability at the conclusion of their tenure. Any inheritance is withheld until such an agreement is signed. Those opposed to the guardianship status quo would like to see this protection for court appointees abolished. These waivers of liability are routinely used in every state and are issued at the conclusion of guardianship and conservatorship cases. They are a major roadblock to anyone who seeks to sue a court appointee for actions taken during the course of their duties.

CHAPTER 13. THE RICHER THE BETTER

1. See Gerald Forbes, "History of the Osage Blanket Lease," *Chronicles of Oklahoma* 19, no. 1 (1941): 72–80.

2. Rennard Strickland, *Indians in Oklahoma: Newcomers to a New Land* (Norman: University of Oklahoma Press, 1980), 72.

3. "25 C.F.R. Part 226—Leasing of Osage Reservation Lands for Oil and Gas Mining," United States Department of the Interior Bureau of Indian Affairs, Tribal Consultation Packet, September 2016, available online at bia.gov.

4. "Chapter 9: Allotment of Indian Lands," USC Title 25—Indians, United States Code, Office of the Law Revision Counsel, available online at uscode .house.gov.

5. Dennis McAuliffe, *Bloodland: A Family Story of Oil, Greed and Murder on the Osage Reservation* (San Francisco: Council Oak Books, 1994).

6. David Grann, *Killers of the Flower Moon: The Osage Murders and the Birth of the FBI* (New York: Doubleday, 2017).

7. Liesl Schillinger, "What Happened to Brooke Astor?," *O Magazine*, December 2008, available online at oprah.com.

8. John Eligon, "Brooke Astor's Son Guilty in Scheme to Defraud Her," *New York Times*, October 8, 2009, available online at nytimes.com.

9. There are five separate trusts involved. Two established by Sharon Disney Lund, one held in the name of Walt Disney's wife, called the Lillian B. Disney Trust, and two others set in 1986 and 1992.

10. Sharon Disney Lund died of breast cancer in 1993. She was fifty-six years old.

11. Eriq Gardner, "Walt Disney Family Feud: Inside His Grandkids' Weird, Sad Battle Over a $400 Million Fortune," *Hollywood Reporter*, May 21, 2014, available online at hollywoodreporter.com.

12. Gardner, "Walt Disney Family Feud."

13. Mike Taibbi and Andrew Blankstein, "The Disneys: Not the Happiest Family on Earth," *NBC News*, November 23, 2013, available online at nbcnews.com.

14. Lund v. Donahoe, 227 Ariz 572 (2011), page 8.

15. Gardner, "Walt Disney Family Feud."

16. During a telephone interview in February 2022, Bill's wife, Sherry, said, "My husband died from what these people did to him. His heart just couldn't take it. She maintained the trustees spread falsehoods about her late husband in a "conspiracy of corruption."

17. Superior Court of California, department 51, page 32 of Judge Mitchell Beckloff's 41-page decision, dated June 3, 2014.

18. Lanny Davis, "Lanny Davis, Attorney to Bradford Lund, Grandson of Walt Disney, Joins Arizona Litigation against Lund's Former Attorney, Jeffrey Shumway Who Is Alleged to Have Charged Lund Over One Million Dollars Only to Secretly Betray Him," *Cision PRNewswire*, July 8, 2020, available online at prnewswire.com.

19. "Disney Family Disney's Grandson Brad Lund and His Family's Fight for Justice," *Court Victim Network*, available online at courtvictim.com.

20. The plaintiffs would spend two more years appealing Judge Oberbillig's ruling. They were unsuccessful.

21. "Sua sponte" means arising from the judge's own initiative and not from any petition presented to the court.

22. See the Theresa Jankowski case in chapter 15: "The Sad Stories of Theresa and Susan," during which Judge Cowan removed two of Jankowski's chosen lawyers. Also see the Britney Spears case in chapter 2: "The Case Heard 'Round the World," during which Judge Riva Goetz refused to allow Spears's chosen attorney to represent her.

23. Lund v Cowan, 5 F, 4th 964 (2021) / 21 Cal. Daily Op. Serve 7100, Daily Journal D.A.R. 7138.

24. See the case of Jenny Hatch in chapter 17: "Possible Solutions to Improve the System."

25. William "Bill" Lund, Brad and Michelle's father, died in 2008 at the age of eighty-three.

26. The Bivins land was situated over part of the so-called Hugoton Field of natural gas, rich in unusually high concentrations of helium. Dwight E. Ward and Arthur P. Pierce, "Helium," in United States Mineral Resources, US Geological Survey, Professional Paper 820 (1973): 285–90.

27. Tom Miller, "The 1904 Arthur Scribner House—No. 39 E. 67th Street," *Daytonian in Manhattan* (blog), April 11, 2013, available online at daytonin manhattan.blogspot.com.

28. Telephone call between John Pacenti and the author on December 19, 2022.

29. John Pacenti, "Jury Hits Lawyers with $16.4 for Doing Senior Wrong in Guardianship," *Palm Beach Post*, August 7, 2017, available online at palmbeach post.com.

30. "Petition for Appointment of Emergency Temporary Guardianship," filed Circuit Court for Palm Beach County, Probate & Guardianship Division, January 5, 2011. They are time-stamped 9:47 and 9:48 a.m. respectively.

31. www.wellness.com/dir/6030725/senior-citizen-counseling/fl/lantana /sonja-kobrin-vip-care-management-mps.

32. For more on the scandal surrounding Judge Colin and his guardian wife, Elizabeth Savitt, see chapter 6: "Guardians from Hell—and Lawyers and Judges Too."

33. Mary E. Bivins Foundation, "Inception of the Mary E. Bivins Foundation," available online at bivinsfoundation.org/about-us/history/.

34. "Bivins v. Rogers et al – 9:15-cv-81298," Florida Southern District Court, Docket Item 1.0, September 17, 2015, available online at pacermonitor.com.

35. Toward the end of 2016, both Judge Colin and his wife would become embroiled in a guardianship scandal. He was removed from hearing guardianship cases and resigned from the bench in November 2016. Her guardian registration was permanently revoked. For more on Judge Colin, see chapter 6: "Guardians from Hell—and Lawyers and Judges Too."

36. Opinion by the Supreme Court of Alabama, July 2, 2020, Petition for Writ of Mandamus, page 15.

37. Ivana Hrynkiw, "Joann Bashinsky, Golden Flake Heiress Who Fought for Control of Estate, Dies at 89," January 5, 2021, updated January 6, 2021, available online at AL.com.

38. Kim Chandler, "Potato Chip Heiress Wins Back Control of Fortune," *Tuscaloosa News*, July 3, 2020, available online at tuscaloosanews.com.

39. Opinion by the Supreme Court of Alabama, July 2, 2020, Petition for Writ of Mandamus, page 48.

40. Ivana Hrynkiw, "Joann Bashinsky, Golden Flake Heiress Who Fought for Control of Estate, Dead at 89," *Advance Local*, January 5, 2021, available online at al.com.

CHAPTER 14. DESPERATE IS AS DESPERATE DOES

1. "Roger Hillygus v. State of Nevada," *Judicialpedia*, August 9, 2019, available online at judicialpedia.com.

2. Terri Russell, "Hillygus Has Extensive History in Family Court," *ABC8 KOLO News Now* (Reno, NV), August 16, 2019, available online at kolotv.com.

3. Bill Dentzer, "Bitter Reno Family Battle Leads to Manhunt, Arrests," *Las Vegas Review-Journal*, August 20, 2019, available online at reviewjournal.com.

4. Heidi Bunch, "Charges Reduced against Former Sheriff in Elderly Kidnapping Case," *Mineral County Independent News*, November 23, 2019, available online at mcindependentnews.com.

5. Kim Burrows, "Judge Orders Former Nevada Lawman to Wear Ankle Monitor ahead of Trial," *NBC News 4* (Reno, NV), January 14, 2022, available online at mynews4.com.

6. "Kidnapping Suspect Wanted in Reno Arrested in Kansas City, Missouri," October 4, 2022, available online at 2news.com.

7. "The Case of Carl DeBrodie: The Guardians," *ABC 17 KMIZ* (Columbia, MO), August 15, 2017, available online at abc17news.com.

8. "In RE: Carl Lee DeBrodie," FindLaw, available online at caselaw.findlaw.com.

CHAPTER 15. THE SAD STORIES OF THERESA AND SUSAN

1. This is the same Jodi Montgomery who, in 2019, would be named as temporary conservator for Britney Spears, replacing Spears's father, who stepped down due to illness. Niamh Cavanagh and Jennifer Roback, "Fresh Start: Who Is Jodi Montgomery?," *The US Sun*, November 15, 2021, available online at the-sun.com.

2. Theresa's attorney, Albert Rasch, believes her estate was worth closer to $900,000.

3. See the official website at www.paismontgomery.com/.

4. See Montgomery's professional profile at www.paismontgomery.com /personnel/jodi-pais-montgomery/.

5. Ethan Wolff-Mann, "Wells Fargo Scandals: The Complete List," *Yahoo! Finance*, March 12, 2019, available online at finance.yahoo.com.

6. Jack Kelly, "Wells Fargo Forced to Pay $3 Billion for the Bank's Fake Account Scandal," *Forbes*, February 24, 2020, available online at forbes.com.

7. This fine would swell over the years to nearly $3 billion, according to *Forbes*. Kelly, "Wells Fargo Forced to Pay."

8. Jonathan Stempel, "Wells Fargo to Pay US $108 Million over Veterans' Loans," *Reuters*, August 4, 2017, available online at reuters.com.

9. Ann Marsh, "Keep Quiet," *Financial Planning*, n.d., available online at financial-planning.com.

10. "Wells Fargo Finds Even More Customers That It Overcharged," *NBC2 News* (Fort Myers, FL), July 13, 2018, available online at nbc-2.com.

11. Montgomery would tell the court that Theresa Jankowski suffered from senile dementia and other mental maladies and should therefore remain at Brookdale. However, as longtime senior adviser Sharon Holmes said in court, the Brookdale facility was not licensed to care for dementia patients and to house such a person there would have been illegal under California law.

12. See Robert George-Foote, et al., v. Affiliated Psychiatric Medical Clinic, Inc, et al., CA-S003030-SO, Opening Brief on the Merits (Supreme Court), L.A. Sup. Ct. No C451467. Statement of Facts, page two.

13. The petition was electronically filed from the law office of Wright Kim Douglas, ALC, and listed Lauriann Wright as the attorney for Jodi Montgomery. The petition was signed by Jodi Montgomery, under penalty of perjury, and affirmed to be "true and correct."

14. Despite the title—Probate Volunteer Panel—participating lawyers receive compensation, either from the estate of the conservatee or from the County of Los Angeles.

15. The revelation about the two Cowan speeches was brought to light in court papers filed by attorney Tom Coleman, executive director of the Spectrum Institute.

16. Under Los Angeles County Superior Court Rules, a PVP attorney is required to zealously represent the interests of his or her client. However, the PVP appointee is also expected to fulfill another duty, according to the rules. "The

PVP attorney's secondary duty is to assist the court in the resolution of the matter to be decided" (section 10.85).

17. Julius Young, "Jodi Montgomery Responds to Jamie's Claims She Felt Britney Was 'Spiraling Out of Control': 'Stop the Attacks,'" *Fox News*, August 6, 2021, available online at foxnews.com.

18. Copies of all emails, court documents, legal letters, and medical evaluations associated with the Terranova case and quoted here were provided by sources who were promised confidentiality.

19. Alzheimer's Association, "Alzheimer's and Dementia," available online at alz.org.

20. "Early Symptoms of Dementia," Dementia.org, February 3, 2014.

21. The National Institute on Aging reports that before the early 2000s Alzheimer's disease could only be positively identified during an autopsy. But medical advances now offer doctors certain imaging and blood tests that can reveal biological signs, or biomarkers, of Alzheimer's in a living person. National Institute on Aging, "How Is Alzheimer's Disease Diagnosed?," available online at nia.nih .gov.

CHAPTER 16. GUARDING AGAINST GUARDIANSHIP

1. Understand that the author is not a lawyer, nor trained in family dynamics, social work, accounting, or trusts. The recommendations in this chapter are borne solely out of her investigations into what can go wrong in a court-ordered guardianship or conservatorship.

2. Massachusetts Council on Family Mediation, "What Is Family Mediation?," available online at mcfm.org.

3. Dr. Sam Sugar, *Guardianships and the Elderly: The Perfect Crime* (New York: Square One Publishers, 2018).

4. Sugar, *Guardianships and the Elderly*, 179.

5. Sugar, *Guardianships and the Elderly*, 180–81.

6. May and Stanley Smith Charitable Trust, "The Story of May & Stanley Smith," https://smithct.org/about-the-trust/may-and-stanley-smith.

7. "Former Anchorage Prosecutor Sentenced to over 13 Years in Prison for Massive Wire Fraud and Money Laundering Scheme," Department of Justice, US Attorney's Office, District of Alaska, press release, May 23, 2016, available online at justice.gov.

8. Sugar, *Guardianships and the Elderly*, 183.

9. Michael Rappaport was named as his mother's healthcare proxy. He was apparently joined in filing the petition by his youngest brother, Richard, and a cousin named Eleanor Burton, who lived in Los Angeles, California. All three Rappaport brothers and the cousin were named as coexecutors of the late David Rapaport's estate.

10. See the property listing at www.zillow.com/homes/11-Oak-Point-Club, -New-Milford,-Connecticut-06776_rb/57809330_zpid/.

11. Report of Guardian ad litem to the Surrogate Court, County of New York, File No.: 2010-2371/F, dated February 1, 2012, page 11, paragraph 43.

12. See Civil Court of the City of New York, Housing Court Clerk, index number 050798-14.

13. IKOR CEO Patricia Maisano testified at the guardianship hearing for Mrs. Bush even though she had not conducted any in-person evaluation of the ward. Maisano relied on the findings of two IKOR staffers. See chapter 1: "The Floodgates Open" for more on Maisano's involvement in the long-running case of Betty Winstanley.

14. In fact, throughout the ten years Mrs. Bush was held in the guardianship system, she never got her day in court, and all legal actions taken to control her life took place without her.

15. Transcript of hearing before the Chester, Pennsylvania, Orphans Court Division, re: the Guardianship of Genevieve Bush, May 6, 2013, page 12.

16. Transcript of hearing before the Pennsylvania Orphans Court Division on January 9, 2014, re: Guardianship of Genevieve Bush, Petition for Contempt against Mary Bush, page 382.

17. "In the Matter of: Genevieve Bush, An Incapacitated Person. Appeal of: Michael and Joseph Bush," Superior Court of Pennsylvania, Court of Common Pleas of Chester County, Orphans' Court at No(s): 1509-1720, February 21, 2017, available online at pacourts.us.

18. Michael Bush, email to the author, August 29, 2022.

19. Marian Kornicki, "Guardianship Destroyed My Family," *NASGA* (blog), January 11, 2022, available online at nasga-stopguardianabuse.blogspot.com.

20. Alisa Partlan, "They Say Legal Guardians Ripped Them Off—and the State AG Let Them Down," *City Limits*, June 5, 2018, available online at city limits.org.

21. Ultimately, Terri Kornicki reached a plea agreement with the district attorney's office. She pleaded guilty to a class A misdemeanor and served no prison time. Marian calls the resolution "a slap on the wrist."

22. In April 2022 Marian said she was still fighting for the guardian to sign over the deed to her parent's home. She told the author she had contacted state lawmakers for help, including the chair of the New York State Assembly's Judiciary Committee.

23. See item seven in Katie J. M. Baker and Heidi Blake, "Here Are 8 Major Takeaways from BuzzFeed News' Investigation into Guardianships," *BuzzFeed News*, September 28, 2021, available online at buzzfeednews.com.

CHAPTER 17. POSSIBLE SOLUTIONS TO IMPROVE THE SYSTEM

1. Theresa Vargas, "Her Case Opened the Way for People with Disabilities to Reclaim Their Freedom. Now, Her Words Open a Book That Could Help Countless More," *Washington Post*, October 12, 2019, available online at washington post.com.

2. Theresa Vargas, "Woman with Down Syndrome Prevails Over Parents in Guardianship Case," *Washington Post*, August 2, 2013, available online at washingtonpost.com.

3. Jonathan Martinis, "From Justice for Jenny to Justice for All: EVERYONE Has the Right to Make Choices," National Resource Center for Supported Decision-Making (blog), n.d., available online at supporteddecisionmaking.org.

4. http://supporteddecisionmaking.org/states.

5. Sam Crane, email message to author, December 19, 2022.

6. For a link to each state's (in)action on SDM laws, see "In Your State," National Resource Center for Supported Decision-Making, available online at supporteddecisionmaking.org.

7. "Fourth National Guardianship Summit: Maximizing Autonomy and Ensuring Accountability," American Bar Association, Recommendations Adopted by Summit Delegates, May 2021, available online at americanbar.org.

8. For more information, visit www.eldercaringcoordination.com, a joint initiative of the Association for Conflict Resolution and the Florida Chapter of the Association of Family and Conciliation Courts.

9. Erin Duffin, "Foster Care and Adoption in the US—Statistics & Facts," September 30, 2022, available online at statista.com.

10. A list of state-by-state guardianship certification requirements can be found here: www.americanbar.org.

11. For example, the Society of Certified Senior Advisors (SCSA), the world's largest membership organization educating and certifying professions who serve senior citizens, requires its members to take continuing education courses that emphasize both a code of ethics and volunteer services to seniors. To become a member, one must first take specific training in the area of elder care, and study various principles of aging, social aspects of aging, society security, taxes, financial and estate planning, and specific caregiving for the elderly.

12. See chapter 8: "Washington Could Help—But It Hasn't."

13. Transcript title: "Abuses in Guardianship of the Elderly and Infirm: A National Disgrace." Available from Superintendent of Documents, Congressional Sales Office, U.S. Government Printing Office, Washington, DC 20402, page 17, September 25, 1987.

14. "Conduct of Law Enforcement Agencies," The United State Department of Justice, Civil Rights Division, Office of the Assistant Attorney General, available online at justice.gov.

15. "Uniform Guardianship, Conservatorship, and Other Protective Arrangements Act," National Conference of Commissioners on Uniform State Laws, July 9, 2018, available online at guardianship.org.

16. See chapter 11: "Turning a Blind Eye: Where's the Legal Community?" for more on the Uniform Law Commission.

17. Nonlawyer stakeholders were also consulted in preparing the document, including representatives from AARP, the National Association to Stop Guardianship Abuse, and the National Disability Rights Network.

18. Marsha Southwick, "Why States Should Pass UGCOPAA," https://stop guardianabuse.org/nasga-legislative-members/.

19. A citizen's right to due process is mentioned in both the Fifth and Fourteenth Amendments to the US Constitution.

20. CEAR's white paper of the UGCOPAA was sent via email from Black to the author in August 2022.

21. "Constructive fraud" is defined as a situation where a person gains an unfair advantage over another by deceitful or unfair methods. For example, a con-

structive fraud would occur when an attorney files a petition for guardianship that contains exaggerations, misinformation, or outright lies.

22. The human impact of the policy of "exclusive jurisdiction globally" can be found in chapter 15: "The Sad Stories of Theresa and Susan," wherein Virginia resident Susan Terranova was forced into an unwanted guardianship in Alabama.

23. Jim Ash, "Bill Creates a Statewide Guardianship Database," March 14, 2022, available online at floridabar.org.

24. "§ 6-1449. Background Checks on Guardians or Conservators; Appointment of Guardian Ad Litem," State of Nebraska Judicial Branch, Supreme Court Rules, Chapter 6: Trial Courts, Article 14, available online at supremecourt .nebraska.gov.

25. The California law was signed the day Britney Spears's conservatorship was ended. Andrew R. Verriere, "California Expands Conservatorship Protections," *Bloomberg Law*, October 12, 2021, available online at news.bloomberglaw .com.

26. "Adult Guardianship Advocacy Program and Minor Guardianship Advocacy Program Year-End Report 2021," 5; www.lacsn.org.

27. Complete text of the "Bill of Rights for Persons Subject to Guardianship or Conservatorship" can be found at the website of the Minnesota Office of the Revisor of Statutes. www.revisor.mn.gov/statutes/cite/524.5-120.

28. Kenneth Farmer, "GAP Act: Mississippi Guardianship and Conservatorship Act," Land Title Association of Mississippi, June 6, 2019, available online at ltams.org.

29. Michelle Chaffee, "Introduction to the Nebraska Office of Public Guardian," *The Nebraska Lawyer*, November/December 2015, available online at supremecourt.nebraska.gov.

30. Bill Kelly, "Guardianship "Scam" Prompts Call for Reform in Nebraska," Nebraska Public Media, December 13, 2013, available online at nebraskapublic media.org.

31. Maunette Loeks, "Bayard Woman Sentenced in Guardianship Theft Case," *Star Herald*, October 15, 2014, available online at starherald.com.

32. Bradley Geller to author during a telephone interview in the spring of 2022.

EPILOGUE

1. Adam Walser, "Former Professional Guardian Abandoned Wards' Mail, Committed Crimes: Inspector General Report," *ABC Action News WFTS* (Tampa Bay, FL), April 8, 2022, available online at abcactionnews.com.

2. To watch video of Lillie White candidly speaking about her guardianship plight, see "In Lillie's Voice," Elder Dignity, https://elderdignity.org/in-lillies -voice/.

3. Arian Campo-Flores and Ashby Jones, *Wall Street Journal*, https:// rethinkingguardianshipnc.org/wp-content/uploads/sites/1731/2021/07

/Abuse-Plagues-System-of-Legal-Guardians-for-Adults-Wall-Street-Journal
-Oct-2015.pdf.

4. Dillon Bergin, "Vulnerable New Mexico Elders Find Themselves Trapped in Guardianship," *Santa Fe New Mexican*, February 27, 2021, available online at santafenewmexican.com.

5. Colleen Heild, "Lawyer Disputes Son's Claims," *Albuquerque Journal*, November 27, 2021, available online at abqjournal.com.

6. Mardi Link and Luca Powell, "Unguarded: Michigan's Guardianship System Leaves Vulnerable Exposed," May 8, 2022, *Record-Eagle*, available online at record-eagle.com.

7. Link and Powell, record-eagle.com

8. Walter F. Roche Jr., "Hendersonville Woman Who Lost Home, Car in Conservatorship Case Dies at 58," *The Tennessean*, July 6, 2017, available online at tennessean.com.

9. Roche, "Hendersonville Woman Who Lost Home."

10. See Marissa Sweeney's personal statement at https://stopguardianabuse
.org/victim-profiles/marissa-sweeney-va/.

11. See the statement by Garr Sanders on behalf of his brother Robert Sanders at https://stopguardianabuse.org/victim-profiles/robert-sanders-mo/.

12. https://stopguardianabuse.org/victim-profiles/robert-sanders-mo/.

INDEX

Brandeis Series in Law and Society

Rosalind Kabrhel, JD, and Daniel Breen, JD, Editors

Justice Louis D. Brandeis once said that "if we desire respect for the law, we must first make the law respectable." For Justice Brandeis, making the law "respectable" meant making it work in the interests of humankind, as a help rather than a hindrance in the manifold struggles of persons of all backgrounds to achieve justice. In that spirit, the Law and Society Series publishes works that take interdisciplinary approaches to law, drawing richly from the social sciences and humanities, with a view towards shedding critical light upon the variety of ways in which legal rules, and the institutions that enforce them, affect our lives. Intended for practitioners, academics, students, and the interested general public, this series will feature titles that contribute robustly to contemporary debates about law and legal reform, all with a view towards adding to efforts of all sorts to make the law "respectable."

For a complete list of books that are available in the series, visit
https://brandeisuniversitypress.com/series/law

We're Here to Help: When Guardianship Goes Wrong
Diane Dimond

The Common Flaw: Needless Complexity in the Courts
and 50 Ways to Reduce It
Thomas Moukawsher

Education Behind the Wall: Why and How We Teach College in Prison
Mneesha Gellman

When Freedom Speaks: The Boundaries and the Boundlessness
of Our First Amendment Right
Lynn Levine Greenky

Pain and Shock in America: Politics, Advocacy, and the
Controversial Treatment of People with Disabilities
Jan A. Nisbet

ABOUT THE AUTHOR

DIANE DIMOND is a freelance journalist, author, syndicated columnist, and veteran television correspondent who specializes in crime and justice topics. Her weekly column, the only nationally syndicated column exclusively devoted to crime and justice issues, has been distributed by Creators Syndicate since 2008. She has been a contributor to *Newsweek, The Daily Beast, Real Clear Investigations, Huffington Post,* and the *New York Post.* For a six-part series on court-approved guardianship exploitation of the elderly done for the *Albuquerque Journal,* Dimond was the recipient of Stanford University's Institute for American Studies' Clark Mollenhoff Award for Outstanding Investigative Journalism (2016), That series also won two major awards from the New Mexico Press Association, including the Best Investigative Public Service Award (2017). Her book *Be Careful Who You Love: Inside the Michael Jackson Case* (2005) chronicles her years investigating Jackson's life and his ultimate fall. She is also the author of *Cirque Du Salahi: Be Careful Who You Trust* (2010) and *Thinking Outside the Crime and Justice Box* (2016). A repository of current information, including a glossary of key terms pertaining to guardianship and conservatorship, contacts for support organizations, and news updates about the topic can be found at www.DianeDimond.com.